P. KASTEN

2495
F

W9-BIJ-668

Other Books of Interest From McGraw-Hill

ISBN	AUTHOR	TITLE
003355-2	Baker	*C Tools for Scientists and Engineers*
003358-7	Baker	*More C Tools for Scientists and Engineers*
026001-X	Hancock et al.	*The C Primer*
707402-5	Ince	*Object-Oriented Software Engineering With C++*
043152-3	Morgan, McGilton	*Introducing UNIX System V*
051216-7	Ranade, Zamir	*C++ Primer for C Programmers*
059177-6	Smith	*Concepts of Object-Oriented Programming*
059180-6	Smith	*C++ for Scientists and Engineers*
062885-8	Tare	*Data Processing in UNIX*
062879-3	Tare	*UNIX Utilities*
062884-X	Tare	*UNIX Utilities* (softcover)

C + C++

Programming With Objects in C and C++

Allen I. Holub

McGraw-Hill, Inc.
New York St. Louis San Francisco Auckland Bogotá
Caracas Lisbon London Madrid Mexico Milan
Montreal New Delhi Paris San Juan Singapore
Sydney Tokyo Toronto

This book is printed on recycled, acid-free paper containing a minimum of 50% recycled de-inked fiber.

Library of Congress Cataloging-in-Publication Data

Holub, Allen I.
    C + C++ : programming with objects in C and C++ / Allen I. Holub.
       p.   cm.
    Includes bibliographical references and index.
    ISBN 0-07-029662-6
    1. Object-oriented programming (Computer science) 2. C (Computer
program language) 3. C++ (Computer program language)   I. Title.
QA76.64.H65   1992
005.1'1—dc20   92-12076
                                                 CIP

2 3 4 5 6 7 8 9 0 DOH DOH 9 7 6 5 4 3 2

ISBN   0-07-029662-6

The sponsoring editor for this book was Neil Levine, the editing supervisor was Joe Bertuna, and the production supervisor was Donald F. Schmidt.

Printed and bound by R. R. Donnelley & Sons Company.

For Philip,

*without whose welcome introduction
to this world,
this book would be a year older.*

Contents

Contents

Preface

This book is an introduction to object-oriented programming (OOP) techniques and to the C++ extensions of the C language. It's geared toward professional-level programmers who know C thoroughly and who have a good working knowledge of basic data structures like trees and linked lists.

I'm approaching the C++ language from a skeptic's perspective—my original title was *A Curmudgeon's Guide to C++*. This book is not OOP or C++ propaganda, but is an objective (so to speak) look at both subjects. Although C++ has many good features, there are also many deficiencies [like a brain-damaged syntax (that's a technical term) and a few serious behavioral problems]. You have to know about these deficiencies in order to write good C++ programs, so I intend to discuss these deficiencies along with the good points. C++ indeed makes it easier to do object-oriented things, but it also gives you just enough rope to shoot yourself in the foot [:-)]. I intend not just to introduce the syntax of C++ but also to demonstrate both how to use C++ effectively and how to use C itself in an object-oriented manner.

Object-Oriented Programming, Hype and Reality

"Object-oriented" is the "new and improved" of computer-software salespersons (the ones with the slicked-back hair, polyester suits, and pointy teeth). The literature presents object-oriented programming as a panacea that will save computer programmers from virtually every conceivable problem. It's supposed to improve performance and make your code both more maintainable and easier to understand. It's supposed to isolate inexperienced programmers from the complexity of a low-level language like C. It's supposed to change the baby and take out the wash. Unfortunately, most of the people who use the term "object-oriented programming" would be hard pressed to define it. Although OOP does have many benefits, you don't get them just by using an object-oriented language.

First, to clear away a little of the hype, object-oriented programming is a collection of programming techniques that are intended to speed program development and improve maintenance. Most of the OOP techniques have been around for a long time—but new buzzwords have been invented to obscure this fact. Moreover, OOP techniques are really language-independent. Some "object-oriented" languages like Smalltalk, Objective C, and C++ can help you do object-oriented things, but you can write assembly language in an object-oriented way if you set your mind to it. Object-oriented programming does not require a radical change in thinking.

Although it's instructive that several studies have shown that non-computer-literate people—especially children—have an easier time picking up OOP concepts and languages than do programmers who are more set in their ways, I strongly believe that the real difficulty is that OOP requires you to organize your thoughts, and unfortunately many programmers find it difficult to get organized. If you're the sort of person who solves a problem by sitting down at a computer and pounding away at the keyboard without first giving considerable thought to what you're trying to accomplish, you'll have a hard time with OOP, and learning any object-oriented programming technique *will* require a major shift in thinking. This isn't because OOP is something new, though. Anyone who regularly uses structured programming techniques should have little difficulty.

The hype surrounding C++ is similar to that of OOP as a whole. C++ is just a few useful extensions to the C language—it is not a radical departure. If you can program in ANSI C, you already know seven-eighths of C++. C++ represents an evolutionary, not a revolutionary, step up from C. Moreover, many of the C++ extensions fall into the "better C" category—things that would be nice to add to the language but nobody thought of doing it. They are not radical additions to the language.

Perhaps the biggest piece of disinformation is that C++ isolates an inexperienced programmer from the pitfalls of C itself. This contention is simply not true. Although you can do things like array-boundary checking (at a considerable execution-speed cost) in C++, you really need to know C thoroughly to do anything with C++. The classic problem of beginners thinking that they understand how a language feature works, and then using that feature incorrectly — thereby creating a bug that's impossible for them to find — is especially true in a C++ environment.

C++ can indeed make an application programmer's life easier because that person can use complex libraries created by someone else. Object-oriented techniques can make these libraries more flexible (and more likely to be used) than would be the case in a procedural language. In this sense, C++ can indeed improve productivity (provided, of course, that you work in an environment that defines productivity as getting the job done faster rather than cranking out the maximum number of lines of code per day).

The existence of a class library does not isolate you from C, however, and the potential for abuse is, if anything, even greater in C++ than in C. Poorly written C++ is probably three or four times harder to maintain than poorly written C. Moreover, writing a good class library is no mean feat—most of this book will be spent explaining how to do it—and considerable knowledge of both C and C++ is required to do so. The final problem is that C++ is not a full object-oriented language in that it's not possible for the user of a class library to be completely ignorant of how that library goes about its tasks, so some knowledge of C++ is required at every programming level.

The purpose of this book is to address all of these problems, while at the same time teaching you how to use OOP and C++ effectively. My main goal is not to vilify C++, but to describe what object-oriented programming is and how to use it in your programs. I believe strongly that object-oriented programming techniques are useful, and that C++ is as good a language as any to use for object-oriented programming.

A Note on the Code

I developed the code in this book was with two compilers, Borland C++ version 2.0 and a beta version of Borland C++ version 3.0. Some of the code was developed with one compiler and some with the other. Unfortunately, The 2.0 compiler doesn't support templates. Moreover, the 3.0 compiler occasionally rejects code that is acceptable to 2.0 and vice versa. I've tried to use code in this book that works in all environments (both Borland versions and other compilers as well), but don't be surprised if your compiler won't accept things exactly as written. You should be able to make the code acceptable to your compiler with only minor modifications—chalk it up to the learning experience. My *turboc.cfg* file (used to configure the Borland compiler) modifies various warning messages emitted by the compiler. The relevant parts of the file are

```
-w-eff
-w-pia
-w-inl
-wpro
-wnod
-wstv
-wuse
```

All the source code in this book is available on IBM/PC disk for $60.00 from

Software Engineering Consultants
P.O. Box 5679
Berkeley, California 94705

Specify the disk size (5¼" or 3½") with your order. California residents add local sales tax. Payment must be made by check or money order drawn on a U.S. bank. (Your own bank should be able to do this.) The author can be reached both at the above address and on internet at *holub@violet.berkeley.edu*.

Acknowledgments

I'd like to thank my neighbor, Bill Wong, who volunteered to learn C++ using an early draft of this book, finding many bugs and offering many useful comments in the process. Les Hancock also read through the book in great depth, finding many bugs and giving me many helpful suggestions along the way. Many many students were subjected to early drafts of the book as their textbook. Their comments (especially those of Peter Youtz) helped shape the book's final form, and I appreciate their indulgence of my using them as guinea pigs. Finally, my wife Deirdre provided welcome emotional support in times of trial and helped enter the editing changes as well.

Allen Holub
Berkeley, California

C + C++:
Programming With
Objects in C and C++

Object-Oriented Programming in C

This chapter presents the mechanics of object-oriented programming (OOP) using both English and C as a vehicle. It seems more reasonable to present new concepts in a familiar environment than to try to do everything at once. Object-oriented programming is really a collection of useful programming techniques that can be applied to any computer language. An "object-oriented language" provides a few primitive mechanisms for operations that you would have to do manually in a non-OOP language. You can program C in an object-oriented way just as easily as you can program C++ in an object-oriented way.

As the chapter progresses, I'll introduce the OOP jargon that's used for the object-oriented concepts. A lot of this jargon is just that—jargon, serving more often to obscure than to clarify the discussion. The vast majority of object-oriented techniques are already in use in every well-structured computer program, and many of the OOP buzzwords simply put a name to (or rename) already familiar concepts. The bad news is that you really do have to learn the OOP terms both because they're used in the literature and because it's handy to have a set of terms that everyone can agree on. The good news is that you're probably already familiar with most of the underlying concepts. Don't look for the "major shift in paradigm" promised by the OOP salespeople with the slick hair and pointy teeth. The path to OOP is evolutionary, not revolutionary, and there are very few truly new concepts at work here. I've seen many students get confused because they actually understand the material, but believe that they shouldn't because the material isn't sufficiently revolutionary: "It couldn't possibly be this easy—I must not understand something." Don't be caught in this trap.

1.2 Data Abstraction

Back at the dawn of history—about three years ago—object-oriented programming was called *data abstraction*, and data abstraction is still central to the loose
collection of programming techniques banded together under the OOP flag. The
main idea of data abstraction is to isolate the data itself (and the mechanics of
manipulating the data) from an application program. You can see what's going on
by looking at nonabstract and abstract ways to do the same thing. A check, for
example, can be represented by a data structure like this one:

```
typedef struct check
{
    char    *payee;
    time_t date;
    float   amount;
}
check;
```

The various subroutines in the program can manipulate the data structure directly,
modifying or reading the various fields as necessary to do their task, and that's the
way it would normally be done in a procedural environment.

In an abstract approach, though, the contents of the data structure are hidden
from the programmer in a manner analogous to a FILE. You, the programmer,
don't know or care what a FILE structure actually looks like. You can go into
stdio.h and find out, but you can't do anything useful with this information because
the contents of the structure are likely to change from compiler to compiler, or
even from release to release of the same compiler. The contents of the FILE structure must be treated as unknown and unknowable. An *object* (a declared instance
of a particular type—you're used to calling objects "variables") is manipulated
entirely by means of subroutines called *methods*. A method is no different from
any other subroutine, except that it must be passed a pointer to the object being
manipulated.

This isolation gives you two real advantages. First, you can modify the contents of the underlying data structure without affecting the application program
that is using that structure. In the case of a FILE, you can completely change the
way that file I/O is done without affecting the rest of the program at all.

Second, you have better control of the data flowing into the structure and
thereby have a more robust program. Take the example of a check object. If you
let anyone access any field in the structure, you have no control over the contents
of the check. It's easy to generate checks with bad dates, or amounts that are too
large, payees named "cash," and so forth. If, however, the only way to set the date
on a check is to call a subroutine called set_date(), which sets the date to the
correct date, then it's impossible to have an incorrect date on the check. Similarly,
a set_amount() subroutine can guarantee that the amount is not above a fixed
ceiling, not negative or zero, and so forth. It's difficult to do this sort of data validation if the date or amount fields are directly accessible to the application program. Moreover, if direct access is possible, the validation code must be duplicated everywhere that a field is accessed, and potential bugs can creep into

your program if the validation criteria are changed in some places but not in others.

1.2 Objects and Messages

The concept of data abstraction has now transmogrified into object-oriented programming. An object-oriented design looks at a program as a group of *black boxes*—such as the FILE and check of the previous section. The boxes communicate by means of *messages* that travel along various communication paths. [Cox] uses the analogy of a printed-circuit board, where the objects are integrated circuits and the message paths are the wires. Another common analogy is a multitasking system in which each object is an independent process that has *I/O (input/output) ports*—queues to which messages are enqueued, or *posted* by one task and dequeued, or *received,* by another.

  A classic example of the black-box model is a database server. The *server* is a program that controls a large database. When an application program (or *client*)—which could be running on the same machine as the server, but could also be communicating across a network or a telephone line—needs to get some information from the database, it sends a stream of characters that requests the data to the server. The server is a black box because all the mechanics of database manipulation are hidden inside it, and you cannot access the database except through the server. The client has no idea how the server works—it just sends a request to the server and gets a reply back. The stream of characters used to communicate with the server is an example of a *message*, an encapsulated packet of data used to communicate with an object. Messages aren't always represented by character streams—I'll look at other mechanisms for message passing in a moment—but character streams are one of the simplest ways to represent a message in a network environment.

  A message might ask the server to do something like "look up all the employees who are paid on the first of the month." The server receives the message and then searches the database for data that matches the incoming specification. If it finds anything, the server sends a message that contains the desired data back to the originating application—in this case, a list of the required employees is sent. The application can then request further information for each employee, such as how much to pay that individual, and then use that additional information to print a check by sending a message to a "check printer" object of the form "print a check to the order of this person for this amount."

black boxes

messages

I/O (input/output) ports

server

client

message

1.3 OOP-Flavored Data Abstraction

Although this example is a good one to get us started, it's not a particularly good model for an object-oriented programming system because it violates one important rule: **An object should never provide external access to its data.** Obeying this rule makes for much more maintainable code, because there will be many fewer changes to make *when* (not if) it comes time to change the way that the data is represented. In the current example, the client application needs to know too much about the organization of the data. In particular, it needs to know which fields to ask for and what to do with the contents of those fields when they come back. In a better system, the application requests the server to give it a packet containing all information needed to print a check for a single employee. This packet is, in turn, routed to the check-printing process. The important issue is that the application does not know (or need to know) the information actually contained in the packet. It just relays the packet from one process (the database server) to another (the printer). Consequently, any change to the contents of the packet will not affect the application at all—only the server and printer are affected. The application ends up much more maintainable as a result. The net effect is another sort of data abstraction in which an abstract "check" packet is used to hide the details of what's actually in a check.

Here's another example of a procedural versus object-oriented approach to the same problem (lifted shamelessly from [Budd]). A program that runs an Automatic Teller Machine can verify the amount of the withdrawal in two ways. A procedural approach to the problem would probably yield a solution like this one:

```
card_number    = read_card();
secret_number  = ask_database( "what is secret number for",
                                                card_number );
entered_number = read_secret_number_from_keyboard();

if( entered_number == secret_number )
{
    switch( get_transaction_type_from_keyboard() )
    {
    /*...*/
    case WITHDRAWAL:
        balance = ask_database("what is account balance for",
                                            card_number );
        amount  = read_withdrawal_amount_from_keyboard();
        if( amount <= balance )
        {
            modify_database("change balance of", card_number,
                            "to", balance - amount );
            distribute_cash( amount );
        }
        else
            error();
        break;
    }
}
```

An object-oriented approach looks like this:

```
card_number   = read_card();
secret_number = read_secret_number_from_keyboard();

if( ask_database( "Is this secret number", secret_number,
                  "valid for this card"  , card_number ) )
{
    switch( get_transaction_type_from_keyboard() )
    {
    /*...*/
    case WITHDRAWAL:
        amount = read_withdrawal_amount_from_keyboard();

        if(ask_database("can_this_user",         card_number,
                        "withdrawal this amount", amount ))
        {
            if( ask_database("perform previous request\n") )
                distribute_cash( amount );
        }
        else
            error( "Insufficient funds" );
        break;
    }
}
```

The latter approach is superior for all the reasons I've been discussing:
- The internal workings of the database are completely isolated from the application. Either can be changed without affecting the other.
- Data validation is implicit in the syntax. For example, it's not possible to debit an amount that's different from the withdrawal amount, as it is in the procedural solution.
- The data itself is more secure because sensitive information like an account balance is not being transmitted over potentially insecure phone lines.
- There's one final but subtle difference. The latter approach requires fewer local variables than the former because less hard information has to be remembered. It is easier to debug and maintain as a consequence.

1.4 Classes and Objects

The central concepts in the preceding sections are those of a "class" and a "message." A *class* has two components. The first is just a data structure, typically a `struct` or equivalent. This component is the "packet" of information I was just discussing. The data component of a class collectively represents the object's *state*, and is sometimes called the *state data*.

    The second component of a class is a group of subroutines, called *methods*, that manipulate the data component of the individual *objects* (the declared instances of the class).

    You communicate with an object by sending it a *message* made up of some sort of method selector and some optional data. That is, the message tells the object to apply one of its methods to itself, perhaps using additional data (that can be part of the message) to do the work. In a properly designed class, the contents of the data

class

object's state, state data

objects

message

structure component are immaterial to the outside world—all manipulation is done through the methods.

In the check-printing example, an "employee database" object contains many complex fields, many of which are actually stored on the disk, and only a few of which are needed to print paychecks. It also contains many method subroutines to manipulate and access that data, and again, only a few of these subroutines are needed to print paychecks. All of this complexity is hidden inside the object, however. To print a list of checks, all you need is a method to respond to a single message of the form "give me a list of checks that need to be printed."

constructor

The returned list of "check" objects contain various fields that represent the contents of the check. Checks need two methods in the current example: an initialization, or *constructor* method that the database object uses to create new checks and a "print yourself" method that tells the check to print a representation of itself.

The check-printing process can then be done in pseudocode like this:

```
list = database <- "give me checks for everyone who
                                        needs to be paid"
foreach ( check in list )
    check <- "print yourself";
```

The pseudocode x<-"message" means pass a message to x. The important point is that all you have to do is modify the "check" object's internal methods if the information contained in a check changes. The application itself doesn't have to change.

1.5 Implementing Messages and Objects

A message has three parts:

method selector

1. A *method selector* that tells the receiving object what to do—which method function to invoke.

receiver

2. A *receiver*. In the earlier example pseudocode x<-"message", x is the receiver. At a high level, the receiver is something like a database server—a process that receives a physical message—a stream of characters across a network. The receiver can also be a physical data structure—I'll discuss the mechanics in a moment.

optional data

3. *Optional data* used by the method to do its task.

An operating-system model like the database server I've been discussing has points in its favor. The internal state data is really isolated from other objects, for example. In a multitasking operating system like UNIX, a check object can be implemented by spawning a check process that receives messages over a pipe or socket and sends messages to other processes via other pipes or sockets. The database object (which is another process) responds to the "give me a list of checks for all employees who need to be paid" message by creating and initializing some large number of "check" processes and the database object then returns their names to the client. The client then prints the checks by piping a "print yourself" message to each of the 1,000 check processes and then kills the process. The problem with this approach is that 1,000 check processes running in tandem are not cheap in terms of system resources. Moreover, communication over pipes or sockets is not particularly fast.

It is often better to implement the object-oriented paradigm within a single program. For example, you can implement a check object with a module—a source file in C. Look at the file as a single object that represents its internal state data with `static` global variables. The methods are simply subroutines in the file that manipulate the `static` globals. There's a bit more flexibility than in a process-based approach. In particular, the object can decide which data and subroutines are *private* (cannot be accessed from outside the current object/file) by declaring them `static`. Nonstatic data is *public*—it can be accessed from anywhere.

private
public

There's also a slight notational shift. Syntax such as

```
check <- "print yourself"
```

makes sense in an operating-system model where the "database" object is an independent process receiving a character stream. In a procedural OOP system you can do the same thing in one of two ways. This syntax

```
check( "print yourself" );
```

encodes the receiver in the function name and the method selector as the argument. Additional data can be passed to the object by adding additional arguments to the function call.

The main problem with this approach is that you can have only one instance of the object. The linker won't let you link the same object file into the program more than once, after all. The only alternative to having only one "check" object per program is to write two almost identical modules in which the method-subroutine names are slightly different. Two check objects would require this:

```
check1("print yourself"); /* subroutine in module check1.c */
check2("print yourself"); /* subroutine in module check2.c */
```

It's not really acceptable to have many almost identical subroutines in the same program just to get more than one check.

The process of creating an instance of an object is called *instantiation* in OOPeese, and it's an important characteristic of any object-oriented system. In a language like C, the easiest way to instantiate more than one object is to not use global data at all; rather, the formerly global data is all concentrated into a structure. The methods that formerly manipulated the global data directly are now all passed a pointer to the specific structure that contains the state data for a particular object.

instantiation

To get more concrete, you can implement multiple `check` objects by defining a `check` structure that is manipulated by various methods, all of which are passed a pointer to the specific `check` they're modifying (the message's receiver). The method-selector component of the message is encoded into the function name. For example:

```
/* class definition: */

typedef struct check                        /* data component */
{
    /*...*/
}
check;
void print_yourself( check *this ); /* method component */

check check1, check2;              /* Two objects             */
    /*...*/

print_yourself( &check1 );    /* Send the print_yourself */
print_yourself( &check2 );    /* message to the object.   */
```

Data structure 'receives' a message

The individual objects are each represented by the two check structs (check1 and check2). In OOPeese, you'd call the structures *instances* or *objects* of *class* check. Rather than saying "call the print_yourself() function, passing it a pointer to a structure that represents the check," a native speaker of OOPeese says: "the check1 structure "receives" the ("print yourself") message." In C, you'd say that the check structure contains fields. In OOPeese, you'd say that "An object of class check has certain *attributes*." Note that a *class* in OOPeese is actually a bit more than the structure declaration because the methods that manipulate the structure are considered part of the class, so a *class definition* is both a structure declaration and a bunch of subroutine definitions as well.

Frankly, the OOP terminology probably does more to obscure than to clarify, but the advantages of the approach, if not the terminology, are obvious. Although the object has both a data and method component, you have only one set of methods that manipulate all the objects.

1.6 Inheritance

The next buzzword of interest is *inheritance*. The various fields in a structure and the subroutines that manipulate those fields (in OOPeese: a class' attributes and methods) are shared by all kinds of checks: employee paychecks, checks used to pay vendors, and so forth, even though the various kinds of checks need to contain information not contained in a vanilla check object. A paycheck, for example, needs all the fields in a normal check, but it also needs fields to represent the amount of withholding that was removed from the gross salary, a health-plan contribution amount, and so forth.

You deal with this problem by creating a "paycheck" class that has all the attributes and methods of the "check" class, but also has a few special attributes that are applicable only to paychecks. By knowing something about checks, you automatically know something about paychecks, too. In other words, a "paycheck" has a set of characteristics that are shared by all "checks" as well as a set of characteristics that are uniquely its own. In OOPeese, you'd say that a "paycheck" has a set of attributes that are *inherited* from a "check" and a set of unique attributes as well.

inherited

You can express this relationship in C, again using structures. You can fill in the check structure from the previous example to look like this:

```
#define CHECK 0          /* Used to differentiate simple      */
                         /* checks from other kinds of checks. */
typedef struct check /* "check" tag for documentation only.*/
{
    int     what_am_i;
    char    payee[80];
    double  amount;
    time_t  date;
}
check;
```

You need to provide a few "method" subroutines to manipulate check objects as well. Every object needs a *constructor* subroutine that initializes the object. A check constructor looks like this:

```
void check_construct( check *this, char *payee, double amount,
                                                time_t date )
{
    this->payee    = payee;
    this->amount   = amount;
    this->date     = date;
    this->what_am_i = CHECK;
}
```

The following method prints a check—I've changed the name from print_yourself():

```
void check_print( check *this )
{
    printf("                         %3.2f\n", this->date );
    printf("Pay to the order of %s  %3.2f\n", this->payee,
                                              this->amount );
    printf("%s\n",              spell_out( this->amount));
}
```

And the following method accesses the check's value:

```
double check_amount( check *this )
{
    return this->amount;
}
```

The initial this argument to all three methods points at the message's "receiver"—the object being manipulated. An object-oriented language like C++ provides access to the this pointer automatically—I'll describe the process below—but you must pass it around explicitly in C.

As I mentioned at the beginning of the current chapter, the main goal of the current approach is *data abstraction*—direct access to the data is prevented. Only the methods can access the data. This way you can change the internal organization of the object without affecting the programs that use the object (as long as the methods—the *interface*—don't change), and data validation is made easier as well. Ideally, the typedef check is local to the file in which the methods are declared

data abstraction

interface

so that direct access to the fields is impossible. Unfortunately, this degree of isolation is often impossible in C, where the data hiding is done more by gentleman's
agreement than by fiat.

In order to restrict access to the internal data of the check, I've provided a subroutine, check_amount(), to provide read-only access to one of the fields. Again,
I've done this for maintenance reasons. If, for example, I decide to store the
amount internally as a fixed-point number (say, in a long, with the value scaled up
by 100), I can make that change without affecting anything in the program except
the check_amount() subroutine (and the other check methods, of course). This
sort of function—a function that does nothing but provide safe access to an
access function   object's data—is called an *access function*. Access functions have to be used quite
carefully in practice, and I'll discuss them in more detail later on in the book.

Moving on to "paychecks," since a "paycheck" object is a kind of "check,"
you can model a paycheck by adding fields to the check structure. Rather than
just duplicate the check's fields in a new structure, you can effectively add fields
to a check as follows:

```
#define PAYCHECK CHECK+1
typedef struct paycheck
{
    check  base_class;
    double withholding;
    double health_contribution;
}
paycheck;
```

The paycheck definition effectively adds fields to a check because the first field of
a paycheck is a check structure—the first few fields of a check and a paycheck
are identical. The process of making a structure larger by adding fields to it is
derivation, base   called *derivation* in OOPeese. The initial structure (the check) is called the *base*
class, derived class   *class*. The expanded structure (the paycheck) is called the *derived class*.

You will need a new constructor subroutine for the new class:

```
void paycheck_construct( paycheck *this,       char   *payee,
                         double   amount,      time_t date,
                         double   withholding, double health
                     )
{
    check_construct( (check *)this, payee, amount, date );
    (check *)this->what_am_i = PAYCHECK;

    this->withholding        = withholding;
    this->health_contribution = health;
}
```

Note that the first thing the constructor does is call the constructor for the check
class. It's important to initialize the check component of the paycheck first
because code in the constructor might want to call methods associated with a
check.

The paycheck constructor also modifies one of the fields in the check directly
(on the second line of the subroutine) by casting the incoming this argument to a

check pointer. This modification is done directly rather than through a subroutine because the what_am_i field is intended to be modified only by derived-class objects, not by the application program. If a subroutine were available, the application program could call it. The structure definition is treated as if it were not available by the application program, however, so an application may not modify or examine this field directly. A field that is intended to be used by the derived class but not by the outside world is called a *protected* field. It's neither public nor private because its access is neither completely uncontrolled nor completely controlled.

protected

The remainder of the constructor subroutine just initializes the local fields.

It's important to remember that the base class is effectively part of the derived class (in C++, at least). All functions that manipulate a base-class object can also manipulate the base-class component of a derived-class object. Since the structure that holds a base-class's data is at the top of the derived-class object, a pointer to a derived-class object can safely be cast into a pointer to the base-class object and then be passed to a base-class function. The speaker of idiomatic OOPeese describes this process by saying that all objects of a derived class can be *promoted* to the base class. To my mind, "demoted" is a better term because you are treating a larger structure as if it were a smaller one, but it's rarely used.

manipulate derived-class objects with base-class functions

promoted

Note that the opposite of the foregoing is not usually safe—you can't use a derived-class pointer (a pointer to the expanded structure) to access a base-class object (an object of the original, unexpanded structure) because the base-class object has fewer fields than the derived-class object. Using a derived-class pointer to access a base-class object lets you access derived-class fields that don't physically exist in the base-class object.

dangerous to manipulate base-class object through derived-class pointer

Getting back to the concrete example, since the check is the first field of the paycheck structure, all subroutines that manipulate a check can also manipulate paycheck. A pointer to a paycheck has the same value as a pointer to the check component of the paycheck. You just need to cast one pointer to the other to get the types to match. Consequently, you don't need a new check_amount() function for a paycheck because you can access the amount field with a cast:

```
paycheck  pc;
paycheck_construct( &pc,
                    "Fred Flintstone",
                    1000.00, time(), 10.00, 10.00 );

check_amount( (check*)&pc );
```

You do need a new output function, because a paycheck has to output fields that check_print() doesn't know about. The new function can call the base-class print function to print its own base-class component, however:

```
paycheck_print( paycheck *this )
{
    check_print( (check *)this );
    printf("\n");
    printf("%3.2f withholding\n", this->withholding        );
    printf("%3.2f health\n",     this->health_contribution );
    printf("%3.2f salary\n",     check_amount( this )
                                 + this->withholding
                                 + this->health_contribution );
}
```

There are two final issues. A C++ compiler might not use the system shown to represent the base-class/derived-class relationship. It might keep the two structures separate, in which case a field in the derived-class object must point at the base-class object.

Also note that a base-class/derived-class relationship is not the same thing as simply nesting one structure (or class) inside another. You can represent this relationship by nesting structures, but you can represent it in other ways as well.

instance variable

A structure or class that is a field in another structure or class is usually called an *instance variable* in OOPeese. The important difference between a base class and an instance variable is that the base-class methods can be passed derived-class objects or pointers. Not so with the methods associated with instance variables— you can't just pass a pointer to the structure within which the instance variable is found to an instance variable's method, because the instance variable isn't guaranteed to be at the top of the structure. A C implementation confuses the issue because an instance variable that happens to be at the top of a structure could conceivably be used as if it's a base class. Nonetheless, there's an important conceptual difference between extending the definition of a structure by adding fields to it and simply using one structure as a field in another. The base-class/derived-class relationship applies only to the former situation.

1.7 Polymorphism and Virtual Functions

The next topic approaches inheritance from the other direction. The check and paycheck objects both have a print function associated with them. What if you want to write a small subroutine that can print checks of any sort, normal checks and paychecks both? As things stand now, you'd have to do something like this:

```
print_check( check *p )
{
    switch( p->what_am_i )
    {
    case CHECK:    check_print(p);                        break;
    case PAYCHECK: paycheck_print((paycheck*) p); break;
    }
}
```

The what_am_i field is part of the check structure. It's initialized to CHECK in check_construct(). The paycheck_construct() subroutine changes it to PAYCHECK. This printing procedure is both ungainly and hard to maintain. First of all, you need to define a new macro (such as PAYCHECK) every time you derive a new class from check. Next, switches such as the foregoing will probably be scattered throughout your code. Every time you derive a new class from check, you'll have to find and modify every one of those switch statements.

This last problem really makes the situation untenable. Fortunately, the problem can be solved by redefining the check class—replacing the what_am_i field with a function pointer as follows:

```
typedef struct check
{
    char    payee[80];
    double  amount;
    time_t  date;
    void    (*print)( struct check *this );
}
check;
```

You also need to modify check's initialization routine like this:

```
void check_construct(check *this, char *payee, double amount,
                                                time_t date )
{
    this->payee  = payee;
    this->amount = amount;
    this->date   = date;
    this->print  = check_print; /*<-- This line replaces the
                                 *  what_am_i initialization.
                                 */
}
```

And modify the one for paycheck as well:

```
paycheck_construct( paycheck *this,
                    char *payee, double amount, time_t date,
                    double withholding, double health
                  )
{
    check_construct( (check *)this, payee, amount, date );
    (check *)this->print = paycheck_print; /*<-- This line
                                            * replaces the
                                            * what_am_i
                                            * initialization.
                                            */
    this->withholding        = withholding;
    this->health_contribution = health;
}
```

The printing routine is now considerably simplified. It looks like this:

```
print_check( check *p )
{
    (*p->print)( p );
}
```

No switches, no what_am_i fields, no macros to maintain—the situation is vastly improved. The important point is that the same code is used to print any sort of check. Sometimes that code will call one print function, sometimes another, depending on the value of the print-function pointer, but the code that calls the print function never changes.

In OOPEESE, you'd say that both check and paycheck objects can receive the same message ("print yourself"), but they might execute the request in slightly different ways. Some kinds of checks print one thing, and other kinds print something else, but that's immaterial from the perspective of the requester as long as the check gets printed. The application just sends a "print yourself" message by calling the print_check() subroutine; the receiving check-type object interprets the message in a way that makes sense for itself. It's important to note that the code in the function that does the printing [print_check()] doesn't even know that it's printing two different sorts of derived-class objects, it just calls whatever function has a pointer in the proper place in the base-class structure.

This property—that all members of a class and its subclasses can receive and act on a certain message, but they may interpret the same message in slightly different ways—is called *polymorphism*. In biology, a polymorphic species has more than one adult form. Bees, for example, differentiate into queen bees, workers, drones, and so forth. They're all bees, though. In botany, broccoli and cauliflower represent a polymorphic plant—they're both *Brassica oleracea*; they just look different. Mineralogically, the term refers to a substance that crystallizes in more than one way like carbon, which crystallizes into diamonds, graphite, and Buckey balls. In C++, polymorphic functions such as the print function just discussed are called *virtual functions* because they're called through pointers rather than directly.

> polymorphism

> virtual functions

1.8 Abstract Types and Code Reuse

Another important advantage to an object-oriented approach is that it lets you write a solution to a general problem without needing any information about a specific application. Once you've written the general code, you can use it in various unrelated applications by customizing it at run time (by passing the general-purpose function pointers to a few auxiliary functions that give it the information it needs about the current application).

> code reuse

Using a general-purpose set of subroutines to solve a whole class of problems is called *code reuse* in OOPeese. Code reuse is a very different thing than just relinking the same library code into several programs. My point is that having solved a problem once, you don't need to solve it again. It's the general-purpose nature of the code that makes it reusable, not the fact that it is linked into several programs. The ANSI qsort() and bsearch() functions are examples of true reusable code in the standard C library. qsort(), for example, can sort arrays of any type—arrays of int, of char pointers, of structs—it doesn't matter what. You pass it the application-specific information that it needs to do the sort by means of function arguments. (It is passed the base address of the array, the size of one element in bytes, the number of elements, and a pointer to a comparison function that compares two elements.) For example, this code sorts argv:

```
int argvcmp( char **s1, char **s2 )
{
    /* Like strcmp(), but is passed pointers to two
     * argv elements and compares them. Same return
     * value as strcmp(), though.
     */
    return strcmp( *s1, *s2 );
}

main( int argc, char **argv )
{
    qsort( argv, argc, sizeof(*argv), argvcmp );
}
```

You can sort an array of ints like this:

```
int intcmp( int *i1, int *i2 ){ return *i1 - *i2; }
f()
{
    int intarray[ ASIZE ];
    ...
    qsort( intarray, ASIZE, sizeof(int), intcmp );
}
```

The concept of code reuse can be combined to good effect with that of derivation and virtual functions (polymorphism). The techniques that I'm about to discuss are the same ones I discussed in the previous section, but a slight shift in the way you look at the problem lets you use these techniques in a new way.

An *abstract class* is one that has virtual-function pointers, but no virtual func-   abstract class
tions. That is, there are slots in the structure definition for pointers to various workhorse functions, but those slots are initially empty. The slots are filled when a derived-class object is created by the derived-class initialization code. It's never safe to create an instance of the abstract base class because you don't want to set up a situation where a function pointer that contains a garbage value is actually used. Derived-class objects are safe because they fill in the virtual-function pointers that are empty in the abstract base class. The base class definition exists only so that you can derive something from it. That's why it's called "abstract."

The classic textbook example of this sort of abstract class is a shape class that represents graphic drawing elements. The shape class contains data common to all drawing elements: line width, color, location, and so forth. The shape is eventually specialized by deriving a second class (a circle or a box, for example) from it. Virtual functions can be used here to allow you to write base-class-level functions that can manipulate shapes of any sort without having to know anything about those shapes in advance. I'll demonstrate the process with a concrete example. A drawing can be represented by a linked list of shapes that can be defined with the following class and methods:

```
typedef struct shape
{
    struct shape *next;  /* next list element, NULL=none */
    int linewidth;
    int color;           /* drawing attributes.         */
    int row;             /* Position on page.           */
    int col;

    void (*draw)( void *app_area );
} shape ;

shape_construct( shape *this, void (*draw)(void *) )
{
    ...  /* Initialize the various shape fields to */
         /* reasonable defaults here               */

    this->draw = draw;
}

shape_row( shape *this ){ return this->row; } /* access    */
shape_col( shape *this ){ return this->col; } /* functions */

/* Other functions that modify the 'shape' from its defaults
 * to other values (eg.: to change the color) go here.
 */
```

Given these definitions, you can now write a general-purpose function to print an entire drawing made up of various shapes. Do it like this:

```
shape_print( shape *this )
{
    for(; this ; this = this->next )
        (*this->draw)( (void *)this );
}
```

This general-purpose function is a base-class method. It is passed a base-class pointer as its receiver.

To complete the example, the base class has to be specialized by deriving a class from it. A circle class derives from shape as follows:

```
typedef struct circle
{
    shape base; /* base class, must come first         */
    int radius; /* additional information needed to */
                /* represent a circle               */
} circle;
```

Various methods are required to manipulate circles. The important one for the current example is

```
void circle_draw( circle *this )   /* draw a circle */
{
    /* Get the row and column from the base class
     * and the radius from the derived class:
     */

    int row = shape_row( (shape *)this );
    int col = shape_col( (shape *)this );
    int rad = this->radius;

    /* draw the circle here */
}
```

You also need a constructor function that initializes the base class, at the same time modifying the `draw` field of the base class to address the derived-class's draw function:

```
circle_construct( circle *this, int rad )
{
    shape_construct( (shape *)this, circle_draw );
    this->radius = rad;
}
```

That's all that the derived class needs to do. You can print a circle (or a linked list of several circles) by calling `shape_print()`, passing it a pointer to the circle (or to the head of the list). `shape_print()` just calls `circle`'s print function indirectly to do the real work.

The point is that the original `shape`-class creator can write a general-purpose function that draws shapes of any sort without having to know anything about the characteristics of those shapes beyond the fact that they can be drawn. The programmer who is writing the `shape` class doesn't need to know in advance what the shapes are or how to draw them—the information is provided by a derived-class function, a pointer to which is stored in the base class. Moreover, you can modify the system by adding a new shape at any time, and you don't have to modify the definition of a `shape` to do it. All you need do is provide a specialized draw function for the new shape and pass a pointer to that function to the `shape`-class constructor. Finally, the application programmer who is using the `shape` classes can write general-purpose functions that can manipulate shapes of any sort, without having to know which shape is actually being manipulated. In the current example, the application programmer can effectively tell any shape to draw itself without having to know what real drawing element the `shape` represents.

The linked-list functions described at the end of this chapter make heavy use of the technique I just discussed, and since the technique is so important—it's really central to object-oriented programming—I'll review it in the context of the linked-list class.

1.9 Class Hierarchies and Inheritance

1.9.1 Single Inheritance

The interdependence of a class and its base class or classes is usually called a *class hierarchy* and is represented as a kind of graph called a *DAG* (directed acyclic graph). A DAG is a tree in which a node can have multiple parents, but there can be no cycles. That is, a node can never point up at one of its ancestors. In the case of a class hierarchy, a base class is usually represented at the top of the DAG, and the classes that derive from it are represented as its children.

Figure 1.1 shows a simple class hierarchy in which a collection of records for various employees will be placed into a linked list. The arrows point from the base class (the original structure) to the derived class (the extended structure).[1] The two data structures represented by this hierarchy are pictured at the right of the figure. At the top of the hierarchy is the `list_element` class (i.e., `struct`) which contains only those fields needed to manipulate a linked list (a pointer to the next element in the list, for example). A plain `list_element` is not very useful, however, because it has no contents. It's just a list of structures that contain nothing but pointers to other list elements. Nonetheless, it <u>is</u> useful in defining a set of subroutines (methods) that can manipulate lists at this level. For example, you can write methods that add elements to the list and remove elements from the list without caring about anything but the pointers in a `list_element`. The other fields are immaterial.

Figure 1.1. A Simple Class Hierarchy

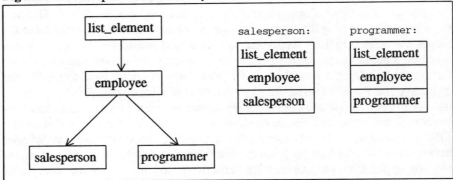

An `employee` class derives from `list_element` in Figure 1.1. In other words, those fields necessary to represent a generic employee have been tacked onto the end of the `list_element` structure. The derived-class relationship means that all subroutines that can manipulate list elements can also manipulate `employee`s, so

---

[1] Some authors use arrows pointing in the other direction (from the derived class to the base class).

(margin note:) class hierarchy, DAG

the simple act of derivation gives us several useful subroutines without having to do anything special. That is, we can declare a variable of type `employee` (in OOPeese: instantiate an object of class `employee`) and then add it to a linked list by passing an `employee` pointer to an add-to-list function that expects a `list_element`. Derivation usually works this way: a derived-class object (or pointer) can usually be converted to a base-class object (or pointer) without difficulty. Remember the earlier discussion of the mechanics of derivation—it's as if the derived-class object has a base-class object at its top. Consequently, a function that's expecting a base-class object but is passed a derived-class object can happily manipulate the base-class component of the derived-class object without even knowing that it's manipulating a derived-class object.

The relationship between a base and its derived classes is called an *inheritance* relationship because the characteristics (i.e., the data and methods) of the base class are inherited by the derived class. The DAG that represents the class hierarchy is often called an *inheritance graph*.

inheritance

inheritance graph

Continuing down the DAG in Figure 1.1, the derivation path now splits off into two distinct subclasses. Both a `salesperson` and a `programmer` are `employee`s, so there will be many common data fields shared by the records (employee name, address, salary, and so forth). This common data is stored in the `employee` class. Similarly, all the functions that can manipulate `list_element`s and all the functions that can manipulate `employee`s can also manipulate `programmer`s and `salesperson`s. The `salesperson` extension to the `employee` class might contain data that's of use only to salespeople, however (the dollar amount of sales that's used to figure a commission, for example). This data is in the `salesperson` class, but not in the `programmer` class. **In general, if two data structures have fields that do the same thing, the shared fields should be in a common base class and the unique components should be in derived classes.**

1.9.2 Multiple Inheritance

The earlier class system is okay in simple situations, but what if you want the `employee` and its subclasses to be members of two data structures at the same time? For example, you want the `employee` simultaneously to be in a tree and a list—in the tree so that you can search for a particular `employee` quickly, and in a list that is presorted by some criteria. In other words, you want the `employee` to have the characteristics of both a linked-list element and a tree node. This dual nature is called *multiple inheritance* and is achieved by specifying multiple base classes for some given class.

multiple inheritance

Figure 1.2 shows how a multiple inheritance relationship such as the foregoing is expressed in an inheritance graph. The resulting data structures are at the right of the figure, as before. The `tree_node` class contains fields and methods used for manipulating binary-tree nodes and `list_element` does the same thing for linked-list elements. The graph then comes back together into the `employee` record. That is, an `employee` record contains both a `list_element` and a `tree_node`.

Figure 1.2 also shows how an object of type `programmer` can be represented at run time. The implementation of multiple inheritance is more complex than that of

Figure 1.2. A More Complex Class Hierarchy

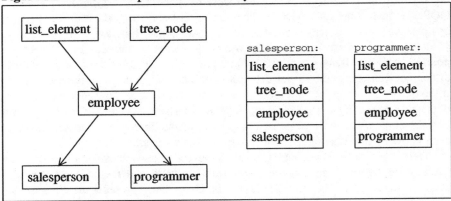

single inheritance. In particular, the compiler can no longer just pass a derived-class pointer to a base-class subroutine and assume that everything will work. It must actually know which base class the base-class subroutine thinks it's manipulating, and then modify the incoming argument accordingly. This is not a simple problem, but is well within the ability of a C++ compiler, for example, to handle. It's difficult to simulate this behavior in simple C, however. Moreover, multiple inheritance tends to lead toward very complex class hierarchies that are difficult to maintain, so the technique must be used with care. C++ supports multiple inheritance, but a host of problems can be introduced into the code as a consequence. (I'll discuss these later on when I talk about the C++ implementation.)

1.9.3 A Few Class-Hierarchy Design Issues

Designing a good class hierarchy is a nontrivial task. I'll discuss this topic throughout the book as you learn more about the mechanics of class manipulation, but I can give you a few basic rules now. There is no good solution to the design problem beyond a few rather fuzzy rules of thumb. Always remember that the main point of classes and object-oriented programming is to make the code more maintainable. If your class hierarchy is too complex, you will have not achieved this end, so you must constantly ask yourself whether a certain solution will be more or less maintainable than another solution. It is a common, though serious, error to use classes (or any other language feature) just because a language supports them. Classes and derivation should be used only if the resulting code is easier to understand and easier to maintain, not just because they're there. On the other side of the coin, classes *can* make the code easier to understand, so don't avoid them just because they're unfamiliar.

The first rule is useful when you're in the middle of the design/development cycle and are refining existing code. If you notice that two data structures in your program have many similar fields and many similar functions that manipulate them, then you have a good candidate for inheritance. Implement the common things as a base class that is customized by deriving two distinct classes from the common base class. Of course, this merging of functionality can be done at the initial design stage, too, but it's often not obvious that there is something in common between two processes until you actually start coding.

The next rule is the *"is-a" versus "has-a"* test. The question is whether something "is-a" something or does it "have-a" something. In the first instance, you'll use derivation. In the second, you'll probably use an object of one class as a field of another class, rather like one structure nested inside a second structure. Some languages call this sort of enclosed class an *instance variable*.

'is-a' versus 'has-a'

instance variable

For example, an employee record "is-a" linked-list element. On the other hand, a window "has-a" color. It is not a color. Consequently, it's not a good idea to derive a `blue_window` class from a `window` class. Rather, a `window` should have a `color` attribute that is changed by calling a method attached to the `window` class.

Often, however, the relationship is not nearly so straightforward. Take, for example, a linked-list class. You can use a linked list to represent a stack, a queue, and a sorted list. That is, stacks, queues, and sorted lists <u>are</u> linked lists; they do not contain linked lists. Consequently, a derived-class relationship could be a reasonable choice here. On the other hand, if you use derived classes, it won't be easy to convert a sorted list into a queue in order to print it out. Similarly, insertion into a sorted list is likely to be an inefficient process because the insert function will have to find the proper place in the list for each inserted element. It is more efficient to insert a group of elements into a queue, and then convert the queue to a sorted list, doing the sorting as part of the type conversion. Although it's possible to define a conversion from queue to sorted list, the resulting code is likely to be more difficult to maintain than a more general `list` class that had a "list type" attribute that can be set to `queue`, `stack`, or `sorted_list`.

Another example of a problematic situation is a scrollbar. Is a scrollbar a type of window, or does a scrollable window contain a scrollbar? In the first approach, scrollbar is a class of its own that derives from a window class ("a scrollbar *is a* window"). Manipulating the scrollbar with a mouse causes it to send messages to another window telling the second window what to do. [For example, it can call a `scroll_window()` function that was passed a pointer to the window to scroll.] Since a scrollbar is a window in its own right, it can be manipulated like one (moved around, made to disappear, etc.) just by calling existing window functions. You can also attach several scrollbars to a given window, one to move the text large distances and another for finer movement, for example.

An alternate approach makes a scrollbar an attribute of the "window" class. Here, a window *has a* scrollbar that is much more tightly coupled to the window than before. The advantage is easier maintenance—it's a simpler process to create the scrollbar when you create a window (and getting rid of it when you delete the window). Also, the external interface to the window class is now simplified because there's no need for a `scroll()` function; all scrolling is handled internally. Both solutions are viable—there is really no correct answer.

The next issue is the size of a class. Class definitions tend to grow if not carefully controlled. Be careful about getting carried away and making a base class too general. Don't solve problems that don't exist. It's common to define a very

fat class definition

general base class that contains a lot of functionality—this is called a *fat class definition*. It's a mistake, though, to add fields or methods to a base class, not because they're required in the current application, but because that *might* be required by some future application. This misdirected zeal generally gives you bloated and hard-to-maintain programs in which a large body of the code is never used. You can almost always add additional data or methods by deriving a class, provided the interface to the base class is designed in a thoughtful manner. A class implementation, typically, should do one thing well.

Smalltalk

The final issue worth mentioning is the overall structure of a class hierarchy or hierarchies. Smalltalk was one of the first object-oriented languages, and in Smalltalk all classes must derive from a common base class called `object`. That means that a Smalltalk program will have only one class hierarchy rooted in the `object` class. For reasons that have to do with the way Smalltalk works, this sort of design has real advantages in the Smalltalk environment.[2] This does not mean that the same organization works effectively in any other environment, however. One of the biggest mistakes I've seen in C++ class hierarchies is a tendency to mimic Smalltalk hierarchies, even when a Smalltalk-like design makes no sense.

flat class hierarchy

C++ lends itself much more to a *flat class hierarchy*—in which several unrelated, not very deep, class hierarchies are used—than it does to a Smalltalk model, that tends to give you a very deep tree-like structure.[3]

First of all, in order to use a Smalltalk model, you need to come up with a root base-class definition that contains functionality needed by every class in the system. I'm not sure this can ever be done in a C++ environment. Can you think of a data field or a method that will be needed by every data structure in every program that you write? I sure can't.

---

[2] First, all functions in a Smalltalk program must be a method in some class. The class system, then, is used not only for data-structure definition but also for Pascal-style nested subroutine declarations. A Smalltalk program consists entirely of class objects that send messages to one another. I see this structure as a deficiency of the language, not an asset. C++ lets you have functions that are just plain functions, thereby letting you use class hierarchies where they make sense, and use normal functions everywhere else. A C++ program is really a C program that uses classes to introduce new types into the language. Since a C++ program doesn't require a single hierarchy, there's no advantage to deriving from a single `object` class.

The other important difference is that Smalltalk is an interpretive, not a compiled language. Messages are passed from class to class at run time by the Smalltalk interpreter. If the class to which a message is sent can't handle that message, the interpreter passes it up the hierarchy to that class's base class. A system like this needs a single class from which all classes derive in order to handle errors—to intercept messages that can't be handled by any of the derived class. C++ resolves the message passing issues at compile time, though. For example, Smalltalk translates a+b as "look up the +b message in a's method table (at run time) and call the appropriate method if one is there. If a has no such message, repeat the lookup in a's base class, and so forth." C++ just translates a+b into a function call, examining the compiler's symbol table (at compile time) to see if the receiving class or one of its base classes has a method function that can deal with the message.

[3] If it makes any of you Smalltalk people feel better, just think of a C++ program's global level as being the definition of the `object` class. Since the roots of all class hierarchy are defined within the global level, they effectively derive from the global-level `object`.

Moreover, too much generality at the highest level in the hierarchy does not come without a price. Remember, in a language like C++, the base class is physically part of the derived class. Consequently, every derived-class object must carry around all the base class's data fields, even if the derived-class object doesn't use the fields. I've met programmers who argue that this isn't a real problem. ("Well, I can't help it if *your* machine doesn't support a 32-bit linear address space and 10 gigabytes of virtual memory; go out and get a *real* machine.") This attitude works to no one's benefit in the long run. The vast majority of computers are not so ideal, and you'll have real difficulty porting your code to an environment that has a paltry three or four megabytes of memory.

The real issue here is a philosophical one. Every Smalltalk data type—even an integer—is a class of some sort. Smalltalk is a pure object-oriented language in this respect—it's entirely object-based. All classes in Smalltalk are related to one another by definition—they all must derive from `object`—so only one hierarchy is possible. C++, however, is a hybrid language: part C and part object-oriented. A C++ program is really a C program that uses classes to add new types to C. There's no reason to put those classes into a single hierarchy if those classes are unrelated to one another.

There are other maintenance issues involved as well. In C++, you can't really derive a class unless you have at least some understanding of the base classes involved—all the way up the hierarchy. Making the hierarchy too deep gives you much harder-to-maintain code, and makes the learning curve for a new programmer very steep, indeed.

The final issue comes back to the idea of a class being a plug-in component that you can interchange with another component later on in the system-development process. If all classes in a commercial class library, for example, derive from a single base class, then this plug-in functionality is impossible. Say, for example, that one store-bought GUI class library has a great mouse-based input system and a lousy window-management system, and another library has a lousy input system and a great window-management system. If the class libraries follow the Smalltalk model and look like this:

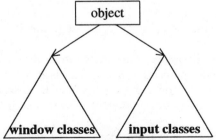

it probably won't be possible to use the input classes from one library and the output classes from the other.

Moreover, you won't be able to use two commercial class libraries in the same program if both of them mimic Smalltalk by deriving everything from a class called `object`.

These last two problems are such a disadvantage that I usually don't purchase Smalltalk-style class libraries. The foregoing notwithstanding, classes, when used correctly, can give you much better maintenance and much better program structure. Writing a good class library is difficult, but it's usually worth the effort.

1.10 Extensibility: Expanding the Language Definition

Language extensibility—the ability to modify the language specification by adding new types and operations to the language—is almost a side effect of an object-oriented approach to programming.

god-like compiler

A compiler for a procedural language looks down on a program in a god-like manner. It knows everything there is to know about the characteristics of possible types and how to manipulate instances of these types. That is, the compiler sees operators and operands, and the compiler generates the code that performs the indicated operations. The characteristics of the data (its size, for example, and how to manipulate it) are built into the compiler itself. You cannot change the width of an `int` without modifying the compiler. Similarly, rules about how to manipulate variables of a particular type, how to convert one type to another, which operations are legal with particular operands, and so forth, are hard-coded into the compiler. The compiler, for example, knows that + must be handled differently with two `int` operands than with a pointer and an `int` operand, or with two pointers. A procedural language like C gives you ways to create aliases for an existing type (the `typedef`), but there's no easy way to introduce an entirely new type into the language. You can't, for example, create a fixed-point arithmetic type called `fixed`, and then declare variables of type `fixed`, use those variables in expressions, and so forth. You'd like for the following to be legal:

```
fixed   a = 1.00,   // Fixed-point number (two decimal places)
        b = 9.99;
double f;
   ...
f = (double)(a + b * 2.0);
```

It's not, though. You have to do it with function calls and `typedef`'s, like the ones in Listing 1.1.

The first form is obviously the more desirable. One of the main differences between an object-oriented language and a procedural one is the ability to introduce real types into a language. An object-oriented language can be extended because it looks at data manipulation in a way that's different from that used by a procedural language.

In a strict object-oriented approach, an expression like a+b is treated as an object (a) that is passed a message (+b). The message has a method selector component (+) and a data field (b). It's up to the object to provide a method that can handle the + message when the data is of the type of b, and to pass back a message that contains the sum of the current object and the b operand. The + operator is not an operator per se. It just selects one of the methods. In a system like this, the

Listing 1.1. *fixed.c*— A C Fixed-Point Arithmetic Package

```
 1  typedef long fixed;
 2  void    fix_assign (fixed *this, double d){ *this = (long)(d * 100.0);     }
 3  fixed   fix_add    (fixed *this, fixed  r){ return (*this += r);           }
 4  fixed   fix_mult   (fixed *this, fixed  r){ return (*this =(*this*r)/100;}
 5  double  fix_double (fixed *this           ){ return ((double)*this/100.0);}
 6
 7  foo()
 8  {
 9      fixed a, b, t0, t1;
10      double f;
11
12      fix_assign ( &a,  1.00 );
13      fix_assign ( &b,  9.99 );
14      fix_assign ( &t0, 0.00 );
15      fix_assign ( &t1, 2.00 );
16      fix_add    ( &t0, t1   );
17      fix_mult   ( &t0, b    );
18      fix_add    ( &t0, a    );
19      f = fix_double( t0 );
20  }
```

only difference between a basic type and a user-defined type is that the methods for the basic types are built into the compiler. Users supply their own methods for their own types.

Looked at another way: in an object-oriented language, the data-description and the data-manipulation rules are combined into the class definition. An object of the class carries around not only the data, as is the case with an int, but also the methods for manipulating the data in the form of method subroutines. A method is invoked by sending a *message* to an object that says "do something to yourself by   message applying the following method subroutine." It's a short step from syntax such as

```
a <- "add b to yourself; return a message holding the result"
```

to

```
a <- "+ b"
```

to

```
add( &a, b )
```

All three are really just different syntaxes for the same thing.

To continue the analogy of sending a message, it's certainly possible to centralize the message dispatching into a single subroutine. Interpretive object-oriented languages work in much this way. The fixed-point arithmetic package from Listing 1.1 is modified to use a message dispatcher in Listings 1.2, 1.3, and 1.4 to show how the dispatcher is used.

Even this primitive sort of message passing yields some notable improvement in the code. The most obvious improvement is that the various send() calls are much more readable than the earlier direct calls to the methods. A more important

Listing 1.2. *fixed.c* — Fixed-Point Arithmetic Functions

```
21   #define PUBLIC   /* empty */
22   #define PRIVATE static
23
24   typedef long fixed;
25
26   PRIVATE fixed *fix_construct()
27   {
28       fixed *this;
29       if( !(this = malloc(sizeof(fixed)) ))
30       {
31           printf("Out of memory\n");
32           exit(1);
33       }
34   }
35   PRIVATE void fix_destroy( fixed *this ){ free(this); }
36
37   PRIVATE void  fix_assign(fixed *this, double d){*this = (long)(d*100.0);}
38   PRIVATE fixed fix_add    (fixed *this, fixed  r){return(*this += r);      }
39   PRIVATE fixed fix_mult   (fixed *this, fixed  r){return(*this *= r);      }
40
41   /* fix_double(), which returns the double value represented by the
42    * fixed operand, is weird in that the returned thing is not the
43    * left operand and is not of type fixed. Be careful with it.
44    */
45
46   PRIVATE double fix_double( fixed *this )
47   {
48       return( (double)*this / 100.0);
49   }
50
51   /* The message-dispatcher function. Called with:
52    *      send( &left_operand, "operator", &right_operand );
53    * Operators are:
54    *    "f"  Initialize fixed left operand.
55    *    "~"  Destroy fixed left operand.
56    *    "="  Assign right to left operand.
57    *    "+"  Add right operand into left operand.
58    *    "*"  Multiply right operand into left operand.
59    *    "d"  Modify double pointed to by left operand to hold
60    *         value of right operand.
61    */
62
63   PUBLIC void *send( fixed* this, char *message, ... )
64   {
65       va_list ap;
66       va_start( ap, message );
67       fixed *right;
68
69       switch( *message )
70       {
```

Listing 1.2. continued. . .

```
71          case 'f': this = fix_construct();
72                    break;
73          case '~': fix_destroy( this );
74                    break;
75          case '=': fix_assign ( this, va_arg(ap, double));
76                    break;
77          case '+': fix_add    ( this, va_arg(ap, fixed*));
78                    break;
79          case '*': fix_mult   ( this, va_arg(ap, fixed*));
80                    break;
81          case 'd': *(double*)this = fix_double(right = va_arg(ap, fixed*));
82                    this = right;
83                    break;
84          }
85          va_end(ap);
86          return this;
87  }
```

Listing 1.3. fixed.h

```
1  typedef long fixed;
2  void *send( fixed* this, char *message, ... );
```

improvement is that the organization of the program has changed dramatically. All the subroutines that are doing the work are isolated in the *fixed.c* file. The only publicly accessible subroutine is send(). Everything else is declared static, so can't be accessed from outside *fixed.c*. Similarly, the typedef for fixed is now also hidden in *fixed.c* and isn't visible to the outside world. That is, this change not only abstracts the data, but the methods as well. It changes both the way that the data is represented and the functions that manipulate it. The send() function must be changed if a function's name or arguments are changed, but everything is concentrated in one file, so the changes are pretty easy to make. The application program is now completely isolated from both the data and the mechanics of manipulating the data.

The code can be improved further by adding a preprocessor that translates input expressions into send() calls. Listing 1.5 shows a UNIX **awk** script that does just that—translates expressions into send() calls.[4] Don't worry about understanding the **awk** syntax if you're not familiar with it—the point is that it's easy to translate one syntax into another. Here, all input lines that take the form

---

[4] Hard-core **awk** programmers will note that the **awk** script isn't as rigorous as it could be about checking the input. White space is required surrounding all operators and operands except the semicolon, for example. I leave cleaning up the script as an exercise.

Listing 1.4. *main.c*— Testing the Fixed-Point Arithmetic Functions

```
1    #include <stdio.h>         /* For NULL definition         */
2    #include "fixed.h"
3
4    main()
5    {
6        fixed *a  = send( NULL, "fixed" );
7        fixed *b  = send( NULL, "fixed" );
8        fixed *t0 = send( NULL, "fixed" );
9        fixed *t1 = send( NULL, "fixed" );
10       double f;
11
12       send ( a,  "=",       1.00 );  /* send "=" message to "a" object */
13       send ( b,  "=",       9.99 );
14       send ( t0, "=",       0.00 );
15       send ( t1, "=",       2.00 );
16       send ( t0, "+=",      t1   );
17       send ( t0, "*=",      b    );
18       send ( t0, "+=",      a    );
19       send ( &f, "double",  t0   );
20
21       send( a,   "~fixed" );
22       send( b,   "~fixed" );
23       send( t0,  "~fixed" );
24       send( t1,  "~fixed" );
25   }
```

```
: fixed name;
```

are converted to

```
fixed * name = send( NULL, "fixed" );
```

(The colon must be the first character on the line.) Lines of the form

```
: name  = value
: name  *= value
: name  += value
```

are converted to

```
send( name , "=",  value );
send( name , "+=", value );
send( name , "*=", value );
```

and a line of the form

```
: value = (double) name
```

is converted to

```
send( name , "double", & value );
```

As an added convenience, calls to

```
send(  name ,  "~fixed" );
```

are automatically generated at the end of the block for every previous declaration.
This way you don't have to worry about forgetting to free the automatically allocated memory. The input file in Listing 1.6, when passed to `awk -f fixed.awk`,
generates the output in Listing 1.7, which can then be compiled and linked
together with *fixed.c* to form a complete program.

Listing 1.5. *fixed.awk*— AWK Script That Translates Simple Expressions into Function Calls

```
 1   #          This block is executed once before any lines are read
 2   BEGIN    {    printf("#include <stdio.h>\n");
 3                 printf("typedef long fixed;\n");
 4                 printf("void * send( fixed* this, char *message, ... );\n");
 5            }
 6
 7   #          This block executed if line begins with an open brace
 8   /^{/     {    Ndecl = 0;              # Number of declarations in block
 9                 printf("{\n");
10            }
11
12   #          This block executed if line begins with a close brace
13   /^}/     {
14                 # Emit the destructors. The Destructor[] array is
15                 # filled when "fixed" declarations are detected, below.
16
17                 while( --Ndecl >= 0 )
18                     printf( "\t%s\n",  Destructor[Ndecl] );
19                 printf("}\n");
20            }
21
22   #          This block executed if the line begins with a colon. The line
23   #          is split into space-delimited fields by awk. The leftmost
24   #          field is named $1, then $2, etc. For example, in the line:
25   #                        : a = 1.0
26   #          $1 is :
27   #          $2 is a
28   #          $3 is =
29   #          $4 is 1.0
30   #
31   /^:/     {
32                 if( $2~/fixed/ )             # if 2nd argument on line
33                 {                            # contains the string "fixed"
34                     sub( /;/, "", $3 );      # remove any semicolon
35                     printf("\tfixed *%s = send( NULL, \"fixed\" );\n", $3 );
36                     Destructor[Ndecl++] = "send( " $3 ", \"~fixed\");"
37                 }
38                 else if( $4 ~ /(double)/ )   # if 4th argument contains
39                 {                            # the string "(double)"
40                     sub( /;/, "", $5 );      # remove semicolon
41                     printf("\tsend( %s, \"double\", &%s );\n", $5, $2 );
42                 }
```

➡

Listing 1.5. continued...

```
43              else if( $3 ~ /^=/ )          # if 3rd argument begins with
44              {                             # equal sign
45                  sub( /;/, "", $4 );       # remove semicolon
46                  printf("\tsend( %s, \"=\", %s );\n", $2, $4 );
47              }
48              else if( $3 ~ /^\+/ )         # if 3rd argument begins with
49              {                             # a plus sign
50                  sub( /;/, "", $4 );       # remove semicolon
51                  printf("\tsend( %s, \"+=\", %s );\n", $2, $4 );
52              }
53              else if( $3 ~ /^\*/ )         # if 3rd argument begins with
54              {                             # a star.
55                  sub( /;/, "", $4 );       # remove semicolon
56                  printf("\tsend( %s, \"*=\", %s );\n", $2, $4 );
57              }
58          }
59
60  /^[^{}:]/ { print } # print lines that begin with anything but {, }, or :
```

Listing 1.6. *fixtst.in*— Test File for AWK Preprocessor

```
1   void main()
2   {
3   :   fixed a;
4   :   fixed b;
5   :   fixed t0;
6   :   fixed t1;
7       double f;
8
9   :   a   =    1.00 ;
10  :   b   =    9.99 ;
11  :   t0  =    0.00 ;
12  :   t1  =    2.00 ;
13  :   t0 +=    t1   ;
14  :   t0 *=    b    ;
15  :   t0 +=    a    ;
16  :   f   = (double) t0;
17  }
```

You can, admittedly, go a lot further in terms of preprocessing. For example, it would be nice if the preprocessor understood the normal C precedence and syntax rules so you wouldn't have to evaluate expressions one operator at a time. It would also be nice if the temporary variables like t0 were generated automatically. If you take this evolution far enough, you'll end up with C++. *Operator overloading*, then, is the ability to get control over how the operators are processed by the compiler; in C++ operator overloading is implemented by translating an expression like a+b into a subroutine call like add(&a,b) in a controlled fashion. I'll discuss the details in Chapter Four.

operator overloading

Listing 1.7. *fixst.out*— Output from AWK Preprocessor

```
 1    #include <stdio.h>
 2    typedef long fixed;
 3    void * send( fixed* this, char *message, ... );
 4    void main()
 5    {
 6            fixed *a  = send( NULL, "fixed" );
 7            fixed *b  = send( NULL, "fixed" );
 8            fixed *t0 = send( NULL, "fixed" );
 9            fixed *t1 = send( NULL, "fixed" );
10    double f;
11            send( a, "=", 1.00 );
12            send( b, "=", 9.99 );
13            send( t0, "=", 0.00 );
14            send( t1, "=", 2.00 );
15            send( t0, "+=", t1 );
16            send( t0, "*=", b );
17            send( t0, "+=", a );
18            send( t0, "double", &f );
19            send( t1, "~fixed");
20            send( t0, "~fixed");
21            send( b, "~fixed");
22            send( a, "~fixed");
23    }
```

Although a single-character message-selector like + is easy to parse, there's no reason why a multiple-character string like add can't be used. In the same way that t0+=a sends a message with send(t0, "+=", a), a function call like do_something(receiver, data) can be mapped to send(receiver, "do_something", data) The moral is that something that looks like a function call can be implemented by the message-passing system in an object-oriented language. The only difference, in fact, between a generic subroutine and a message passed with a function-like syntax is that the message must have a receiver (a structure to manipulate), while a generic subroutine probably won't have one.

Finally, note that once you introduce a preprocessor or compiler into the picture, there's little advantage in using a physical send() subroutine. It's just as easy for the preprocessor to generate calls to the dispatched functions as it is for it to generate send() calls.

1.11 Case Study: Making `malloc()` Safe for Democracy

It's reasonable to come down to earth at this point and demonstrate some of the principles I've been discussing in the context of vanilla C. I'll do that with two case studies (in the current and the next sections). The first is a *wrapper* layer   **wrapper** around malloc(). A wrapper subroutine is one through which a second subroutine is called—the second subroutine is never called directly. The current wrapper solves two serious dynamic-memory problems: (1) it's possible to corrupt the heap used for dynamic storage by passing a pointer to `free()` that wasn't returned from `malloc()`, and (2) it's also possible to corrupt the heap by passing a legitimate pointer to `free()` twice. The wrapper also logs all `malloc()` and `free()` calls to a file so that you can get a handle on the problem when it does spring up.

Most `malloc()` implementations are modeled after the one in Kernighan and Ritchie's *The C Programming Language.*[5] Dynamic memory (the heap) is split up into a group of variable-sized blocks, arranged as a linked list. Each block is headed by a structure like the following one:

```
typedef struct malloc_hdr
{
    struct malloc_hdr *next;
    unsigned int size;
}
malloc_hdr;
```

The `size` field holds the size of the current block, the `ptr` field holds the address of the next block that is not currently in use. A small free list is pictured in Figure 1.3.

Figure 1.3. A Small Free List

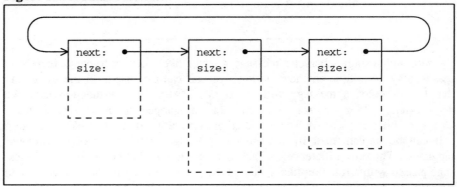

Looked at objectively (so to speak), the free-list header forms a base class.

When you call `malloc()`, it searches along the free list until it finds a big enough block. It then removes this block from the list and returns a pointer to the region of memory just beneath the header, more or less like this:

---

[5] [K&R] pp. 185–189.

```
malloc_hdr *p,                    /* Desired block.           */
           *preceding_block;  /* Block preceding desired  */
                              /* block in the free list.  */

           /* The following call returns a pointer to the */
           /* first available block in the free list and  */
           /* initializes preceding_block to point at the */
           /* block preceding the one addressed by p.      */
p = first_available_block( &preceding_block );

preceding_block->next = p->next; /* Unlink block from list.*/
return ++p;                       /* Return pointer to area */
                                  /* beneath the header.    */
```

The `++` on the last line moves the `malloc_hdr` pointer from the top of the block to the beginning of the application region. The code

```
struct fred {...};
fred *p = malloc( sizeof(fred) );
```

creates an object like this:

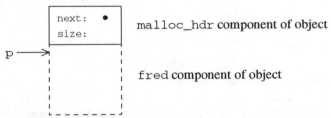

Again, looked at in an object-oriented manner, a call to `malloc()` effectively derives an object from the `malloc_hdr` base class. It adds fields to the base-class structure by tacking memory for a `fred` structure after it. A derived-class method (one that manipulates a `fred` object) can't access the base-class component of the derived class (the `malloc_hdr`), but that's all for the better from a maintenance perspective. All such base-class manipulation must be done through the base-class methods `malloc()` or `free()`. This isolation lets you change the way that `malloc()` and `free()` work without affecting any of the rest of the program. It's all done by agreement, though. There's nothing in the C language itself that prevents you from mucking around with the `malloc_hdr`—it's only your better judgment that does so. This isolation of the base class from the derived class is usually a good idea, even if the language doesn't force you to separate the layers. In an object-oriented language like C++, the compiler can indeed prevent you from accessing the base-class structure, but it doesn't provide this isolation unless you tell it to.

The main advantage of this layered approach is that you can add additional layers to the system more or less transparently. For example, two common problems appear in programs that use `malloc()` and `free()`: memory leaks (situations in which you allocate memory that is never freed) and a corrupted heap [where you pass the same pointer to `free()` more than once, or you pass a pointer to `free()` that was not returned from `malloc()`]. You can—if not solve—at least get a handle on both problems by putting a debugging layer around `malloc()`. That is, the debugging layer derives a class from the `malloc_hdr()` by calling `malloc()` to get memory in a safe way. Your application derives classes from the debugging layer by calling its version of `malloc()` to get memory. You'd never call `malloc()` directly.

You do all this, first by introducing a structure to represent the data component of the derived class. There's one shown in Listing 1.8. A safe-allocation method that uses the derived-class object [called `new()`] is presented in Listing 1.9.

Listing 1.8. *new.h*— A Safer `malloc()`—Definitions

```
 1   typedef long align;                    /* worst-case alignment type */
 2   #define MAGIC ( (align)0xabcd1234L )    /* Arbitrary value          */
 3
 4   typedef struct wrapper
 5   {
 6       align signature;      // Make it first to guarantee alignment.
 7       int   line_number;
 8       char *file_name;
 9   }
10   wrapper;
```

A log file is opened on line 20 of Listing 1.9 if this is the first time that `new()` has been called. (In this case, `Logfile` will have a `NULL` value.) The subroutine logs the current allocation to the file on line 26. The new class is derived on line 28: `malloc()` is called to get the memory, but the requested size is the incoming block size plus the size of the wrapper structure. The wrapper is initialized on lines 30 to 32. The `signature` field is set to an arbitrary value that I'll use in the safe version of `free()` to test for a valid block. Note that the returned pointer is incremented to point past the `wrapper` header (on line 35) so that the derived-class objects don't have to worry about the base-class component of the structure.

The safer version of `free()`, called `delete()`, is in Listing 1.10. The subroutine first tests for an incoming `NULL` pointer (on line 52). If the pointer is valid, it then tests to see if it's pointing at memory that came from `new()`, first by backing up the incoming pointer to the top of the `wrapper` (on line 60) and then by testing for a valid `signature` field (on line 61). If the memory is valid, a message is sent to the log file and the pointer is passed to `free()`. The assignment of ~MAGIC to `signature` ensures that the same pointer can't be passed to `delete()` two times in succession. (~MAGIC is guaranteed to have a value different from that of MAGIC without the tilde.)

As an added convenience, `new()` and `delete()` are mapped to `malloc()` and `free()` using the macros on lines 11 and 12 in Listing 1.11. These macros also take care of providing the input file and line number to both functions by using the ANSI `__LINE__` and `__FILE__` predefined macros.

Rush: _____

Title: C + C++ : programming with objects in C and C++ / Allen I. H
        olub.

                                              Order Date:: 03/01/94
                                              PONumber   :: 0S006134945
                                              Year   :: 1992

Author: Holub Allen I.

Edition::   Volume::   Control # 5020458 Copy bs 404331
Comments::

Publisher::New York :: McGraw-Hill

ISBN:: 0-07-029662-6

Copies::   1   Estimated Cost:: 30.00   Total Charge : _____17.81

Supplier:: Total Information Inc.
            844 Dewey Avenue
            Rochester, NY 14613-0202

Total Info In Stock? yes 00H::   7 Stock Location: COMPUTERS

Listing 1.9. *new.c*— A Safer `malloc()`—Functions

```
1    #include <stdio.h>
2    #include <stdlib.h>
3    #include "new.h"
4
5    #undef malloc    /* Undo macro definitions in new.h that cause trouble.*/
6    #undef free      /* I'll explain what this is all about in a moment.   */
7
8    static FILE *Logfile;    /* Must be global because it's used by both   */
9                             /* new() and delete(). It's static to avoid   */
10                            /* potential conflicts with similarly named   */
11                            /* variables declared in other files.         */
12
13   void *new ( size_t size,    /* Size of requested block in bytes */
14                char *file,     /* File from which call was made    */
15                int line        /* Line number in file              */
16              )
17   {
18       wrapper *wp;
19
20       if( !Logfile && !(Logfile = fopen("new.log", "w")) )
21       {
22           fprintf(stderr,"new: Can't open log file\n");
23           exit(1);
24       }
25
26       fprintf( Logfile, "%s: %d ", file, line );
27
28       if( wp = (wrapper *)malloc( sizeof(wrapper) + size ) )
29       {
30           wp->signature   = MAGIC;
31           wp->line_number = line;
32           wp->file_name   = file;
33
34           fprintf(Logfile,"(Allocating memory at %p)\n", wp );
35           ++wp;
36       }
37       else
38       {
39           fprintf( Logfile,"(Out of memory)\n" );
40           fprintf( stderr, "(Out of memory)\n" );
41       }
42       return (void *)wp;
43   }
```

Listing 1.10. *new.c*— A Safer `free()`

```
44    void delete    ( void *p,      /* Previously allocated block (from new()) */
45                      char *file,   /* File from which call was made           */
46                      int line      /* Line number in file                     */
47                     )
48    {
49        wrapper *wp = (wrapper *)p ;   /* Assign to avoid casts everywhere */
50
51        fprintf( Logfile, "%s: %d ", file, line );
52        if( !p )
53        {
54            fprintf(Logfile, "delete: NULL pointer argument\n");
55            fprintf(stderr , "delete: NULL pointer argument\n");
56            exit( 1 );
57        }
58        else
59        {
60            --wp;                              /* Back up to wrapper */
61            if( wp->signature != MAGIC )       /* Is it valid?        */
62            {
63                fprintf(Logfile, "delete: bad pointer argument (%p)\n", wp);
64                fprintf(stderr,  "delete: bad pointer argument (%p)\n", wp);
65                exit( 1 );
66            }
67            else
68            {
69                fprintf(Logfile, "(Freeing memory @%p, allocated @%s: %d)\n",
70                                   wp, wp->file_name, wp->line_number);
71                wp->signature = ~MAGIC;
72                free(wp);
73            }
74        }
75    }
76
77    #ifdef NEW_MAIN
78    #include "new.h"
79    void main() /* Test routine, not compiled unles NEW_MAIN defined */
80    {
81        char *p = (char *)malloc();
82        void *q = malloc();
83        free( q );
84        free( q );            /* Force an error      */
85        free( ++p );          /* Force another error */
86    }
87    #endif /* MAIN */
```

Listing 1.11. *new.h*— Mapping `malloc()`/`free()` to `new()`/`delete()`

```
1   #define malloc(size)  new    ( (size), __FILE__, __LINE__ )
2   #define free(p)        delete( ( p  ), __FILE__, __LINE__ )
3
4   void *new   ( size_t size, char *file, int line );
5   void delete ( void *p,      char *file, int line );
```

A macro is also provided in *new.h* to let you test for a bad pointer before calling `delete()` to begin with. It's shown in Listing 1.12. The `is_dynamic(p)` macro evaluates false if it doesn't find the magic number in the `signature` field of the `wrapper` located in memory just above the incoming pointer. Note that `p` must be cast to a `(wrapper*)` because it probably won't be declared as such in the application program—it better not be or the data abstraction we're trying to accomplish is a dismal failure. The `[-1]` backs the pointer up a notch and also converts the `wrapper` pointer to a `wrapper` structure, the `signature` field of which is then extracted with the `.signature`.

Listing 1.12. *new.h*— Checking for Dynamic Memory

```
6   #define is_dynamic(p) (((wrapper *)(p))[-1].signature == MAGIC)
```

The `is_dynamic()` macro is also handy if dynamic memory is mixed with declared memory in unpredictable ways. Listing 1.13 demonstrates the problem. I'm creating a simple linked list, but some of the list elements came from dynamic memory [via the `new()` call on line 17 that's hidden in the `malloc()` macro], and others are declared directly (on line 15). The code on lines 27 to 29 discards all the list elements, using the `is_dynamic()` macro to decide where the memory came from, calling `delete()` only if the memory came from `new()`.

Note that this method isn't foolproof. It is possible, although unlikely, that the memory above `declared` on the stack actually does contain `MAGIC`. You can improve matters by putting two magic numbers in the `wrapper` structure (at opposite ends, for example). Alternately, you can put another magic number (whose value was different from `MAGIC`) into the `link` structure, and then test both for `is_dynamic()` to be false and for the `link`'s magic number to be correct. I don't particularly like this second solution because it requires the user of the linked list to do too much work. A third, more robust solution to the problem modifies the `wrapper` structure so that a `wrapper` can also be an element of a binary tree (by adding left- and right-child pointers). `new()` puts the wrapper into the tree as it allocates memory, using the address of the `wrapper` as the key. `delete()` deletes the `wrapper` from the tree when it frees the associated memory. `is_dynamic` looks up the incoming pointer in the tree to test for validity.

This last solution adds a lot of code, though, and isn't particularly fast. The existing solution is a good compromise that works well enough in most applications—when you just want to detect a possible error in a `free()` call that

Listing 1.13. Demonstrate Memory-Allocation Problems

```
1    #include <new.h>
2
3    typedef struct link      /* A linked-list element    */
4    {
5        int key;
6        struct link *next;  /* next element in the list */
7    }
8    link;
9
10   fred()
11   {
12       link *p, *succ;
13       link *head;          /* head of a linked list          */
14       link *dynamic;       /* pointer to one list element    */
15       link declared;       /* a second list element          */
16
17       dynamic = malloc(sizeof(link));  /* Macro---maps to new() call.     */
18       head    = dynamic;               /* Create a two-element linked     */
19                                        /* list, the key indicating the    */
20       dynamic ->key  = 0;              /* distance from the start of the  */
21       dynamic ->next = &declared;      /* list to the current element.    */
22       declared->key  = 1;
23       declared->next = NULL;           /* Last element, pointer is NULL.  */
24                                        /* Delete the entire list:         */
25       for( p = head; p ; p = succ )    /*    foreach( list element )      */
26           if( is_dynamic(p) ) {        /*       if memory came from new() */
27               succ = p->next;          /*                                 */
28               delete(p);               /*              discard it.        */
29           }
30   }
```

would normally go undetected. The worst case is that you don't catch the bug. I would definitely use the tree-based solution if I was doing mixed-allocation such as in Listing 1.13 in a real program. You don't want a computer program to play the odds—you want it to be correct.

We have to look at one final OOP issue before leaving the current example. Incrementing the pointer returned from malloc() to the area below the wrapper header is convenient, but it also makes it impossible to use a base-class subroutine to manipulate a derived-class object. The pointer that's returned from new() cannot be passed to a base-class method like free() without causing a serious error. This sort of relationship—where you have a base-class/derived-class relationship between two structures, but it's not safe to manipulate a derived-class object with a base-class function—comes up occasionally in most object-oriented applications. In OOPeese, the inaccessible base class (the malloc_hdr) is said to be a *private* base class. The normal situation, where the base-class functions *can* manipulate the derived-class objects, describes a *public* base class.

private, public base class

There's no really good solution to the problem of private base classes in C. You can't really require the user of new() to declare a wrapper as the first field in their structure—you're violating the basic rule that the derived-class functions shouldn't need to know anything about the workings of the base-class functions. Consequently, all base classes really must be private in C.

1.12 Case Study: A Linked-List Class in C

The principles of derivation can be extended to data-structure manipulation. This section presents a small linked-list manager implemented in C. I've kept things simple for now not to obfuscate the basic issues with implementation details. Later on in the book, I'll develop a more complex C++ linked-list class that will demonstrate the thorny problems of a more realistic implementation.

The functions in the package let you manipulate the lists as queues (linked lists where the first object inserted is the first removed), stacks (where the last object inserted is the first removed), or arrays (where arbitrary list elements can be accessed by an index). The principles of data abstraction are used heavily in order to isolate the mechanics of list manipulation from the application program, which deals with the list as a high-level object on which a set of operations are defined.

1.12.1 List-Element-Manipulation Methods

Two classes (that is, data structures) work in concert to manage the lists. There is a list class and a _list_ele class.[7] The list class holds information that concerns the entire list, and the methods associated with the list class manipulate the list as a whole (add an element, copy the list, etc.). The _list_ele class holds information about individual elements and the methods manipulate a single element only. Your application program allocates multiple _list_ele objects that are inserted into the list object by means of methods attached to the list itself. A list is a high-level object that organizes a collection of low-level, list-element objects. The relationship between the two classes is illustrated in Figure 1.4.

The _list_ele structure contains only that information that is common to every linked-list element. (Figure 1.4 shows two of these fields—pointers to the next and previous list elements.) Imagine the _list_ele structure as a header for the common data. The list and _list_ele methods manipulate the fields in the header only. For example, you can put an element into a linked list by manipulating the pointers in the _list_ele without knowing anything about the application space.

---

[7] I've used a leading underscore in _list_ele because _list_ele objects are never created by an application program—the struct exists only for use by the linked-list functions themselves. Since application programmers don't use a _list_ele directly, they won't be thinking about potential conflicts when they name their own structs. The underscore makes it less likely that a user-defined struct will have the same name, though there is a potential conflict with a compiler-vendor supplied struct name—ANSI C reserves leading underscores for use by the compiler vendor.

Figure 1.4. List Data Structures

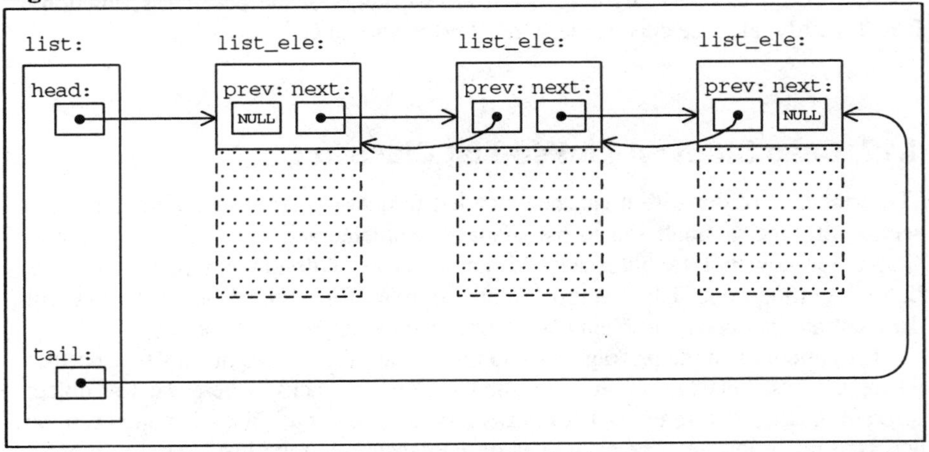

```
list:              list_ele:           list_ele:           list_ele:

head:              prev: next:         prev: next:         prev: next:
  [ • ] ────────►   NULL  [ • ] ─────►  [ • ] [ • ] ────►   [ • ] NULL  ◄──
                                   ◄────                ◄────
tail:
  [ • ] ──────────────────────────────────────────────────────────────────┘
```

abstract class   The _list_ele structure is also an *abstract class*. You'd never declare a _list_ele structure by itself—there's no point, the list doesn't have any data in it, only pointers. To make a _list_ele useful, you must derive a class that contains the data that you're actually putting into the list (the shaded area in the figure). That is, you must add fields to the _list_ele structure. The contents of the derived-class component of the two-part structure change from application to application, but—and this is an important "but"—for the most part no knowledge of the contents of this application area is necessary for the list-class methods to do their work.

      Those few situations in which knowledge of the application region is required by a list-management method are handled by means of functions that you must provide to the list manager. For example, when a list method needs to compare two keys (which are part of the application space) it calls a comparison function that's supplied by the application writer. You pass a pointer to that comparison function to the list-management function, which calls the comparison function indirectly, passing it pointers to the two application areas to be compared. Pointers to the shaded component of the list element are passed to the comparison function—<u>not</u> pointers to the list_ele headers.

      Think of the program as being divided into two regions—I'll call them list space and application space. The parts of the program that comprise the application all work in application space, and all of the application functions work with pointers to the application areas of the list-element structures. These functions don't care what's in the _list_ele header. This situation is identical to the header used by malloc()—malloc() returns a pointer to an application area of a memory block. There's a header just above that memory, but the application doesn't know or care that it's there.

      The functions in list space (rather than application space) manipulate the _list_ele headers. These functions don't care about what's in the application space any more than malloc() or free() cares about how the returned block is used. Since the _list_ele is manipulated entirely by various methods attached to the list and _list_ele class, your application never manipulates the _list_ele structure directly. Everything is done through methods.

What you get out of the foregoing is data abstraction and reusable code. The mechanics of list manipulation are completely hidden from the application program, as is the data that's used for this manipulation. All list manipulation is done by a group of functions that understand about _list_ele headers and know how to turn an application-area pointer into a _list_ele pointer. A _list_ele header is <u>never</u> directly manipulated by an application program, though— everything is done through functions. Moreover, the list-management code is completely general purpose: it works with any sort of list. The general-purpose functions are customized to the specific application by passing them pointers to a few small functions, not by rewriting the list-management code every time that you need a linked list of some sort.

> data abstraction, code reuse in lists

I have deliberately avoided discussing the actual implementation of the list and list_ele classes because the implementation details are immaterial from the perspective of someone who's using the linked-list functions. I'll demonstrate what I mean by implementing a queue of simple structures with character-pointer keys, declared in Listing 1.14.

Listing 1.14. *listtest.c*— Example Application Area

```
1    #include <tools/list.h>
2
3    typedef struct app_area    /* The data component (application area) */
4    {                          /* of a list-element object             */
5        char *key;
6        int  other_stuff;
7    } app_area;
```

As with qsort(), you need to tell the list-manipulation functions how to manipulate an app_area structure by providing object-manipulation methods for the list-element objects (or the method component of the app_area class definition, depending on how you want to look at it). You must supply versions of these methods for each kind of object that you intend to put into a list, just as qsort() was passed one comparison function for int arrays and another for arrays of char pointers.

Several functions are required—the first two are easy. A print function is passed a pointer to the application area of a list element and prints the application-dependent information. One of these for the current test structure is given in Listing 1.15.

A test-for-equality function is passed pointers to two application areas and returns true if the elements are equivalent. An example is presented in Listing 1.16. The third method is a constructor—a subroutine that initializes an object. The first argument to the constructor is a pointer to the object being initialized (this). Additional arguments are also possible, but the number and types of these arguments will vary with the actual structure used for the application space. Typically,

Listing 1.15. *listtest.c*— A Print Method

```
 8   static void print( app_area *p )
 9   {
10       printf( "%s ", p->key );
11   }
```

Listing 1.16. *listtest.c*— The Test-for-Equality Method

```
12   #include <string.h>
13
14   static int equal( app_area *p1,  app_area *p2 )
15   {
16       return strcmp(p1->key, p2->key) == 0 ;
17   }
```

there's either a constructor argument for every field in the application area, or all
fields in the application area are initialized to some default value, and there will be
no additional arguments to the constructor. The constructor returns true only if it
succeeds in initializing the object.

The constructor isn't called directly by the application program; rather, the
application passes the constructor a pointer to a list-element-creation subroutine,
which then calls the constructor indirectly. I'll discuss the reasons for this roundabout process in a moment, but the mechanics of the constructor call are straightforward. The following code is a simplified version of the list-element-creation
subroutine that you normally don't see. That is, the following code is part of the
list-management package; you do not provide this subroutine:

```
void *simplified_allocator(int size, int(*constructor)(),...)
{
    va_list args;
    void    *this;
    if(this = malloc( size )) /* Allocate space for object */
    {
        va_start(args, constructor);
        if( !(*constructor)(this, args)) /*CONSTRUCTOR CALL*/
        {
            free( this );                /* Can't initialize */
            this = NULL;
        }
        va_end(args);
    }
    return this;
}
```

You call the foregoing routine to both allocate space for and initialize a list element, and this subroutine calls the constructor in turn. The actual constructor subroutine, which *you* must provide, is quite simple. A constructor method for the
current `app_area` object takes two arguments and is shown in Listing 1.17. You'd

call the constructor implicitly (using the simplified allocator) as follows:

```
int initial_other_stuff = 10;
app_area *p = simplified_allocator( sizeof(app_area),
        construct, "initial key", initial_other_stuff );
```

Listing 1.17. *listtest.c*— A Constructor

```
18   #include <stdarg.h>
19
20   static int construct( app_area *this, va_list args )
21   {
22       this->key          = strdup( va_arg( args, char* )); /* initial key */
23       this->other_stuff =          va_arg( args, int   );
24       return( this->key != NULL);            /* Return true if we got memory */
25   }
```

You can avoid the roundabout initialization by separating the memory allocation from the construction process—call one subroutine to allocate the structure and then call another to initialize it—but then you won't have the guaranteed initialization. Allocated but uninitialized memory is a bug waiting to happen. It's just too easy to do the allocation and forget the initialization. Moreover, manipulation of an uninitialized object can be a difficult bug to track down, and the error won't show up until run time. By combining the allocation and initialization steps, you make sure that the object is valid and can be manipulated safely. It's not possible to forget the constructor call because it's required by the function prototype for new_list_ele. Consequently, you've transformed a difficult-to-find run-time error into an easier-to-find compile-time error. It is my preference, at least, for the compiler to catch as many errors as possible so that they won't slip into run time at all.

A constructor is matched by a destructor function that destroys the application component of an object. The destructor for the current class is shown in Listing 1.18.

Listing 1.18. *listtest.c*— A Destructor

```
26   static void destruct( app_area *this )
27   {
28       free( this->key );
29   }
```

Finally, two kinds of copy functions are needed. The first of these (in Listing 1.19) copies the application area of an existing object into uninitialized memory, and the second (in Listing 1.20) copies into previously initialized memory.

Listing 1.19. *listtest.c*— A Copy-into-Uninitialized-Memory Method

```
30   static void copy( app_area *this, app_area *src )
31   {
32       this->key        = strdup( src->key );
33       this->other_stuff = src->other_stuff;
34   }
```

Listing 1.20. *listtest.c*— A Copy-into-Initialized-Memory Method

```
35   static void assign( app_area *this, app_area *src )
36   {
37       free( this->key );
38       this->key        = strdup( src->key );
39       this->other_stuff = src->other_stuff;
40   }
```

The problem is the `key` field, which points at dynamic memory that came from `malloc()`. You can't copy one `app_area` to another with a `*this=*src`[8] because you'd end up with two `app_area` structures whose `key` fields both pointed at the same region of memory, like this:

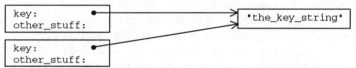

If you called the destructor for both objects (the original one and the copy), you'd `free()` the memory used by the `key` twice.

shallow (memberwise) copy

This superficial copying of the object itself is called *shallow* or *memberwise* copy copying. The shallow-copy problems are solved in the `copy()` and `assign()` functions of Listings 1.19 and 1.20 by allocating a new buffer for the copy's `key`. The resulting data structures look like this:

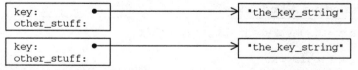

deep copy

This kind of copying is called a *deep copy*. You make copies, not only of the

---

[8] I'm using structure copying. The entire source structure is copied into the destination. You do the same thing with

        `memcpy( this, src, sizeof(*this) );`

if you don't have an ANSI compiler.

structure itself, but of everything that's pointed to by some member of the structure as well.

Note that `assign()`, which is copying into previously initialized memory, must call `free()` on the existing buffer before overwriting the target's `key` field. Otherwise, the original memory is orphaned—the pointer to it is lost, so there is no way to `free()` it. The need for an additional `free()` step explains why two kinds of copy operations are needed, one for copying into initialized memory and a second for copying into uninitialized memory.

While on the subject, this bug is a classic case of a *memory leak*, as discussed in the previous section. Memory leaks are particularly difficult bugs to find because they often won't show up until a program has been running for some time. The bug sometimes doesn't surface until the program is installed in the field and "out of memory" errors mysteriously appear after a few hours (or days) of running. The `malloc()` wrapper discussed in the previous section lets you track down this sort of problem because the log file will show the memory being allocated, but never deleted.

memory leak

1.12.2 Class Derivation: Element Creation and Deletion

The next step is to allocate a `_list_ele` and attach the application area onto the end of it. Looked at in an object-oriented way, we are going to derive an `app_area` class from the `_list_ele` class. In an object-oriented language like C++, you can do this derivation as part of the declaration. In C, you need to use a function call.

First, you need to put the following at the top of your file to use any of the list functions.

```
#include <tools/list.h>
```

The file contains declarations for the `list` and `_list_ele` structures as well as prototypes for the various functions discussed in this and following sections.

The first of these functions is `new_list_ele()`, which allocates space for both the `_list_ele` and `app_area` components of the structure, and initializes both components as well. It is passed pointers to the various methods I just discussed (which are remembered in the `_list_ele` class) and returns a pointer to the `app_area` component of the derived class—to the head of the shaded area in Figure 1.4. A call to `new_list_ele` for the current example looks like this:

```
#include <list.h>

app_area *member ;
member = (app_area *) new_list_ele(
              sizeof(app_area),   /* Size of the object */
              copy,               /* Method  pointers   */
              assign,
              print,
              equal,
              destruct,
              construct, "the_key", 10 );
```

The constructor that's passed to `new_list_ele()` as the seventh (`construct`) argument is used to initialize the object, as was discussed earlier. If this argument is `NULL`, then the application area will not be initialized; you must initialize the object yourself. Use this last feature with caution.

SIGABRT

    `new_list_ele()` raises `SIGABRT` if it can't get memory. Normally, raising `SIGABRT` terminates the program, so `new_list_ele()` won't return in the case of a memory-allocation error. If you modify the `SIGABRT` handler to do nothing [with a call to `signal(SIGABRT, SIG_IGN)`, for example], then `new_list_ele()` works like `malloc()`, returning `NULL` if it can't get memory. If you don't want this `malloc()`-like behavior, make sure that your `SIGABRT` handler doesn't return. For example, you can install a handler to print an error message and then abort the program like this:

```
#include <signal.h>
out_of_mem_handler()
{
    fprintf( stderr, "Out of memory.\n" );
    exit( 3 ); /* terminate program */
}
main()
{
    signal( SIGABRT, out_of_mem_handler );
    ...
}
```

List_ele_err

In order to deal with the situation where `SIGABRT` can be raised by several different events, the global variable `List_ele_err` is set to `LIST_NOMEM` (defined in *list.h*) when `new_list_ele()` raises the signal.

    The pointer returned from `new_list_ele()` can be used by the application program as if it had been returned from a `malloc(sizeof(app_area))` call. Unlike `malloc()`, the returned structure is guaranteed to be initialized by means of the constructor that you provided. The last two arguments of the `new_list_ele()` call are simply passed through to the constructor using the process just discussed.

    Since this `new_list_ele()` call is pretty involved, you should probably hide it in a macro like the following one to clean up the source code a bit:[9]

```
#define new_link(str) ((app_area *) new_list_ele(           \
                                sizeof(app_area),     \
                                copy, assign, print, \
                                equal, destruct,     \
                                construct, (str), 0) )
```

A properly organized program puts the method definitions in the same module as

---

[9] Borland C++ users: A bug in the Borland compiler makes it much too picky about the `void*` type. In particular, a hard type-mismatch error is generated when you do this:

        `int funct ( char *p );`
        `int (*pfi)( void * ) = funct;`

This alleged mismatch happens with all of the methods passed to the `new_list_ele()` subroutine, whose arguments will most likely be pointers to the application-area structure, not `void*` as is shown in the prototype to `new_list_ele()` in *list.h* [discussed below, but #included before calling the `new_link()` call and declares the methods as `static`. Consequently, the methods will not be directly accessible to subroutines in other modules. This way the other modules are forced to look at the list element as a black box—they have no other option since they can't call the methods directly. If new list elements need to be created in other modules, then the earlier macro should be implemented as a non-`static` subroutine, and that subroutine will be called from the other modules to allocate the links.

Since direct access to the methods is undesirable (hopefully impossible), four functions are provided to allow indirect access to four of the list-element methods. Use the functions like this:

```
void   le_copy   (app_area *this, app_area *src);
void   le_assign (app_area *this, app_area *src);
void   le_print  (app_area *this             );
int    le_equal  (app_area *this, app_area *key);

app_area *p1=new_link( "key 1" ); /* Macro (or subroutine) */
app_area *p2=new_link( "key 2" ); /* discussed earlier.    */
   ...
if( le_equal( p1, p2 ) )
{
    le_print(p1);   /* Send "print yourself" message to p1  */
    printf("==");
    le_print(p2);
    printf("\n");
}
```

When you're done with the list element, you can discard the memory with the following call:

```
delete_list_ele( member );
```

which works more or less like `free()`. Unlike `free()`, the destructor method that you passed to `new_list_ele()` is called automatically by `delete_list_ele()`—you don't have to do anything special. Unfortunately, you can't pass a pointer that was allocated by `new_list_ele()` directly to `free()`—

---

new_link()]. Declaring the function pointers without argument lists also generates an error, and the compiler doesn't accept (...) as an argument list in a C function prototype. There are only two ways around this problem: either declare the arguments to the methods as void* (which will complicate the methods themselves with unnecessary code) or cast the arguments to new_list_ele. You can hide these casts inside the new_link() macro as follows:

```
#define new_link(str) ((app_area *) new_list_ele( sizeof(app_area),\
                    (void (*)(void *this, void *src )) copy     ,\
                    (void (*)(void *this, void *src )) assign   ,\
                    (void (*)(void *this             )) print    ,\
                    (int  (*)(void *this, void *key )) equal    ,\
                    (void (*)(void *this             )) destruct ,\
                    (int  (*)(void *this, ...        )) construct,\
                                              (str), 0 ))
```

all deallocation must be done via a `delete_list_ele()` call. Although this restriction introduces a potential bug—someone might try to pass the `new_list_ele()`-allocated pointer to `free()`—the bug can easily be detected by using the debugging versions of `malloc()` and `free()` discussed in the previous section.

1.12.3 List-Manipulation Methods

We're now done with the list-element methods. You can, of course, add a host of additional `app_area`-manipulation methods, but these are not required by the `list` functions. This section continues the development with a discussion of the `list` class and the methods used to manipulate entire lists rather than single elements.

1.12.3.1 List Creation and Destruction. Since you won't be deriving classes from `list`, you don't need to provide any special methods to create `list` objects (instances of the `list` class). The list constructor, which allocates and initializes an empty list, works like this:

```
list    *listp = new_list();
```

Like `new_list_ele()`, `new_list()` aborts the program by raising SIGABRT if it can't get memory. It sets the global variable `List_err` to one of the following values when it raises the signal so the handler can figure out what caused the problem:

Problem	List_err =	Notes
No error	LIST_NOERR	*Evaluates false*
No memory	LIST_NOMEM	—
Constructor failed	LIST_NOINIT	—

The symbolic constants are defined in *list.h*.

The notion of a null list (a `list` pointer that contains NULL) is not supported. Empty lists [the `list` pointer holds an address that was returned from `new_list()`, but nothing has been put into the list yet] are okay. You can't pass a NULL pointer to any of the list functions, though. Consequently, you must <u>always</u> initialize `list` pointers to a value returned from `new_list()` as part of the declaration, as I've done here. This requirement causes problems with global-level lists, which must be initialized in `main()`, but the alternative is to add complexity to the list-management code itself. One of the strengths of C++ is that this global-level initialization problem doesn't exist.

You get rid of a list like this:

```
delete_list( listp );
```

where `listp` is a pointer that was returned by a previous `new_list()` call. If the list isn't empty, then all the elements are discarded as well. The element's destructor function is called for each element as part of the process. You cannot use `free()` to delete without orphaning any existing list elements. A `delete_list()` call should be found at the end of every scope in which a `new_list()` call is present, usually just above the close curly brace.

1.12.3.2 Finding List Elements. Four functions are provided for finding specific list elements. (I'll talk about how they get into the list in a moment.) head(listp) returns a pointer to the application area of the object currently at the head of the list (or NULL if the list is empty); tail(listp) returns a pointer to the object at the end of the list (or NULL if it's empty); and list_empty(listp) returns true if the indicated list is empty (has no elements). Finally, list_find() finds a list element whose key matches a specified key and returns a pointer to the application area of the found element (if it's in the list—NULL is returned if it isn't). The calling syntax is

```
void *list_find(list *listp, void *obj );
```

The function uses the equal() method discussed earlier to compare objects in the list with the desired element. The first argument to equal() is an element in the list. The second argument to equal() is the second argument to list_find(). You can look for an arbitrary key in our example list as follows:

```
app_area *member;
app_area look_for_this = { "match this key", 0 };

if( !(member = list_find( listp, &look_for_this )) )
    printf("NOT IN LIST");
```

Note that you don't have to use new_list_ele() to allocate the space for the template, look_for_this. A simple declaration suffices. You cannot insert the template into the list unless you use new_list_ele() for the allocation, however.

The final find function is list_index(listp,n), which lets you use the list as if it were an array. It returns a pointer to the *n*th element of the list or NULL if the list isn't that large. A list_size(listp) is also provided. It returns the number of elements currently in the list, zero if the list is empty. You can use both functions to traverse a list like this:

```
for( i = 0; i < list_size(listp); ++i )
    mangez( list_index(listp, i ) ); /* mangez( listp[i] ) */
```

1.12.3.3 Duplicating and Copying Lists. Two functions are used for copying lists. The first function, list_dup(listp), returns a clone of a list (or NULL if it can't get memory). All the elements of the target list are duplicated in the copy. The copy() method that was passed to new_ele() is used to initialize the new elements. In a heterogeneous list, the different list elements will each have their own copy() functions, so the duplication will work fine.

The second copying function, list_assign(), is called like this:

```
list source      = new_list();
list destination = new_list();

... /* add members to source list */

list_assign( destination, source );
```

It overwrites all members of the destination list with the members of the source list in order (destination[0] = source[0], etc.). If the destination list is larger than the source list, the extra elements are discarded. If the destination list is smaller than the source list, additional elements are added to the destination. The source list is not modified in any way. The `copy()` method is used for uninitialized (i.e., added) list elements, the `assign()` method is used for existing elements.

1.12.3.4 Adding and Removing List Elements. You can enqueue (add to the tail of the list) any structure that was created by `new_list_ele()` [but not `malloc()`] as follows:

```
app_area *member = new_list_ele( ... );
  ...
if( !enqueue(listp, member) )
    printf("%s is already in a list\n", member->key );
```

`enqueue()` returns false if `member` is already in a list. That is, an element can be in only one list at a time, and it can be in any given list only one time.

You can remove an object from the head of the list by calling `dequeue()`, which normally removes the head-of-queue element and returns a pointer to it. It returns NULL if the list is empty. The calling syntax looks like this:

```
app_area *member;
  ...
if( !(member = dequeue(listp)) )
    printf("queue is empty");
```

Two other list-management functions let you treat the list as a stack. A call to

```
push( listp, &object );
```

works just like `enqueue()`. It adds an element to the tail end of the queue. [In fact, `push()` is just mapped to an `enqueue()` call via a macro in *list.h*.] A call to `pop()` removes the object currently at the *tail* of the list (the most recently enqueued object). The syntax is as follows:

```
app_area *member;

if( !(member = pop( listp )))
    printf("queue is empty");
```

A fifth function lets you remove an arbitrary element from the list, provided that you have a pointer to that element. The syntax is

```
app_area *member;  /* Points to an active list element
                    * (one that is currently in the list.)
                    */
member = list_find( ... );  /* find an element          */
list_unlink( listp, member ); /* remove it from the list */
```

This function is passed (in the second argument) a pointer to the application area of an object that's currently in the list. It returns NULL if `member` isn't in a list. Otherwise, `list_unlink()` removes that element from the list and returns a pointer to it (which is the same thing as the incoming second argument, but it's occasionally useful). This function can work with any of the list elements, including ones in the middle of the list. `dequeue()` and `pop()` work only on objects at the two ends of the list. `list_unlink()` doesn't delete the memory for the element—you have to use `delete_list_ele()` to do that.

   Note that `list_unlink()` doesn't check to see if the incoming `member` is in the list pointed to by `listp`. It just checks that `member` is in some list somewhere. This is a potential bug, but the alternative is scanning the list to ensure membership, and this scanning is too inefficient a process. A second alternative combines the functionality of `list_unlink()` and `find()` into a single subroutine, but this solution adds inefficiencies in situations where you already have the required pointer and don't want to search for it a second time. The current behavior is, admittedly, a compromise, but it does find the most likely bug—that the element isn't in any list at all.

1.12.3.5 Printing the List.
The final list function prints an entire list. The prototype looks like this:

```
void list_print( list *listp, int forward );
```

This function walks through the list from head to tail (if the `forward` argument is true) or from tail to head (if `forward` is false). It calls the `print()` method that was passed to `new_ele()` for each list element, passing `print()` a pointer to the application area for that element. You can print the entire example list from front to back like this:

```
list_print( listp, 1 );
```

1.12.4 Implementing the List Class

1.12.4.1 Class Definitions.
The implementation for the list class starts out with *list.h* in Listing 1.21. The `#ifndef` and `#define` on lines two and three (and the matching `#endif` on line 79) assure that the remainder of the code is included only once in a given compilation. The first time the file is included, `__LIST_H` won't exist, so it's defined on line three and the rest of the code is processed. If *list.h* is included a second time, `__LIST_H` will exist, and the compiler ignores the remainder of the file. I'll use this mechanism in all my files so that I don't have to worry about problems caused by nested `#include` statements referencing the same file more than once.

   List.h continues on line seven with a definition of the `_list_ele`. I've added a leading underscore because an application program never needs to declare a `_list_ele` directly; rather, the application declares a structure to represent the application area of the list element and the `_list_ele` component is supplied in the background by `new_list_ele()`. The class has three data components: pointers to the previous and next element in the linked list (`prev` and `next`) and the size of the application area in bytes (`app_size`).

   The `_list_ele` structure in Listing 1.21 also contains pointers to the six list-element-manipulation methods discussed earlier (on lines 70 to 14). These pointers are virtual-function pointers, such as the ones that were discussed earlier. The entire list of function pointers constitutes the *virtual-function table*. It is more space efficient to isolate the virtual-function table into a separate array, only one of which exists in the entire program. Pointers to this array can then be carried around by each object, and every object of a given type carries around a pointer to

virtual-function table

Listing 1.21. *list.h*— List-Management Definitions and Macros

```
1    /* List management definitions.  (c) 1990 Allen I. Holub. */
2    #ifndef __LIST_H
3    #define __LIST_H
4
5    #include <stdlib.h>
6
7    typedef struct _list_ele
8    {
9        struct _list_ele *next;        /* Next element in list        */
10       struct _list_ele *prev;        /* Preceding element in list   */
11       size_t app_size;               /* size of one element         */
12
13                                       /* Virtual functions:       */
14       void (*copy    )(void *this, void *src); /* *this=*src, this uninit.*/
15       void (*assign  )(void *this, void *src); /* *this=*src, this init.  */
16       void (*print   )(void *this           ); /* print list element      */
17       int  (*equal   )(void *this, void *key); /* true if this == key     */
18       void (*destruct)(void *this           ); /* destroy current object  */
19   } _list_ele;
20
21   typedef struct list
22   {
23       _list_ele *head;               /* first ele in list           */
24       _list_ele *tail;               /* last  ele in list           */
25       int   num_ele;                 /* Number of elements in the list */
26
27       struct _list_ele *current;     /* Most recently accessed element  */
28       int               index;       /* Index (list position) of *current. */
29   } list;
30   /*-------------------------------------------------------------------*/
31   void _delete_chain ( _list_ele *head           );
32   int    enqueue      ( list *this, void *usr_space );
33   void  list_assign  ( list *this, const list *src );
34   void  list_dup     ( list *this                );
35   void *list_find    ( list *this, void *obj     );
36   void *list_index   ( list *this, int n         );
37   void  list_print   ( list *this, int forward   );
38   void *list_unlink  ( list *this, void *usr_space );
39   list *new_list     ( void                      );
40
41   void *new_list_ele ( size_t app_size,
42                        void (*copy     )(void *this, void *src ),
43                        void (*assign   )(void *this, void *src ),
44                        void (*print    )(void *this            ),
45                        int  (*equal    )(void *this, void *key ),
46                        void (*destruct )(void *this            ),
47                        int  (*construct)(void *this, ...       ),
48                        ...
49                      );
50
```

```
Listing 1.21. continued...
51    extern int List_ele_err;/* Set by new_list_ele() before raising SIGABRT*/
52    extern int List_err;    /* Set by new_list() before raising SIGABRT      */
53
54    #define LIST_NOERR        0        /* Values for List_ele_err and List_err */
55    #define LIST_NOMEM        1
56    #define LIST_NOINIT       2
57    /*--------------------------------------------------------------------*/
58    #define list_size( this ) ((this)->num_ele      )
59    #define list_empty(this ) ((this)->head == NULL )
60
61    #define le_copy(  this, src) (*((_list_ele*)(this)-1)->copy   )(this,src)
62    #define le_assign(this, src) (*((_list_ele*)(this)-1)->assign)(this,src)
63    #define le_print( this     ) (*((_list_ele*)(this)-1)->print  )(this,src)
64    #define le_equal( this, key) (*((_list_ele*)(this)-1)->equal  )(this,src)
65
66    #define head(    this    ) ((this)->head ? (void*)((this)->head+1):NULL)
67    #define tail(    this    ) ((this)->tail ? (void*)((this)->tail+1):NULL)
68    #define push(    this, p ) enqueue((this),(p))
69    #define pop(     this    ) list_unlink( (this), tail(this) )
70    #define dequeue( this    ) list_unlink( (this), head(this) )
71
72    #define delete_list(this) ( _delete_chain( ((_list_ele*) this)->head ),\
73                                 free(this) \
74                               )
75
76    #define delete_list_ele(this) ( ((_list_ele *)(this)-1)->destruct(this),\
77                                 free( (_list_ele *)(this) - 1 ) \
78                               )
79    #endif /* __LIST_H */
```

the same table. This is, in fact, what most C++ compilers actually do. Here, though, it's easier to put the actual pointers into the structure, even though the structure is made larger as a consequence.

The macros on lines 61 to 64 provide indirect access to the virtual functions. The complexity results from `this` being a pointer to the application area, not to the `_list_ele` header. Consequently, `this` must be cast into a `_list_ele` pointer and then decremented to get it to point back up at the header.

There is a good reason to go through all this trouble to provide indirect access to the methods: support for heterogeneous lists—lists in which the elements are of different types. Say, for example, that you want to represent a graphic image as a list of "drawing elements," each of which represents a specific shape (circle, line, text, etc.). If a different print method is bound to each list element, the `list_print()` function can traverse the list, telling each element to print itself with a call to `le_print()`. In the case of a list of "drawing elements," the individual print methods draw the appropriate shape on the screen. The only reasonable way to do this is to have a pointer to the `print()` method carried around by each list element. You can print an entire drawing like this:

```
for( i = 0; i < list_size(listp); ++i )
    le_draw( list_index(listp, i) );
```

The other alternative is a `what_am_i` field in every list element that's set to arbitrary symbolic values like `CIRCLE`, `LINE`, and so forth. A `switch(what_am_i)` in the foregoing loop selects the correct print method. This alternative is pretty messy, though. It's also hard to maintain. You'd have to modify every one of those switches every time you added a new shape to your program, for one thing.

Since heterogeneity isn't always required, let's pause a moment and look at the design issues. First, I could have passed the workhorse-function pointers to the list functions that use them rather than to `new_list_ele()`. For example, the only list function that uses the `print()` method is `list_print()`. Consequently, I could have passed the pointer to `print()` directly to `list_print()`. This approach would have saved memory because I wouldn't have to carry around the method pointers with each list element. On the other hand, the interface to the list functions would now be more complicated. I opted for simplicity in the interests of easier maintenance.

I could also have used hard function calls in the list-management functions rather than pointers, requiring the application programmer to provide functions with specific names to do specific things. For example, instead of calling the `print()` method indirectly through a pointer, I could have a call to `list_element_print()` hard-coded into the list-printing function. The programmer would then have to provide a function called `list_element_print()` and

static (early) binding   link that function into the final program. The linker, then, would *bind* these functions to the list manager when it put together the final program. This solution— where the linker attaches methods to a class—is called *static* (or *early*) *binding*. The disadvantage of a static binding in the current situation is lack of flexibility. The list routines could manipulate only one type of list because the subroutines that manipulated individual list elements couldn't change at run time—they're statically bound to the class by the linker. Similarly, macros like `le_print()` would now be impossible to write—you'd have to use a `what_am_i` field in the list element, which would be passed to a general-purpose print function, to print a heterogeneous list. The advantage of static binding is smaller code size; a method needs to be called into the final program only if it is actually used.

Static binding is really unacceptable in the current application, though. It seems quite reasonable that a program would want to manipulate various lists made up of various kinds of objects. The solution is to call the relevant methods indirectly through function pointers that will be carried along with the list-element

dynamic (late) binding   object. This binding method is called *dynamic* (or *late*) *binding*—the method subroutine is not bound to the class until it is actually called at run time. Again, a

virtual function   method function that's dynamically bound to a class is called a *virtual function*.

There's a third binding issue. To what class should the element-manipulation subroutines be bound? Binding the method pointers to the list element effectively increases the size of every list element. (In the worst case, the size is increased by as many pointers as there are virtual functions attached to the class—the best case is by the size of a single pointer, which will point at an array of virtual-function pointers that is shared by all instances of the class.) In this situation, the `list` class methods print an element, for example, by indirectly calling the "print" function, a pointer to which is in some known place in the list-element structure. The "print" function is passed a pointer to the structure within which its pointer was found.

Alternatively, you can bind the element-manipulation methods to the list class rather than the list element. Here, the list structure contains the pointer to the "print" function and calls that function indirectly, passing it a pointer to the particular element to print. Since there are usually many fewer list structures than list elements, the size penalty is not nearly so severe. The main disadvantage is that lists all have to be homogeneous—all the list elements have to be structures of the same type. The print method has to know about every kind of list element that could logically be printed in order to handle a heterogeneous list, and maintenance is more difficult as a consequence—you have to modify the print method every time you add a new kind of list element to the program.

Moving back to Listing 1.21, the next data structure of interest is the list on line 21. This structure holds the data component of the list class: pointers to the head and tail of the list and the number of elements in the list. The current and index fields are used to make nonrandom list accesses a bit more efficient. I'll discuss them in a moment. There's no leading underscore because the application programmer actually declares lists (or at least list pointers).

The remainder of the file contains prototypes for the _list_ele and list methods. One of these (_delete_chain() on line 31) starts with an underscore because this function is intended for internal use only, as was the case with a _list_ele. _delete_chain() is called by other methods, but never directly by a user. Functions that are intended only for internal use are called *private* functions. By the same token, all the data fields in both a _list_ele and a list are used only by the methods. They are never accessed directly by a user (with a . or -> operator). Consequently, these fields comprise *private* data. The functions that are intended for use by the application are called *public functions*, and any fields that were intended to be accessed directly (there aren't any here) are *public* data.

private

public functions and data

1.12.4.2 Function Macros. Listing 1.21 finishes up with a few macro definitions that implement methods too small to be real subroutines. Taking them in sequence, the list_size() macro (on line 58 of Listing 1.21) is passed a list pointer and just extracts the num_ele field of the structure. This access is done by means of a macro in order to isolate the internal structure of the list from the application program, which should never access a list field directly (in a manner similar to a FILE). I've made list_size() a macro for efficiency reasons, but making this macro a subroutine gives you one important benefit: the subroutine gives you read-only access to the field. A statement like

```
list_size( listp ) = 10;
```

is legal with the macro, although it will corrupt the list so shouldn't be used. Making list_size() a subroutine assures that it can't be used in this manner.

The next two macros also provide read-only access to various fields in the list structure. list_empty() (on line 59 of Listing 1.21) just tests for a NULL list-head pointer. head() and tail() (on lines 66 and 67) return pointers to the application area of the list elements at the head and tail of the list. Both macros evaluate to NULL if the list is empty, otherwise they get at the application space of the required element with a statement like ((listp)->head + 1). The head pointer is a pointer to a _list_ele, so incrementing it by one skips us past the entire _list_ele structure to the application area that follows the header. The resulting pointer is then cast back to (**void** *) to avoid possible type conflicts.

The macros on lines 68 to 70 of Listing 1.21 implement the push, pop, and dequeue functions. They all just map to some other list function: push() to enqueue() and pop() and dequeue() to the more general list_unlink() function. push() is mapped in this way because it's really an alias for an enqueue operation. pop() and dequeue() are mapped because list_unlink() contains error-processing and other maintenance-related code that otherwise would be duplicated in the other functions. Concentrating everything in the more general-purpose function allows for better maintenance.

1.12.4.3 List and List-Element Destruction.

The final two macros [delete_list() and delete_list_ele() on lines 72 and 76 of Listing 1.21] destroy objects of the list and list-element classes, respectively. They both use the sequence (comma) operator to link together two statements, and since this operator isn't used very much outside of a for statement, it seems that an explanation is in order. It's not possible to use a semicolon in these macros. A statement such as

doing two things in
a macro

```
#define do_two_things    thing(1); thing(2)

if( condition )
    do_two_things();
else
    do_something_else();
```

expands as follows (I've modified the formatting to demonstrate the problems):

```
if( condition )
    thing(1);
thing(2);
else                          /* ERROR: MISSING "IF" FOR "ELSE" */
    do_something_else();
```

The problem doesn't exist if you use a sequence operator.

The delete_list() macro on line 72 of Listing 1.21 calls a subroutine [_delete_chain(), Listing 1.22] to delete any list members. It then calls free() to delete the list itself. delete_list_ele() on line 76 is similar in that it calls the destructor for the list element and then deletes the memory for the element. The incoming this pointer addresses an application area, so it must be cast into a pointer to a _list_ele and decremented in order to be used. This process must be done twice—once to call the destructor, a pointer to which is stored in _list_element.destruct, and the second time to pass the correct pointer through to free()—you must pass the address of the _list_ele header, not of the application area to free().

Listing 1.22. _*delete*_.c— Delete a Chain of Linked-List Elements

```
1    #include <tools/list.h>
2
3    void _delete_chain( _list_ele *head )
4    {
5        _list_ele *next;
6        for(; head ; head = next )
7        {
8            next = head->next;
9            delete_list_ele( head );
10       }
11   }
```

1.12.4.4 List and List-Element Creation. The list package continues with *new_list.c* in Listing 1.23, which contains the list and list-element creation routines [new_list() and new_list_ele()] and definitions for the two global variables used by these functions to communicate with the SIGABRT handler (List_err and List_ele_err).

new_list() is the more straightforward of the two functions, It uses calloc() to allocate the memory because all the fields will be initialized to zeros anyway. It raises SIGABRT on the event of a memory failure, as promised. If the SIGABRT handler doesn't exit() the program, raise() returns and NULL is returned from new_list().

Listing 1.23. *new_list.c*— Create New Lists

```
1    #include <tools/list.h>
2    #include <signal.h>
3    #include <stdarg.h>
4
5    /* public */ int List_ele_err; /* To communicate with SIGABRT handler */
6    /* public */ int List_err;
7
8    list  *new_list( void )              /* Allocate an object of class list */
9    {
10       list *this ;
11       List_err = LIST_NOERR;
12       if( !(this = (list *) calloc( 1, sizeof(list) )) )
13       {
14           List_err = LIST_NOMEM;
15           raise( SIGABRT );
16       }
17       return this;
18   }
19                                   /* Allocate an object of class _list_ele */
20   void *new_list_ele( size_t app_size,
21               void (*copy     )(void *this, void *src ),
22               void (*assign   )(void *this, void *src ),
23               void (*print    )(void *this              ),
24               int  (*equal    )(void *this, void *key ),
```
→

Listing 1.23. continued. . .

```
25                       void (*destruct )(void *this               ),
26                       int  (*construct)(void *this, ...           ),
27                       ...        /* arguments to constructor */   )
28    {
29         /* Create a new list element. If the construct argument is non-NULL,
30          * use the constructor to initialize the element, otherwise the
31          * contents of the application space are undefined.
32          */
33
34         va_list args;
35         _list_ele *this;
36
37         List_ele_err = LIST_NOERR;
38
39         va_start(args, construct);
40         if( !(this = (_list_ele *) malloc( sizeof(_list_ele) + app_size )) )
41             List_ele_err = LIST_NOMEM;
42         else
43         {
44             if( construct  &&  !(*construct)( this + 1, args )  )
45             {
46                 List_ele_err = LIST_NOINIT;
47                 free( this );                  /* Can't initialize, deallocate */
48                 this = NULL;                   /* memory and return NULL.       */
49             }
50             else
51             {
52                 this->next      = NULL;        /* Normal data fields       */
53                 this->prev      = NULL;
54                 this->app_size  = app_size;
55                 this->copy      = copy;        /* virtual function table   */
56                 this->assign    = assign;
57                 this->print     = print;
58                 this->equal     = equal;
59                 this->destruct  = destruct;
60                 this += 1;                     /* Skip to application area */
61             }
62         }
63         va_end(args);
64         if( List_ele_err )
65             raise( SIGABRT );
66         return this;
67    }
```

new_list_ele() (on line 13 of Listing 1.23) is more complicated than new_list() for two reasons. First, it has to call the list-element constructor (on line 44). The constructor function is called only if construct isn't NULL and the function is passed a pointer to the application area of the structure, not to the _list_ele header. (That's what the +1 is doing on line 44.) The else clause is executed only if the constructor succeeds or if there is no constructor.

The virtual-function table is initialized on line 55. Finally, the this pointer is incremented on line 60 so that the returned pointer will address the application region of the list element rather than the _list_ele header.

1.12.4.5 Finding List Elements. The next group of functions are used to find arbitrary list elements. The list_find() function looks for a list element that matches the one pointed to by the incoming obj pointer. It calls the equal() method to compare elements on line 13 of Listing 1.24. If it finds a match, list_find() modifies current and index to reference the found object (on lines 15 and 16) and then returns a pointer to the application space of the object.

Listing 1.24. *list_fin.c*— Find an Arbitrary List Element

```
1    #include <tools/list.h>
2
3    void *list_find( list *this, void *obj )
4    {
5        /* Look for a list element that matches obj, using the equal()
6         * method to compare elements. Return a pointer to the application
7         * area of the found element, or NULL if there's no match.
8         */
9
10       _list_ele *cur;
11       int index = 0;
12       for(cur = this->head; cur ; cur = cur->next, ++index )
13           if( (*cur->equal)( (void *)(cur + 1), obj ) )
14           {
15               this->index   = index;
16               this->current = cur;
17               return( cur + 1 );
18           }
19       return NULL;
20   }
```

The list_index() function in Listing 1.25 works in a similar manner, but it uses current and index to make the list traversal more efficient. Always counting from the head of the list to the required element is very inefficient if you're traversing the list sequentially. (You'll need to skip on the order of $n!$ list elements, where n is the list size.) I've attempted to improve the situation by using the previously remembered current and index information. If the distance from the start of the list to the desired element is less than the distance from the previously accessed element, then the subroutine counts from the start of the list with the for loop on line 24. Otherwise, it goes either left or right from the most recent element with one of the loops on line 34 or 39, as appropriate. The code on lines 45 and 46 adjust current and index to reference the new element if there is one.

Listing 1.25. *list_ind.c*— Find the *n*th Element

```
1    #include <tools/list.h>
2
3    void *list_index( list *this, int index )
4    {
5        /* Return a pointer to the index-th element of the list (counting
6         * from head to tail, the element at the left edge of the list is
7         * element 0) or NULL if the list doesn't have that many elements
8         * in it.
9         */
10       _list_ele *cur = this->current;
11       int n          = index;
12
13       if( !(0 <= index && index < this->num_ele) )   /* out of bounds */
14           cur = NULL;
15
16       else if( cur == NULL || abs(this->index - n) >= n )
17       {
18           /* If there's no previously remembered index or the distance
19            * from the index to the desired position is greater than the
20            * distance from the head of the list to the desired position,
21            * then count over from the head of the list.
22            */
23
24           for( cur = this->head; cur && --n >= 0; cur = cur->next )
25               ;
26       }
27       else if( (n -= this->index) < 0 ) /* n=the distance from current */
28       {                                 /* element to desired element. */
29
30           /* The desired element is to the left of the most recently
31            * accessed element, go left.
32            */
33
34           while( cur  &&  ++n <= 0  )
35               cur = cur->prev;
36       }
37       else                             /* If n==0, the while loop doesn't  */
38       {                                /* do anything. otherwise, go right */
39           while( --n >= 0 && cur )
40               cur = cur->next;
41       }
42
43       if( cur )                        /* Element wasn't in the list   */
44       {                                /* Adjust current and index to  */
45           this->current = cur;         /* reference the new element.   */
46           this->index   = index;
47       }
48       return cur ? cur + 1 : NULL ;
49   }
```

1.12.4.6 Adding and Removing List Elements. The next group of functions add and remove list elements. The enqueue function is given in Listing 1.26. It has to decrement the pointer to the new element (user_space) on line five because the incoming pointer addresses the application area. The user_space pointer was returned from a previous new_list_ele() call, and the -1 here complements the +1 on line 48 of Listing 1.25. The test on line seven checks to see that the incoming element isn't already in a list. An element can be in only one list at a time. The current-element pointer is updated to reference the newly added element on lines 23 and 24, and the element count is incremented on line 25.

Listing 1.26. *enqueue.c*— Enqueue a List Element

```
 1   #include <tools/list.h>
 2
 3   int enqueue( list *this, void *usr_space )        /* (push) add to tail */
 4   {
 5       _list_ele *ele = (_list_ele *)usr_space - 1;
 6
 7       if( ele->next || ele->prev )
 8           return 0;
 9
10       if( !this->head )                              /* List is empty */
11       {
12           ele->next = NULL;
13           ele->prev = NULL;
14           this->head = this->tail = ele;
15       }
16       else                                           /* List not empty */
17       {                                              /* add to tail of list */
18           ele->next        = NULL;
19           ele->prev        = this->tail;
20           this->tail->next = ele;
21           this->tail       = ele;
22       }
23       this->current = ele;
24       this->index   = this->num_ele;
25       this->num_ele ++;
26       return 1;
27   }
```

All of the list-element removal is done by list_unlink() in Listing 1.27. (dequeue() and pop() both are mapped to list_unlink() calls in *list.h*.) The code on line 13 of Listing 1.27 handles the situation where the most recently accessed member of the list is being removed. Since the member won't be in the list after the removal, current has to be adjusted to reference an element that's in the list. Operating on the assumption that the next access is likely to be in the same vicinity as the current one, current and index are modified to point at the member following the one that is being deleted in most situations. If the last element of the list is being deleted, the preceding member is used. If the list has no members, current is set to NULL and index is set to zero. The remainder of the subroutine just juggles around pointers to remove the required element. Note that this routine just assumes that the incoming usr_space pointer address a valid list element. It's a serious bug if it doesn't.

1.12.4.7 Duplicating and Copying Lists. The two list copying functions are presented in Listings 1.28 and 1.29. The first of these, list_dup() in Listing 1.28, is the simpler of the two because it always copies from the source list into uninitialized memory. Note that the new_list_ele() call on lines 11 to 17 is passed a NULL construct argument, so it will allocate, but not initialize, the application area. The initialization happens on the next line with a call to the copy() method.

The list_assign() function in Listing 1.29 overwrites an existing list, recycling the memory used for the existing list elements as much as possible. The outermost loop on line 14 goes through the source loop one element at a time, copying the source members over to the target list. The code on lines 18 and 26 is executed as long as there are members in the destination list into which the source elements can be copied. Since these are previously initialized list elements, the assign() method is used to do the copying. If the source list is larger than the target list, the code on lines 30 to 38 takes over once the destination list is exhausted. It creates new list elements, using the copy() method to initialize them, and then calls enqueue() to tack them onto the end of the target list. Note that once dst_ele goes to NULL as the result of the assignment on line 26, it will stay that way for the duration of the subroutine. Consequently, enqueue() is safe to use on line 38. The if statements on lines 40 to 44 and lines 20 to 24 update the current-element pointer and index of the new list to reference the same cell as in the old list. The final if statement on line 49 handles the situation where the target list is larger than the source list. All the extra elements are removed from the list and discarded in this case.

1.12.4.8 Printing the List. The last method of interest is the print-list function in Listing 1.30. It is pretty straightforward, going through the list in the indicated direction calling the "print" method of each element to print the individual elements. Note that in a heterogeneous list, different types of elements will have different print methods, so everything's hunky-dory. The code on lines 13 to 14 and 19 to 20 prints out the normally hidden parts of the list and _list_ele structures when debugging is enabled.

Listing 1.27. *list_unl.c*— Delete an Arbitrary Element from the List

```
1    #include <tools/list.h>
2
3    void *list_unlink(list *this, void *usr_space) /* remove arbitrary ele.*/
4    {                                               /* returns 2nd argument */
5        _list_ele *ele = (_list_ele *)usr_space -1;
6
7        if( !usr_space )      /* This happens if the dequeue() or pop()     */
8            return NULL;      /* macros are passed empty lists.             */
9
10       if( this->head != ele &&  !ele->prev  &&  !ele->next )
11           return NULL;                       /* Element isn't in a list   */
12
13       if( ele == this->current )             /* Deleting current element: */
14       {                                      /* There's an element to      */
15           if( this->current = ele->next )    /* the right of the one       */
16               ++this->index;                 /* we're deleting. Use it.    */
17           else
18           {                                  /* Use the element preceding */
19               this->current = ele->prev;     /* the one we're deleting.   */
20               --this->index;                 /* current=NUL and index=0   */
21           }                                  /* if the initial list has   */
22       }                                      /* only one element.         */
23       --this->num_ele;                       /* Reduce element count       */
24
25       if( this->head == this->tail )         /* only 1 element in the list */
26       {
27           this->head = this->tail = NULL;
28       }
29       else if( ele == this->head )           /* dequeue */
30       {
31           this->head = ele->next;
32           this->head->prev = NULL;
33       }
34       else if( ele == this->tail )           /* pop */
35       {
36           this->tail = ele->prev;
37           this->tail->next = NULL;
38       }
39       else                                   /* get a middle element */
40       {
41           ele->prev->next = ele->next;
42           ele->next->prev = ele->prev;
43       }
44       ele->prev = ele->next = NULL;     /* Mark element as "not in list" */
45       return usr_space;
46   }
```

Listing 1.28. *list_dup.c*— Duplicate a List

```
1    #include <tools/list.h>
2
3    void list_dup( list *this )
4    {
5        _list_ele *cur;              /* Current source-list element  */
6        void   *member;             /* New destination-list element */
7        list  *new = new_list();    /* The new, generated list      */
8
9        for(cur = this->head; cur; cur = cur->next) /* for each element  */
10       {                                           /* of existing list, */
11           member = new_list_ele( cur->app_size,   /* get a new element */
12                                  cur->copy,
13                                  cur->assign,
14                                  cur->print,
15                                  cur->equal,
16                                  cur->destruct,
17                                  NULL );  /* don't initialize */
18
19           (*cur->copy)( member, cur + 1 );     /* initialize new element */
20           enqueue(new, member);                /* put it into the list   */
21
22           if( this->current == cur )  /* Update current-element pointer */
23           {
24               new->current = (_list_ele *)member - 1;
25               new->index   = this->index;
26           }
27       }
28   }
```

Listing 1.29. *list_ass.c*— Duplicate a List

```
1    #include <tools/list.h>
2
3    void list_assign( list *this, const list *src )
4    {
5        /* Overwrite all elements of the current list (this) with elements
6         * from the source list. Change the current list's size as necessary
7         * to accommodate the source list size.
8         */
9
10       _list_ele *src_ele, *dst_ele, *new_ele;
11       list  *new = new_list();    /* the generated list */
12
13       dst_ele = this->head;
14       for( src_ele = src->head; src_ele; src_ele = src_ele->next )
15       {
```

Listing 1.29. continued. . .

```
16            if( dst_ele )     /* There's a destination element to use */
17            {
18                (*src_ele->assign)( dst_ele + 1, src_ele + 1 );
19
20                if( src->current == src_ele )
21                {
22                    new->current = dst_ele;
23                    new->index    = src->index;
24                }
25
26                dst_ele = dst_ele->next;
27            }
28            else
29            {
30                new_ele = new_list_ele( src_ele->app_size,
31                                        src_ele->copy,
32                                        src_ele->assign,
33                                        src_ele->print,
34                                        src_ele->equal,
35                                        src_ele->destruct,
36                                        NULL );
37                (*src_ele->copy)( new_ele, src_ele + 1 );
38                enqueue(new, new_ele);
39
40                if( src->current == src_ele )
41                {
42                    new->current = new_ele - 1;
43                    new->index    = src->index;
44                }
45            }
46
47        }
48
49    if( dst_ele )        /* Then there are more elements in the current */
50    {                    /* list than are in the source list.          */
51
52        if( dst_ele == this->head )         /* Truncate entire list */
53        {
54            this->head    = this->tail = this->current = NULL;
55            this->num_ele = this->index = 0;
56        }
57        else
58        {
59            this->tail = dst_ele->prev;       /* Truncate partial list */
60            dst_ele->prev->next = NULL;
61        }
62        _delete_chain( dst_ele );             /* Discard extra elements */
63    }
64  }
```

Listing 1.30. *list_pri.c*— Print a List

```
1    #include <tools/list.h>
2
3    #ifdef DEBUG
4    #define D(x) x              /* D(printf(...)) expands to printf(...)      */
5    #else
6    #define D(x) /*empty*/   /* D(printf(...)) expands to an empty string */
7    #endif
8
9    void list_print( list *this, int forward )
10   {
11        _list_ele *p;
12
13        D(  printf("list @%08p, head=%04x, tail=%04x, num_ele=%d\n", \
14                          this, this->head, this->tail, this->num_ele ); )
15
16        p = forward ? this->head : this->tail ;
17        for( ; p ; p = forward ? p->next : p->prev )
18        {
19            D( printf("\t(@%04x): next=%04x prev=%04x -> ", \
20                                            p, p->next, p->prev ); )
21            (*p->print)( p + 1 );
22        }
23   }
```

C++: Small Differences from C

C++ is a set of extensions to the C language that attempts, with mixed success, to solve some of the programming problems implicit in the examples at the end of the last chapter. In general, the good points (such as language-level support for derivation and virtual functions) outweigh the bad sufficiently that using C++ makes sense when a program lends itself to an object-oriented solution.

This chapter starts our look at C++ by discussing the little features of the language that fall into the "better C" category—small additions to the language that just improve the way C works. For the most part ANSI C is a proper subset of C++. (There are a few minor differences in the way the defaults are handled in function prototypes, and const global variables are processed slightly differently.) This conformance is generally good because you can move properly written C code into C++ with minimal effort. On the other hand, some of the obvious flaws of C—such as the botched precedence of the bitwise operators[1]—have not been fixed in C++.

---

[1] The bitwise operators (&, ^, and |) are much too low in the precedence chart. A statement like

```
if( getchar() & 0x7f == 'a')
```

won't work as expected because == is higher precedence than &. Since 0x7f is never equal to a, the primary subexpression evaluates to zero, which is ANDed with getchar()s return value to yield zero. Parentheses fix the problem, but they shouldn't be necessary.

2.1 New Keywords

None of the following C++ keywords are in C, and a few of them are not supported by all C++ compilers:

```
asm      delete   new        private     template   try
catch    friend   operator   protected   this       virtual
class    inline   overload   public      throw
```

I'll describe what these keywords do as the book progresses. The important issue for now is that you shouldn't use them for variable or subroutine names.[2] Because there's serious talk of using C++ as ANSI C 2.0, you should avoid the C++ names even in straight C programs so that future portability won't be a problem. This is a particular annoyance for new and delete, which are pretty common names in C programs.

Note that not all of the keywords in the foregoing list are treated as keywords by all compilers. overload, for example, is considered obsolete and is often unsupported. Moreover, many compilers treat the following as keywords, so they should be avoided as well:

```
cdecl    fortran   interrupt
entry    handle    near
far      huge      pascal
```

In addition, identifiers should generally not begin with an underscore in order to avoid conflicts with that ANSI name space, which is intended for use by the compiler vendor. I occasionally use leading underscores (as I did with _list_ele in Chapter 1) for identifiers that I don't want an application programmer to know about, but this is a potentially risky practice because the compiler vendor might use the same identifier for some other purpose.

2.2 End-of-Line Comments

C++ supports C-style comments, but it also introduces an end-of-line-style comment that looks like this:

```
some_code();   // this is a comment
```

The // and everything following it on the line is ignored. This form is particularly useful for commenting variable declarations, and so forth. For readability, it's still a good idea to line up the start-of-comment designator in nice columns. Compare this code:

---

[2] I used this, new, and delete in Chapter 1 only to demonstrate how they're used in C++.

```
char *numbuf[10];//array of strings to process
unsigned char *pointer;//pointer to current string
static double result;//place to put translated string
```

to this:

```
char            *numbuf[10]; // array of strings to process
unsigned char   *pointer;    // pointer to current string
static   double result;      // place to put translated string
```

The second form is much easier to read, you can find the variable name that you're looking for by running your finger down a column, comments don't confuse things by being mixed up visually with the code, and so forth.

2.3 The Scope Operator (::)

The `::` operator (usually pronounced "colon colon") is used for many purposes in C++, so I'll bring it up again later in the book. It is always used to specify some sort of scope. For example, given the global-variable definition

```
int var;
```

The notation `::var` always accesses the global variable, even if it is shadowed by a local variable with the same name. (It does not just go to the previous level, but goes to the outermost scope.) The code

accessing global scope

```
int x = 0;
main()
{
    int x = 1;        printf("Level 1, ::x is %d\n", ::x );
    {
        int x = 2;    printf("Level 2, ::x is %d\n", ::x );
    }
}
```

prints

```
Level 1, ::x is 0
Level 2, ::x is 0
```

2.4 The const Storage Class

The `const` storage class, although officially part of ANSI C, isn't used as often as it should be, and as a consequence a lot of C programmers don't know how to use it. You must use `const` in many C++ applications, however, so a review of the keyword is in order. You can skip past this section if you know how `const` works. The same goes for the next section, which describes `volatile`—skip it if you don't need the review.

The `const` keyword satisfies a philosophical point in C++: that a language that requires a preprocessor has something wrong with it. The idea is that the preprocessor is used only to make up the deficiencies in a language.

Declaring a variable as `const` tells the compiler that the variable may not be modified—it's a constant. As a consequence, an initialization must be part of the declaration. For example, the following code declares an `int` constant with the value 5.

```
const int rocky = 5;
```

The declaration is effectively the same as

```
#define rocky 5
```

The compiler won't permit an expression like

```
rocky = 10;
```

in either situation. Unlike the macro, the `const` declaration has a type associated with it, so type checking operations can be applied to a `const` that cannot be applied to a macro.

In C, space is always allocated for the constant, but you're not allowed to modify the space. In C++, space is allocated only if necessary. Consequently, the compiler is free to treat a `const` as if it were a macro and just substitute the value for the variable name. A call like

```
bullwinkle( rocky );
```

can be translated into

```
bullwinkle( 5 );
```

Space *will* have to be allocated in several situations—if you take rocky's address, for example.

In order to allow the compiler to treat the `const` as a macro, C++ diverges from C in one important respect: the default storage class of a global-level `const` is `static`, not `extern`. This means that the `const` definition can (actually, it must) be put into a *.h* file, just like a macro, if you intend to use the constant in more than one source file. The down side of this practice is that the compiler decides whether to allocate space for the `const` on a file-by-file basis, and it could conceivably decide to allocate space in every file. Multiple allocation is harmless from a code-correctness point of view because all the instances of the constant have the same type and value. You will waste a small amount of space, though.

The advantages of macro-like expansion usually outweigh the space issue. If you want to guarantee that only one instance of the constant is expanded, however, you can declare an explicit `extern const`, which is accessible from other modules. Use the following declaration syntax for this purpose:

```
extern const int fred = 10;
```

The compiler always allocates space for an `extern const`. The `extern const` declaration with an explicit initializer may appear only once in the entire program; everywhere else, you must omit the initializer. The initialized `extern const` declaration is illegal in ANSI C because you may not initialize an explicit `extern`.

The rules for declaring a `const` variable are complicated by the fact that `const` can be used in two ways. All declarations can be broken up into two parts. The

specifier is an initial list of words (int, unsigned, static, and so forth). The
words can appear in any order. The *declarator* is the object's name and any *s,
[]s, and parentheses. A definition can have only one specifier, but it can have
several comma-delimited declarators.[1]

specifier
declarator

One problem with const is that it can appear in both the declarator and specifier portion of the declaration. If it appears in the specifier, it modifies the basic
type described by the specifier. For example, in

```
const unsigned int  i = 10;
```

the const is applied to the int. Since the int variable cannot be changed, it must
be initialized as part of the declaration. Similarly, in

```
const unsigned int *xp;
```

the const modifies the int. It is the int pointed to by xp (*xp) that cannot be
changed. xp is just a normal pointer and can be modified to your heart's content.
For example

```
const int array[10];
const int *xp;

xp = array;          // okay
putchar( *xp++ );    // okay
*xp = '\0';          // **** ILLEGAL, you may not modify *xp
```

Note that xp does not have to be initialized in the declaration because it is not a
constant.

In C++, a const is actually a different type than a variable that is otherwise
identical. A variable is silently promoted to a const to make an assignment or call
a function. You can't go the other way, though. For example, this is okay:

```
betty( const char *x ){...}
   ...
char *p = malloc(some_size);
betty( p );
```

The buffer passed to betty() via the p can't be modified by betty() because
betty()s argument is a pointer to a const string. The actual argument in the call,
which is a normal char*, is silently promoted to const char* by the compiler.

---

[1] As an aside. I've seen many books use the following syntax for pointer declarations:

```
int*     p;
```

This syntax is misleading at best—the * is part of the declarator, not the specifier. This develop-
mentally challenged formatting implies that

```
int*     p, q;
```

declares two pointers, which is simply not true. Don't use it.

Consider the following code, however:

```
wilma( char *x ){...}
const char bam_bam[] = { 'a', 'b', 'c' };
wilma( bam_bam );   // ILLEGAL
```

`wilma()` takes a normal character-pointer argument. Consequently, it can modify the array addressed by the p argument. `bam_bam` is an array of three constants, however. Those three elements may not be modified. Consequently, you cannot pass `bam_bam` to `wilma` because `wilma` might modify it.

By the same token, a call like

```
wilma("constant string");
```

is also illegal. You may not modify the contents of a constant string. You can fix the problem by declaring `wilma`'s argument as a **const char*** rather than a simple **char***.

When you need to pass an array to a function for examination purposes only, you should declare the corresponding argument as a pointer to a **const** of some sort; otherwise, you won't be able to pass arrays of true **const** objects to the function.

The **const** keyword can also modify a * that's found in a declarator. The syntax is

```
char s[] = "a string" ;
char *const pebbles = s;
```

Here, `pebbles` is a constant pointer to a variable character. You can modify *pebbles, but you cannot modify `pebbles` itself. Note that the **const** follows the * so it cannot possibly be confused with a **const** that's part of the specifier.

A ***const** is usually used to access memory-mapped hardware. For example, the video memory in an IBM-PC monochrome card can be treated as a 25×80 array of **int** based at physical address B000:0000. You can do this in a C or C++ program as follows:[4]

```
typedef int ROW[80];                          // one row
ROW *const display = (ROW *const)0xb0000000;  // video memory
display[24][79]   = c; // bottom-right corner of screen = c
```

Since the display isn't going to move around, the pointer to it is declared **const**.

You can put a **const** in both the declarator and the specifier if you like. You'd do this with a read-only memory-mapped register, for example. The syntax is

```
const int       x = 5;  // constant int
const int *const p = &x; // constant pointer to constant int
```

---

[4] I'm assuming the 8086 compact, large, or huge model, so have not used an explicit **far** keyword.

2.5 The `volatile` **Storage Class**

The `volatile` keyword is not nearly so important as `const` in most applications. Nonetheless, it's indispensable when you're writing to memory-mapped hardware or are sharing memory with another process in a multitasking operating system.

`volatile` is syntactically identical to `const`. It can appear in either the declarator or specifier component of the declaration. `volatile` tells the compiler not to optimize expressions involving a given variable.

Here's a classic case of when you need to use it. A printer might be hooked up to a CPU through an eight-bit parallel port as shown in Figure 2.1. The parallel port is masquerading as two bytes in memory. When you write to memory locations 0x10000 or 0x10001, you are really writing out to the hardware. Memory location 0x10000 is a status port and 0x10001 is a data port. The low bit of the status port is used to communicate with the hardware. Everything written onto the low bit of that location is transferred to a wire that's hooked up to the printer's "data available" line. When you read the port, the low bit is modified to reflect the state of the "busy" line.

Figure 2.1. A Hardware Printer Interface

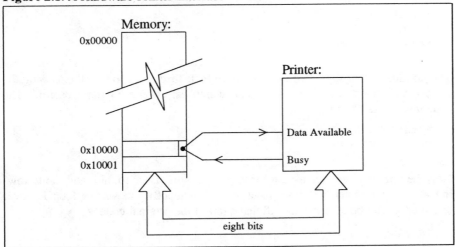

Initially, everything is set low (to zeros). You send a byte to the printer as follows:
- Put the data onto the bus by writing it out to memory location 0x10001.
- Tell the printer that the data is available by writing a 1 to memory location 0x10000, thereby setting the "data available" line high.
- The printer responds by setting it's "busy" line high (to 1) to indicate that a read is in progress.
- The CPU reads location 0x10000 to check the printer status. Seeing that the printer is busy, the CPU sets the "data available" bit low to acknowledge that the bus is being read.
- After a few microseconds have passed, the printer signals the CPU that it is finished reading the data by setting its "busy" line low again (to zero).

This process is called a *handshake*. A first attempt to code the foregoing might look like this:

```
, char *const status = (char *const)0x10000 ; // status port
  char *const data   = (char *const)0x10001 ; // data port

  *data   = the_data;
  *status = 1;        // Set the data-available bit
  while( !*status )   // Wait for printer to start reading
      ;
  *status = 0;        // Clear the data-available bit
  while( *status )    // Wait for the printer to finish reading
      ;
```

The two pointers are `*const` because the port addresses don't change; the contents do change, though, so the pointers are not declared `const char`. The foregoing code is perfectly good C (and C++). Then the optimizer gets its metaphorical hands on it. "Well," the optimizer says, twisting its pointy moustache, "you've set `*status` to 1 and then have looped waiting for it to go to 1. Since it's already there, the test in the first `while` will fail immediately and the body will never be executed." The optimizer then removes the first `while` loop, leaving this:

```
  *status = 1;
  *status = 0;
  while( *status )
      ;
```

The optimizer now says, "you set `*status` to 1, then set it to 0 without using the 1, so I can remove the first assignment, which isn't doing anything useful." The code now looks like this:

```
  *status = 0;
  while( *status )
      ;
```

Now the optimizer applies the earlier logic. `*status` is set to false and the following `while` fails when `*status` is false. Consequently, the `while` loop is never executed so can be eliminated. All that's left of the original code is

```
  *status = 0;
```

This lamentable situation is fixed with the `volatile` keyword, which tells the compiler that a variable can change its value at any time without the compiler doing anything to effect the change. All the earlier optimizations are disabled when you redefine the pointers as follows:

```
  volatile char *const status = (volatile char *const) 0x10000;
  volatile char *const data   = (volatile char *const) 0x10001;
```

Both pointers are still `const`—they cannot be modified—but the `char` that they point to is `volatile`—it can change at any time.

You can also combine the keywords. A `volatile const` is a read-only hardware register, for example. You can't modify it but its value can change at any time.

A handshaking process is also used in multitasking operating systems to pass data from one process to another through a shared region of memory. The sending process sets a byte in memory called a *semaphore* to some condition that means "I have control of the shared memory." It writes to the shared memory, clears the earlier semaphore, and then sets another semaphore that says "I have put data into shared memory that you should read." The semaphores must both be declared `volatile` or the compiler is likely to optimize the references to them out of existence. For many of the same reasons, `volatile` is also handy when you're reading a memory location that is modified by an interrupt-service routine. This memory is modified by an external process—the interrupt-service routine.

semaphore

Finally, you need to use `volatile` when you use `setjmp()` and `longjmp()`. (Which I do not recommend—code that uses `setjmp()`/`longjmp()` is difficult to maintain at best, and the presence of these subroutines is usually a sign of ill-conceived program structure.) The problem is that all memory that's visible after you `longjmp()` to somewhere (including local variables) will have unknown values because the memory may have been modified between the `setjmp()` and `longjmp()` calls:

```
#include <setjmp.h>
main()
{
    int local = 0;

    jmp_buf vector;
    setjmp( vector );

    printf("%d\n", local );
    ...
    local = 1;
    longjmp( vector );      // Jumps to the instruction that
                            // follows the setjmp()
}
```

The first time `printf()` is called, it prints 0. The code then modifies `local` and calls `longjmp()` to return to the instruction immediately following the previous `setjmp()`. The `printf()` statement should now print 1, but it might not if the optimizer substitutes the reference to `local` with its initial value (0) in the `printf()` call. All variables (local and global) visible after a `longjmp()` call must be declared `volatile`.

2.6 The `inline` Storage Class

C++ introduces a new storage class that can be applied only to functions. This is the `inline` storage class which tells the compiler to expand a subroutine in line (as if it were a parameterized macro) in place of the call. Unlike a macro, an `inline` function does not have side effects. For example

```
#define toupper(c) (islower(c) ? (c) + ('a'-'A') : (c))
```

when invoked with

```
toupper( *p++ )
```

expands to

```
(islower(*p++) ? (*p++) + ('a'-'A') : (*p++))
```

and increments p twice. An **inline** function doesn't exhibit this behavior, though. Declare it like this:

```
inline toupper(int c){ return islower(c)? c+('a'-'A'): c; }
```

The earlier toupper() call now works correctly—p is incremented only once. Moreover, you now have a function prototype for toupper(), so the compiler can do argument checking—impossible with a macro implementation.

An **inline** function also solves the multiple-line macro problem discussed on page 56. You can't do the following with a macro:

```
inline two_things() { int ret = a(); b() ; return ret; }
```

The closest you could get is

```
#define two_things() (a(), b())
```

but the macro incorrectly evaluates to b()'s return value, not a()'s.

As with a **const**, you can't link to an **inline** function. Its default storage class is **static**, so the entire function declaration (body and all) must be put into a *.h* file if you intend to use it in more than one module.

inline is a suggestion
out-of-lining

inline is only a suggestion. The compiler might actually treat the definition as a normal **static** function definition and generate calls to it in the normal way. (This process is called *out-of-lining*.) The **inline** is always ignored if you take the function's address somewhere. It might also be ignored if the function is too complex. Many compilers, for example, won't **inline** functions that have **for** loops in them.

out-of-lining can create duplicate **static** functions

In most real code, the compiler doesn't usually out-of-line an **inline** function—remember that inline functions are meant to replace parameterized macros, and how many parameterized macros do you write with loops in them? An overlarge **inline** function that's expanded every time it's called would probably generate an unacceptable amount of code. Nonetheless, you may end up with multiple **static** copies of the function in the program if the compiler out-of-lines a function in multiple files. Since the source files are compiled independently, the compiler can't know if the **inline** function has been expanded elsewhere in the program, so it must expand the **inline** function in every file that the function is used. Some linkers are smart enough to recognize multiple instances of the same function and link only one into the final program. Others aren't.

local **statics** in **inline** functions

This multiple expansion won't cause linkage problems because the individual instances of the function are **static**. The multiple expansion *will* cause problems if the function uses local **static** variables, though. Each instance will have its own set of local **statics**. **Never use local static variables in inline functions.**

2.7 The `char` Type

Moving from storage classes and the like to types, `char` is a basic type in C++, and there is no automatic conversion from `char` to `int` in expressions. For example, there are no type conversions in the following code:

`char` is a basic type

```
char x, y, z;
x = y + z;
```

A `char` is silently converted to an `int` when either operand is an `int`, however. Similarly, a `char` is converted to `int` when it is passed to a function in the place of an `int` argument in the prototype.

2.8 NULL **and Zero**

C++ silently converts zero to NULL if the zero is assigned to a pointer or if it corresponds to a pointer in a function prototype. For example, in C, the following code is legal, but it will produce a serious run-time error if you have a 32-bit pointer and a 16-bit `int`:

```
main() { fred( 0 ); }
fred( void *p ) { ... }
```

A 16-bit `int` is pushed onto the stack by the call, but `fred()` expects a 32-bit pointer. In C, you can detect the problem either by providing a function prototype for `fred()` or by swapping the position of `fred()` and `main()` so that the prototype that's implicit in the function definition comes before the call:

```
fred( void *p ) { ... }
main() { fred( 0 ); }
```

Having seen the foregoing, a C compiler will usually give you a type-mismatch warning. (It's not a hard error in ANSI C.) A C++ compiler will silently convert the 0 to NULL and call the function. I still prefer an explicit NULL in the call rather than 0—it makes for better documentation.

2.9 void **Pointers**

The next issue is `void*`. A C compiler silently allows conversion from any pointer to and from `void*`. A C++ compiler requires a cast:

```
char *cp;
void *vp;

cp = vp;          // Legal in C, illegal in C++
vp = cp;          // Legal in C, illegal in C++
cp = (char*)vp;   // Legal in both languages
vp = (void*)cp;   // Legal in both languages
```

This requirement yields better type checking, but is a pain in the neck[5] in some function prototypes—I'll discuss the problem in a moment.

Note that, as in C, a `void*` is a data pointer. For example, in the 8086-family medium model—where a function pointer is 32 bits and a data pointer is 16 bits— it's a serious error to convert a function pointer to `void*`. The top 16 bits of the pointer will be lost.

2.10 `struct` and `union`

Additions to the functionality of the `struct` in order to support OOP classes is one of the fundamental differences between C and C++, and I'll spend most of this book talking about those changes. There are a few less earth-shattering differences between the ways that C and C++ handle `struct`s and `union`s, however. Since there's no syntactic difference between `struct` and `union`, I'll use `struct` in the following discussion. Everything I say applies to `union`s as well.

automatic `typedef` *for* `struct`

First, the compiler treats a `struct` tag as an implicit `typedef` for the `struct`. A C declaration such as

```
typedef struct george
{
    int fella;
    struct george *ursula;
}
george ;
```

can be written as follows in C++:

```
struct george
{
    int fella;
    george *ursula;
};
```

Not only is no `typedef` required, but the self-referential pointer declaration for `ursula` doesn't need the redundant `struct` keyword, either.

For now, it's best to look at this implicit `typedef` in a C-like way, as a simple name alias. As we'll see later on in the book, a `struct` definition is really more than a name alias, however. `struct` actually introduces a new type to the language. You will be able to provide type-conversion operators, control how normal operators like + work on the new type, and so forth. But for now, think of it as a `typedef`.

The automatic `typedef` means that it's unnatural to use the `struct` keyword to declare two structures that point at each other. Two mutually referential structures can be declared as follows in C:

---

[5] That's another technical term.

```
struct B { struct A *p; };
struct A { struct B *p; };
```

In C++, however, the interior **struct** (the one for the pointer) is rarely used. Unfortunately, a definition like this is illegal:

```
struct B { A *p; }; // ERROR: "type required" (A undefined)
struct A { B *p; }; // Okay because B has been defined
```

You can solve the problem as follows:

struct A;

```
struct A;              // Tell the compiler that A is a struct.
struct B { A *p; };    // Now the declaration is okay.
struct A { B *p; };
```

The **struct** A; carries with it a promise that you will define a body for A sometime before the end of the current compilation unit. It is a hard error if you fail to do so—you can't define A in a different module. This mechanism is also supported by ANSI C, but it isn't used very often.

Moving on to **unions**, a very useful modification to the **union** syntax is the *anonymous* **union**. You can define a union without a tag or name, like this:

anonymous **union**

```
union
{
    int  afl;
    long cio;
};
```

thereby giving two labels (and types) to the same region in memory. Your program can now access these labels as if they were normal variables—as if the surrounding **union** weren't there—but they do actually overlap in memory, so only one can be active at once. This mechanism is particularly useful when the **union** is nested in a structure:

```
struct
{
    int which_one;
    union
    {
        int  afl;
        long cio;
    };
}
afl_cio;
```

You can now say `afl_cio.afl` and `afl_cio.cio` without calling out a name for the union field, as would be required in C. Usually, you need a selector field like `which_one` to tell you which field of the **union** is active. The mechanism is much like a Pascal variant record.

2.11 Variable Declarations

declarations can go
anywhere

There are a few minor differences in variable-declaration syntax in addition to the `struct` and `union` issues. First, a variable declaration in C++ can go anywhere that a statement can go—it does not have to be at the top of a block (immediately following a curly brace).

declarations in `for`
statement

A common way that this feature is exploited is to declare a loop-control variable as part of a `for` statement:

```
for( int i = 0 ; i < 10 ; ++i )
{
    f( i );
}
f( i ); // Illegal in C++ 2.1, legal in C++ 2.0
```

As you can see from the above comment, this mechanism is risky in portable code. The scope of i is the body of the `for` statement, but only in version 2.1 of C++. In earlier releases of the language, the scope of the i was the <u>outer</u> block, not the `for` loop. Consequently, the following is illegal in the earlier versions of the language because the first i is still in scope when the second `for` statement is encountered:

```
for( int i = 0 ; i < 10 ; ++i )
    ...
for( int i = 0 ; i < 10 ; ++i )
    ...
```

Many popular C++ compilers are version 2.0 implementations at this writing, so it's best to avoid the construct altogether if your target is one of those compilers.

There are code-maintenance issues as well. I dislike scattering declarations all over the code. One school of thought states that an uninitialized variable is a potential bug. Consequently, all variables should be initialized as they are defined. Often, though, you don't know the initial value of a variable until you've done some computation. Therefore, the reasoning goes, you should delay the declaration until all that computation is complete, and then declare and initialize the new variable simultaneously. A related thought is that a variable that is used only locally in a loop should be declared in that loop, like this:

```
while( ... )
{
    int i;   // Used in body of while loop only.
}
```

On reflection, I've come to the conclusion that the maintenance becomes more difficult when declarations are scattered all over the place. It's too hard to find a declaration when you need to see a variable's type because the declaration could be anywhere on the page. Moreover, you can have several variables in different blocks of a single subroutine, all of which have the same name, but are different variables. Since the resulting confusion is easily avoided by giving the variables different names, you might as well declare them all at the top of the subroutine where you can find them. Finally, note that the locally-used-variable problem I mentioned earlier (with the i in the `while` loop) is easily solved by breaking the loop out into a small subroutine and declaring i local to that subroutine.

A final variable-related issue is that global variables do not have to be initialized to constants in C++. Something like the following is perfectly acceptable at the global level:

global variables
initialized with
nonconstants

```
const int color = get_color_from_configuration_file();
```

The initial value is fetched from a configuration file by the subroutine call, and color cannot be modified anywhere in the program because it is a const.

You can also call library functions in global declarations. Code like the following is occasionally useful:

```
double Angle  = 10.0;
double Radius = 20;
double End_x  = cos(Angle) * Radius;
double End_y  = sin(Angle) * Radius;
```

Lifting the "must be initialized with a constant" restriction also solves the "initializing global objects" problem discussed in Chapter 1. You can now declare a list element at the global level, for example, and initialize it there by calling an initialization subroutine in the declaration.

Be careful, though. All globals are created and initialized before main() is called, so library-level initializations performed in main() (such as setting up the video environment for a windowing system) will not have been done yet. It's best to do these library-level initializations in the subroutine that initializes individual objects. For example, here is the wrong way to do it:

```
window menu = create_window();
    ...
main()
{
    initialize_window_environment();
}
```

This is wrong because the initialization in main() doesn't happen until after menu is initialized. You can solve the problem by moving the library-level initialization into the subroutine that initializes individual objects:

```
static int Instance_count; // Number of active windows
window *create_window()
{
    if( ++Instance_count == 1 )
        initialize_window_environment();
}
```

Doing the library-level cleanup in a destructor is also a good idea. This way you don't have to worry about forgetting to do it:

```
destroy_window( window *p )
{
    if( --Instance_count == 0 )
        shut_down_window_environment();
}
```

There's one more caveat. Global-level variables should never be initialized to values held by other global-level variables in different files. For example, your guess is as good as mine as to the values to which x and y are initialized in the following code:

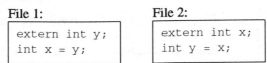

File 1:
```
extern int y;
int x = y;
```

File 2:
```
extern int x;
int y = x;
```

The compiler accepts the foregoing without comment. Be careful.

2.12 Dynamic-Memory Allocation

For reasons that will be discussed in the next chapter, C++ can't manage dynamic memory with function calls like malloc() and free()—the compiler must do the allocation itself. (You *can* call malloc() and free() in a C++ program, but you shouldn't.) Although I don't want to discuss the reasons at this stage, it is useful to look at the syntax now.

new, delete   C++ allocates dynamic memory using the **new** and **delete** keywords. Table 2.1 demonstrates how to use them. Allocate storage by using **new** followed by a type name. A **new** statement evaluates to a pointer to the allocated object or NULL if the system can't get the memory [much like malloc()]. Deallocate storage using **delete**, the argument to which must be a pointer extracted from a previous **new**. Unlike free(), **delete** should accept and ignore an incoming NULL pointer. Some C++ implementations do not handle this feature correctly, though, so you should test your compiler before relying on it. It's possible to get control over how **new** and **delete** do memory allocation—the process is discussed in a future chapter.

Table 2.1. Using **new** and **delete**

C	C++

`int *ip = malloc(sizeof int);`
`struct fred *sp=malloc(sizeof(struct fred));`
`free(ip);`
`free(sp);`
	`int *ip = new int;`
	`fred *sp = new fred;`
	`delete ip;`
	`delete sp;`

`int *ia=malloc(sizeof(int) * array_size);`
`struct fred *fa=malloc(sizeof(struct fred)`
`                         * array_size);`
`free(ia)`
`free(fa)`
	`int *ia=new int[array_size];`
	`fred *fa=new fred[array_size];`
	
	`delete [array_size] ia;`
	`delete [array_size] fa;`

The array-allocation syntax is the biggest difference between the two systems. using new to allocate arrays The array size in a `new` statement must also be part of the matching `delete` statement. It's passed in brackets following the type indicator. Unlike `free()`, you must pass the array size to the matching `delete`. Note the weird syntax here. The array size goes between the `delete` and the pointer.[6] The brackets must follow the `delete` rather than the pointer name because you can have an array of pointers to dynamic objects. For example:

`delete` [n] p;

```
int *array[2];

array[0] = new int;       // pointer to a single int
array[1] = new int[3];    // pointer to first element of
                          //            three-element array
// ...
delete    array[0]; // free single int addressed by array[0]
delete[3] array[1]; // free array of three ints addressed by
                    //                              array[1]
```

This requirement that a size be passed to `delete` makes it important to do something that you should already be doing in C, but probably aren't. A `free()` call or `delete` statement should, if at all possible, be in the same subroutine as the matching `malloc()` call or `new` statement. In other words, treat memory returned from `malloc()` or `new` as if it were allocated locally with a normal declaration. You should deallocate the memory when the pointer used to keep track of the memory goes out of scope.

There are two reasons for this practice. First, it makes it much easier to reconcile the array-size argument in a `delete` statement with the matching `new` if both statements are in the same subroutine. Second, it is more difficult to orphan the memory. As with `malloc()` and `free()`, every `new` statement must have a matching `delete` statement. Otherwise, the memory is lost. It's much easier to guarantee this matching if the allocation and deallocation happen in the same subroutine.

The foregoing is not always possible, of course. A program might build a tree using a complex system of subroutine calls, for example. It will probably be impossible to free each tree node in the same subroutine that allocated that node. Nonetheless, it's worth following the same-subroutine rule if you can.

One final point for now: you can't mix `new` and `delete` with `malloc()` and `free()`. A program can use both systems, but memory allocated by `new` must be deallocated by `delete`; memory from `malloc()` must be deallocated by `free()`. Passing a pointer that was returned from `malloc()` to `delete` [or a pointer that came from `new` to `free()`] will yield unpredictable results.

---

[6] C++ 2.1 lets you leave out the array size in a `delete` statement, but you can't leave out the brackets. This is okay:

```
int *ip = new int[10];
delete [] ip;
```

but a plain `delete` ia, without the brackets, isn't. It's best, for now, to use the explicit array size to keep your code portable.

2.13 Function Prototypes and Forward References

forward references
not permitted

Forward references are not permitted in C++. A full-function prototype (not just a simple **extern** statement) must be given to the compiler before a function may be called. As with ANSI C, a prototype-style function definition constitutes a function prototype for the purpose of resolving forward references.

differences from C
function prototypes

C++ function prototypes work just like C prototypes with three exceptions, shown in Table 2.2. Note that the first problem can be rectified simply by not using the defaults—you should always specify a return value and argument types as part of the prototype.

Table 2.2. Differences Between C and C++ Function Prototypes

Prototype	Treated like this in C:	Treated like this in C++:
f(void);	int f(void); *function returns int*	void f(void); *function does not return a value*
int f( );	int f( ); *don't check function arguments*	int f(void) *function takes no arguments*
int f(...);	— *not recognized by most C compilers*	int f(...) *don't check function arguments.*

2.14 Default Arguments

default function
arguments

C++ provides a controversial feature that can affect function prototypes—default arguments. (I strongly suggest that you don't use this feature in your own programs, but you'll see it in other books and existing code, so a discussion of it is in order.) You can provide default values for arguments in a prototype and then omit the actual argument from the call. The compiler will effectively add an argument having the default value to the call. The syntax is as follows:

```
int   pebbles( int a = 5, int b = 6 );
```

Thereafter:

A call to	pebbles()	is the same as	pebbles(5,6)
A call to	pebbles(10)	is the same as	pebbles(10,6)
A call to	pebbles(10,20)	is the same as	pebbles(10,20)

only trailing
arguments can be
supplied

Only trailing arguments can be supplied in this way. [pebbles(,y) is illegal.] Similarly, you can't provide default values for an argument unless you've also provided default values for all arguments to its right. [int   pebbles(int a = 5, int b); is illegal.]

The main difficulty is maintenance. I, at least, can never remember what the default values are. Consequently, as I read the code, if an argument is missing, I have to go find the prototype to find out what the argument really is. What you're really doing is defeating one of the maintenance advantages that function prototyping gives you—that you are required to provide the correct number of arguments of the correct type in a function call. If you use default arguments, you are now permitted to provide too-few arguments as part of the call, creating confusion all around. If you insist on using default arguments, always default them to 0 or NULL so you at least know what they are.

Unfortunately, things are permitted to get even more confusing. A default initializer for a given argument can be supplied only once in a file, typically as part of the function prototype in a header file. For example, redefining one of the arguments to x() is illegal:

.h file:	`int pebbles(int a=5, int b=6);`
file that includes the .h file:	`int pebbles(int y, int z=0); //ILLEGAL`

You can supply a default argument in a redefinition if an explicit one isn't in the first prototype, however. This is legal:

redefinition of default arguments

.h file:	`int bam_bam(int a, int b=0);`
file that includes the .h file:	`int bam_bam(int a=1, int b);`

Frankly, this redefinition only adds to the confusion. A redeclaration like

```
bam_bam(int a=1, int b);
```

is normally illegal, so the person maintaining the code is put in the position of looking at a normally illegal definition that is nonetheless accepted by the compiler. In order to see what's really going on, the maintainer now has to search through all the included *.h* files, looking for the original definition.

2.15 Function Definitions

The old K&R style function definition

```
int pebbles( arg1, arg2 )
long arg1;                      /* arg2 defaults to int */
{
}
```

is not permitted in C++. A full prototype-style definition is required:

```
int pebbles( long arg1, int arg2 )
{
}
```

Argument names are optional in the list, both in a prototype (a function declaration) and in the function definition, where the body of the function is found. You should always use the argument names in the prototype for documentation purposes.

You need to use the names in a function definition in order to access the arguments from the function. If an argument is deliberately not used, you should not give it a name. The most common use of this mechanism is a stub subroutine used in the initial development stage of a program. A *stub* is a small subroutine that exists only to test a higher-level function that calls it. The stub doesn't do anything but return a reasonable value, but its existence lets you debug the higher-

stub

level routine without needing to write an entire program. A stub could look like this:

```
void stub( int, int ){ printf("in stub()\n"); }
```

thereby requiring the caller to pass it two `int` arguments, but the arguments aren't given names in the definition because they are not actually used. The compiler won't generate an "argument not used" warning, either. Later on, when the stub is replaced by a real subroutine, the arguments will be given names.

omit name for
function argument,
_doprnt()

Situations also come up where you never intend to provide a name. Consider, for example, a general-purpose display function that is passed a pointer to a single-character output function that takes an optional argument. A few early versions of `_doprnt()` (which became `vfprintf()` in ANSI C) worked like

```
void _doprnt( char *format, va_list args,
              int (*output_function)(int c, void *arg),
              void *arg );
```

The output function is called indirectly by `_doprnt()` to output a single character. It is called like this:

```
(*output_function)( c, arg );
```

where `arg` is the fourth argument to `_doprnt()`. You can use this routine to implement `fprintf()` as follows:

```
#include <stdarg.h>
fprintf( FILE *stream, char *format, ... )
{
    fputc( int c, FILE *stream );
    va_list args;
    va_start(args, format);

    _doprnt( format, args, (int(*)(int,void *)) fputc, stream );

    va_end( args );
}
```

But what happens when the output function needs only one argument? You need to declare the output function with a bogus second argument that holds the place of the second argument to `fputc()`. Since that argument is never used, it is not given a name. For example:

```
output_funct( int character,  void* );
```

A pointer to `output_funct()` can be passed to `_doprnt()` without the horrible cast in the previous example because the argument types and number of arguments match the prototype exactly. If the second argument had been given a name, the compiler would probably complain that the argument was never used. Since there's no name, the argument is clearly intended by the programmer to be unused, so the compiler won't complain.

Finally, because the name component of an argument in a function prototype is optional, the following strange syntax is permitted:

```
void f( int x, int = 0 );
```

The reasoning is that a default value will be in place to test a function when you provide a name for the second argument in the actual function definition. The syntax has little to recommend it, though, and should be treated as an artifact of the compiler, not as a feature.

2.16 Function Pointers

Function pointers work pretty much the same in C++ as in C. There are a few things to watch out for, though. First of all, an explicit dereference is not required to call a function through a pointer in C++. (This is also a feature of ANSI C, but most people don't know it.) For example, given

explicit function-pointer dereference optional

```
int (*pfi)( int x, long y ); // function pointer
int    foo ( int x, long y ); // function
pfi = foo;
```

both of the following are legal:

```
foo( 10, 20L );
pfi( 10, 20L );
```

You can still use `(*pfi)(10,20L)` [or `(*foo)(10,20L)`] if you want, but it's less readable.

Note that function arguments must be supplied for function pointers, too:

must supply function arguments for function pointers

```
int (*pf)();   // *pf is a function with a void argument list

int g( void );
int f( int x );

pf = g; // okay-----g() has a void argument list
pf = f; // ILLEGAL--f() has an int argument
```

The idea is that function prototyping must guarantee that the function is being passed the correct arguments, even if the function is being called indirectly through a pointer. All of the foregoing applies to C as well as C++, but C programmers tend to be sloppy about the arguments to functions that are called indirectly because the compiler is equally sloppy about argument checking. You don't have that luxury in C++.

Although requiring the function arguments to be spelled out in the prototype and matched in the assigned function is more often than not what you want, it's a real nuisance with functions that take function-pointer arguments. The last case in Table 2.2 [`f(...)`] is sometimes a useful solution to the problem. Consider a definition like the following:

```
qsort( void *base, int nel, int ele_size,
                    int (*cmp)(void*, void*) );
```

The argument types for the `cmp` pointer must be provided in C++ or the compiler assumes a `void` argument list. The writer of `qsort()`, who doesn't know the actual argument types at compile time, has to declare these arguments as `void*`.

The real comparison function will hardly ever have **void*** arguments. Consider the following comparison function, which could be used to sort an array of **int**s:

```
int int_cmp( int *e1, int *e2 ){ return *e1 - *e2; }
```

You have to use the following ugly cast to pass int_cmp to qsort():

```
int array[10];
   ...
qsort(array, 10, sizeof(int), (int(*)(void*,void*)) compare);
```

The real difficulty is that C++ does not silently convert to and from **void***, even in a function call. The cast is required because a function with two **int*** arguments does not match the function with **void*** arguments in the prototype.

In this situation, the type checking is more of an annoyance than a help. In theory, you can turn it off by changing the prototype to

```
qsort( void *base, int nel, int ele_size, int (*cmp)(...) );
```

but not all compilers accept this construct.

There's one final annoyance. The actual definition of qsort() will probably look like the earlier prototype (with the **void*** arguments), not like the one with the ellipses. If so, the ellipses version of the prototype must not be visible to the compiler when it's working on qsort() itself or you'll get a "type mismatch in redefinition" error—ellipses in a prototype do not match an explicit argument in the definition. You must have ellipses in both places. The net result is that the ugly cast will probably be required every time you need to pass a function pointer to a function like qsort().

2.17 Function Overloading

overloaded

A function name is *overloaded* when you provide more than one version of the function. The different versions must have different argument types, however. For example:

```
double sqrt ( double arg ); // called with:  sqrt( 16.0 );
int    sqrt ( int arg    ); // called with:  sqrt( 16   );
```

The first function is the normal library function. The second version must be provided by you. The compiler decides which version to use by looking at the argument types in the call. The first overload, with the **double** argument in the prototype, is called when the argument actually passed to the function is of type **double**. The second version is called when the argument is an **int**. Unfortunately, the return value is not considered when determining which function to call, only the arguments are taken into account.[7] The following is illegal, given the

---

[7] The reasons for this restriction lie in the way that compilers work. Suffice it to say that it's difficult for the compiler to know what was to the left of the equal sign when it's processing the code on the right of the equals sign. That is, the return value of a function overload would be important in a situation like this:

```
int  f(void), int_var;
```

earlier definitions:

```
double sqrt( int arg );      // ILLEGAL
```

because it conflicts with the

```
int sqrt( int arg );
```

that was defined earlier.

when function call
doesn't match
prototype exactly

C++ provides a host of rules that define the compiler's behavior when the argument types in the call don't match any of the overloads exactly. Ellis and Stroustrup use 15 pages to describe the actual rules.[8] With only a few exceptions, the rules aren't worth learning, though. Probably one out of a hundred (if that many) C++ programmers completely understand how the conversion rules work. Consequently, code that makes assumptions about what the compiler is going to do is effectively unmaintainable.

In any event, any compiler with pretensions of being a production compiler will print a warning if it has to do an implicit type conversion to get a call to match a prototype. Your C compiler probably works this way already. The only exceptions will be automatic conversions like char to int and float to double. C++ compilers should exhibit the same behavior. Since you don't want useless warnings hanging around on the screen obscuring the warnings that are telling you that something's really wrong, you should eliminate prototype-generated warning messages by using cast operators. That is, **make the argument types in all function calls match one or the other of the overloads exactly by using cast operators if necessary.** This way there is no ambiguity.

Note that a cast can sometimes mask a real problem in the code—and it's easy to toss a cast into code to shut up the compiler without solving the actual problem. Use casts with care. Here's an example of the sort of problem I'm talking about: The following code correctly generates a warning because I'm passing a long int to a function that expects a normal int.

cast can mask real
problem

```
long nose = 65535L; // Value won't fit into 16-bit int
babar( int nose );  // Function prototype
//...
babar( nose );      // WARNING: type conversion in argument
```

I can turn off the warning with a cast, as follows:

```
babar( (int)nose );
```

```
long f(void), long_var;
long_var = f();      // call long f(void);
```
Unfortunately, the compiler has effectively forgotten that it's seen the long_var when it's processing the f(). It's possible for the compiler to get around this difficulty, but it requires extra work with which, I assume, the original implementers of C++ didn't want to be bothered.

[8] [Ellis and Stroustrup], pp. 312–327.

but the cast doesn't solve the real problem: a 32-bit `long` can hold a value that won't fit into a 16-bit `int`. Casting `nose` to `int` suppresses the warning, but a garbage value is still passed to `babar()`. (The decimal number 65,535 has the hex value 0xffff, a value treated as −1 when it's placed into a 16-bit `int`.) Use casts carefully to solve specific problems, not just to turn off warning messages.

Because of the foregoing cast issues, and because casts are not always desirable, you do need to know a few of the basic type-conversion rules used to make a call match a prototype. Here's a summary of the process that the compiler goes through:

1. First, the compiler tries to find an exact match between the arguments in the call and the arguments in the various prototypes.
2. If no exact match is found, the compiler applies standard C conversions to arguments of call, attempting to get them to match the argument of one of the overloaded functions. The standard conversions are
   - `char`, `unsigned char`, and `short` are converted to `int`.
   - `unsigned short` is converted to `int` if an `int` is larger than a `short`; otherwise, it's converted to `unsigned int`.
   - `float` is converted to `double`

   No standard conversion is considered better than any other standard conversion.[9]

   In general, an ambiguity results, and the compiler generates an error, when a conversion needs to be applied to more than one argument. Use casts to create an exact match.
3. Finally, user-defined conversions (the mechanics for which are discussed in the next two chapters) are applied if nothing else works.

no C conversion is better than any other

The most important of these rules is: No C type conversion is considered better than another C type conversion. Consider the following:

```
void fred( double x );
void fred( long   x );
    . . .
fred( 10 );     // ERROR
```

The problem is that `10` is an `int`, so it must be converted to be used. Conversions from `int` to `long` and `int` to `double` are both possible, however, and neither is considered superior to the other. The compiler refuses to accept the call in this case—it's a hard error.

---

[9] This note is skipping ahead a bit to the topic of references, but some compilers consider a conversion of a reference variable that doesn't generate a temporary to be better than a conversion that does create a temporary. For example:

```
extern ff( long &c_ref );      // version 1
extern ff( unsigned &s );      // version 2
int i;
ff( i ); // Conversion from int to unsigned is used because no
         // temporary needs to be generated to make the call.
```

The foregoing example isn't much different than C, because most C compilers will at least give a warning if they have to convert an **int** to some other type in order to match a function prototype. The following code doesn't behave like C, though:

```
void barney( int  x );
void barney( long x );
 ...
barney( 'c' ); // ERROR
```

A **char** is a basic type in C++. The automatic conversion from **char** to **int** does not happen, as it does in C. Consequently, the compiler has to choose between converting the **char** to an **int** and converting it to a **long** and it won't be able to make the decision. If the second version of barney() (with the **long** argument) was missing, the compiler would happily (and silently) convert the **char** to an **int**, however.

Also note that keywords you're used to thinking of as unimportant become very important when function overloads are possible. All six of the following functions are different:

```
betty( char tok                 );
betty( const char tok           );
betty( unsigned char tok        );
betty( const unsigned char tok  );
betty( int tok                  );
betty( const int tok            );
```

It will be almost impossible for the compiler to pick the correct one in most applications. (Probably the best solution to the foregoing is to get rid of all but the last one.) Note that this example depends on the compiler distinguishing between a normal argument and a **const** version of the same argument. The following code should work:

```
ff( const char *p );
ff(       char *p );
 ...
char *cp;               // Variable pointer to variable char
const char *const_cp;   // Variable pointer to constant char
 ...
ff( cp );        // calls non const version
ff( const_cp ); // calls const version
```

Some compilers don't handle the foregoing correctly, though, so be careful with it.

A **void*** argument matches all pointer types that aren't covered by explicit pointers in other declarations—it's a none-of-the-above situation:

```
foo( int  *p );
foo( long *p );
foo( void *p );

int  *int_ptr;
long *long_ptr;
char *char_ptr;
  ...
foo( int_ptr  ); // calls int*  version
foo( long_ptr ); // calls long* version
foo( char_ptr ); // calls void* version
```

Since there is no defined conversion (in C or C++) from `char*` to `int*` or `long*`, the third call would be illegal if the `void*` overload were not present. But be careful of the following:

```
void wilma( void *p );
void wilma( int x   );
  // ...
wilma( 10   );  // okay, 10 is an int
wilma( NULL );  // okay, NULL is a pointer
wilma( 0 );     // ERROR
```

The last line is an error because 0 can be converted to a pointer type in C++ — 0 and NULL are interchangeable. Consequently, the compiler doesn't know whether to call the `int` or pointer version of the function.

It's possible for you to set up a situation where a correct decision is literally impossible. Consider the following:

```
dino( long x, int  y );
dino( int  x, long y );

dino( 10, 10 );
```

It's impossible for the compiler to decide whether to convert the first 10 to a `long` to match the first call or to convert the second 10 to a `long` to match the second. The compiler generates a hard error in this situation.

Default arguments in a prototype effectively create function overloads. Given a declaration such as

```
int x( int y = 0 );
```

you cannot provide an explicit overload like

```
int x( void );
```

because the compiler won't know whether to call your explicit `void` function or to call the earlier `int` function with a default value of zero when it sees the call `x()`. This is another good reason not to use default arguments.

Confusion can also be added if some overloads of a function have a different number of arguments than other overloads, and default values are used as well. For example:

```
void f( int  x );                // version 1
void f( long x, int y = 0 );     // version 2
     // ...
f(  2L );  // calls ver. 2: exact match of first argument
f(  0  );  // calls ver. 1: exact match of first argument
f( 0,0 );  // calls ver. 2: two args are present.
f( 'c' );  // ambiguous: char->long no better than char->int
```

As a last word (for now) about function overloading, it is function overloading that makes function prototypes absolutely necessary. In order to determine which overload of a function to call, the compiler must know what all the possibilities are and the prototype gives the compiler this information.

2.18 Function Templates

Although `inline` functions are a great improvement over macros because of the lack of side effects and argument-type checking, the argument-type checking can sometimes cause problems. Consider the C `min()` macro, which is usually defined like this:

```
#define min(a,b) ((a) < (b) ? (a) : (b))
```

This macro works with arguments of any type. You can, for example, compare two `int`s, two `long`s, an `int` and a `long`, and so forth (barring the usual type-conversion issues like sign extension on conversion from `char` to `int`).

An equivalent `inline` function that might look like this:

```
inline int min( int a, int b ){ return a < b ? a : b ; }
```

has a big problem—it can only compare two ints. You'd get a type-conversion error (or at least a warning) if you tried to pass two `long`s to it (for good reason—the truncation will probably yield a garbage return value).

type conversion problems with inline-function arguments

There are two solutions to this problem. The first is to provide a host of overloads for `min()`:

```
inline int    min(int a,    int b   ){ return a < b ? a : b;}
inline long   min(long a,   long b  ){ return a < b ? a : b;}
inline double min(double a, double b){ return a < b ? a : b;}
```

This solution creates an awful lot of redundant code to maintain, however. An alternate solution is to generate the overloads with a function-generation macro. For example, the following macro generates overloads of the `min()` function:

function-generation macro

```
#define min_gen( type ) \
    inline type min(type a, type b){ return a < b ? a : b ;}
```

The three `min()` overloads can now be generated like this:

```
min_gen( int    ) // generate min overload for int args
min_gen( long   ) // generate min overload for long args
min_gen( double ) // generate min overload for double args
```

The only real problem is the weird syntax: There's no semicolon following the template

macro invocation, for example, and a programmer probably won't expect a macro to expand to a function definition.

C++ corrects these problems by means of the *template* mechanism. (Templates are a new feature to C++, and are not supported by all compilers.) A template for a `min()` function looks like this:

```
template <class type>
inline type min( type a, type b )
{
    return a < b ? a : b ;
}
```

function template

The **template** statement attaches itself to the next declaration in the file, in this case the definition for the `min()` function. The combined definition—the **template** statement and attached function definition—is collectively called a *function template.*

It's convenient to look at the template as a fancy version of the earlier function-generation macro. In reality, though, it is a mechanism for telling the compiler to generate a potentially infinite number of overloads of the attached function on an as-needed basis. The `<class type>` in the **template** statement tells the compiler to treat `type` as if it were a special kind of **typedef** that exists only long enough to generate a version of the function.

The use of **class** in the **template** statement is unfortunate. The **class** in `<class x>` says that `x` specifies a type of some sort. A better design solution would introduce a `type` keyword into the language so you could say `<type x>`. Unfortunately, the **class** keyword is recycled for this purpose.

A template is not an actual function, it's just a model that the compiler uses to generate overloads of a function as necessary. The easy way to cause the compiler to generate an overload is to just call the function. For example, the calls

```
int   a, b, c;
long lb, lc;
   . . .
a = min( b,  c );
a = min( lb, lc);
```

template functions

cause the compiler to generate two versions of `min()`, one with two **int** arguments and another with two **long** arguments. These generated functions are called *template functions.*[10]

Look at the process as follows: The compiler, when it sees a call to a template function, generates short-lived **typedefs** for each type in the **template** statement's type list. It does this by matching the argument types actually used in the call with those in the template. When an argument is found that matches a type

---

[10] The potential confusion—between a "function template" (the model used to generate the template) and a "template function" (the generated function)—is truly unfortunate. It's akin to the definition (allocates space) versus declaration (give information to the compiler) disaster that is accepted C terminology. The terms are in common use, though.

in the `template` statement, it generates a `typedef` for that type using the actual type passed. In the current case, the compiler looks at the <u>calls</u> and finds an `int` argument that corresponds to a in the earlier definition for `min()`. It sees that a is declared as a `type`, however, not an `int`. It then consults the `template <class type>` statement and finds `type` listed there. So it generates a short-lived `typedef` of the form `typedef int` `type`. It now creates a version of `min()` using this `typedef`, and then destroys the `typedef`. The same process is followed for the second call, but now `type` is recast as a `long` because `min()` is called with a `long` first argument.

A function prototype also forces the compiler to expand the template into a function. For example, a prototype like

force
function-template
expansion with
function prototype

```
double min( double a, double b );
```

tells the compiler to produce a `double` version of `min()`.

Forcing the expansion of a template in this way is useful in one situation. The compiler doesn't do **any** of the normal type conversions in the template expansion. Since `min()` is defined as having two arguments of type `type`, the compiler will not be able to process the call

```
int  x;
long y;
 ...
min( x, y ); // ERROR
```

because `type` is mapped to `int` when the first argument is processed, and there is no defined conversion from a `long` to a `type`. Consequently, the second argument cannot be processed.

There are two ways around the problem. The first (and best) is to provide a prototype of the form

```
long min( long x, long y );
```

thereby forcing the compiler to create an instance of `min()` with `long` arguments. The earlier call will now work because a `long-long` overload of `min()` exists, so the compiler can convert the x in `min(x,y)` to `long` in the normal way.

Alternately, you can provide a template for `min()` that looks like this:

```
template <class left_arg, class right_arg >
inline left_arg min( left_arg a, right_arg b )
{
    return a < b ? a : b ;
}
```

When multiple types are present in the `template` definition, as is the case here, all of them must be used at least once in the argument list of the attached function definition. You cannot, for example, declare a type in the `template` statement that is used as the function's return type, but not as an argument.

The foregoing approach has problems with regard to the mismatched-arguments issue. The first is the return value, which is arbitrarily defined as having the same type as `left_arg`—`right_arg` could be used just as well, though. The second problem is that the compiler can generate a tremendous number of overloads of the `min()` function—a new overload is generated every time a call has arguments that aren't of the same type as a previous call. You'll also get occasional errors when you try to use some of the expanded templates. For example, the compiler will happily expand a version of the template for `min(1,"one")`. The generated function, which declares `a` as an **int** and `b` as a **char***, won't work because C++ won't let you compare an **int** against a pointer with a < operator. Forcing generation with a prototype is generally a better solution.

an explicit version of a function overrides a function template

There's one final situation that's addressed with templates. What if you want a special-purpose version of `min()` that will do lexicographic comparisons on two strings? You can't use the general-purpose template because that will just expand to a less-than operation. The function will return whichever string is at the lowest address, not the one with the smallest lexical value. Get around the problem simply by providing an explicit overload such as the following somewhere in your program:

```
char *min( char *a, char *b )
{
    return (strcmp(a,b) < 0) ? a : b ;
}
```

If the special-purpose definition is in another file, just put a prototype for it in the file where the call is found. The compiler (or more precisely, the linker) will use your explicit overloads rather than the ones provided by template expansion. The formal rules say that if an explicit overload of a function and a template-generated version both exist, the explicit overload is used.

portability problems with function templates

There is a portability caveat. In theory, the function template (the **template** statement and attached function definition) can be in any file in the program, and calls to the generated template functions can also be scattered around the code—both in the module that contains the function template and elsewhere. Similarly, explicitly declared overloads such as the **char*** version of `min()` can be anywhere in the program—they don't need to be in the same module as the template. When a compiler sees a function prototype that could match a function template, it doesn't actually know whether the prototype is a directive to expand the template with the specified arguments or whether it is a prototype for an explicit overload function that's declared in another file. This means that the potential conflicts between explicit versions of a function and template-generated versions must be sorted out by the linker, not the compiler, and not all linkers are this smart.

For example, at least one compiler that I know of does not support the earlier template-function generation mechanism where the simple presence of a prototype causes a template function to be generated. This compiler always assumes that a function prototype references an explicit overload somewhere else in the program. Consequently, the presence of the prototype causes exactly the opposite effect as the behavior just described—it tells the compiler not to generate a template function, assuming that an explicit overload exists and will be picked up by the linker.

Templates are still very much in flux in terms of the evolution of the language. They are a very useful feature of the language, and should certainly be used, but you should use them with care and with the foreknowledge that the compiler's behavior might change at any point and that not all compilers support them.

As usual, there are a few small implementation details that you need to know to finish up the topic. First, the `inline` keyword that I used in the earlier examples is not required in a template. A template can expand to a real function in addition to an `inline` one, although an `inline` expansion will give you more efficient code.

Also, the scope of the `type` is the declaration that follows the `template` statement. This is okay:

```
template <class type>
inline type min( type a, type b ){ ... }

typedef int type;    // The "type" in the template doesn't apply
type x;              // x is always an int
```

2.19 Type-Safe Linkage

Function overloading adds a very useful feature to the language, almost as a side effect. In a C program, even if you provide prototypes for all functions before calling them, there is no guarantee that the prototype is correct. It's possible to change the actual function and forget to change the prototype in a separate header file. Other modules that then call the function, using the unmodified header file, will not be passing the correct arguments and the compiler will not detect the problem. One way to attack this problem is to `#include` all header files that hold prototypes for a given function in the source file where the function is actually defined. This way, the compiler will flag mismatches between the declaration and definition when you recompile the source file. Since not everyone will do the foregoing, the only real solution to this problem in C is to use a global-level syntax checker like **lint**, which examines the entire program at once rather than one module at a time, as is the case with a compiler.

prototype may not match function definition

Fortunately, this problem is solved in C++ because of function overloading. Since you can't really have two functions with the same name, the compiler must generate a unique name for each of the overloads. It usually does so by appending a string of characters representing the argument types to the end of the user-supplied name. For example, the encoding scheme suggested in Ellis and Stroustrup,[11] encodes the function names

```
int  fred( char *x, unsigned x )
long fred( unsigned x, long y  )
```

like this:

```
_fred__FPScUi
_fred__FUiSl
```

---

[11] A suggested encoding scheme is described on pp. 122–127.

You can break the encoded name up as follows:

`__`	introduces the string that represents the arguments
`F`	indicates function
`PSc`	stands for pointer to signed char
`Ui`	stands for unsigned int
`Sl`	stands for signed long

name mangling

Ellis and Stroustrup call this process "name encoding," but most C++ programmers call it *name mangling*. Ellis and Stroustrup's system calls for two underscores separating the function name from the string representing the arguments. Since many compilers use their scheme, it's a good idea to avoid double underscores in your own function names.

signature

The encoded function name is called the function's *signature*. The compiler decides which of several overloads to call by using the declared types of the arguments that are actually passed to the function to create a signature from the call. It then compares the generated signature against the signatures of the various overloads and chooses the appropriate one.

name mangling
means safer linking

Name mangling yields an important benefit. Since the name will be mangled at both the call and in the function definition itself, it's now impossible to call a function improperly by using a bad function prototype. For example, if a function is defined as f(**int** x), its name is mangled to f__FSi when the definition is processed. A call like f(0L) is also mangled by the compiler. Since a **long** argument is passed, the name is mangled to f__FSLi. None of this will cause errors at compile time, but when you go to link, there will be no function named f__FSLi—the function itself is named f__FSi—so the linker kicks out an error. It's impossible to call a function with the wrong argument types in C++.

suppress mangling
with **extern** "C"

There's one difficulty with name mangling. You can't call a C function (which has an unmangled name) from C++ (which will mangle the name as part of processing the call), or vice versa. Since it's useful to be able to write a hybrid C and C++ program, a mechanism is provided to suppress mangling. A prototype like this:

```
extern "C" short boris( int x );
```

tells the compiler not to mangle the function name boris in a call or a definition. Consequently, boris() can be called from either C or C++. An alternate form of **extern** "C" lets you direct the compiler to suppress mangling for a whole group of declarations:

```
extern "C"
{
    short boris   ( int x );
    long  natasha ( long y );
}
```

Note that the curly braces don't form a compound statement in the normal sense. There is no semicolon following the close brace and the curly braces do not form a scope. It's just a grouping mechanism. Also **extern** "C" is not an "escape to C for a while" mechanism. It just disables mangling.

Any sort of statement can be processed with an **extern** "C". You can have typedefs and so forth inside the braces. The **extern** "C" just tells the compiler not to mangle any function names found in the block. Consequently, a statement like the following is both legal and useful:

```
extern "C"
{
    #include "header.h"  // prototypes for C functions
}
```

All of the C functions declared in *header.h* can now be called directly from a C++ program. (Note that most compiler vendors put the **extern** "C" inside header files like *stdio.h* for you, so an explicit **extern** "C" on your part isn't required.)

It's possible to suppress mangling on only one overload of a function. The following is perfectly legal:

```
extern "C" int strcmp(char *s1, char *s2 ); // C library ver.
extern     int strcmp(string s1, string s2); // string-class ver.
    ...
string s1,   s2;
char   *cp1, *cp2;
    ...
strcmp( cp1, cp2 ); // call the C-library version
strcmp( s1,  s2  ); // call the C++ version that you supply
```

You can't turn off mangling on two overloads, though. Something like the following causes problems because you can't have two functions with the same name at the assembly-language level:

```
extern "C" int rocky(int  x);
extern "C" int rocky(long x);   // ERROR, only one rocky()
                       //            may be "C"
```

There is one potential problem with using name mangling. If a function's signature is very complex—with 8 or 10 arguments that are of different user-defined types, for example—then it's possible for the mangled name to have more characters than can be handled by the underlying assembly language. If two signatures differ only in the types of the rightmost arguments, and if the mangled names are so long that the rightmost characters in the name are effectively truncated, then it's possible to end up with two conflicting function names. This truncation is not generally a problem, but it's worth considering if the linker is printing messages about conflicting labels or subroutine names when no such conflict should exist.

name mangling can produce too-long identifiers

As a final note, some compilers provide support for languages other than C using the **extern** mechanism (such as **extern** "Pascal"). The compiler has to do a lot more than just suppress mangling to call a Pascal subroutine from a C++ subroutine and vice versa. Pascal subroutine arguments are usually pushed onto the stack in the reverse order of C subroutine arguments, for example. So, the **extern** "whatever" really says: make a C++ subroutine callable from the "whatever" language and allow the C++ compiler to call a subroutine written in the "whatever" language.

2.20 References

I'm reluctant to introduce references at this point because it's difficult to explain
what they're good for until I demonstrate how to use them in a class implementation, something I won't do until the next few chapters. I've put this section here
because it simplifies future discussion to have all the information up front. I didn't
want to plop an eight-page digression on the subject of references into the middle
of a discussion of how to form a class. So, please bear with me for a bit and take it
on faith that the following material is actually useful in practice. (References are
required in the language because you can't do operator overloads without them.)

2.20.1 Reference Variables

Although it sounds rather ominous in the context of the previous paragraph, reference variables are hardly ever used in practice. Reference arguments to functions,
which are discussed in the next section, are used all the time, however, and
explaining references in terms of variable declarations simplifies the discussion
a bit.

reference

A *reference* is a mechanism for providing a name alias for a variable. The
declaration syntax mirrors that of a pointer, and looks like this:

```
int x;           // an int
int &rx = x;     // a reference to an int
```

the & (reference)
operator

The second definition establishes rx as an alternate name for x. The ampersand in
the declaration for rx is treated syntactically just like a *, but it is translated as
"reference to" rather than "pointer to."

Using the & to mean "reference" is, to my mind, a syntactic mistake on the part
of the language designers. The & usually means "address of" and using for "reference to" just adds unnecessary confusion. A new operator (@ is a good candidate)
should have been introduced to mean "reference to." Anyway, keep in mind that
an ampersand that's part of a declarator means "reference to." It means "address
of" only when it's part of an initializer or an expression.

initializing
references

The assignment in **int** &rx=x is <u>not</u> like a normal initialization. It specifies
the variable that rx references. All reference variables must be made to reference
a real variable at declaration time by using the assignment-like syntax shown.

Thereafter, the variable itself and the reference to that variable are treated
identically. The situation (at least with respect to reference *variables*) is similar to

```
union
{
    int x;
    int rx;
};
```

References are not **unions**, however.

Given the earlier declaration, rx is an alternate name for x. The compiler *can*
treat it just like a macro (it might not). For example, an expression like rx=y can
effectively be translated by the compiler into x=y. There is no way to modify the
reference itself because it has no physical existence. Every time you say rx, you're

really talking about x. That's why the =x that tells the compiler the name of the referenced variable has to be part of the declaration—in any other context an rx=x would be the same as x=x.

References are sometimes very difficult for C programmers to understand because they try to make them more complicated than they are. Do not think "pointers." A reference is a reference—a name alias—not a pointer. C programmers tend to think that references must be implemented as pointers, so should be treated as such, and that way lies madness.

a reference is not a
pointer

Here are a couple examples. Given the earlier definition,

```
int *p = &rx;
```

puts the address of x into p. rx is just an alternate name for x—it has no physical address. &rx evaluates to the address of the referenced object. Something like

```
int *p = rx;
```

is illegal: p is of type pointer-to-int and rx is of type int (the same type as x—the referenced object).

Here's another example. Something like

```
*rx = 10;
```

does not work. Neither x nor rx are pointers. x is an int and rx is a reference to (an alternate name for) x—an int. Consequently, the expression *rx is trying to dereference an int, as if you had said *x. The compiler gives you a hard error if you try it. Similarly, the following code does not work:

```
int x;
int &rx = &x;
```

rx is a reference to an int—an alternate name for an existing int. &x, however, is a pointer to an int, so there is a type mismatch. Moreover, the assignment-like part of the declaration is not an assignment—it tells the compiler what object the reference aliases. &x, however, is not a declared object, it's a temporary variable that holds the address of x. Consequently, you'll end up with an alternate name for a temporary variable that will probably cease to exist after the declaration is processed. Subsequent code that used rx would be modifying the memory location where the temporary variable used to be. Unpredictable things will happen if the same space has been recycled for something else in the meantime.

The declaration syntax for a reference follows the normal rules of C declarations. For some reason, C programmers forget everything they know about how declarations work and try to read reference declarations from left to right rather than inside out. The & used for reference is at the same precedence level as the * used for pointers, and it associates right to left. Consequently, a declaration like

reference to
pointers, pointers to
references

```
int *p;
int *&rp = p;
```

is parenthesized as

```
int *p;
int   *(&rp) = p;
```

and reading from the inside out, you get "rp is a reference to an int pointer." A declaration such as

```
int &*rp;
```

has no meaning. It defines a pointer to a reference, but references don't have addresses because they have no physical existence. You can't have pointers to them. (You can have a pointer to the thing that the reference references, but not to the reference itself.)

2.20.2 Reference Arguments

Although reference variables are not of much use, reference arguments to (and return values from) functions are common, particularly in operator overloads (discussed in a subsequent chapter), but sometimes in normal functions as well.

calls by reference

C++ allows a function to be passed an argument by reference as well as by value. C passes all arguments except arrays by value—a copy of a variable is passed to a function on the stack.[12] When you pass a variable by reference, it's as if the variable itself is passed rather than a copy. The called function can actually modify the variable's contents as if it had been declared local to itself. The basic syntax is like this:

```
set_to_ten( int &xr )
{
    xr = 10; // modify caller's variable, not the local copy
}
main()
{
    int x = 0;
    set_to_ten( x );
    printf("%d", x); // prints 10
}
```

The declaration syntax is similar to that of a reference variable, but the initialization happens at run time, as part of the call, rather than at compile time, as part of the declaration. That is, xr is initialized to reference x when the call is made at run time. Although it's true that the compiler will most likely use a pointer to implement a reference argument, don't think of it as a pointer or you'll fall into the extraneous-star-and-ampersand traps discussed in the previous section.

reference arguments in operator overloading

The main use of reference arguments is in operator overloading. "Operator overloading," you'll remember from the previous chapter, is the automatic translation by the compiler of an expression of the form a <op> b into a function call like operator_op(a, b). (This is not the actual C++ syntax, but you get the idea.)

---

[12] You could argue—correctly—that arrays are not really an exception because C passes the pointer to the first element by value, but that's not the way that most books present it.

Say you have a large user-defined arithmetic type, such as a `matrix`, and `*` is overloaded to do matrix multiplication. The compiler sees the code

```
matrix a, b;
// ...
a *= b; // Multiply the a by the b matrix,
        // with a modified to hold the result
```

and it maps the `a*=b` into a function call like `operator_star_equals(a,b)`. The two rather large structures used as operands are passed by value—the entire structures are copied onto the stack—by default. Moreover, you can't modify the contents of the original `a` to hold the product because `a` is passed by value—a copy of `a` is passed. Defining the operator-overload function to get its arguments by reference

```
operator_star_equals(matrix &a, const matrix &b)
```

solves both problems.

The foregoing is one of the few situations in which reference arguments are reasonable. I read a magazine article once in which the author, who was clearly a Pascal programmer, waxed poetic about calls by reference, touting them as the main reason why C++ was a "better" language than C. The author of the article missed a critical point, however. Calls by reference can make your code virtually unmaintainable.

avoid reference arguments if possible

When you pass an argument by value, you are guaranteed that the variable used for that argument will have the same value after the call that it had before the call. The only way for a C function to modify a local variable in the caller is for the caller to pass the variable's address to the function, in which case you'll see a `&` in the call to clue you in to the fact that the function might modify the variable.

Not so with calls by references. In the earlier example, `f()` might have been declared in a separate file and the prototype would probably be buried in a *.h* file as a consequence. This puts you in the position of looking at the call [`f(x)`] and having no idea whether `x` will have its original value after the function returns. You are forced to look up the function definition to see whether the argument is passed by reference or by value. The maintenance ramifications are enormous. If all calls were by reference, you'd have to save all of the variables passed to a function in other local variables, call the function, and then restore the original values to make sure that those values were intact.

This problem leads to a few rules of thumb that you should follow religiously. First, **a function that needs to modify an object in the calling function should be passed a pointer to that object, not a reference.** This way you get an ampersand in the call to tell a reader of the code that the object might be modified.

rules for using reference arguments

Next, **references should be used only for passing around large objects.** Never use a reference to pass an `int` to a subroutine, for example. The primary use of references is to pass larger data structures (`structs` or `classes`) in and out of subroutines. Passing a structure by value is possible in both C and C++, but it's inefficient—at the very least, stack space must be allocated for the object and the space needs to be initialized by copying the source object onto the stack. Returning a `struct` has the same problems. Although you can usually get around this problem by passing (and returning) pointers to structures, we'll see in a following section that this is not always possible in C++.

There's also an important conceptual reason to sometimes use references rather than pointers. C++ uses the class mechanism discussed in the next chapter to introduce new types to the language. Just as a C program wouldn't use a pointer to pass an `int` into a function, a C++ program wouldn't use a pointer to pass an object of a user-defined type. Say, for example, that you have introduced a new `string` type into the language. You would like to pass an object of type `string` to a function like this:

```
string s = "initial value" ;
do_something_with( s );
```

just like you'd say

```
int x = 10;
do_something_else_with( x );
```

A third rule of thumb is required to ensure that the foregoing works as expected: **Reference arguments should be declared const**. Just as a nonreference argument declaration like

```
bjarne( const char *str );
```

guarantees that `bjarne()` cannot modify the string addressed by `str`, a reference argument such as

```
void do_something_with( const string &s );
```

guarantees that the local version of `s` (in the caller) cannot be modified by `do_something_with()`. Again, if `do_something_with()` needs to modify `s`, pass it a pointer in the normal way. This way, you'll have all the usual indications that `x` might come back modified.

As usual, there are occasional legitimate reasons to violate some of the foregoing rules, and I'll discuss those reasons in future chapters. It's generally in your best interest to obey the rules, though.

2.20.3 Returning References

A function can also return a reference value. Here's a simple, though unrealistic, example that demonstrates what's happening:

```
int &peabody()
{
    static int x;
    return x;
}
sherman()
{
    peabody() = 10;
    printf("%d", peabody());
}
```

Since peabody() returns a reference to an **int**, then a call to peabody() is a name
alias for the **int**. In this case, peabody() returns a reference to a local **static**
variable (x), so a call to peabody() is effectively a name alias for that variable.
The peabody()=10 sets x to 10. The printf() statement prints the value of x. If
peabody() were declared **inline**, the call really would be just a name alias for x.
That is, the statements in the earlier main() subroutine would generate essentially
the same code that the following source would generate:

```
int x;   // (Originally local to peabody())
//...
x = 10;
printf("%d", x);
```

Note that there's no "reference to" operator. The function declaration is the only
thing that tells you that a reference is being returned; you can't tell what's happening by looking only at the **return** statement. The compiler uses the declaration to
determine that a reference must be returned, and then modifies the code generated
by the **return** statement accordingly.

Be very careful to ensure that the referenced object actually exists after the
function returns. You can—but must not—return a reference to a local variable,
for example. The following code is legal, but will give you unpredictable results:

**references to local
variables**

```
some_class &f( void )
{
    some_class local;
    ...
    return local;
}
```

because local won't exist after the function returns. The situation is analogous to
a function that returns a pointer to a local automatic variable. Declaring local as
static would fix the problem in both situations, but might introduce other problems. Several active references to the same **static** variable could be scattered all
over the code, for example.

You also must be very careful with references to memory allocated by **new**.
The following code works fine but is virtually unmaintainable (if you understand
the following, you *really* understand references—it will take a few moments to
figure it out):

**references to
dynamic (new)
memory**

```
#include <stdio.h>
int &f( void )
{
    int *ip = new int;
    return *ip; // return reference to int addressed by ip
}
```

```
void main( void )
{
    int *p;
    p = &f();      // Assign address of the int, a reference
                   // to which was returned by f(). &f() is the
                   // same as &(*ip), which is the same as ip
                   // (because the & and * cancel each other).
    delete p;      // Now delete the memory.
}
```

Since `f()` returns a reference to an `int`, a call to `f()` is a name alias for the `int` returned from **new**—not to the pointer, but to the `int` itself. Consequently, `&f()` gets the address of the `int`, which is the pointer that **new** returned.

In practice, returning a reference to something is useful primarily when you need to return a large object, a reference to which was passed into the function as an argument. For example:

```
some_class &f( some_class &ref_obj )
{
    // ...
    return ref_obj;
}
```

2.20.4 Problems with References

references to
temporary variables

references to
constants

Over and above maintenance, the problems with references all have the same underlying cause: it's possible for a reference to alias a temporary variable rather than a real variable. These problems all generate hard errors in version 2.1 of the language. Compilers for earlier versions of the language often let the error go without even a warning, however.

The first problem is initializing a reference with a constant. It's important that a C++ function call work like a C function call—there should be no surprises in your code. Since you can't tell that a function is passed a reference argument at the point of call, it's important that you be able to pass constants to the function in the normal way; otherwise, you'll get mysterious errors from the compiler for seemingly reasonable function calls like the following call to `wally()`:

```
wally( int &ri )
{
    ri = 0;
}
beaver()
{
    wally( 10 );
}
```

The difficulty is that a constant may not have any physical existence. To reference it, the compiler must create an anonymous temporary and initialize that temporary to the constant value, passing the function a reference to the temporary. It's as if the compiler does the following:

```
int t0 = 10;
wally( t0 );
```

In the current example, the `ri=0` in `wally()` modifies the temporary, thinking that it's modifying something real, and this modification is considered to be a hard error in version 2.1 compilers. The solution to the problem lies in following the earlier rule of thumb about **const** references. Redefining `wally()` as follows makes the call of `wally(10)` legal:

```
wally( const int &ri )
```

The **const** tells the compiler that the object referenced by `ri` will not be modified in the function itself. Of course, the `ri=0` inside `wally()` is now illegal, but that's probably all for the better.

The next problem is an extension of the earlier one. The compiler must also generate a temporary variable when it does a type conversion, which is really an implicit cast. The function call in this code

references and type conversion

```
ward( long &rl )
{
    ++rl;
}
june()
{
    int i;
    ward( i );
}
```

is treated by the compiler as follows:

```
int i;
long t0;          // generated by compiler
t0 = (long) i;    // Implicit type conversion
ward( t0 );
```

Consequently, `i` will not have been modified when `ward()` returns. This is a more serious problem than the earlier one because you wouldn't expect a constant to change its value, and you probably won't be thinking about type conversions when you write the code.

Again, you can fix the problem (in C++ version 2.1, you *must* fix the problem) with a **const**. Redefining `ward()` to `ward(const long &rl)` makes the call legal, but also makes the `++rl` illegal.

The next problem is more subtle than the previous ones. Most C programmers know that an array name is treated as a pointer to the first array element. Usually, though, you don't stop and think about how the compiler implements this feature. Conceptually, when you use an array name in your code, the compiler creates a temporary variable of type "pointer to array element." It then initializes that temporary with the address of the first element. Thereafter, the temporary is used for all computation. (Again, the optimizer might clean up an unnecessary temporary, but the compiler and optimizer are different things. Think "compiler," here.)

problems with references to arrays

The upshot of all this is that the following code will not work as expected:

```
george( char *&p ) { ++p; } // p references a char pointer
shep()
{
    char buf[128];
    george( buf );
}
```

When you pass buf to george(), you're really passing a reference to a temporary variable of type pointer to **char**. The ++p in george() modifies the temporary. Arrays in C++ are, in any event, passed by reference by default—just as in C. The easiest way to solve the temporary-variable problem is to remove the & from the declaration for p argument to george(). You can also redefine p as **const char** *&p, but that's a lot of work that yields little benefit.

The rule of thumb to use in all of the foregoing situations is: **A reference should be initialized with an lvalue.** (If you need to review lvalues, they are discussed at the beginning of Chapter Four.) Even this rule can't always help, though. The following is legal, but weird, and doesn't work as expected:[1]

```
int x, y;
int *p  = &x;
int &pr = *p;    // Reference the object addressed by p.

pr      = 0;     // Assigns 0 to x.
p       = &y;    // Modifies p, but not the reference.
pr      = 0;     // Assigns 0 to x again.
```

Once a reference is initialized to alias a specific object, it will continue to reference that object for its entire lifetime. pr is initialized to reference the thing that p points at when pr is initialized. Modifying p does not affect the reference—it continues to reference the original target (x). A reference is not a macro that hides a * from the programmer. A reference is an object in its own right, and once it's initialized, it stays initialized.

2.21 I/O Streams

Although it's not officially part of the language, all C++ implementations that I know support AT&T's stream I/O library. I've omitted an in-depth discussion of the library from this book for two reasons. I don't much like the library, so I don't use it very often, and the library is not standardized beyond the basic functions—different compilers implement it in different ways. I'll explain the basic system, including its deficiencies, here. You should refer to your compiler's documentation or to Chapter 10 of Ellis and Stroustrup (pp. 325–359) for further details of how the system works.

---

[1] This code will probably also give the optimizer fits as well.

One of the big problems with the stream functions is that they *overload* the shift operators to do their work. A simple output statement looks like this:

overload`<<` for output

```
#include <iostream.h>
extern ostream cout; // contained in <iostream.h>
  ...
int i = 10;
cout << i ; // prints "10"
```

The compiler translates the expression `cout << i` into a call to an output function that's passed `cout` and `i` as its arguments—the shift operator means "output" in this context. The compiler distinguishes between this use of the shift and a standard shift by looking at the operand types. The compiler translates the operation into a function call only if the left operand is of type `ostream`—a type that's defined in the *iostream.h* file that's included at the top of the example. It wouldn't do so if the left operand were an `int`, for example. The `cout` variable is a predefined object of class `ostream`. It's the equivalent of `stdout` in the C standard I/O system. (Be careful not to misspell `cout` as `count`—I do it all the time.) There's also a `cerr` for standard error.

You can chain output operations together. For example:

```
cout <<  "i has the value" <<  i  <<  "\n" ;
```

is the equivalent of

```
printf( "i has the value %d\n, i );
```

There's also an equivalent input system. For example

```
char ch;
cin >> ch;
```

works like `scanf("%c", &ch)`, and

```
int i;
char array[80];
cin >> i >> array;
```

works like

```
scanf("%d%s", &i, array);
```

Unfortunately, `cin` has all the usual maintenance problems of `scanf()` except one: you at least don't have to worry about forgetting an `&` in front of a nonarray argument to `scanf()`. You do have to worry about all the "white space is ignored" problems, however. The earlier `cin >> ch` doesn't work like `getchar()` because it skips white space.

can't translate - `iostream` to `FILE`

I'm putting off a full discussion of how operator overloading is implemented in C++ to a future chapter because you need to understand a lot of the language before you can make sense of the mechanics. Nonetheless, the basic process—if not the mechanics of implementing that process—should be clear to you. I frankly think that the current abuse of the shift operator is a classic example of how not to use operator overloading. Operator overloading is valuable when you are implementing a new arithmetic type, such as the `fixed` type in the previous chapter, and

`iostream` **problems, a bad use of operator overloading**

need to define arithmetic operations on the new type. In the current case, however, all operator overloading does is obscure what's going on. It's a basic tenet of structured programming that **a function name should describe what the function does.** Using a shift operator to mean "output" violates this rule. It's as if you called `printf()` `formatted_left_shift()`. I've heard the argument that an expression involving shift, but with no equal sign on the left, is not doing anything useful.[14] Consequently, using << for output is clarified by the context—an arithmetic use has been ruled out. I don't buy it.

The root cause of all these difficulties is that C++ does not allow you to add any operators to C. The language does let you overload existing operators, but you can't introduce new ones. Consequently, the real solution to the problem—add a low-precedence "output" operator to the language—is not available. An existing operator had to be pressed into service.

Unfortunately, not only can you not introduce new operators, you can't change the precedence or associativity of the existing ones, either. The following C expression prints `"NULL"` if a pointer is NULL; otherwise, it prints the string addressed by the pointer:

```
char *p;
...
printf("%s",  p ? p : "NULL" );
```

You might be tempted to do the same thing with

```
cout << p ? p : "NULL" ;
```

but shift is <u>higher</u> precedence than ?:. The expression binds like this:

```
(cout << p) ? p : "NULL" ;
```

So, you'll always try to print the string—garbage is printed if the pointer is NULL—and the rest of the expression is silently discarded. You need to parenthesize the expression as follows for it to work properly:

```
cout << (p ? p : "NULL" );
```

The precedence problems just discussed can be avoided by rewriting the I/O system to use a low-precedence assignment operator for output rather than shift. You can write a small I/O system, for example, that defines a `file` type and uses uses += to output to the file like this:

---

[14] Expressions such as
```
        a << b;
        a + b;
        x ? y : z ;
```
are all perfectly legal in both C and C++. None of them does anything useful because there's no assignment, but the compiler accepts them without errors. The first two are particular problems because you probably meant to say <<= and +=.

```
file  file1;         // create anonymous temporary file
file  file2="fred";  // open file "fred" in default "w+" mode
file1 += "string";   // output string to file1
int i  = a_file ;    // Get an int from the file2
```

The main difficulty with an assignment operator is that += associates right to left, so a statement like file += y += z adds z to y then outputs the result. The sources for a system like this one aren't discussed in the current book, but the implementation is a simple matter (and a good exercise) for you to pursue after you've learned C++.

The final big problem with the C++ I/O stream system is that explicitly formatted output is possible, but the necessary code isn't particularly readable. A C statement like

formatting iostream output

```
#include <stdio.h>
printf("0x%10x %d\n", i, j);
```

is done like this:

```
#include <iostream.h>
#include <iomanip.h>
cout << "0x" << setw(10) << hex << i << " "
                         << setw(1) << dec << j;
```

I leave it to you to decide which is more workable, but I find the printf()-family functions more to my taste. The iostream method is too hard to read—it's too difficult to see what you're actually printing.

Unfortunately, there is no way to translate an ostream into a printf()-style FILE—there isn't even an equivalent to fileno()—so you can't mix the C I/O system with the C++, even if you're sending output to standard output. The two systems might be buffering characters independently, so the output could get mixed up in surprising ways. An unsatisfactory situation all around.

cannot convert ostream to FILE

The only advantage to the C++ I/O stream system—and it is a real advantage—is that you can easily add a new type to the system. In C, for example, you'd have to modify printf() itself to get it to output a fixed-point number, perhaps introducing a %F for this purpose. It's really unacceptable to require the writer of a new arithmetic type to modify existing library code to support that type, however. On the other hand, it's easy to use the operator overloading mechanism described in Chapter Four to provide an alternate version of the function that handles the << operator. (The left operand to this new function is still an ostream, but the right operand is of your new type. The function prints its right operand.) You can do the same thing, however, by providing a print() method in your new class, and I think that this approach is usually better.

Simple Classes

Probably the most significant feature that C++ adds to C is direct support for data abstraction using a system of classes. We saw in Chapter One that classes can indeed be implemented in C, but there's a lot of overhead involved that is better done by the compiler. C++'s additions to C make that overhead a bit less tiresome and error-prone. This chapter introduces basic classes, both by describing the language semantics and by developing a small string class.

The approach I've taken looks at the string class in fragments, discussing them one part at a time. Unfortunately, a complete class definition looks pretty confusing until you understand what all the parts are doing, so it seemed reasonable to look at the parts first, deferring a look at a complete class definition until the end of the chapter.

3.1 Classes as Black Boxes

C++ adds support for classes by extending the definition of a struct. It introduces the class keyword into the language to provide some semantic differentiation between a normal struct and a structure that's used to implement a class, but with one exception discussed below, class and struct are synonyms. All the extensions to struct that are discussed apply to unions as well.

A C++ class is an internal template, rather like a structure tag. An object is an instance of a class, occupying memory.

a class definition introduces a new type

A class definition conceptually introduces a new type into the language. For example, you might use a class to represent a string, and although the actual data structure will be a class or struct with many fields in it, you'll think of a string object as a single entity, not as a collection of fields. The situation is analogous to a floating-point number in C, which has three internal components (a sign bit, a mantissa, and an exponent). You look at a floating-point number as a single entity, though. A new arithmetic type in C++ works the same way, but you use a struct or `class` to store the various parts.

One important ramification of this shift in thinking (from a collection of fields to an object, the inner structure of which is immaterial) is that you will treat class objects the same way as you treat objects of a basic type like `double`. For example, you typically don't pass the address of an object to a function any more than you pass the address of a `double` to a function. You pass the object itself in both cases—by value. This practice, of course, gives you a significant benefit: you don't have to worry about a function modifying an object's value when the object is passed by value because a copy is passed to the function. Just as you declare an `int` and pass it to a function like this

```
int x;
printf( "%d",  x );
```

you declare a `string` and pass it to a function like this:

```
string x;
print( x );
```

In both cases, the function uses the information in `x` to do something, but the mechanics of that "something" are unknown to you.

Although the syntax is usually nicer, passing objects by value can get pretty inefficient because of the overhead of allocating space and then copying the object onto the stack. Generally, it's better to pass a reference, as was discussed in Chapter Two. For example, you'd use

references used to pass large objects

```
print( const string &obj );
```

rather than

```
print( string obj );
```

to declare the print function. Changing the argument from a value to a reference doesn't change the calling syntax at all. Calls to both functions will look the same. Since the reference is also a `const`, you can guarantee that the call by reference won't have side effects. The reference is more efficient, though, and thus is preferable.

3.2 Member-Function (Method) Definitions

A C++ `class`, `struct`, and `union` differ from their C counterparts in one important respect: they can contain member functions as well as member data. The member function can be declared inside the class body, but it is usually declared in prototype form in the structure/class/union definition and is defined later on. For example, a first attempt to implement a `string` class is shown in Listing 3.1. (Just look at the definitions for now—don't worry about how the functions work yet.)

The `string::` in `string::makeupper()` and `string::concat()` on lines 13 and 21 of Listing 3.1 identifies these functions as members of the `string` class. The function's names are the entire strings `string::makeupper()` and `string::concat()`. You need the `string::` because member-function names follow the same rules as do member data, so several different structures can have

the :: (scope resolution) operator

Listing 3.1. *string1.cpp*— A First-Attempt `string` Class

```
1    struct string
2    {
3        char *buf;      // Buffer that holds string, NULL for null string.
4        int str_len;    // String length.
5
6        void print     (void)  { printf("%s", buf); }
7        int  len       (void)  { return str_len;    }
8        void makeupper(void);
9        void concat    (char*);
10       // ...
11   };
12
13   void string::makeupper( void )   // Map all characters in string
14   {                                // to upper case.
15       char *p = buf;
16       if( p )
17           for(; *p ; ++p )
18               *p = toupper( *p );
19   }
20
21   void string::concat( char *str )   // Concatenate "str" to string.
22   {
23       buf = realloc( buf, (str_len += strlen(str)) + 1 );
24       strcat( buf, str );
25   }
```

inline member
functions

fields or member functions with identical names. The `string::` tells the compiler to which structure the function is attached.

Other member functions are defined in the class definition itself, not by using a prototype in the **struct** declaration and then defining the actual function later on, as was the case with `string::makeupper()` and `string::concat()`. Examples are `string::print()` and `string::len()` on lines six and seven of Listing 3.1. Functions declared in this way—with the function body actually inside the **struct**, **class**, or **union** definition—are **inline** by default, so they should be kept short. My general rule of thumb is: **Inline member functions should never be more than two statements long. Ideally, they should fit onto a single line.** You can get the best of both worlds by declaring an **inline** prototype and using a later definition:

```
class fred
{
    inline int f(void);
};

inline int fred::f(void){ /* body of f() }
```

The first `inline` (the one in the `class` declaration) is optional, but makes for good documentation.

source-file
organization

More often than not, the class definition will be in a *.h* file and the member functions will be declared in *.cpp* (for C++) files that `#include` the *.h* file. The normal considerations of library-function modularity apply. A member function is not called into the final program unless it's actually used. Consequently, member functions are usually put into individual files—one function per file—in order not to inflate the final program with unused code.

An `inline` member function is the one exception to the foregoing. You can't link to an `inline` function because it's expanded in line—there's nothing to which to link. Consequently, an `inline` function definition (the complete body of the function, not just a prototype) must be visible to the compiler in every module that the function is used. If an `inline` function definition is not physically part of the `struct` or `class` definition (as was `fred::f()`, above), it must go into the *.h* file along with the `struct` or `class` definition.

3.3 Accessing Members: The `this` Pointer

The `.` and `->` operators access `struct` and `class` members in the usual way. For example:

```
string   str_obj;                   // An actual string object.
string   *str_ptr= &str_obj;        // A pointer to a string.
int      len    = str_obj.str_len;  // Get the string length.
int      len2   = str_ptr->str_len;
```

A member function is accessed the same way:

```
str_obj.print();             // Print the string.
str_ptr->concat( "tail" );   // Concatenate "tail" to string.
```

member functions
modify the internal
state of an object

The main difference between a member function and a normal function, is that the member function is intended to implement a method—a function that manipulates the inner state of an object of the `class` of which it's a member. In fact, all member functions should either modify or access some or all of the member data of a `class`, otherwise it has no business being a member.

Since the member function manipulates member data, it must be passed the address of the object being manipulated. In C, you have to do this by passing the function the address of an object. In C++, a member function is passed that address automatically. For example, the call

```
str_obj.print();
```

passes the address of `str_obj` to `print()` implicitly as part of the call. Similarly, the compiler passes the contents of `str_ptr` to `concat()` when it processes

```
str_ptr->concat( "tail" );
```

message selector

receiver

In OOPeese, the function name is acting as a *message selector*, and the object being manipulated (the subexpression to the left of the `.` or `->`) is the message's *receiver*. The data component of the message is the function arguments.

The receiver's address is available inside a member function through a predefined variable called **this**. (**this** is a keyword in the language.) The **this** pointer is defined anew in every member function as a pointer to an object of the current class—the class of which the function is a member.

It is convenient to look at **this** as an implicit first argument that is passed to all member functions by the compiler as part of processing the . or -> operator in the function call. A . causes the compiler to pass the address of the object whose name is to the left of the dot, a -> causes the compiler to pass the contents of the pointer to the left of the arrow. It's as if the compiler translates

```
str_obj.print();
str_ptr->concat( "tail" );
```

into the following C code:

```
string_print ( &str_obj        );
string_concat( str_ptr, "tail" );
```

calling the first argument **this**. The linked-list subroutines in Chapter One used an explicit argument named **this** in exactly this way. All of these subroutines could be moved from C to C++ simply by removing the definition of **this** from the argument list, letting the compiler's implicit definition take over.

Although looking at **this** as an implicit first argument is convenient, **this** must really be treated in C++ as a preexisting local variable—one that you don't have to declare explicitly, but can use anyway—not as an argument. It's illegal for you to declare an argument called **this**, for example. It's really immaterial how the value of **this** gets into the member function. It might not <u>really</u> be the first argument to the function. It can be passed on the stack, in a register, in a static variable, and so forth. There's no reliable way to call a C++ member function from another language, for example, because you can't know how the compiler actually passes the value of **this** to the function. The **extern** "C" mechanism probably won't work with member functions.

When inside the member function, **this**->field can be used to access a field of the class of which the function is a member. You can call another function with the expression **this**->function(). Putting the foregoing into context, a member function of the string class can use **this**->str_len to get the string length and can print the current object with **this**->print().

Note that the earlier description of how **this** is passed applies here, too. For example, the call **this**->print() causes the current value of **this** to be passed to print() as its own **this** pointer. In other words, all member functions have the same **this** pointer at run time, so one method can call another without having to pass the pointer explicitly.

Although an explicit **this**-> is occasionally handy, you'll notice that it is not used by any of the code in Listing 3.1. In order to clean up the code a bit, the C++ compiler automatically adds an implicit **this**-> to the left of every reference to the member data or member functions of the current class that's found in a member function of that class. You can say **this**->field or **this**->function() if you like, but the **this**-> is redundant and can be omitted to simplify the code.

Because all member functions must act on a specific object—there must be a valid value to pass to the function as `this`—all member-function calls must be attached to an object. To use the `string` functions for an example, you can't say

call member
functions via objects

```
f()     // Not a member of the string class
{
    print();
}
```

or

```
f()     // Not a member of the string class
{
    string::print();
}
```

any more than you can access the member data with

```
f()     // Not a member of the string class
{
    int y = str_length;
}
```

You must declare an object in both cases, and use the dot or arrow to access the object:

```
f()
{
    string s   = "some value";
    string *p  = &s;
    int    len = s.str_length;
    s.print();
    p->print();
}
```

A member-function call that's issued in another member function does not violate the foregoing rule because of the implicit `this->`:

```
class x
{
    int y;
    int g(){...}

    f(){  y = g();  } // Really is "this->y = this->g()"
}
```

I've heard people who don't understand the real object-oriented issues grumble about the restriction that all member functions must be accessed through an object and then try to get around the restriction with misguided code such as the following:

do not cast a
constant to an
object pointer

```
class fred
{
    int   field;
    void funct( void ){...}
};

((fred *)0 )-> funct();
```

Zero is cast into a `fred` pointer, which is then used to call one of `fred`'s member functions. This code is misguided, dangerous, and—unfortunately—legal C++. First of all, consider the results of the foregoing on a data field. Zero is used as the `this` pointer—the base address of the structure. A statement like

```
y = ((fred *)0 )-> field;
```

tells the compiler to fetch an `int` from some offset from base address zero. The odds of a legitimate `fred` structure being located at absolute-address zero are pretty small. The same applies to

```
((fred *)0 )-> funct( 10L );
```

The `this` pointer passed to `fred::funct()` has the value zero, so any member data that `fred::funct()` accesses will be garbage—it will be fetched relative to absolute-address zero.

Moreover, if `fred::funct()` is virtual—you'll remember from Chapter One that virtual functions are called indirectly through a pointer stored in the object— the compiler won't call it directly; rather, it will call it through a pointer that's effectively stored in the `fred` structure. Here, the compiler assumes that there's a `fred` object at absolute-address zero, it gets a pointer to the virtual function from that structure (the pointer will be garbage), and it then attempts to call the function through that pointer. You'll end up executing in outer space someplace. If you're lucky, you'll get a core dump or your machine will lock up. If you're not lucky, you'll damage your hard disk directory or something equally catastrophic.

The real issue is one of design. The whole point of a member function is to manipulate the member data. The foregoing cast of zero to a `fred` pointer is effectively passing a NULL pointer to the method. If the function can handle this situation (a NULL `this` pointer), then it's not manipulating member data, and has no business being a member function in the first place.

out-of-lining `inline` member functions.

There's one final caveat here. In theory, only one instance of a member function will exist in the program. That is, if you declare a normal, non-`inline` member function, only one version of that function will exist—the single function will be shared by all objects of the class. That's why you need a `this` pointer—so the function can tell which object it's supposed to manipulate. If the compiler decides to ignore the `inline` keyword of a member function—as it might do if the function is too complex or too long—then the foregoing won't apply. That is, if the compiler ignores the `inline` keyword when processing a class member function, it might generate a `static` version of that function in every module that uses that class, making the resulting executable image larger than necessary. Same goes if the compiler chooses not to treat a function as `inline` even though the function body is declared in the body of the class definiton, as it might do if the function is too complex. There won't be linker conflicts because these multiple versions are all `static`, but there might be problems if the function contains `static` local variables. Each instance of the function could have its own set of local `statics`. Avoid `static` local variables in `inline` functions.

3.4 Access Protection

In C, access to the contents of a structure that's used as an object (such as a `FILE`) is restricted only by your good sense. C++ gives you better control over access. The fields in a class can be given one of three *protection modes*:   protection modes

`public`   `public` data and functions can be accessed from anywhere in the program, just like a normal C `struct`.

`private`   `private` data can be accessed only by member functions. `private` member functions can be called only by other member functions.

`protected`   `protected` data and functions are `public` to derived-class objects and `private` to everyone else. The mechanics of derivation will be discussed in Chapter Five, but remember from Chapter One that derivation is the process of making a `struct` or `class` larger by adding fields (and member functions) to it. Protected data and functions provide an interface to a derived-class object that is not available to the rest of the program. I'll discuss this protection mode in greater depth in Chapter Five.

You specify the protection mode of the various fields like this:

```
class name
{
private:
        int private_data;
        int private_function();
        int more_private_data;
public:
        int public_data;
        int public_function();
protected:
        int protected_data;
        int protected_function();
};
```

The mode stays in effect until another mode-change directive is specified. The default protection mode of a `struct` is `public`. The default mode in a `class` is   **struct** versus **class** `private`. That's the only difference between them.

Although nothing in the language requires it, **all member data should be private in a class** definition. This is the only way to guarantee that the `class` is used in an object-oriented way—as a black box. The `public` and `protected` modes should be used only for member functions. As with most rules of thumb, there will always be exceptions to the foregoing. Nonetheless, you'll be able to maintain your programs much more easily if you follow this rule.

The order of declaration of fields is unimportant (except that you generally get optimal alignment if you declare data members in order of increasing size). Although a class can have any number of `public:`, `private:`, or `protected:`

specifiers, I usually prefer to limit them. I try to put all the data at the top of a class definition, `private` data, followed by `protected` data, followed by `public` data. I then list all the member functions, organized by protection mode in the same order as the data.

3.5 Constructors

constructor

There are several special member functions in a class, the first of which is the *constructor* function. The constructor initializes a newly created object. It is called implicitly by the compiler when an object is created, thereby making it difficult to forget to do the initialization. I say "difficult" rather than "impossible" because the compiler does not require a constructor to exist. For example, a normal `struct` that isn't used to implement a class will probably not have a constructor. Initialization, in this case, will be done just like a C structure initialization.

constructors have
the same name as
the class

Constructors are member functions that have the same name as the class. Member functions can be overloaded just like normal functions, so a class can have several constructors that are used in different circumstances provided that the constructors have different arguments. Listing 3.2 shows a few for our string class. (I'll explain them all in depth in a moment.)

Listing 3.2. *string2.cpp*— Constructors for the `string` Class

```
 1   #include <stdio.h> // for NULL definition
 2
 3   class string
 4   {
 5       char *buf;
 6       int  str_len;
 7   public:
 8       string( void           ){ buf=NULL;           str_len=0;           }
 9       string( const string &s ){ buf=strdup(s.buf); str_len=s.str_len;   }
10       string( const char *str ){ buf=strdup( str ); str_len=strlen(str); }
11       string( const char *s1, const char *s2 );
12       // ...
13   };
14
15   string::string( const char *s1, const char *s2 )
16   {
17       // Concatenation constructor, creates a string initialized
18       // to the concatenation of s1 and s2.
19
20       if( buf = malloc((str_len = strlen(s1) + strlen(s2)) +1) )
21           sprintf(buf, "%s%s", s1, s2 );
22   }
```

You'll note that all the constructors in Listing 3.2 are `public`. The problem is that a constructor call is implicit in a declaration. In other words, a declaration is treated as if you declared space for the object and then called the constructor to initialize that space. A `private` function can be accessed only by other member functions. If a class's constructor is `private`, then the only functions that can create instances of the class are member functions of the same class. `private` functions—including the constructor—can be called only by other member functions and the constructor call that's implicit in the declaration is still a call, so the normal rules apply. Consequently, a constructor is almost always `public` so that instances of the class can be created by nonmember functions. There are, believe it or not, occasional uses for `private` constructors that I'll discuss later, but for the most part, constructors must be `public`.

Also, a constructor must not specify return type (or use `return` with a value attached) because you can't call it in the normal way. The compiler calls it implicitly as part of the allocation process, but you can't call it explicitly. Consequently, the constructor doesn't return in the normal way, and a return value is meaningless.

only the compiler can call a constructor

3.5.1 The Default Constructor

The first constructor of interest in Listing 3.2 is the *default constructor*, defined as follows on line eight of Listing 3.2:

default constructor

```
string( void )
{
    buf     = NULL;
    str_len = 0;
}
```

A default constructor is one that either has no arguments or has arguments which all default to some value in the prototype. The default constructor is used in two situations. A declaration like

```
string s;
```

causes the default constructor to be called to initialize `s`. The default constructor is also used in both of the following:

```
string *p  = new string;
string *pa = new string[10];
```

That is, `new` implies a constructor call. In the second example, the constructor is called 10 times, once for each array element. This behavior explains why C++ needs the `new` and `delete` keywords. `new` not only allocates memory, as does `malloc()`; it initializes the memory by calling the constructor.

why C++ needs `new` and `delete`

The compiler will supply a default constructor if you don't, and this constructor follows the normal rules under C: Memory is initialized to zeros if it is global or a local `static`; otherwise, it is uninitialized.

The default constructor for the `string` class initializes the string as a null string (one with a `NULL` buffer pointer), as differentiated from an empty string, in which a non-`NULL` buffer pointer addresses a string containing a single `'\0'`.

3.5.2 The Copy Constructor

The second special constructor is the copy constructor, defined as follows for the `string` class (on line nine of Listing 3.2):

```
string( const string &s )
{
    buf     = strdup( s.buf );
    str_len = s.str_len;
}
```

copy constructor

The *copy constructor* is a constructor whose argument is a reference to the current class. (The & in the argument means "reference.") The copy constructor is used in two situations. The first is a declaration like this:

```
string s1;      // Use default constructor.
string s2 = s1; // Use copy constructor.
```

One `string` object is being initialized from another, already extant, `string` object. The constructor code on line nine of Listing 3.2 uses the incoming string to initialize the new one, copying the source string's buffer with `buf = strdup(s.buf)` and the length with `str_len = s.str_len`.

Note that a dot is used to reference a field, not an arrow. `s` is a reference to a `string`, not a pointer to it. This distinction is often hard for a C programmer who is learning C++ to understand. The problem is that you know too much about the implementation details. The compiler must, after all, use a pointer to implement the reference. This may well be the case, but a reference is not a pointer; don't confuse them.[1]

The copy constructor is a special case because, like the default constructor, it is called implicitly by the compiler in certain situations; the compiler uses the copy constructor to copy an object into <u>uninitialized</u> memory. The copy constructor is not used for assignment, which copies into previously initialized memory—we

---

[1] I'm skipping ahead a bit in this footnote, but there's nothing to stop you from using a pointer in a constructor by introducing a `string*`, type-conversion constructor like this:

```
class string
{
    // ...
    string( string *s )
    {
        buf=strdup( s->buf );
        str_len=s->str_len;
    }
}
```

You'd have to use it like this, though:

```
string s1;
string s2 = &s1;    // Note the &
```

Moreover, the `string*` constructor is not a "copy constructor" according to the official definition. Consequently, it will exhibit none of the characteristics of a copy constructor described in the paragraphs that follow.

looked at these two situations back in Chapter One. I'll describe how to get control of assignment in a future chapter.

The compiler uses implicit copy-constructor calls in two situations: when you pass an object to a function by value (when you pass an actual `struct` or `class` object rather than passing its address) and when you return an object (as compared to returning a pointer or reference to an object). Consider this code:

implicit
copy-constructor
calls when passing
or returning objects

```
string str_toupper( string str )
{
    str.makeupper();
    return str;
}

f()
{
    string s1 = "a string";
    string s2 = str_toupper( s1 );

    s2.print();                 // Print the string.
    str_toupper( s1 ).print();  // This also works because
                        //------// str_toupper() returns a
                        // string object. It's just as if a
                        // C function returns a structure
                        // and you use a dot to access a
                        // field in that structure.
}
```

The `str_toupper()` function returns an uppercase version of the string that's passed into it as an argument. (The `string` object returned by `str_toupper()`— as is the case with all temporary variables generated by the compiler as part of processing a `return` statement—is freed automatically by the compiler.) It does not modify the original string. `makeupper()`, which was defined on lines 13 to 19 of Listing 3.1 and is used by `str_toupper()` to do the mapping, indeed modifies the object to the left of the dot, mapping all characters in the string to uppercase. Since the string was passed by value, `str_toupper()` is passed a `string` object, however, not a pointer to a `string`. Consequently, the compiler must copy the argument to `str_toupper()` onto the stack, and it uses the copy constructor for this purpose. The `makeupper()` call in `str_toupper()` modifies the copy, not the original version in `f()`.

`str_toupper` also returns `str`—it returns a copy of the local automatic variable. It can't return a pointer or reference to `str` because `str` will not exist after the function returns and the stack frame is cleaned up, so it must return a copy. The compiler, again, uses the copy constructor to make this copy as it processes the `return` statement.

There's no difference from what goes on in ANSI C, which permits `struct` assignment, passing a `struct` by value, and returning a `struct` by value. C++, however, gives you control over how the object is passed. C just uses `memcpy()` to pass and return the `struct`—it does a shallow copy. C++ uses the copy constructor if there is one; otherwise, it uses `memcpy()`. Consequently, C++ allows for a deep copy if you need one, as is the case with a `string`. A shallow copy just copies the `buf` field of the `string` in `f()` (`s1`) into the `string` on the stack (the `str` argument to `str_toupper()`), giving you the situation in Figure 3.1 If a shallow copy were used to pass `str` to `str_toupper()`, the function would modify the buffer component of the local variable in the caller (`s1`)—an undesirable side effect. The current copy constructor gets around the problem with an `strdup()` call that copies the string itself, not just the pointer, giving you the situation in Figure 3.2.

Figure 3.1. A Shallow **string** Copy

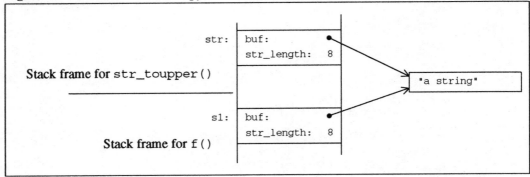

Figure 3.2. A Deep **string** Copy

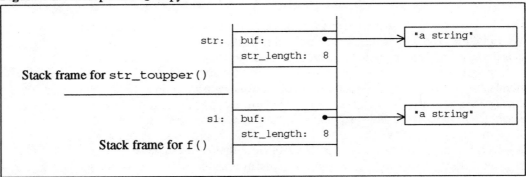

call by reference required in copy constructor

The copy constructor is one situation where a call by reference is required by the language. The problem is that the compiler always uses the copy constructor to pass objects by value, even to a constructor. The compiler doesn't need to copy anything to pass an argument by reference, though. A constructor definition like

```
string( string s );
```

can't work as a copy constructor because the copy constructor must call itself to pass an argument to itself—an Orobourus-like conundrum.

shallow copy used if argument matches elipsis

There's one final caveat about copy constructors. I mentioned earlier that the compiler uses the copy constructor to pass a function an object by value. There is one exception to this rule: the compiler uses C-like (shallow) structure copying to pass a function an argument of some class in a position that corresponds to an elipsis in a prototype. Given these declarations

```
class cls
{
    cls(){ /* constructor body */ };
};

foo( cls y, ... );
cls instance;
```

this is safe:

```
foo( instance, 10 );
```

but this is not:

```
foo( instance, instance );
```

The problem is that the compiler uses information in the prototype to determine
how to pass the object to the function. If the prototype tells the compiler that the
argument is of a class that has a copy constructor, then the copy constructor is used
to copy the object onto the stack. If the object is passed in place of the ellipsis,
though, the compiler has no information as to whether the object has a copy constructor. Rather than making this situation a hard error (which is, to my mind, the
sensible approach), the compiler happily processes the call, but it uses C-like
structure copying (shallow copying, that is) to pass the object. This can, of course,
cause serious problems if you don't want anything about the passed object to be
modified in the function. Hopefully, your compiler will print a warning if you try
the foregoing, but it might not.

3.5.3 Type-Conversion Constructors

The next constructor of interest is the type-conversion constructor on line ten of
Listing 3.2. This sort of constructor takes as its argument an object of a different
type than the one being constructed. Here, for example, I'm creating a string, but
the constructor takes a char* argument.

A type-conversion constructor is used by the compiler in several situations.
The first are declarations like the following (only the first one will look familiar):

```
string s1 = "initial string"; // best form here
string s2("initial string");   // not good in current context
```

The first and second forms are treated identically by the compiler, but they are
used in different situations. The first form is used when true initialization is indicated. Here, for example, the string has the initial value "initial string".
We're also converting a C-like string represented by a char pointer into an object
of the string class as part of the declaration, but that's really immaterial in the
current context.

The second form is useful when the passed information is used to create the
object, but not to initialize it. Consider an implementation of an array class that
uses a constructor to specify the array size.

```
class int_array
{
    int *buf;
    int size;
    int_array( int array_size )
    {
        size = 0;
        if( buf = new int[ array_size ] )
        {
            size = array_size;
            memset( buf, 0, array_size * sizeof(int) );
        }
    }
}
```

Create a 10-element `int_array` that is initialized to zeros like this:

```
int_array  fred(10);     /* 10-element array */
```

(A declaration like `int_array fred[10]` allocates a 10-element array of
`int_array`s, which isn't what we want.) The alternative syntax:

```
int_array fred = 10;
```

has the same effect, but doesn't make any sense visually. This syntax implies that
the array (or perhaps the first element of the array) is being initialized to 10, which
is not the case at all. The 10 is used to create the object, but not to initialize it.
    Be careful, by the way, of

```
string fred();
```

This statement declares a function that returns a `string`—it does not call the
default constructor. The foregoing declaration is semantically identical to

```
string fred(void);
```

type-conversion
constructors and
new

The next declaration of interest is one that uses **new**:

```
string *sp = new string( "initial string" );
```

Here, something that looks rather like a constructor call—an argument list
attached to the type name—selects the actual constructor to call. This is not a
direct call to the constructor, though; the compiler must first allocate space and
then pass the correct **this** pointer through to the constructor function. (There is no
object yet, so a . or -> that is required to call a normal member function isn't possible.) The parenthesized list following the type name is used only to decide
which constructor to call and what arguments to pass to the constructor.
    Note that creating a pointer does not involve construction of an object. This is
just like C—allocating a pointer just gets you the pointer; you have to allocate the
thing that it points at with a separate operation, usually a **new** invocation. Consequently, a cast to a pointer-to-object type is permitted, even when there's no
matching constructor:

```
void *vp, string *sp;

sp = new string("..."); // Construction happens here, in the new
vp = (void    *)sp;     // okay, no construction
sp = (string *)vp;      // okay, no construction
```

A little analysis of the foregoing yields an interesting observation—the `new` `string("...")` is effectively a cast operation. It is allocating memory to hold a `string` and then initializing that memory from an object of a different type. The only difference, in fact, between the `new` statement and a cast is that you must explicitly `delete` the memory that came from `new`, but the compiler will implicitly `delete` the temporary variable generated by the cast.

constructors define
type conversions

Since a cast is one of the more misunderstood operators in C a minor digression is in order at this juncture. Many C programmers assume, incorrectly, that the cast is a directive that tells the compiler to treat the cast's operand as if it had been declared in the target type. In fact, the cast is a run-time operator. A cast of the form `(type)x` tells the compiler to allocate a temporary variable of the indicated `type`, then copy the operand (x) into that temporary, doing any necessary type conversions. The optimizer may well clean up the process by eliminating all of the code involved. For example, a cast from `void*` to some other pointer probably doesn't need to go through the whole song and dance. But this is the optimizer at work, not the compiler.

casts generate
temporaries

It's the fact that the cast generates a temporary variable that makes an expression like `++(int)x` illegal, even if x starts out as an `int`. You are trying to apply the `++` to a temporary variable, not to x itself. A cast, then, is much like a normal variable allocation, except that the resulting temporary is anonymous—it has no name.

So, in C++ a type-conversion constructor indeed defines a conversion from the argument type to the class of which it is a constructor, and can be used as such. The syntax is just like the earlier `new` statement, but without the `new`:

```
string( "initial string" );
```

The lack of an explicit `new` tells the compiler that it must both allocate and destroy the memory. If the `new` is present, you must do the `delete` explicitly. C-style cast also works if the constructor has only one argument. (I'll look at multiple-argument constructors in a moment.)

```
void f( string s );    // Function takes a string argument.
char buf[128] = gets(); // get input using gets().

f( string (buf) ); // These calls are processed identically
f( (string) buf );
```

The last two statements both cast `buf` into a string in order to call the function. The compiler uses the `char*` constructor for this purpose. It then uses the copy constructor to pass the argument to f(), copying from the temporary generated by the cast into the uninitialized memory on the stack.

There's a big difference, by the way, between the declarations

```
string *sp = new string( "initial string" );
string  s1 (  "initial string"  );
string  s2 =  "initial string"   ;
```

and the declaration

```
string s3 = string( "initial string" );
```

The first three declarations just tell the compiler to call the **char*** constructor to initialize the object. The s3 declaration is also declaring a string object, but that object is initialized by evaluating an expression (the cast) and then using the result of that evaluation. The process might be made clearer if the declaration is restated in a more familiar, C-like notation:

```
string s = (string)"initial string";
```

The compiler starts by calling the **char*** constructor to process the cast, thereby generating a temporary variable. The compiler then calls the copy constructor to initialize s, copying the contents of the temporary into s. (The destructor, which is discussed below, must also be called to destroy the memory allocated by the cast.)

In addition to explicit casts, the compiler also uses the constructor-defined conversions to call functions whose prototypes don't match the call exactly. For example, this code works fine:

```
f( const string &s ){ ... }
   // ...
f( "a char pointer" );
```

because the compiler uses the string class's **char*** constructor to convert f()'s argument to a string. Hopefully, the compiler will generate a warning in this situation, but it might not. An explicit cast (which just replaces the implicit one supplied by the compiler) eliminates the warning in the usual way:

```
f( string("a char pointer") );
```

This implicit conversion goes to only one level, though. For example

```
class A
{   // ...
    public: A( int x ); // conversion from int to A
};

struct B
{   // ...
    public: B( A x );   // conversion from A to B
};

void bob( B x ){...}    // Bob requires an argument of type B

f()
{
    A a_obj;
    B b_obj;
```

```
    bob( b_obj );  // okay, exact match
    bob( a_obj );  // okay, conversion from A to B is defined,
                   // compiler uses B::B(A) to convert argument.
    bob( 1 );      // ERROR: There is a conversion from int
                   // to A and another from A to B, but the
                   // compiler can apply only one level of
}                  // user-supplied conversion.
```

There's one final caveat. I mentioned earlier that you cannot call a constructor directly—the compiler calls it indirectly to initialize an object that it creates. Nonetheless, the compiler happily accepts a statement like the following:

```
class goofy
{
public:
    goofy(){ ... }  // default constructor:

    pluto()
    {
        goofy();    // DOES NOT reconstruct current object
    }
}
```

The thing that looks like a constructor call in `pluto()` is not a call at all—it's a cast operation that invokes the default constructor. The programmer probably thought that the `goofy();` statement would reinitialize the current object to its default values. That's not what happens. The compiler processes the cast by allocating space for a new `goofy`, and then calls the default constructor to initialize that space. The temporary variable so created is destroyed when `pluto()` exits. Here's the way to do what's required:

```
class goofy
{
    init(){ /* initialize current object to some default state */ }
public:
    goofy(){ init(); }  // default constructor

    pluto()
    {
        init();
    }
}
```

3.5.4 Type-Conversion Default Constructors

A constructor, all of whose arguments default to some value, can also be used as the default constructor. I could have provided a default constructor for a `string` like this:

implicit default constructors

```
class string
{
public:
        string( const char *s = NULL )    // Assume NULL if
        {                                  // no argument.
            str_len = 0;
            if( !s )
                buf = NULL;
            else if( buf = strdup( s.buf ) )
                str_len = strlen(buf);
        }
        // ...
}
```

default arguments in
constructors

instead of the true default constructor—the one with no arguments. I didn't do the
foregoing for two reasons. First, the combined code is not as easy to understand as
the original version. Having two constructors makes it crystal clear what's going
on. Second, a class can have only one default constructor; otherwise, the compiler
won't know which one to call when it sees a declaration like string s;. If you
use default arguments, it's tempting to use them in more than one constructor, and
if all the arguments in two or more constructors default to some value, or if all the
arguments in one function default and you also have a true default constructor
(with no arguments), then you have more than one default constructor. The compiler then kicks out an error when it sees a declaration like string s because it
won't know which default constructor to use. (Note that the error is generated
when the definition for s is processed, not when class string declaration is processed.)

You can use a default argument effectively in some situations. For example, if
the concept of a null string (in which the buf pointer is NULL) as compared to an
empty string (in which the buf pointer addresses a zero-length string) was not
important, you can eliminate null-string support and use a constructor like this:

```
class string
{
        char *buf;
        int   str_len;
public:
        string( void )
        {
            if( buf = strdup( "" ) )
                str_len = strlen(buf);
            else
                str_len = 0;
        }
```

```
        string( const char *s );
        {
            if( buf = strdup( s ) )
                str_len = strlen(buf);
            else
                str_len = 0;
        }
        // ...
    }
```

A default argument can now be used to improve the code, by folding the two almost identical constructors into a single subroutine:

```
    class string
    {
            char *buf;
            int  str_len;
    public:
            string( const char *s = "" )
            {
                if( buf = strdup( s ) )
                    str_len = strlen(buf);
                else
                    str_len = 0;
            }
            // ...
    }
```

A default argument is appealing in the current context because you can't call a constructor. The following code does not work as you might expect:

you can't call a constructor

```
    class string
    {
            char *buf;
            int   str_len;
    public:
            string( void          ) { string(""); }
            string( const char *s )
            {
                str_len = (buf = strdup(s)) ? strlen(s) : 0 ;
            }
            // ...
    }
```

The `string("")` in the default constructor is not a call to the constructor with a `char*` argument; rather, it's a cast from `char*` to `string`. That is, it creates a temporary variable of class `string`, initializing that variable to `""`. This cast does not initialize the current string—the one addressed by `this`. It creates a second `string`—the temporary—and then initializes that temporary. Consequently, the default constructor in the foregoing code does nothing useful. The current object is still uninitialized after the default constructor is executed.

The solution to this problem is to make both constructors call a common subroutine to do the initialization. A solution such as the following one is perhaps better than the default-argument solution:

```
class string
{
        char  *buf;
        int    str_len;

        init_char_ptr( const char *s )
        {
            str_len = (buf = strdup(s)) ? strlen(s) : 0 ;
        }
public:
        string( void            ) { init_char_ptr( "" ); }
        string( const char *s ) { init_char_ptr( s  ); }
        // ...
}
```

Everything is `inline`, so there's no performance penalty.

3.5.5 Constructors with Multiple Arguments

Multiple-argument constructors are also possible—there's one declared on line 11 (and defined on lines 15 to 22) of Listing 3.2. A multiple-argument constructor is invoked like this:

```
string s( "prefix", "suffix" );
string *sp = new string( "prefix", "suffix" );

void f( string s );
f( string( "prefix", "suffix" ) );         // Cast to string
```

Note that the cast can't use the C-style syntax because of the multiple arguments. This doesn't work:

```
(string) "prefix", "suffix"  // ERROR
```

It casts `"prefix"` into a `string` and then tries to apply the comma operator with a `string` left operand and `char*` right operand. Since no such operation is defined, you'll get a hard error from the compiler.

I suppose it wouldn't hurt to use the newer style cast everywhere for consistency's sake. I tend to use C-style casts when basic C types like `int` or `char*` are involved and use the newer-style casts when classes are involved, although I have no rational reason for preferring one method over another.

3.5.6 Constructors and Control Flow

Because a class declaration implies a constructor call, it's risky to skip over a declaration. Here's the obvious case:

```
        goto label;
        some_class ret_value = 10;
        // ...
label:
        return ret_value;               // ret_value doesn't exist!
```

The declaration not only allocates space, but also initializes the object with a constructor call. When you jump over it, you at the very least will be dealing with an uninitialized object because the constructor call is certainly omitted. The space allocation may have been omitted as well.

The `goto` is not solely responsible for the current problem; the location of the declaration—in an inner block rather than at the top of the subroutine—is also responsible.

3.5.7 Constructors and `unions`

Constructors affect unions in two ways. First, you cannot have a `union` of `class` objects if the classes involved have constructors or destructors. The problem is that the compiler can't know which constructor to call when it creates an object. The same goes for a `union` of `structs` and a `union` of `unions`.

Constructors are useful in the `union` definition itself, though. The problem we're solving is that C++ (just like C) allows declaration-time initialization of only the first field in a `union`:

```
union fred
{
    long    shoreman;
    double teamster;
};
union fred baily = 0L;   // okay
union fred meany = 0.0; // ILLEGAL, can initialize first
                         // field only
```

You can solve this problem with a constructor:

```
union union_member
{
    long    shoreman;
    double teamster;

    union_member( const double init_teamster )
    {
        teamster = init_teamster;
    }
    union_member( const long init_shoreman )
    {
        shoreman = init_shoreman;
    }
};
```

Given these constructors, declarations like the following are now legal:

```
union_member fred     = 10L;    // initialize shoreman field
union_member frank    = 10.0;   // initialize teamster field

union_member chapter[]={20L, 20.0}; // Creates a two-element
                                    // array of union_members.
                                    ////// The first member uses
                                    //   the shoreman field and
                                    //   the second uses teamster.
```

3.6 Destructors

The next special-purpose member function is the destructor function. Destructors complement constructors—they are called automatically when an object goes out of scope or is deleted (by you or by the compiler). Just as `new` implies a constructor call, `delete` implies a destructor call if the object passed to `delete` has one. Destructors are not called when a reference or pointer goes out of scope, only when the real object does so. In other words, if you allocate memory using `new`, the memory will not be deallocated or destroyed unless there's a matching `delete`. The memory is orphaned if the pointer goes out of scope without an explicit `delete` call or equivalent.

delete calls destructor

A destructor, like the constructor, has the same name as the class, but the destructor's name is preceded by a tilde. A destructor for the `string` class looks like this (I've left one of the constructors in so you can see the relationship between it and the destructor, which is at the bottom):

```
class string
{
    // ...
    string( const char *str ){ buf     = strdup( str );
                               str_len = strlen( str );   }
    // ...
    ~string( void )    // Destructor
    {
      if( buf )        // If a non-NULL string
          free(buf);   // Free memory used for buffer.
    };
}
```

A class may have only one destructor, which takes no arguments and has no return value.

calling a destructor

Although you cannot call a constructor, you <u>can</u> call a destructor, but you must use a strange-looking, fully qualified syntax. Calls to the `string` class's destructor look like this:

```
string object, *p_object = &object;

   object. string::~string();
p_object->string::~string();
```

The call must have an explicit receiver (`object` and `p_object`, above) to supply a `this` pointer. The `string::` class identifier is really superfluous because the compiler ought to be able to figure out that it's dealing with an object of class `string` by looking at the receiver's type and the destructor name. The class identifier is required by many compilers, however, so it's a good idea to put it in for portability's sake.

Strictly speaking, the class identifier should not be required if the destructor is called from a member function:

```
class string
{
public:
    string::replace( char *s )
    {
        // String member function to replace string's
        //                               contents with s.
        this->~string(); // Clear all fields, this-> required
        buf = strdup( s );
        str_len = strlen(str);


    }
};
```

The `this->` in the destructor call is required, though. The rationale (which I do not agree with) is that a simple

```
~string();
```

looks to the compiler like either a call to the default constructor with a ˜ applied to the result or an expression that consists of a cast operation that uses the default constructor, again with a ˜ applied to the result. Neither operation is ever likely to come up in real code—calling a constructor just isn't possible and applying ˜ to a cast isn't useful—it's the equivalant to the following C expression:

```
~(int)x ;
```

Consequently, it's easy enough for the compiler to figure out what's going on—that you intend to call the destructor. The extraneous `this->` is, nonetheless, required.

In general, explicit destructor calls are confusing and should be avoided. The earlier example is improved by using a member function called by both the destructor and `replace()`:

```
class string
{
    // ...
    void clear_all_fields( void )
    {
        if( buf )        // If a non-NULL string
            free(buf);   // Free memory used for buffer.
        buf = NULL;
    };
public:
    ~string(){ clear_all_fields(); }  // destructor
    string::replace( char *s )                    // replace function
    {
        clear_all_fields();
        buf = strdup( s );
        str_len = strlen(str);
    }
    // ...
};
```

3.7 Arrays of Objects

An object that has **private** data must be initialized by a constructor. Similarly, objects that have constructors must be initialized by the constructor. The foregoing means that only a C-style **struct** declaration, with no **private** data or constructor, can be initialized with a brace-delimited list in the normal way. Other objects must be initialized by means of a constructor, using one of the syntaxes that I've been discussing.

The only complication to this process is arrays of objects. A simple array declaration like

```
string array[10];
```

causes the default constructor (either the one with no arguments or the one all of whose arguments default to some value) to be called for each array element. The destructor is called for each element when the array goes out of scope.

new class[] and
delete[]p

Allocation with **new** does essentially the same thing. The declaration

```
string *p = new string[10];
```

allocates space for 10 string objects and initializes each of them in turn with 10 calls to the string class's default constructor. The compiler won't let you allocate an array of objects unless the class has a default constructor, which leads to another rule of thumb: **All classes should have a default constructor.**

You delete an array of objects like this:

```
delete [10] p;
```

brackets in **delete**
tell compiler how
many times to call
destructor

The compiler calls the destructor for each array element. The brackets to the right of the **delete** statement tell the compiler how many times to call the destructor. (The size is optional in version 2.1 compilers—it's stored internally by **new**—but the brackets are mandatory. Some 2.1 compilers print a warning if the size is present.) A simple **delete** p—without brackets—frees the memory correctly, but incorrectly calls the destructor for only the first of the 10 elements.

Arrays allocated at compile time (created with declarations rather than **new** statements) may specify constructor arguments as part of the declaration. The syntax looks much like a standard array allocation. Here's a declaration for an array of string objects:

```
string array[4] = { "string 1", "string 2", "string 3" };
```

This is not an initialization in the normal sense, though. You're telling the compiler to call the **char*** constructor for the first three array elements, passing the **char*** constructor the strings "string 1", "string 2", and "string 3" in turn. The fourth array element is initialized by the default constructor since the initialization list is shorter than the array. If a class has no default constructor, then all array elements <u>must</u> be explicitly initialized.

Other constructors can be called as follows:

```
string s = "not an array";
string array[] =
{
    string(),              // Use default constructor
    "hello",               // Use char* constructor
    string("there"),       // Use char* constructor
    s,                     // Use copy (string&) constructor
    string(s),             // Use copy constructor
    string("two", "strings") // Use 2-argument concatenation constructor
};
```

The initialization-list element's type is just compared against the list of constructors, and the proper constructor is called when a match is found.

3.8 `static` Member Data and Functions

Members of C++ classes and structures are also permitted to have attributes not allowed by C. First, a **struct** or **class** can have **static** members—both data and functions. Static data members are shared among all instances of a class. That is, the **static** data member is physically a single global variable, but that global variable is treated as if it were physically inside the **struct** or **class** in all other respects. It's accessed with a . or ->, and so forth. If the **static** member is **private**, it's as if the member functions have access to a global variable (the **static** member) that no nonmember functions can access.

Static data has many uses, but one of the main ones is to keep an *instance count*—a running count of the number of objects that are in existence at any given moment. A constructor can use this information to do library-level initialization and cleanup operations. Listing 3.3 shows a skeleton for a window class that uses an instance count for this purpose.

instance count

A **static int** member called num_objects tracks the number of objects that exist. It's incremented in the constructor every time an instance of class window is created (on line ten of Listing 3.3). A matching decrement is in the destructor on line 16. start_up_video_system() is called once, when the first window is created. shut_down_video_system() is called when the last window is deleted. This way, the library-level initializations are done transparently; there's no explicit initialization function to forget to call.

The declaration on line 23 of Listing 3.3 should be required only if you want the static member to have an initial value other than zero. Some implementations require space for all **static** members to be explicitly allocated in this way, though, even if a zero initial value is acceptable. This declaration must be treated like a normal global-variable declaration in other ways—it has to be compiled exactly once. That's what the **#ifdef** above line 23 is doing. Exactly one module of the program will look like this:

```
#define _WINDOW_HPP_COMPILE 1
#include "window.hpp"
```

All other modules **#include** *window.hpp* without the preceding macro definition. You'll get an error from the linker if a real definition for the **static** member—one

Listing 3.3. *window.hpp*— Using an Instance Count

```
1    class window
2    {
3        void start_up_video_system (void);
4        void shut_down_video_system(void);
5    public:
6        static int num_objects;
7
8        window(void)
9        {
10           if( ++num_objects == 1 )
11               start_up_video_system();
12       }
13
14       ~window(void)
15       {
16           if( num_objects-- == 1 )
17               shut_down_video_system();
18       }
19       // ...
20   };
21
22   #ifdef _WINDOW_HPP_COMPILE
23   int window::num_objects = 0;
24   #endif _WINDOW_HPP_COMPILE
```

that allocates space—doesn't exist.

accessing static members

A **static** member can be accessed in the normal way—through an object or pointer:

```
window w, *wp = w;

... w.num_objects ...
... wp->num_objects ...
```

use :: to access static members

Unlike a normal member data, a nonmember function can access a public **static** class member even if no object exists. Use the :: operator for this purpose:

```
void main( void )
{
    //...
    if( window::num_objects != 0 )
    {
        cerr << "internal error: windows exist at exit");
        exit(1);
    }
    exit(0);
}
```

You have to specify a class name as well as a field name because several classes can all have **static** members with the same name. They are different variables, however, and the class name serves to differentiate them. Note that direct access to `window::num_objects` would not be permitted if it were declared **private** on line six of Listing 3.3.

A member function can also be declared **static**. For example, read-only access to `num_objects` can be implemented with a **static** member function like this:

```
class window
{
private:
    static int num_objects;
public:
    window()   { /*...*/ }
    ~window()  { /*...*/ }
    static int num_windows( void )
    {
        return num_objects;
    }
};
```

An application program can now call `num_windows()` to get an instance count, but it cannot modify the instance count except by creating or deleting windows in the normal way. (Remember, `num_objects` was initialized to zero in the declaration on line 23 of Listing 3.3 and is modified by the constructor and destructor functions, the bodies of which are shown in Listing 3.3.)

A **static** member function does not have to be **inline**, although that's convenient here. As was the case with **static** data, a **static** member function can be called without an explicit object by using the `::` operator:

```
main()
{
    //...
    if( window::num_windows() != 0 )
    {
        cerr << "internal error: windows exist at exit";
        exit(1);
    }
    exit(0);
}
```

This behavior leads to one serious restriction on **static** member functions—they do not have **this** pointers. Consequently, a **static** function may access only the **static** data fields of the class of which it is a member. Since the only real use of a **static** function is to access the **static** data, this restriction doesn't pose any problems in practice.

3.9 const Member Data and Member-Initialization Lists

It's also possible for a **struct** or **class** to have a **const** member. A **const** member works just like a normal data member, but it can't be modified. It's useful for holding information that is fixed at object-creation time, such as a window's color. You can add a `color` field to the `window` structure like this:

```
class fred
{
private:
    const int color;
    //...
public:
    void fred( int init_color );
}
```

The astute reader (that's you) will have noticed that there's one problem here. If a `const` member cannot be modified, how do you initialize it? You can't do the following in the constructor

```
fred::fred( int init_color )
{
    color = init_color; // ERROR
}
```

because `color` can't appear to the left of an equal sign.

C++ solves this problem by introducing an alternative mechanism that a constructor can use to initialize member data called the *member-initialization list*. The member-initialization list is attached to the constructor definition (where the function body is found), not to the prototype. It looks like this for the current `window` class:

```
fred::fred( int init_color ) : color( init_color ) {}
```

The list is introduced by a colon[2] and ends with the open curly brace that starts the function body. The syntax is as you see it: the field name comes first and is followed by a parenthesized expression that is evaluated at declaration time and then used for the initial value. Constructor arguments can be used in the initialization expression. In fact, the expression can be arbitrarily complex—it can even include function calls:

```
fred::fred( int init_color ): color(encode(init_color-1)){}
```

Note that the constructor body must be present in order to differentiate the declaration from a prototype. The body can be empty, though, as is the case here.

Member-initialization lists can specify more than one field. Just separate the initializers with commas:

---

[2] I assume that the colon is an anachronism from a time when K&R C-style declarations were permitted for function arguments. Since the full declaration must now be part of the argument list, there's no rational reason why the colon should still be needed, but it's required nonetheless.

```
class string
{
    char *buf;
    int  str_len;
public:
    string( void ) : buf(NULL), str_len(0) {}
}
```

A `static const` member is both legal and useful—it takes up no space in the object, has an unmodifiable value, but still can be initialized at program-load time. The following example uses a `static const` to specify a default array size for an array class, getting the default size from somewhere (perhaps the command line) by making a function call.

static const members

```
class int_array
{
    static const int default_array_size ;
    int actual_size;
    int *buf;
public:
    int_array( void ) : actual_size( default_array_size   ),
                        buf( new int[ default_array_size ] ) {}
};

const int_array::default_array_size =
                    get_default_size_from_somewhere();
```

If `int_array::default_array_size` were initialized to a constant, it's possible that the compiler won't have to allocate any space for it at all, just as if it were a global-level `const` of some sort. It's more probable that space will be allocated, though.

If the default array size is a true constant—one whose value is known at compile time—an enumerated type is a better choice than a `static const` because the enumerated type never requires the compiler to allocate any space. Here's the previous example, reworked to use an enumerated type:

Use enum for local constants in a class

```
class int_array
{
    enum { DEFAULT_SIZE = 128 };
    int actual_size;
    int *buf;
public:
    int_array( void ) : actual_size( DEFAULT_SIZE   ),
                        buf( new int[ DEFAULT_SIZE ] ) {}
};
```

Since the `enum` is both local and private to the class, access is restricted to members of the current class. This access restriction could not be achieved with a

```
#define DEFAULT_SIZE 128
```

which would potentially be available to the entire program.

3.10 Designating Member Functions for `const` Objects

The `const` keyword affects objects in yet another way. In C, the compiler knows that some operations are safe to perform on a `const` object and others are not. For example, it will happily let you add two `const ints` together because addition doesn't affect either operand's value. It will not let you apply `++` to a `const int`, though, because `++` will modify the value.

Member functions are really just an extension of the idea of an operator since member functions either access or modify member data. C++ provides a mechanism for telling the compiler that it's safe to call a member function when the object itself is declared `const`. That is, given a definition like

```
const string s = "a constant string";
```

the compiler must know that it's safe to call member functions that just examine the object, such as

```
s.len();
s.print();
```

but the compiler must also know that it is not safe to call functions that actually modify the internal state of the object, such as:

```
s.makeupper();
```

The default assumption is that it *is not* safe to call a member function of an object that is itself declared `const`. You must tell the compiler that the function call *is* safe by putting the `const` keyword between the argument list and the open curly brace of the member-function definition. The `string` class definition from Listing 3.1, modified to designate a few functions as safe for `const` objects, is presented in Listing 3.4.

`const` to right of arguments

`const` definitions like the ones on lines 15 and 23 of Listing 3.4 can be applied only to member functions. That is, you can look at the `const` to the right of the argument list as modifying the `this`-pointer declaration inside that function. A constant function of the form

```
some_class::f() const {...}
```

effectively (and implicitly) declares `this` as follows:

```
const some_class *this;
```

Most compilers specify that a function that is declared `const` in this way may call only those member functions that are also declared `const`; otherwise, you'd effectively be converting `this` from a pointer to a `const` object to a pointer to a variable simply by making a function call.

`const` part of a function's signature

The `const` attribute is part of the function's signature. It must be present in both the prototype and the definition, as is the case with `string::print()` on lines 15 and 23 of Listing 3.4. The inclusion of `const` in the signature means that you can have two overloads of a member function, one of which is used with `const` objects and the other of which is used with variables. I've done that with the `print` function. The version for variables is declared on line 16 and defined on line 28 of Listing 3.4. The `main()` on lines 33 to 43 prints

Listing 3.4. *string2.cpp*— **const** Member Functions

```
 1   #include <string.h>
 2   #include <stdio.h>
 3
 4   class string
 5   {
 6       char *buf;
 7       int str_len;
 8   public:
 9       string(char* s)
10       {
11           buf = strdup(s);
12           str_len = buf ? strlen(buf) : 0 ;
13       }
14
15       void print    (void)  const ;
16       void print    (void);
17       int  len      (void)  const { return str_len; }
18       void makeupper(void)  ;
19       void concat   (char*) ;
20       // ...
21   };
22
23   void string::print( void ) const
24   {
25       printf("%s (CONSTANT)\n", buf);
26   }
27
28   void string::print( void )
29   {
30       printf("%s (VARIABLE)\n", buf);
31   }
32
33   main()
34   {
35       const string s = "constant";
36       string       q = "variable";
37
38       s.print();
39       q.print();
40
41   //  s.makeupper()        // ILLEGAL, s is a const
42       q.makeupper()        // okay.
43   }
```

```
constant (CONSTANT)
variable (VARIABLE)
```

I feel compelled to inject yet another polemic here. The rationale for the weird positioning of the **const** keyword is that a **const** in the declarator means that the function returns a **const** object, not that the function is safe to call when a **const** object is being manipulated. This rationale doesn't hold much water, though.

First, the vast majority of member functions, at least in my own code, are safe to call on `const` objects. The default, then, is backward. It would have been better to introduce a `var` keyword into the language to indicate that a function can safely be called for a variable object. Since `var` would never refer to a function's return value, it could be moved to the specifier (to the far left of the definition) where it belongs. An alternative approach would allow an optional, explicit declaration of `this` as a local variable in a member function:

```
some_class::some_function()
{
    const some_class *this;   // Can't modify current object
}
```

The existing syntax does little but add to the confusion.

3.11 A Very Simple Example: The `tracer` Class

Although we still need a little more information before we can look at a realistic class definition, it is possible at this point to look at a few very simple classes.

library-level
initializations

The example a few pages back of using a `static` instance count is the most common way to do library-level initializations. What if you need to initialize a library that is not tightly coupled to a class, however? That is, there is no one object to which an instance count can be attached.

The usual way to solve this problem is to do the initialization with a function call in `main()`. It's easy to forget the function call, though. ANSI C provides an `atexit()` function that lets you specify a series of function calls to make when the program terminates. There's no `atentrance()`, though, and even if there were, there'd be no way to call it before `main()` was executed. In any event, `atexit()` [and our theoretical `atentrance()`] don't solve the more likely problem of simply forgetting to do the initialization or cleanup.

What's needed is a way to do the initializations automatically without going to the extremes of rewriting your startup module to initialize the library before calling `main()`. C++ gives you this ability in the guise of a constructor. You create an initialization class, only one global-level object of which will exist in the entire program. Since global objects must be initialized before `main()` is invoked (because `main()` might access them), the class's constructor is called automatically by the run-time system before invoking `main()`. Similarly, the destructor for this special class is called as the program terminates. A skeleton for an initialization class looks something like this:

```
class init
{
public:
    init() { /* do library-level initializations */ }
    ~init(){ /* do library-level cleanup          */ }
};
static init only_instance;
```

The global variable (only_instance) is declared only once, typically in the same module as the class definition. This way, both the class definition itself and the single object of that class will be inaccessible to the rest of the program. You don't have to do anything beyond declaring the global-level object. The compiler takes care of providing the constructor and destructor calls at the right time.

This principle of using a constructor and destructor to do useful external work can be applied at the local level, too. A good example is a tracer class like the one shown in Listing 3.5. (I got the idea of this class from Ellis and Stroustrup. I've elaborated on their idea a bit by adding the automatic indenting.)

tracers

A tracer is a mechanism for tracing subroutine execution. It is particularly useful in tracking recursive systems of subroutine calls. The one presented here prints the name of a subroutine on entrance, with the name indented by an amount proportional to the subroutine-calling depth. It prints a similar message, at the same indent level, when the subroutine exits.

Listing 3.5. *trace.hpp*— A Tracer Class

```
1    // Print a message showing when a subroutine is entered or exited (but
2    // only when DEBUG is defined) by putting the following at the top of
3    // the subroutine:
4    //                     trace("function name");
5    //
6    // (in with the variable declarations).
7    //
8
9    #ifndef __TRACE_HPP
10   #define __TRACE_HPP
11
12   #include <stdio.h>
13
14   #ifdef DEBUG
15   class tracer
16   {
17         char *name;
18         static int lev;
19     public:
20         tracer(char *s){printf("%*senter %s\n", lev++ * 4, "", name=s);}
21         ~tracer()      {printf("%*sleave %s\n", --lev * 4, "", name  );}
22   };
23   int tracer::lev;
24
25   #     define trace(s) tracer trace_trace_trace(s)
26
27   #else // DEBUG
28
29   #     define trace(s) // empty
30
31   #endif // DEBUG
32   #endif // __TRACE_HPP
33
```

➡

Listing 3.5. continued. . .

```
34   #ifdef TRACE_MAIN
35   void level2()
36   {
37       trace("level2");
38   }
39
40   void level1( int first_time )
41   {
42       trace("level1");
43       if( first_time )
44           level1( 0 );      // recursive call
45       level2();             // nonrecursive call
46   }
47
48   main()
49   {
50       trace("main");
51       level1( 1 );
52   }
53   #endif
```

The test subroutines on lines 35 to 52 of Listing 3.5 demonstrate the process. They print the following on the screen:

```
enter main
    enter level1
        enter level1
            enter level2
            leave level2
        leave level1
        enter level2
        leave level2
    leave level1
leave main
```

The nicest feature is that the "leave" message is printed automatically when the subroutine exits, no matter how many exit points there are.

The code works by using constructors, destructors, and **static** members. When DEBUG is defined, a tracer class (tracer) is defined on lines 15 to 23 of Listing 3.5. The **static** variable (lev) keeps track of the subroutine nesting level. Since it's **static**, it's shared by all instances of the class. Space is allocated for the variable on line 23.

The lone constructor[3] is passed a string, which must be specified when an object of class tracer is declared. The constructor prints this string at an indent

---

[3] High ho!, Silver.

level proportional to the current value of lev, at the same time incrementing lev. (The %*s gets the field from the argument list [lev++*4], and then prints an empty string [the " " argument to printf()] in a field that many characters wide.) At the same time, the constructor stores the string pointer in the local name field. Since name is not **static**, every active object will remember a unique name.

The destructor is invoked when the function exits and the tracer goes out of scope. It prints the "leave" message at the current indent level, decrementing the level at the same time.

The preprocessor controls tracer printing. A tracer is declared with trace("function_name"), which is a macro defined either on line 25 or 29 of Listing 3.5, depending on whether DEBUG is also defined. When not debugging, trace() expands to an empty string, so the entire macro invocation effectively disappears. When DEBUG is defined, the macro declares an object of class tracer with the name trace_trace_trace, a name not likely to be used by a local variable. It is the existence of this object that brings the tracer's constructors and destructors into play to do the work.

Note that since the scope of a compiler-generated temporary variable should be the enclosing scope of the statement in which the temporary is generated, it should be possible to redefine the macro on line 25 as follows:

```
#define trace tracer
```

The trace("string") statement would be mapped to tracer("string"), which would be treated as a cast operation, and a tracer object would be created. This object would then stay in existence until the current block—the function —exits. Some compilers, though, will optimize the foregoing and destroy the temporary before the function exits, so defining a named object is more reliable than using an anonymous, cast-generated temporary.

Operator Overloading

operator overloading

In order to aid in the creation of arithmetic types, C++ provides a mechanism, called *operator overloading*, that lets you get control of how operators are processed. You tell the compiler that, when it encounters an operator with specified operand types, it should call a subroutine of your devising to perform the operation. This mechanism can be used only to add user-defined operand types (i.e., the class that you've created) to existing operators—you can't add operators to the existing system and you can't redefine the way that basic C operations (like adding two ints) work. The first few sections of this chapter discuss the syntax of declaring an operator overload. The remainder of the chapter discusses how to implement and use the operator-overload functions.

Operator overloading is one of the most abused features of C++, but also one of the most useful when applied properly. Operator overloading can make code that manipulates objects of arithmetic classes that you create dramatically more readable. Moreover, almost every class implementation overloads the assignment (=), equality (==), and inequality (!=) operators; otherwise, you couldn't assign one object to another or compare two objects. Most other applications of operator overloading serve only to obfuscate the code, though, not improve it. Don't overload operators just because you can.

4.1 General Considerations in Operator Overloading

There are several general concerns about operator overloading.

one operand must be of a user-defined type

At least one operand of the overloaded operation must be of a user-defined type created by a previous class, struct, or union definition. A typedef, which is just a type alias, not a true type in its own right, is not sufficient. This rule prevents you from changing the way that + works on two ints, for example. You can be sure that if the foregoing *were* possible, some idiot would do it—thank heaven for small favors.

You can get control over all operators except ?:, ., ::, and .* (I'll discuss .* in a future chapter). Many compilers prohibit the overloading of `sizeof` as well.

can overload everything but ?:, ., ::, and .*

In order to minimize confusion, you cannot change the precedence level or associativity of an operator. You can't introduce new operators into the language, either. This feature would occasionally be handy, but there are a lot of problems. For example, you could introduce a FORTRAN-like ** operator to do exponentiation, but would `x**p` be x raised to the pth power or x times the contents of *p? Stroustrup and coworkers chose to avoid the issue entirely by making new operators illegal.

introducing new operators

You can always introduce new operators into the language using a preprocessor like awk if you like. For example, you can introduce the operator "(**)" to do exponentiation, using a preprocessor like **awk** to map "(**)" either to a standard operator or, even better, to a function call. Unfortunately, C++ provides no such built-in capability, even if there are no ambiguity problems between your new operator and existing C operators.

In general, operator overloading must be used with great care, or it will introduce more problems than it solves. In an extreme case, you can look at an expression like x=a+b and have absolutely no idea what the code is going to do. For example, if x, a, and b are objects of class database, x=a+b could merge the a and b databases together, putting the result in a database named x. Hundreds of subroutine calls could be used to do this operation.

operator overloading can obfuscate

There are several rules of thumb you can use to avoid these problems. First and foremost, **there should be no surprises.** Something that looks like a C expression should act like a C expression. This rule has a corollary: **Use operator overloads only to define arithmetic operations.** Do not use an operator overload in place of a subroutine call just because it's cute. A subroutine name has a very valuable use in a program. It tells the reader what the subroutine does, thereby providing self-documentation. An operator like + is not just an arbitrary symbol. It too has a specific meaning—"add" something to something else. Look at + as an abbreviation for "add," not as an arbitrary squiggle. Pressing + into some other service—to implement a subroutine that is not adding two operands—does nothing but make the program hard to read.

I discussed this problem in Chapter Two with respect to the stream I/O system that overloads >> and << as input and output operators. This practice is a mistake, and should be avoided in your own code at all costs. Stroustrup should have provided `read` and `print` member functions to do I/O. He should not have tried to make "left shift" mean print. Using << for output is like renaming `printf()` to `left_shift()`.

Moreover, once you start overloading operators to do random things, even more confusion can result. For some reason beginning C++ programmers love to overload + to concatenate two string operands. You could rationalize this particular overload as reasonable, but then what does - do? or *? + should do some sort of addition, not concatenation.

Since overloaded operators look like C operators, it's critical for maintenance purposes that **overloaded operators act as much like the equivalent C operators as possible.** Not only should they behave functionally, but they should be well behaved in terms of generated temporaries as well. If you overloaded [] in a two-dimensional-array class, for example, it must be possible to say a[y][z] to get a single array element. (I'll discuss how to do this in a moment.)

4.2 Operator-Overload Definitions

This section lays out the syntax of operator overloading. I'll show you how the functions work in a little while.

global-level
overloads

At the global level (outside of a **class** definition), an operator overload is created by creating a subroutine called **operator** *<op>*, where *<op>* is the operator that you want to overload. For example, use **operator+** as the name of the function that overloads the binary + operator; **operator**[] overloads the array-bracket operator, and so forth.

Operand types are specified using the function's arguments. Global-level unary (monadic) operator-overload functions take a single argument representing the operand. For example, this global-level function overloads unary minus:

```
some_class operator-(some_class x);
```

When the compiler sees code like this

```
some_class an_obj;
x = -an_obj
```

it calls **operator-**(some_class) to process the operator.

name mangling in
operator overloads

An operator overload is just a special case of a function overload. It has a funny name, but that's the only difference. You can have several overloads of the same operator, for example, as long as they have different argument types. This means that name mangling must go on in an operator overload; the compiler provides a valid name as well as an argument signature, though. For example:

```
some_type operator - ( some_type x )
```

is encoded to

```
__mi__F9some_type
```

in Ellis and Stroustrup's system. Decipher the name as follows:

__mi	represents **operator-**
__	introduces the signature
F	indicates a function
9	indicates a user-defined type with a nine-character name
some_type	the user-defined type name

I mention the mangling issues because some compilers and some linkers use the mangled name for error messages. When the linker tells you that it can't find __mi__F9some_type(), you have to know enough about the mangling algorithm used by your compiler to see that it's looking for **operator-**(some_type). Fortunately, most compilers' documentation describes how names are mangled by that compiler.

Binary operators are overloaded much like unary operators, but there are two operands—one for each argument. The left argument corresponds to the left operand; the right argument corresponds to the right operand. When you use a function name like `operator-` to specify both the unary and binary operators, the compiler tells which is which by counting the number of arguments in the definition. For example, when you add a global-level binary overload of the minus operator to the earlier unary overload with a function like

global
binary-operator
overloads

```
some_type operator-( some_type left, some_type right );
```

you then call the function like this:

```
some_type x, y;
... x - y;      // call operator-( some_type, some_type );
```

At least one operand of the function must be a user-defined type (a **class**, **struct**, or **union**), but one of the operands can be a basic type. For example, the function

```
some_type operator-( some_type left, int right );
```

overloads binary minus for a `some_type` left operand and an **int** right operand. This one goes in the other direction:

```
some_type operator-( int left, some_type right );
```

The compiler can now handle these situations:

```
some_type x;
int       i;
... x - i;      // call operator-( some_type, int      );
... i - x;      // call operator-( int,      some_type );
```

Operators can also be overloaded by class member functions. The only difference is that the left operand—the only operand in unary-operator overloads—is replaced by **this**, so is not listed in the operator-overload function's argument list. Binary-operator member-function overloads have one argument; unary-operator member-function overloads have no arguments. The previous overloads can be implemented as member functions as follows:

member-function
operator overloads

```
class some_class
{
public:
   some_class operator-( void );        // -some_class
   some_class operator-( some_class &r ); // some_class - some_class
   some_class operator-( int r );         // some_class - int
};
```

Since the left operand is always **this**, the global-level overload

```
some_type operator-( int left, some_type right );
```

cannot be implemented as a member function—it must be done at the global level.

4.3 Type Conversion and Operator Overloads

defining cast from
class to arbitrary
type; **operator** *type*

We've already seen one way to effectively overload a cast: a constructor defines a cast from the argument type to the class of which it is a constructor. You can also go in the other direction—cast from the current class to a specific type. You do this with an overload of **operator** *type* where *type* is the target type. For example, the code

```
class act
{
-public:
    operator int  (){ ... }      /* Convert act to int   */
    operator char*(){ ... }      /* Convert act to char* */
};
```

provides overloads of the cast operators (**int**) and (**char***) for operands of class act. Operator overloads of this sort cannot take arguments (because they're unary operators) or specify a return value (because the return value is implicit in what the operator does—you don't want a cast to **char*** to evaluate to an **int**, for example).

You must be careful of ambiguity when two or more classes are involved:

```
class rags;
class riches
{
public:
    riches( rags &x ){...}        // Convert from rags to riches
};

class rags
{
public:
    operator riches(){...}        // Convert from rags to riches
};

f()
{
    riches loaded;
    rags   horatio_alger;

    loaded = (riches) horatio_alger; // ERROR: Which conversion?
}
```

As was the case in the earlier discussion of type-conversion constructors, the compiler uses cast operators to convert objects of one type to another type in order to get a function call to match a function prototype. Given the earlier **class** act, which provided a conversion from act to **char*** using **operator char***(), you can print an object by saying

```
act one;
puts( one );
```

because puts() takes a **char*** argument and you've provided a conversion from act to **char***.

This implicit use of a type-conversion operator to call functions can cause problems when there are too many possibilities. For example, the stream I/O system supplies overloads of the left-shift operator for all the basic types, including `int` and `char*`. The relevant overloads look like

problems with too many conversions

```
ostream &ostream::operator << ( long  print_this );
ostream &ostream::operator << ( char* print_this );
```

and allow you do this:

```
cout << 10  ;
cout << "\n";
```

which is effectively the same as the following calls:[1]

```
operator<<( 10   );
operator<<( "\n" );
```

A problem arises when you try to output an `act` object using this system:

```
act one;
cout << one;    // ERROR, ambiguous conversion
```

The compiler doesn't know whether to convert `one` to `int` in order to call `operator<< (ostream, int)` or to convert `one` to `char*` to call `operator<< (ostream, char*)`. Fix the problem either by eliminating one of the conversions or by supplying an additional overload of left shift for the current type:[2]

```
ostream &operator << ( act &print_this );
```

The compiler also uses supplied conversions (both constructors and overloaded cast operators) to evaluate expressions within the framework of existing operator overloads. Unlike C, which converts the smaller operand to the larger, the C++ compiler usually[3] attempts to make the type of the right operand match that of the left when it's processing an overloaded operator. Think of this process in terms of the overload-function calls that actually underlie the expression processing—an expression like a+b is mapped to a.operator+(b). When the compiler processes a+b, it is not doing type conversion in the normal sense of an expression; rather, it

user-supplied conversion in expressions

---

[1] I'll discuss this in greater depth in a moment, but both functions return references to the output stream—they return references rather than `ostream` objects for efficiency's sake—so statements like this are possible:

```
cout << 10 << "\n" ;
```

This statement maps to function calls as follows:

```
operator<<(10).operator<<("\n");
```

The left call returns a reference to an `ostream`, a member function of which [`operator<<(char*)`] is called via the dot.

[2] Note that I'm using references—described in Chapter Two—to both pass an `act` object to the function and to return an `ostream` object from the function, thereby eliminating the overhead of passing an object by value (i.e. copying the entire thing onto the stack) and returning one by value (which involves a copy as well).

[3] But not always. I'll discuss a problem case when I discussed the `fixed` class, below.

is trying to get the arguments in a function call to match one of the prototypes for that function. Consequently, it cannot change the type of a in the earlier expression. It can convert b to a type that matches a prototype for an `operator+()` function, though.

This conversion is done silently, without an error message. Consider

```
class fixed      // A fixed-point number
{
public:
    operator int()  { ... }     // Convert fixed to int.
};

f()
{
    fixed f;
    int   i, j;

    i = f;       // Compiler uses fixed-to-int conversion to
                 // convert f to int.

    j = i + f;   // Compiler uses fixed-to-int conversion
                 // when processing + to convert f to int.
                 // Result is an int so no conversion is
                 // needed to do the assignment.

    j = f + i;   // ILLEGAL, compiler has no way to make the
                 // type of the right operand (i, an int)
                 // match that of the left (f, a fixed). You
                 // must supply an operator+(int x) function
                 // in the fixed class for this expression to
                 // work.

    j = (int)f + i; // An explicit cast solves the problem.
}
```

The `operator int()` function is also used in implicit tests against zero such as the following:

```
fixed x = 0; //...

if( x )   // Uses operator int() to convert x to an int
    //...
```

Most compilers will also use `operator int()` to process logical statements like

```
if( !x )  // Uses operator int() to convert x to an int
    //...
```

provided that there is no explicit overload of the ! operator [in which case `operator!()` is used].

Automatic type conversion is also used when conversions are done through a constructor rather than an overloaded `operator` *type*. Consider the following:

```
class A
{
public:
    int operator-( const A &right )  // Subtract two A's
};

class B
{
public:
    B( A aobj ){...}   // Constructor converts A to B
    int operator-( const B &right )  // Subtract two Bs
};

f()
{
    A aobj;
    B bobj;

    i = bobj - aobj;  // Okay. Compiler converts aobj to a B
                      // using supplied constructor (in B).
                      // Then uses B::operator-() to do the
                   // operation.
    i = aobj - bobj;  // ILLEGAL, Compiler attempts to
                      // convert to class of LEFT operand,
                      // but there's no conversion from a B
                   // to an A.

}
```

There's one final caveat. Only one level of user-supplied conversions work. The following code is illegal:

```
class A { ... };

class B
{
public: B( A aobj ); // convert A to B
};

class C
{
public: C( B aobj ); // convert B to C
};

g()
{
    B bobj;
    A aobj;
    void f( C cobj );  // Function requires C argument

    f( bobj );    // Okay, C constructor used to make B-to-C
               // conversion
    f( aobj );    // ILLEGAL, can only go one level. You
                  // can't convert A to B to C, only A to B
               // and B to C.
```

```
f( (B)aobj ); // Fixes the problem; cast converts aobj
             // to B, which can be converted to C by
             // the compiler. You can also define an A-
             // to-C conversion by adding a constructor
             // to C that takes an A argument.
}
```

4.4 The operator++() Function

The operator++() and operator--() functions also present a few problems. In
version 2.0 compilers, there's no way to differentiate between prefix and postfix
operations. The operator++() and operator--() define a prefix operation, but
these functions are called even if the triggering expression is postfix. That is, both
++x and x++ causes operator++() to be called as if ++x were always
processed—x++ and ++x are handled identically as prefix operators. This, of
course, causes real problems if you expect x++ to be a postfix operator. Consequently, I suggest that you do not overload ++ or -- if you have a version 2.0 compiler.

The problem has been fixed in version 2.1 of the language, but unfortunately
it's been fixed with a kludge. Rather than introduce a postfix or prefix keyword into the language,[4] Stroustrup and Co. opted to use the function arguments
to specify how the function is to be applied. At the global level, a prefix ++ is
specified like this

```
some_class operator++( some_class operand )
```

and a postfix operator is specified like this:

```
some_class operator++( some_class operand, int dummy );
```

The second, dummy argument tells the compiler to use the postfix form. Zero is
passed to the function in place of the dummy. The member-function implementation replaces the first argument by this in the usual way, so

```
class some_class
{
    some_class operator++( void );        // ++x
    some_class operator++( int dummy ); // x++
}
```

4.5 The operator()() and operator->() Functions

The operator()() and operator->() functions are also somewhat weird. They
are both described later on in the book in the context of real applications so you
can see how they're actually used. The rules for using them are straightforward,

---

[4] Or use syntax like **operator**++() for postfix and ++**operator**() for prefix.

although restrictive, and I've included them here for completeness' sake.

The `operator()()` function overloads the function-call operator. That is, C++ treats a function call like `f(x)` as a function-call operator `[(x)]` applied to a function pointer operand (`f`). C++ allows you to overload the operator, but it must be a member function, so the left operand—which is the function pointer in the normal call—must be a class object of some sort. The other operands to `operator()()` are the function arguments. Here's how you'd define one: *`operator()()`*

```
class perhaps_a_two_dimensional_array
{
    int x[10][10];
public:
    int &operator()( int row, int col ) // Function-call operator.
    {                                   // Call with: obj(r,c)
        //...
        return x[row][col];  // Returns a reference to desired cell.
    }
}
```

Called like this

```
perhaps_a_two_dimensional_array ar;
ar(i,j) = 0;
```

The statement `ar(i,j)` returns a reference to the indicated cell so that cell can be modified. *returning a reference*

The second weird function is `operator->()`. It's difficult to explain this one out of context, so I'll defer an in-depth discussion of what it's good for until I discuss iterators in Chapter Seven. The rules for using it are as follows: *`operator->()`*

- `operator->()` is treated as a unary operator, the operand of which is to the left of the `->`. It also must be a member function. These rules mean that the function can take no arguments and the operand is always `this`. *`operator->()`*
- `operator->()` must return a pointer to a `class`, `struct`, or `union`.
- The argument to the right of the `->` must be a field in the object that was returned from the function.

Again, these rules will make more sense when they're put into context in Chapter Seven.

4.6 Lvalues and Rvalues

Before talking about how to write the body of a function that implements an operator overload, it's important to start with a solid understanding of how the compiler itself handles expression processing. When you overload an operator, you are putting yourself in the place of the compiler writer—you are actually extending the capabilities of the compiler. In order for your code to be maintainable, you must make your operations behave as much as possible like the standard set of C operations. Consequently, you have to know how the compiler goes about its task.

A compiler translates an expression into assembly language in a two-step process. It starts with an analysis phase in which it organizes an expression into a special kind of tree, called a *syntax tree*, that represents the internal structure of the *syntax tree* expression. A syntax tree for the expression x= (a+b) *c is shown in Figure 4.1

Figure 4.1. A Syntax Tree for x= (a+b) *c

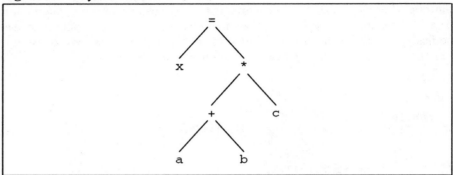

how a compiler
processes
expressions
The compiler then traverses the tree in post order. (It visits the left subtree recursively, then the right subtree recursively, then the root.) The subscripts in Figure 4.2 show the order in which it visits the nodes for the current tree.

Figure 4.2. An Annotated Syntax Tree for x= (a+b) *c

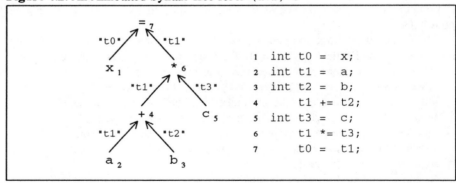

```
1   int t0 =   x;
2   int t1 =   a;
3   int t2 =   b;
4       t1 += t2;
5   int t3 =   c;
6       t1 *= t3;
7       t0 =   t1;
```

Look at the code generation as a series of subroutine calls. A subroutine is called as each node is visited, and the same subroutine is called for each type of node. A node that holds an identifier, for instance, is processed by calling subroutine identifier(), a node that contains a plus sign is processed by calling subroutine plus(), multiply() handles the star, and so forth. Each subroutine calls the subroutines beneath it in the tree, so plus() calls identifier() twice (once for a and once for b). Similarly, multiply() calls plus() and identifier(). All code-generation actions are done in the subroutines <u>after</u> all the subroutines beneath it in the tree are called and each of those lower-level calls returns something to the caller. This process is represented in Figure 4.2 by the upward-pointing arrows which are labeled by the return values—the names of the temporary variables that hold the result of the operation that was handled by the code generated in the current node. Each inner subroutine uses the information returned from the lower-level subroutines to do its work.

The generated code—I'm using pseudo C in place of assembly language—is on the right of Figure 4.2. The number preceding each line of code matches the subscript identifying the order in which the nodes are visited. To see how things work, the compiler starts out in subroutine `equal()`, which calls subroutine `identifier()`. `identifier()` generates code to move the identifier into a temporary variable: `t0=x`. `identifier()` then returns the temporary-variable name (`t0`) to the caller. `equal()` now calls `multiply()`, which calls `plus()`, which calls `identifier()` again. This time `identifier` generates `t1=a` and returns `t1` to the caller. `plus()` now calls `identifier()` yet again, and this time it generates `t2=b` and returns the `t2` to its caller. `plus()` is now done with the lower-level routines, so it can do its work, generating `t1+=t2`. It gets these names (`t1` and `t2`) from the previous `identifier()` calls. Finally, `plus()` returns the name of the temporary that holds the result of the addition (`t1`) up to its caller, `multiply()`. Processing continues in this manner until all the nodes are visited.

temporary-variable generation

The problem is the last of the generated instructions, which should put `t1` into `x`, but puts it into a temporary variable instead.

The problem here is that there are two kinds of temporary variables used for expression processing, and the current example uses the wrong kind. At the source-code level, an expression forms an lvalue if it can go to the left of an equals sign. (that's what the "l" stands for, "left"). An expression forms an rvalue if it can go to the right of an equals sign. The current example incorrectly uses rvalues in places where it should use lvalues.

two kinds of temporary variables

Looked at more formally, an *rvalue* is a temporary variable that holds the value of something. For example, `t1` holds the value of a initially. Later on, `t1` holds the actual value that results from performing the addition operation. The problem is that t0 holds the *contents* of `x`, and those contents are of little use when you need to modify `x`.

rvalue

Clearly, a compiler that can't do assignment properly won't be of much use, so a new strategy is in order. The assignment problem can be solved by generating the other kind of temporary, an lvalue. An *lvalue* is a temporary variable that references the place that has the value rather than actually containing the value. If you are using a C-like syntax, an rvalue is a temporary that holds the value; and an lvalue is a temporary that holds the address of the cell that holds the value. In a C++ framework, an rvalue is an object of some sort, and an lvalue is a reference to an object. Remember from Chapter Two that when you use a reference in an expression, you are actually using the referenced object, not the reference itself. The same applies here. When you use an lvalue in an expression, you actually use the thing that the lvalue references, not the lvalue itself.

lvalue

rvalues are objects; lvalues reference objects

Figure 4.3 shows how code is generated once lvalues are introduced into the picture. Rvalue temporaries are marked with an `r`, and lvalues with an `l` in the figure. Most of the generated temporaries form lvalues that reference identifiers, `t3` is an rvalue that holds the result of the addition and multiplication operations. The generated code (at the right) shows both C-style and C++-style ways to do the evaluation. Remember, the reference variables on the C++ sides are effectively name aliases. `t0` is an alternate name for `x`, and so forth. Step 4 (the addition) requires that an rvalue (`t4`) be generated since both of the incoming temporaries

160   Operator Overloading —Chapter 4

are lvalues. Addition generates an rvalue by definition, so it returns t3. The multiplication code doesn't need to create a second rvalue because it can recycle the incoming t4. Like addition, it generates an rvalue—it returns t4 to its caller.

Figure 4.3. Using Lvalues

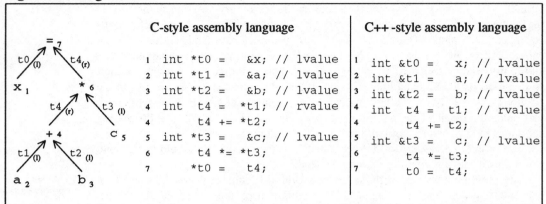

4   t4 += *t2;

| C-style assembly language | C++-style assembly language |

```
1   int *t0 =    &x;  // lvalue
2   int *t1 =    &a;  // lvalue
3   int *t2 =    &b;  // lvalue
4   int  t4 =   *t1;  // rvalue
4        t4 += *t2;
5   int *t3 =    &c;  // lvalue
6        t4 *= *t3;
7       *t0 =    t4;
```

```
1   int &t0 =     x;  // lvalue
2   int &t1 =     a;  // lvalue
3   int &t2 =     b;  // lvalue
4   int  t4 =    t1;  // rvalue
4        t4 += t2;
5   int &t3 =     c;  // lvalue
6        t4 *= t3;
7        t0 =    t4;
```

4.7 Generated Temporaries

In C, all variable references evaluate to lvalues that reference the variable.[5] Most operators in C generate rvalues; exceptions are *, ->, ., and [], which usually generate lvalues. (They won't if the referenced object is an array, but that's the only exception.) Similarly, all assignment operators (including ++ and --, which imply assignment) require lvalue operands. Other operators can take either lvalue or rvalue operands.

As we've seen, an operator is overloaded in C++ by providing a subroutine that the compiler calls to perform the operation. The operands are passed into the subroutine as arguments. Expression processing involves more than isolated subroutine calls, though. The subroutines must work together to evaluate a complete expression. Expressions are evaluated one operator at a time, with the precedence and associativity rules determining the order of evaluation to a large extent. The C++ compiler then maps each operator into an equivalent function call.

return objects for rvalues; references for lvalues

Similarly, each evaluated operator generates a temporary of some sort to hold the value of the subexpression, and that temporary is the value returned from the overload function. As we saw in the last section, the temporary can be either an rvalue or an lvalue. The function returns an actual object for an rvalue, a reference

---

[5] Array names evaluate to rvalues—temporary variables that hold the address of the first element of the array. An lvalue in this case would reference the entire array, but that's not what goes on. Structure references in ANSI C <u>do</u> generate lvalues. They did not in K&R C.

to an object for an lvalue. An overload of +, for example, should return an actual object that holds the result of the addition. Overloads of [] or * should return lvalues—references to the selected array elements.

To put all this into even more concrete terms: Assuming that the =, + and * operators are all overloaded for a fixed left operand, the C++ compiler translates an expression like the following

```
fixed x, a, b, c;
x = (a + b) * c
```

into this code:

```
x.operator=( (a.operator+(b)).operator*(c) );
```

Note that there are two sorts of things going on. At the inner level, the (a+b) generates an rvalue of type fixed. That is, the operator+() function returns a fixed object. It returns the actual structure. Consequently, the *c is processed with

```
(a.operator+(b)).operator*(c)
```

The rightmost dot is applied to the fixed structure returned from operator+(). On the other hand, the entire expression to the right of the equals sign evaluates to a single rvalue that is the right operand to =. Consequently, the return value from operator*() is just passed to operator=() as an argument—there are no dots.

The foregoing discussion of return values also applies to arguments. Subroutines that implement operators that require lvalue operands must take reference arguments; subroutines that implement operators that don't care whether the operand is an lvalue or rvalue can take either references or actual objects as arguments—references are usually more efficient, though.

4.8 Operators That Generate Lvalues

Moving from declarations to definitions, this section demonstrates how to code an operator-overload function that generates an lvalue using the small implementation of an array-of-int type in Listing 4.1. (I'll discuss this listing over the next few pages, so don't be shocked if lots of it looks unfamiliar.) I've overloaded the array-index operator so you can use brackets to access an array element. Unlike a normal array of int, however, the overloaded bracket function checks for an index-out-of-bounds error before it permits the access.

overloading[];
operator[]()

Starting at the beginning, the following declaration:

```
int_array x( 10 );          // A ten-element array.
```

invokes the int constructor, which uses new to allocate a size-element array of ints and initializes the internal buf pointer to address the array. The matching delete on line 23 is executed when x goes out of scope and the destructor is called.

An array element is accessed with an expression such as

Listing 4.1. *int_array.cpp*— An Array of **int** Type

```
 1    // A simple array-of-int implementation. I've left out allocation-error
 2    // checking to simplify things.
 3
 4    class int_array
 5    {
 6    private:
 7        int *buf;
 8        int size;
 9    public:
10        int_array( int size )
11        {
12            buf = new int[ this->size = size ];
13        }
14
15        int_array( const int_array &s )
16        {
17            buf = new int[s.size];
18            memcpy( buf, s.buf, s.size * sizeof(int) );
19        }
20
21        ~int_array()
22        {
23            delete buf;
24        }
25
26        int &operator[]( int index )
27        {
28            if( !(0 <= index && index < size) )       // index out of bounds
29                fatal_error("array out of bounds\n"); // error
30            else
31                return buf[index];                    // return reference to cell
32        }
33
34        const int_array &operator=( const int_array &s )
35        {
36            if( size != s.size )
37            {                                   // Replace current buffer with one
38                delete buf;                     // that's the same size as the source.
39                buf = new int[size = s.size];
40            }
41            memcpy( buf, s.buf, size * sizeof(int) ); // copy s to current
42            return *this;
43        }
44    };
```

```
int i;
x[i] = 0;
```

which is processed by the **operator**[]() function on line 26 of Listing 4.1. The
index **argument** to **operator**[] is the right operand (the i in [i]). Since **operator**[] is a member function, the left operand (the x) is **this**—this in

`operator[]()` holds the address of x in the current example. The function tests that the index is out of bounds on line 28. If the index is okay, a reference to the specified array element is returned on line 31. Note that you can't tell from the `return` statement whether the subroutine returns a value or a reference; you must look at the function definition on line 26.

So, `x[i]` is translated by the compiler into a call to `operator[]()`, which returns a reference to the *i*th array element. The `=0` now modifies the referenced element in the normal way. This assignment would be impossible if `operator[]()` returned the value of the `index`th element rather than a reference to it—it would be like saying `2=0` (if `2` were the previous contents of `x[i]`).

This example also demonstrates why references are so important in C++. You could do the foregoing with pointers by redefining `operator[]()` as follows:

```
class string{
    //...
    int *operator[]( int index )
    {
        //...
        return &buf[i];
    }
};
```

Now, however, the `x[i]` in

```
int_array x( 10 );        // A ten-element array.
*( x[i] ) = 0;
```

evaluates to a pointer to the *i*th element, not a reference to it. Consequently, an additional star is required to get the cell itself [thus the `*(x[i])`]. Just mentally substitute the `x[i]` for the real call to `x.operator[](i)` to see what's going on. That star is not only messy, it causes maintenance problems because nobody expects a star to be required when brackets are used.

4.9 Assignment Overloads

Another example of returning lvalues is an overload of the assignment operator. Almost every class gets control of the assignment process by providing an `operator=()` function. Remember, the copy constructor is used only when the compiler copies into uninitialized memory, as when an object is created, passed to a function by value, and returned from a function by value. The copy constructor on line 15 of Listing 4.1 allocates memory from **new** and then copies the source array's contents into the new memory.

overloading=;
operator{=()}

Assignment overloads are used for the other sort of copying—into previously initialized memory, as in

```
int_array x(10);
//...
int_array y(10) = x;      // call copy constructor
//...
x = y;                    // call x.operator=( y )
```

<parel>T

shallow copy

The compiler does a C-like shallow copy for classes that don't provide an `opera-tor=()` function. It just overwrites the target structure with the source structure's contents.

use **operator=**() for deep copy

The `operator=()` function for an `int_array`, on line 34 of Listing 4.1, does a deep copy—just like the copy constructor. `operator=()` differs from the copy constructor in that it must replace the memory used for the target array if the target array is the wrong size.

The source operand is defined on line 34 of Listing 4.1 as a reference to a `const int_array` object. It's passed as a reference for efficiency's sake—to avoid copying the entire source object onto the stack. It's declared `const` both to guarantee that the source operand cannot be modified by `operator=()`, even though it's passed by reference, but also to allow the following code:

```
const int_array x(10);
int_array y;
y = x;
```

You cannot pass a `const` object to a function by reference unless the matching argument in the function is declared `const`; otherwise, the function could modify the `const` object through the reference.

returning ***this**

The `return *this` on line 42 of Listing 4.1 also needs some comment. All operator overloads must return a value to be used as the generated temporary. Moreover, an expression like `x=y=z`, in which the return value from one operator-overload function is used as an argument to another operator-overload function, must be possible. That, is the expression `x=y=z` parenthesizes to `x=(y=z)`, the `y=z` is mapped to a call to `y.operator=(z)`, and the return value is used in evaluating the next subexpression. The entire expression is mapped to the following by the compiler:

```
x.operator=( y.operator=(z) );
```

The return value from the first `=` is passed to the second as its argument. Since the argument to `operator=()` is an `int_array` reference, `operator=()` must evaluate to an `int_array` reference to make the foregoing work.

The `operator=()` function *could* handle this situation as follows:

```
const int_array operator=( const int_array &s )
{
    int_array ret_val = *this;
    return ret_val;
}
```

but there's a lot of overhead. The compiler must create a new object of type `int_array` at the top of the function. It initializes the object by assigning `*this` to it. (`this` is a <u>pointer</u> to an `int_array` in the current context, so `*this` <u>is</u> an `int_array`.) The copy constructor is used to create the object. Finally, the function returns an actual `int_array` object—an rvalue. To do so, the compiler must create a second `int_array` object to hold the return value. (It can't use `ret_val` itself for this purpose because `ret_val` is an automatic variable—on the stack— and so is destroyed when the function returns.) The copy constructor must be called a second time to process the `return` statement. Finally, note that this version of the function can't return a reference to `ret_val` for the same reason that it had to make a copy earlier—`ret_val` doesn't exist after the function returns.

The situation is improved in the real `operator=()` function (on line 34 of Listing 4.1) by dispensing with the explicit temporary. Since the left operand (`*this`) already has the correct value in it, there's no reason to make a copy of it. The function can just return a reference to `*this` directly. Since a reference is returned, no copying needs to be done.

The only problem to this approach is that the expression `(x=y)=z` is now legal. This code expands to

```
(x.operator=(y)).operator=(z)
```

First, `y` is assigned to `x` in the normal way. The `x.operator=(y)` call evaluates to a reference to an `int_array`, which is treated just like an actual `int_array`. The second `operator=()` call uses the address of `x` (a reference to which was returned from `x.operator=(y)`) as its `this` pointer.

As a final note, there is no situation where modifying `this` makes sense. Modifying `*this` can occasionally be useful when you need to change all of the fields in the current object to have the same values as the fields in another object of the same type. That is, assigning to `*this` with an equal sign, as in `*this = an_obj` (where `an_obj` is the same type as `*this`) modifies the current structure, overwriting it with the contents of `an_obj`.

modifying `*this`

There's one caveat. An assignment to `*this` uses `operator=()` if a class has one; otherwise, C-style structure copying is used. The following `operator=()` implementation, which attempts to do a simple structure copy of `right` on top of the current object, is actually recursive and will crash the program:

```
some_class &some_class::operator=( some_class &right )
{
    return *this = right; // uses operator=() to do the copy.
}
```

4.10 Operators That Generate Rvalues

Unfortunately, most operators do not generate lvalues. The `fixed` class defined in Listing 4.2 demonstrates a generated rvalue. It implements a fixed-point numeric type—numbers have two decimal points of precision and are stored, scaled up by a factor of 100, in a `long`. The fixed-point number 1.23 is stored as 123 in the `num` field of a `fixed` object, for example. (Listing 4.2 is a simplified, and rather inefficient, version of an example we'll look at more closely in a moment.)

`fixed` **class**

```
class fixed
{
    long num;
public:
    fixed( double f ){ num = (long)(f * 100.0); }
                                        // fixed x = 100.0;
    fixed(          ){ num = 0L; }      // fixed x;
    ...
    fixed operator+(fixed &right);
};

inline fixed fixed::operator+(fixed &right)
{
    fixed temporary;
    temporary.num = num + right.num;
    return temporary;
}
```

fixed::**operator**+()
generates rvalue

The `operator+()` function returns a `fixed` *object*, not a reference. That is, an entire structure is returned. This is exactly what we were trying to avoid in the `operator=()` overload discussed in the previous section. Here, however, we've no choice. There is no convenient object that has the correct value (the sum of the two operands) already in it.

operator-overload
efficiency problems

The code just presented is easy to understand, but it has considerable efficiency problems. First, an expression like x+y can be mapped into a function call, with all the overhead implied by any function call. (It shouldn't be mapped to a function in the current implementation because it's declared `inline`. The compiler can choose to ignore the `inline` directive, though.)

The compiler incurs even more overhead as it executes `operator+()`. It starts by calling the default constructor to create `temporary` on the stack. It then must create an anonymous temporary to process the `return` statement, using the copy constructor for this purpose. Finally, it must call the destructor when `temporary` goes out of scope at the bottom of the subroutine. Moreover, memory for the anonymous temporary has to be created somehow; ideally, it will be on the stack, but there could be an implicit **new** statement, which implies a `malloc()` call. All of this flailing around takes time, of course.

implementing
operator overloads
as aliases for
private
constructors

Listing 4.2 shows how some of these problems can be solved. The main change is that I've made the `operator+()` function an **inline** alias for a cast operation, which is itself an **inline** alias for the code num=val. The processing happens much like several nested macro expansions:

```
x + y
```

expands to

```
x.operator+( y )
```

which expands to

```
fixed( x.num + y.num , XX );
```

which expands to

```
x.num = x.num + y.num;
```

Listing 4.2. *fixed0.cpp*— A Simplified Fixed-Point Arithmetic Class

```
 1    class fixed
 2    {
 3        long num;
 4        enum marker { XX };
 5        fixed( long val, marker ){ num = val; }
 6    public:
 7        fixed( double f ){ num = (long)(f * 100.0); } // fixed x = 100.0;
 8        fixed(            ){ num = 0L;                } // fixed x;
 9        ...
10        fixed operator+( const fixed &right )
11        {
12            return fixed( num + right.num, XX );
13        }
14    };
```

The main issue is that making `operator+()` an inline alias for a cast makes it more likely that the compiler will avoid creating an unnecessary temporary variable. Since the operand to the `return` statement in `operator+()` is itself a temporary, the compiler does not have to create a second temporary—which would, in any event, be an exact copy of the first one—to execute the `return`. It can just use the one returned from the cast operation. Consequently, the overhead is lower than in the earlier solution. The compiler needs to make only a single constructor call to an `inline` constructor. In general, it's best that an overload of an operator that generates an rvalue be an `inline` alias for a cast operation.

I must say at this juncture that just because a compiler <u>can</u> handle the foregoing efficiently, there's no guarantee that it will. In fact, at this writing, most compilers are pretty stupid about operator-overload code. Generating two temporaries to handle the code in Listing 4.2 (one for the cast and one for the `return` statement) is common. One of the biggest drawbacks to viable operator overloading in C++ is the inefficiency of the generated code. It's great that you can manipulate complex types with operators rather than explicit function calls, but many applications simply can't afford the overhead that you put up with to get readability. The moral is that no language exists in isolation from its compilers, although many proponents of C++ look at the language in just this way, talking about how an ideal compiler will behave without bothering about how real compilers actually do behave. If you intend to use C++ for arithmetic operations, it's important to evaluate several compilers carefully, looking at the generated code and deciding if the extra overhead is acceptable.

Returning to Listing 4.2, you'll note that the constructor that's used by `operator+()` is not a normal constructor. First of all, it's `private`, so nonmember

private
(special-purpose)
constructor

functions cannot call it to create an object. This is an important characteristic. The special-purpose constructor on line five of Listing 4.2 does not scale its operand as does the normal constructor on line seven. This way, it doesn't have to waste time multiplying and dividing. If an external subroutine could call the special-purpose constructor, it could create an object with an incorrect value—off by a factor of 100. Making the constructor `private` saves you from this potential bug by disallowing external (nonmember function) access.

The next issue is that the special-purpose constructor has an extra argument (of type `marker`, declared as an `enum` on line four). The argument isn't used, but it's required in the call. This extra argument is here for two reasons. First, a function's access privileges (`public`, `private`, `protected`) are not part of its signature. You can't have two versions of a function, one `private` and one `public`. Adding the dummy argument to the `private` function lets you introduce a normal type-conversion constructor, such as the following one, that has a single `long` argument:

```
fixed( long f ){ num = f * 100L; } // fixed x = 10L;
```

privacy does not give you invisibility

The second reason is more subtle, but equally important. If you tried the following with the existing constructors:

```
fixed x = 10L;
```

you'd get back an error message on the order of "you can't do this because there's no constructor." If the dummy argument were missing from the constructor definition, the error message would say, "there's a `long` constructor present, but you can't use it" (nyeah, nyeah, nyeah). Privacy does not make a function invisible; it just prevents external access (external to the class, that is). The first error message is clearly preferable from a debugging point of view—it is much less mysterious to someone who is debugging code that uses the class, but who doesn't have the class definition in front of him or her.

enum in class definition

Finally, note that the `enum` marker statement is internal to the class as well as being `private`. This makes it impossible for a nonmember function to use a value of type marker because the scope of the `enum` is the class. If a nonmember function tried to use XX in a constructor call, the compiler would kick out an "unknown identifier" error because it would assume that XX was a reference to an undeclared variable of some sort—the local `enum` declaration is not visible to non-member functions.

operator-overload strategies that don't work

Before leaving the subject of rvalues, I'd like to demonstrate that the two options just discussed (creating an internal named temporary and returning it, and making the operator overload an `inline` alias for a cast) are the only options available. I'll do this by showing you various ways that I've seen it done incorrectly and describing what's wrong.

don't use static temporaries

The first wrong solution is to use a `static` variable for the temporary. The main problem is that the solution does work—sometimes. You could incorrectly redefine `operator+()` as follows:

```
fixed &fixed::operator+( const fixed &right )
{
    static fixed tmp;            // Added "static"
    tmp.num = num + right.num;
    return tmp;
}
```

The expression

```
fixed x, y, z;
//...
x + y + z;
```

maps to these function calls:

```
x.operator+( y ).operator+( z )
```

The x+y is done first, it returns a reference to the local temporary (tmp), which holds x+y. operator+() is now applied again, this time with the temporary as the left operand (**this**) and z as the right operand. This also happens to work because the temporary has the correct sum in it.

The only reason why the foregoing seems to work is that we're going across the expression left to right, collecting the sum as we go. But what happens when you do the following:

```
fixed x = 1.0;
fixed y = 2.0;
fixed z = 3.0;
fixed i = (x + y) + (y + z);
```

i should end up with $(1+2)+(2+3) = (3+5) = 8$ in it. The answer that you actually get is 10, however. The

```
(x + y) + (y + z);
```

maps to these function calls:

```
( x.operator+(y) ).operator+( y.operator+(z) )
```

The compiler evaluates the left subexpression first, loading tmp [the local **static** in operator+()] with 3. The compiler next evaluates the right subexpression with a second call to operator+(), which overwrites the 3 in tmp with 5. The compiler now processes the middle addition with a third operator+() call. Since both operands are references that were returned from previous operator+() calls, both operands reference the same variable (tmp), so the both have the same value (5). Consequently, the compiler adds 5 to itself, yielding 10, not 8 as required.

The next "solution" that won't work is to use a pointer. (I've discussed this one before, but it's worth repeating.) Let's redefine operator+() like this:

don't use pointers
for temporaries

```
fixed *fixed::operator+( const fixed &right )
{
    fixed *p = new fixed( right );   // calls copy constructor
    p->num += num;
    return p;
}
```

The first problem is one of syntax. Since `operator+()` returns a pointer, you'll have to use a star in the normal way to access the returned object. The following code works correctly because a+b evaluates to a call to `operator+()`, which evaluates to a pointer to the object that holds the result.

```
fixed a = 1.0, b = 2.0, c = 3.0;
fixed *p;
// ...
p = a + b; // result is in *p
delete p;
```

You have to say *p to get the sum, though. Moreover, since the function used **new** to get the memory, you need to provide an explicit **delete** statement to get rid of it. You can do the foregoing here, but it's messy. But consider an expression like a+b+c, which you'd have to process with this monstrosity:

```
fixed *t1, *t2;

t2 = ( *(t1 = (a + b)) + c);
delete t1;
delete t2;
```

The internal subexpression (a+b) generates a pointer to a fixed object, which you have to remember in t1 so that you can free it later on. Next, you have to add c, but the left operand of `operator+()` is an <u>object</u> of type fixed, not a pointer to an object. Consequently, you need a star to convert the pointer into an actual object. Finally, the pointer returned from the second call to `operator+()` has to be remembered in t2 so the memory can be deleted.

You cannot fix this problem by returning a reference to the memory that came from **new**. The following code works fine:

```
#include <stdio.h>
int &f( void )
{
    int *p = new int;
    return *p;
}

void main( void )
{
    int *p = &f();
    delete p;
}
```

f() returns a reference to *p, to the actual object. Consequently, the &f() in main() yields the address of *p—the original pointer. You can't do this in an operator overload, however, because there's still no reasonable way to **delete** the memory that is returned from **new**. Consider this code:

```
fixed &fixed::operator+( const fixed &right )
{
    fixed *p = new fixed( right );   // uses copy constructor
    p->num += num;
    return *p;
}
```

You'd have to do a simple x=y+z like this:

```
void main( void )
{
    fixed x, y=2.0, z=3.0;

    x = *(p = &(y + z));
    delete p;
}
```

which is too ugly for words. Returning an actual object is the only real solution.

4.11 The Scope of a Temporary

When the compiler creates a temporary variable, the compiler also destroys it. A temporary variable of a user-defined type that's generated by a **return** statement stays in existence from the moment the **return** is processed (at run time) until the program exits the enclosing scope of the <u>call</u> (not of the subroutine in which the **return** is found). This rule applies to temporaries that are used for operator overloads as well as normal function calls. For example, in

temporary variable lifetime is the block of the call

```
f()
{
    fixed x, y, z;
    x = y + z;
    // ...
}
```

processing y+z generates a temporary because the expression is mapped to a call to fixed::operator+(), which returns a fixed object (not a pointer or reference). That temporary stays in existence until the program leaves the enclosing scope of the call—the block in which the y+z is found. In the current example, it persists until f() returns.

The one (reasonable) exception to the preceding behavior is that a loop body is considered to be an inner scope even if braces aren't present. For example, the following code is handled identically, regardless of whether the inner braces are present:

temporary variables in loops

```
main()
{
    fixed a=0.0, b=1.0, c=2.0;
    int i;
    for( i=3; --i >= 0 ;)
    {
      a = b + c;
    }
}
```

This means that the temporary variable that's created to hold the result of the b+c is destroyed and then recreated on each loop iteration. The alternative—to leave all the temporaries in existence until the loop terminates—is not really viable because you could have thousands of the things hanging around using up dynamic memory. Moreover, there'd be no speed advantage because you still have to create them one at a time in each loop iteration. Similarly, all the deletes could happen at once after the loop terminates, but you'd have the same number of deletes as before. The compiler can't recycle the same temporary without deleting because the temporary is not generated in the loop—it's generated in the function that's called by the b+c processing. This function could be in a different module than the one that holds the loop and compiled at a different time. Consequently, it's difficult to pass that function information about temporaries to be used for return values. The easiest solution—and the one used by C++—is to free the temporary in the calling routine and then reallocate the memory in the operator-overload function.

overlong lifetime of a temporary

More often than not, this overlong lifetime of temporaries causes problems rather than solving them. If the temporary objects are large, it's easy to run out of dynamic memory. You can deal with the problem with the following strange-looking code, which encloses each expression in its own scope so that temporaries are freed at the end of the expression:

```
bam_bam()
{
    // ...
    { x = a + b;  }
    { pebbles(x);  }
}
```

The problem that the overlong lifetime is attempting to solve shows up only if you violate all OOP precepts and provide public access to private data. Consider the following seemingly reasonable addition to the string class from Chapter Three.

```
class string
{
    char *buf;
public:
    string( const char *str ){ buf     = strdup( str );
                               str_len = strlen(str);
                             }
    ~string( void           ){ free( buf ); }
    // ...
    operator char* (){ return buf; }
};
```

I've added the `operator char*` function to provide a conversion from `string` to
`char*`. Now I can use standard C functions to manipulate a `string`:

```
string s = "some string";
printf("%s", (char*) s );
```

The problem is `operator char*()`, which gives public access to `buf`. Consider
this seemingly innocuous code:

don't give public access to private pointers

```
char *Glob_p;
abelard()
{
    string s = "doo wha";
    Glob_p = (char *) s;
}
heloise()
{
    abelard();
    //...
    printf("%s\n", Glob_p); // Prints garbage
}
```

`abelard()` creates a `string` object (`s`) and then effectively copies the `buf` pointer
from the `string` into `Glob_p` using a cast operation that invokes `operator`
`char*`. Then `s` goes out of scope as `abelard()` returns, and is destroyed at that
time, and a `delete` statement in the destructor frees the memory. From this point
on, `Glob_p` points at deleted memory—at garbage. The behavior of the `printf()`
statement in `heloise()` is unpredictable as a consequence. A more serious error
would be a statement like `*Glob_p='\0'` in `main()`, which would be modifying
memory that has been `deleted`, and then perhaps reallocated for some other purpose.

The point of this exercise is twofold. First, I really want to drive home the following rule: **Never provide public access to private data.** Second, given the
foregoing, it's never absolutely safe to destroy a temporary variable. Temporaries
would have to hang around for the life of the program to guarantee that the previous code would work. Since that's clearly not a viable solution, Stroustrup and
coworkers compromised with the decision to keep temporary variables around as
long as the current scope exists.

To my mind, the decision to leave a temporary in existence for such a long time
only serves to protect incompetent programmers from themselves. I don't think
much of this reasoning—it's not used anywhere else in the language, so isn't even

internally consistent. Efficiency should be the main consideration, so, to my mind, a temporary should stay in existence only until the end of the enclosing statement, not the enclosing scope. Some compilers indeed destroy temporaries sooner than the end of the enclosing block, but for your code to be portable, you have to obey the basic rule of porting code: you can't expect the nonstandard behavior unless you don't want it. We all have to live with the way the language actually works.

Unfortunately there's no really good solution to this problem in C++, although there are not-so-good solutions. One thing that won't work is redefining the cast so that it returns a duplicate of the string rather than the internal buf pointer:

```
char *string::operator char*(){ return strdup(p); }
```

It's just too easy to forget to free the returned memory when you use a cast operation to allocate the memory. It's natural to say this:

```
string str;
printf("%s", (char *)str );
```

Requiring the code to look like this:

```
string str;
char    *p;
printf("%s",  p = (char *)str );
free(p);
```

is just setting yourself up to lose the memory. Even worse, consider this code:

```
string str;
extern void hildegard( char *p );
// ...
hildegard( str );
```

The compiler uses **operator char*()** implicitly to convert the string to a char* in order to call the function. An explicit cast like

```
hildegard( p = (char*)str );
free(p);
```

doesn't help much—it at least makes the problem visible, but the code is still ugly.

One real solution is to get rid of the operator char* entirely, and replace it with a function that does the same thing in a more manageable way. For example:

use export function
to access indirect
data

```
char *string::export( char *dst )
{
    strcpy( dst, buf );
    return dst;
}
// ...
bernard()
{
    char buf[128];
    string str;
    // ...
    printf("%s",  str.export( buf )  );
}
```

`export()` is never called implicitly by the compiler, and since it's now your responsibility to allocate the memory used for the target, you're much less likely to forget to free the memory. In the current case, the memory in question is a local variable, so no special actions to free it are necessary.

4.13 Friends

We saw a few pages back that it's not always possible to implement an operator overload as a member function. Say, for example, that you wanted to overload + in this expression:

```
some_class obj;
int i, j;
j = i + obj;
```

The problem is that a member function requires the left operand to be of the same type as the current class, but here the left operand (i) is an `int`.

C++ provides a mechanism to deal with this problem, a `friend` function. A function that is a *friend* of a class can access the `private` parts of that class,[6] as if the friend were a member function. The `friend` is not a member, however. I'll demonstrate what `friends` are good for with an example.

friend

I discussed the `iostream` I/O system briefly at the end of Chapter Two. After a long litany of problems with it, I did mention one real advantage: you can extend the I/O system to include a newly created class without having to modify any of the existing I/O-system code. You do this by providing your own overload of the left- or right-shift operator to take care of I/O operations.

extending `iostream` classes with `friend` functions

To see the problem, a simple output statement looks like

```
#include <iostream.h>
some_class obj;
//...
cout << obj << "\n" ;
```

where `cout` is a predeclared member of the `ostream` class, defined in *<iostream.h>*. The << operator associates from left to right so it parenthesizes as

```
(cout << obj) << "\n" ;
```

Consequently, the function that processes the overloaded << must evaluate to `cout`—its left operand—for the expression to work correctly. Moreover, the function must take an `ostream` left operand and a right operand of whatever class `obj` is. Given the foregoing, you cannot overload << as a member function because the left operand of a member function is always `this`—a member of the current class, not of the `ostream` class.

---

[6] Let's hope it's a good friend—accessing one's private parts is no laughing matter.

You solve the problem with a `friend` function as follows:

```
class some_class
{
    friend ostream &operator<<( ostream &os, some_class &obj );
    int the_data;
    // ...
};

ostream &operator << ( ostream &os, some_class &obj )
{
    os << obj.the_data ;
    return stream;
}
```

The global-level `operator<<()` function is declared as a `friend` in the `some_class` definition. The function itself follows. It is called every time the left operand of `<<` is an `ostream` and the right operand is of type `some_class`. It's not a member function, so there's no `some_class::` in the function name. It is a friend, though, so it can access the normally private parts of `some_class` as if it were a member.

The function uses this ability to print `the_data`, which is an `int`, using the predefined `<<` operator (with an `int` right operand). Since it's not a member function, there's no implicit `this` pointer in `operator<<()`—the left operand is supplied explicitly as the left argument. The function returns a reference to its left argument, so can be used in a string of `<<` operators, as was discussed earlier.

overloads of =, [], (), and -> must be member functions

The only restrictions to overloading operators as friends rather than member functions is that overloads of `=`, `[]`, `()`, and `->` must be member functions— `operator=()` is illegal at the global level, for example (but `operator+=`, `operator-=`, and so forth, can be friends—this is an inconsistency that I don't much like).

member functions of one class as friends of another

In theory, a member function of one class can be a friend of another. The following code should work:

```
class tweedledee;
class tweedledum;
class tweedledee { int data;
                        friend  void tweedledum::f(tweedledee e);
                 };
class tweedledum { public: void f( tweedledee e )
                          {
                                e.data = 0;
                          }
                 };
```

This way `tweedledum::f()` can access all private data in both `tweedledum` and `tweedledee`. The declaration in `tweedledee` is saying "`tweedledum::f()` is my friend, so he can access my data." Unfortunately, some compilers reject the foregoing because of forward-reference problems. You can fix the problem by moving things around as follows:

```
class tweedledee;
class tweedledum { public: void f( tweedledee e ); };
class tweedledee { int data;
                   friend  void tweedledum::f( tweedledee e );
                 };
```

```
tweedledum::f( tweedledee e ){ e.data = 0; };
```

I've moved the definition (as compared to the prototype) for f() beneath the declaration for tweedledee so that the compiler can see that tweedledee indeed has a data field. This move has the obvious maintenance problem of placing a member-function definition a long distance from the point of declaration. There's no technical reason why the compiler can't assume that a data field exists—as it is already assuming that tweedledee will be defined—and then print an error message at the end of the file if it hasn't seen a data field inside a tweedledee definition, but this degree of sophistocation would be exceptional and is not required by the language.

ordering friend member functions to avoid order-of-declaration problems

There is an alternate syntax that allows *all* members of one class to access the private data of another. You do it like this:

```
class tweedledum;
class tweedledee {  int data;
                    friend  class tweedledum;
                 };
class tweedledum {  public: void f( tweedledee e )
                           {
                               e.data = 0;
                           }
                 };
```

A linked-list class serves as a practical example of what a **friend** class is good for. A C++ linked-list manager can mirror the structure of the C linked-list manager in Chapter One. That is, a linked-list class is really two classes that work in tandem, one that controls the list as a whole (it holds the head-of-list pointer, for example), and another class that controls a single linked-list element (which holds pointers to the previous and next elements of the list). The situation is really one in which two physical data structures (a list and a list_ele) are required to manage a single conceptual object (a linked list). You want to add a member to a list like this

```
list the_list;
list_ele *p = new list_ele;
// ...
the_list.add( p );
```

using a member function of the list class to add new elements to a list. This function has to access pointers in the list_ele to do its work, though. The easy way out is to make one class a **friend** of the other:

```
class list;
class list_ele
{
    friend class list; // All members of class list can
                        // access next and prev, even though
                        // they're private.
    list_ele *next;     // Next list element, NULL if none.
    list_ele *prev;     // Previous element, NULL if none.
}

class list
{
    list_ele *head;
public:
    add( list_ele *p )  // Add to head of list
    {
        p->prev = NULL;
        p->next = head;
        head    = p;
    }
}
```

avoid friends if
possible to
guarantee privacy

Although friends have their uses, there are problems as well. One school of thought holds that you shouldn't use them at all. The main difficulty is illustrated by the previous linked-list example. A `friend` designation, in granting private access, is violating the black-box rule, that you should never give public access to private data. The violation is selective, but it's a violation nonetheless. If, for example, you change the way that a list-element is represented, you must modify two sets of classes to reflect the change. Ideally, you would like to be able to freely modify the `list_ele` representation without affecting any of the functions in the `list` class. This is, if not easy to do, at least possible. Listing 4.3 shows one method. The main idea is that the `list_ele` class has an "insert yourself into the list" function, which is called from a `list`-class function when it needs to insert an element. You also need a "delete yourself from list" function, and so forth. None of the functions in the `list` class have any direct knowledge of the inner structure of a `list_ele`. Everything is—properly—done through function calls, and the maintenance of a `list_ele` is restricted to a `list_ele's` member functions.

Note that the `list` constructor can call `list_ele::init()` directly on line 28 of Listing 4.3 because `list_ele::init()` is declared `static` on line six. Were this not the case, a `list_ele` object would have to exist so that `init()` could be called through the object in a manner similar to `insert()` on line 29.

A similar solution can be applied to the printing problem. A class can have a `public` member function called `print()` that is called from a global-level overload of the `<<` operator:

Listing 4.3. *list_ele.cpp*— A `friendless` Linked-List Implementation

```
1    class list_ele
2    {
3        list_ele *next;      // next list element
4        list_ele *prev;      // address of "next" pointer in previous element
5    public:
6        static init( list_ele **headp )       // initialize list pointer.
7        {
8            *headp = NULL;
9        }
10       void insert( list_ele **headp );      // Insert current node into list.
11   }
12
13   void list_ele::insert( list_ele **headp )
14   {
15       insert( list_ele **headp )  // Insert current node into list at head.
16       {
17           prev = NULL;
18           if( next = *headp )
19               (*headp)->prev = this;
20           *headp = this;
21       }
22   }
23
24   class list
25   {
26       list_ele *head;
27   public:
28       list( void        ){ list_ele::init( &head ); } // constructor
29       add ( list_ele *p ){ p->insert       ( &head ); } // add p to list
30   }
```

```
class some_class
{
  int the_data;
  // ...
public:
  print( ostream stream ){ stream << the_data;  }
};

ostream &operator << ( ostream stream, some_class obj )
{
    obj.print( stream );
    return stream;
}
```

Since no internal data is used by `operator<<()`, it doesn't need to be a `friend` of
class `some_class`.

4.13 A Fixed-Point Arithmetic Package

The remainder of this chapter demonstrates operator overloading by presenting several small, but realistic, class implementations. The first of these is a pretty characteristic arithmetic class—the fixed-point arithmetic class that I used as an example earlier in the chapter.

fixed-point numbers   Fixed-point numbers, as implemented here, have a limited amount of precision—there are always a fixed number of places to the right of the decimal point. The main advantage of a fixed-point number is that many of the round-off errors that occur regularly in floating-point arithmetic do not occur. In financial calculations, for example, you won't gain or lose pennies. The other advantage is that a fixed-point number can be stored more efficiently on the disk than can most floating-point numbers because you need to store only the number of bits that are actually used in the largest number. A typical 32-bit floating-point representation requires you to store all 32 bits, even if they are not needed.

Fixed-point numbers are used much like `floats`. You declare one with or without a type-`double` initializer like this:

```
fixed x;
fixed y = 1.0;
```

The current implementation (in Listing 4.4) has 32 bits of precision and two places to the right of the decimal point. (Numbers are stored in a 32-bit `long`, scaled up by a factor of 100.) The following operators are supported:

```
+      -      /      *      +=      -=      *=      /=
```

Fixed-point numbers can be mixed freely with `doubles` in expressions. When one operand is of type `fixed` and the other is a `double`, the result is of type `fixed`. No provision has been made for `int`, `longs`, and so forth—although you can add support for these types with little difficulty. You can also convert oddball operands to `double` with a cast if you need to mix them into fixed-point calculations.

member-
initialization list   To refresh your memory of the syntax before looking at the code itself, I'm using perhaps confusing C++ syntax in several places The `:num(0L)` on line 17 of Listing 4.4 is an example of a small (one element) member-initialization list that tells the compiler to initialize the `num` field to zero. The similar one-element list on line 14 initializes `num` to `x`. The other construction that you may have forgotten is the `const` between the argument list and the open brace on line 25˙ (among other places) of Listing 4.4. This `const` tells the compiler that the function is safe to call if the declared object is declared `const`. It effectively declares `*this` as a constant within the body of the subroutine.

class fixed
special-purpose
private constructor   Moving on to the code itself, the special-purpose constructor on line 14 of Listing 4.4 was described earlier on page 168. It's used by the operator-overload functions on lines 25 to 40 to make memory allocation a bit more efficient. The default constructor is on line 17. It just initializes the number to zero. The `double` constructor declared on line 18 is used both to initialize a `fixed` object from a `double` (`fixed x = 1.0`) and to cast a `double` into a `fixed`. The function definition starts on line 83. The number is scaled on line 85. The constructor then uses a slightly nonstandard approach (in order to speed up the code a bit) to isolate the

integer component of the number and round if necessary. [A more standard approach would use `fmod()`, `floor()`, and `ceil()` for this purpose.] The integer component is extracted by casting d to **long** on line 86. The d-num on the next line isolates the fraction, and the ++num on line 88 rounds up if the fraction was bigger than .50.

Listing 4.4. *fixed.hpp*— A Fixed-Point Arithmetic Class

```
 1    #ifndef __FIXED_HPP
 2    #define __FIXED_HPP
 3
 4    #include <math.h>          // note, modf() (used below) is a not ANSI
 5    #include <stdlib.h>
 6    #include <iostream.h>
 7
 8    class fixed
 9    {
10    private:
11        long num;                   // This is the only data element.
12
13        enum marker { X };
14        fixed( const long x, marker ) : num( x ) {}   // used locally
15
16    public:
17        fixed( void      ) : num( 0L ){}
18        fixed( double d );
19
20        // Since there are no pointers, memberwise copy is okay, and you
21        // don't need an explicit copy constructor or operator=() function.
22
23        operator double() const { return (double)num / 100.0; }
24
25        fixed operator+(const fixed &r) const
26        {
27            return fixed( num + r.num, X );
28        }
29        fixed operator-(const fixed &r) const
30        {
31            return fixed( num - r.num, X );
32        }
33        fixed operator*(const fixed &r) const
34        {
35            return fixed( (num*r.num)/100L, X );
36        }
37        fixed operator/(const fixed &r) const
38        {
39            return fixed( (num*100L)/r.num, X );
40        }
41        const fixed &operator+=(const fixed &r){ num += r.num; return *this;}
42        const fixed &operator-=(const fixed &r){ num -= r.num; return *this;}
43        const fixed &operator*=(const fixed &r){ num = (num * r.num) / 100L;
44                                                 return *this;
45                                               }
46        const fixed &operator/=(const fixed &r){ num = (num * 100L)/ r.num;
```

Listing 4.4. continued…

```
47                                                           return *this;
48                                                         }
49       const fixed &operator++( void           ){ num += 100L;   return *this;}
50       const fixed &operator--( void           ){ num -= 100L;   return *this;}
51       const fixed  operator++( int /*dummy*/){ num += 100L;
52                                                           return fixed(num-100L,X);
53                                                         }
54       const fixed  operator--( int /*dummy*/){ num -= 100L;
55                                                           return fixed(num+100L,X);
56                                                         }
57
58       // Provide relational operators to avoid unnecessary conversion
59       // to double:
60
61       int operator< (const fixed &r) const { return num <  r.num; }
62       int operator<=(const fixed &r) const { return num <= r.num; }
63       int operator> (const fixed &r) const { return num >  r.num; }
64       int operator>=(const fixed &r) const { return num >= r.num; }
65       int operator==(const fixed &r) const { return num == r.num; }
66       int operator!=(const fixed &r) const { return num != r.num; }
67       int operator! ( void         ) const { return !num;         }
68  };
69  //---------------------------------------------------------------
70  inline fixed operator- (double l,const fixed &r){return fixed(l) -= r;  }
71  inline fixed operator/ (double l,const fixed &r){return fixed(l) /= r;  }
72  inline fixed operator+ (double l,const fixed &r){return r.operator+ (l);}
73  inline fixed operator* (double l,const fixed &r){return r.operator* (l);}
74  inline int   operator< (double l,const fixed &r){return r.operator> (l);}
75  inline int   operator<=(double l,const fixed &r){return r.operator>=(l);}
76  inline int   operator> (double l,const fixed &r){return r.operator< (l);}
77  inline int   operator>=(double l,const fixed &r){return r.operator<=(l);}
78  inline int   operator==(double l,const fixed &r){return r.operator==(l);}
79  inline int   operator!=(double l,const fixed &r){return r.operator!=(l);}
80  //---------------------------------------------------------------
81  #ifdef __FIXED_COMPILE_METHODS
82
83  fixed::fixed( double d )          // Convert double to scaled long
84  {
85       d *= 100.0;                  // scale (decimal left shift 2 digits)
86       num = (long)d;               // num = integer component of d
87       if( d - num > .50 )          // if( fraction component of d > .5)
88           ++num;                   //      round up to next integer.
89  }
90
91  #endif // __FIXED_COMPILE_METHODS
92  //---------------------------------------------------------------
93  #ifdef __FIXED_MAIN      // Compile a test program
94  void main( void )
95  {
96       fixed x = 10.001;
97       fixed y = 11.00 ;
98       double ix;
99
```

Listing 4.4. continued...

```
100        int i;
101        cout << "10 * " << double(x) << " + 12 == " << i << "\n" ;
102
103        cout<< "x = " << double(x) << "\n" ;
104        cout<< "y = " << double(y) << "\n" ;
105
106        cout << "x <  y = " << (x <  y) << "\n" ;
107        cout << "x <= y = " << (x <= y) << "\n" ;
108        cout << "x >  y = " << (x >  y) << "\n" ;
109        cout << "x >= y = " << (x >= y) << "\n" ;
110        cout << "x == y = " << (x == y) << "\n" ;
111        cout << "x != y = " << (x != y) << "\n" ;
112        cout << "!x     = " << (!x )    << "\n" ;
113        cout << "!y     = " << (!y )    << "\n" ;
114
115        cout << "11.0 <  y = " << (11.0 <  y) << "\n" ;
116        cout << "11.0 <= y = " << (11.0 <= y) << "\n" ;
117        cout << "11.0 >  y = " << (11.0 >  y) << "\n" ;
118        cout << "11.0 >= y = " << (11.0 >= y) << "\n" ;
119        cout << "11.0 == y = " << (11.0 == y) << "\n" ;
120        cout << "11.0 != y = " << (11.0 != y) << "\n" ;
121
122        cout << "y <  11.0 = " << (y <  11.0) << "\n" ;
123        cout << "y <= 11.0 = " << (y <= 11.0) << "\n" ;
124        cout << "y >  11.0 = " << (y >  11.0) << "\n" ;
125        cout << "y >= 11.0 = " << (y >= 11.0) << "\n" ;
126        cout << "y == 11.0 = " << (y == 11.0) << "\n" ;
127        cout << "y != 11.0 = " << (y != 11.0) << "\n" ;
128
129        ix = 12.34;
130        x = ix;
131        cout << "ix == "        << ix                  << "\n" ;
132        cout << "x  == "        << double(x)           << "\n" ;
133        cout << "ix *  0.01 = " <<         (ix *  0.01) << "\n" ;
134        cout << "x  *= 0.01 = " << double( x *= 0.01) << "\n\n" ;
135
136        ix = 12.34;
137        x = ix;
138        cout << "ix == "        << ix                  << "\n" ;
139        cout << "x  == "        << double(x)           << "\n" ;
140        cout << "ix /  0.01 = " <<         (ix /  0.01) << "\n" ;
141        cout << "x  /= 0.01 = " << double( x /= 0.01) << "\n\n" ;
142
143        ix = 12.34;
144        x = ix;
145        cout << "ix == "        << ix                  << "\n" ;
146        cout << "x  == "        << double(x)           << "\n" ;
147        cout << "ix +  0.01 = " <<         (ix +  0.01) << "\n" ;
148        cout << "x  += 0.01 = " << double( x += 0.01) << "\n\n" ;
149
150        ix = 12.34;
151        x = ix;
152        cout << "ix == "        << ix                  << "\n" ;
```

➡

```
Listing 4.4. continued...
153        cout << "x   == "        << double(x)            << "\n" ;
154        cout << "ix -  0.01 = " <<        (ix -  0.01) << "\n" ;
155        cout << "x  -= 0.01 = " << double( x -= 0.01) << "\n\n" ;
156
157        ix = 12.34;
158        x = ix;
159        cout << "ix == "         << ix                   << "\n" ;
160        cout << "x   == "        << double(x)            << "\n" ;
161        cout << "ix -  34.56 = " <<        (ix -  34.56) << "\n" ;
162        cout << "x  -= 34.56 = " << double( x -= 34.56) << "\n\n" ;
163   }
164   #endif // __FIXED_MAIN
165   #endif // __FIXED_HPP
```

fixed class operator overloads

The class definition continues with various operator overloads, the mechanics of which were described earlier. The overloads of ++ and -- on lines 49 to 56 of Listing 4.4 are exceptions. The prefix versions (without the dummy argument) can return *this because the operation is done first. Since the modified object holds the required return value, these functions can return *this to save some work. Not so with the postfix versions, which must return the unmodified value. The operator++() function, for example, increments the current object first, but then compensates for the addition by passing num-100L to the cast used to create the returned object. This way, a temporary holding the unmodified value is returned.

use global-level overloads to avoid conversions

Some words about the global-level operator overloads on lines 70 to 79 are necessary. In theory these overloads aren't required because the operator double() function can be used by the compiler to convert all fixed objects to double before doing evaluation. For example, the compiler can still evaluate an expression like the following one when the overloads on lines 70 to 79 aren't present:

```
double doub;
fixed  fix1, fix2;

fix1 = doub + fix2;
```

It uses operator double to convert fix2 to double to do the addition, and then uses the fixed(double) constructor to convert the result back to fixed to do the assignment.

These conversions, in addition to being a lot of needless work, cause a more serious complication: The very floating-point errors that we're trying to avoid by having a fixed type are reintroduced in mixed-type expressions which will now use double operands for intermediate temporaries. By overloading the operators for double left operands on lines 70 to 79, we're forcing all intermediate temporary variables to be of type fixed rather than double, forcing rounding to occur at every stage of the arithmetic process.

These functions don't have to be friends because they don't access any private data — they just use the previously overloaded operators. For example, the operator+() function on line 72 does the addition by flipping around the two operands. It returns r+1, and since r is of type fixed, the member-function overload of `operator+()` is used to do the work. This transposition is done with an `inline` mapping, so there's no loss of efficiency. The only exceptions are the overloads of - and /, which must convert the left (`double`) operand to `fixed` because these operators aren't commutative.

As a final issue here, some compilers do not handle operator overloads as if they were functions, thereby making implicit, user-defined conversion almost worthless. These compilers will refuse to accept the following code, given the earlier definitions:

too-flexible type conversions cause problems

```
double dvar;
fixed  fixvar;
fixvar = fixvar + dvar;
```

The compiler considers a conversion of the left operand to be acceptable, and as a consequence gets confused when processing the + operator. Here are the possibilities:

- Convert `dvar` to `fixed`, using the constructor, and then call `fixed::operator+(fixed)` to do the add.
- Convert `fixvar` to `double` using `operator double()` and then use normal floating-point arithmetic.
- Convert `fixvar` to `double` and `dvar` to `fixed`, then use `operator+(double, fixed)`.

If your compiler works in this way, you'll have to provide a third set of operator-overload member functions to handle the `fixed`-left-operand-and-`double`-right-operand situation. Since an exact match of a function's arguments takes precedence over a user-supplied conversion, an operator-overload function whose arguments match the operand types exactly is always called and no ambiguity exists.

4.14 A Random-Number Class

The next example is a little less commonplace. It implements a special sort of class called a *data source*. These classes contain little or no internal state information. (The current example has no data fields in the `class` definition, for example.) They consist primarily of member functions.

data source

Typically, a data source (and its opposite number, a *data sink*) is used in I/O-system implementations. The idea is that every time an object of the class is used, it evaluates to a different value. In the case of `cin`, for example, it will evaluate to the next thing in the input stream. Similarly, data is sent to a data sink such as `cout`. The sink is a bottomless pit that collects data (and in the case of `cout`, prints it). You can never get data back out of a data sink, though—it's a write-only object. A statement like `char *s = cout;` is conceptually meaningless.

data sink

The current example is a random-number class. An object of class `rand_num` evaluates to a different value every time it's used in an expression. You use it like this (I'll discuss the mechanics in a moment):

```
main()
{
    rand_num rnum;              // Unconstrained random number.
    rand_num constrained(100); // Random number whose value is
                               // in the range 0 <= x <= 100.
    int    x, y;
    x  = rnum;     // Compiler uses an implicit rand-to-int
    x += rnum;     // conversion to make the left operand
    y = x * rnum;  // match the right one on these three lines.
    x = rnum * y;  // Here, however, it uses operator*().
}
```

class rand_num

The random-number class is implemented in *random.hpp*, in Listing 4.5. The constructor on line 13 calls `srand()` to seed the random number generator, using the current time for the seed value. It also sets the range limit (`range`) to the value supplied as an argument. If the constructor is called without arguments, then the maximum random-number value that `rand()` uses is defined. (This value is defined by the RAND_MAX macro in *<stdlib.h>*). Otherwise, the random-number value is in the range zero to whatever value is passed to the constructor.

rand_num:: **operator int()**

Most of the work is done by **operator int** on line 20, which converts a `rand_num` to an **int**. Since every access yields a different result, there's no member data to convert; rather, every conversion to **int** calls to the `rand()` function to get a value, and then MODs this value by the current range. In the earlier example, all three of the statements

```
x  = rnum ;
x += rnum ;
y = x * rnum ;
```

use **operator int**() to do their work. The first one because the compiler must convert `rnum` to an **int** to do the assignment, the second two because the left operand is of type **int**, and the compiler converts the right operand to match the type of the left operand when user-defined types are involved.

The four operator overloads on lines 25 to 28 of Listing 4.5 handle expressions like

```
y = rnum * x;
```

where the left operand is a `rand_num`. Note that all of these operator-overload functions must actually do the arithmetic, as compared to just returning a random value. Consider the following code:

```
rand_num  bool(1); // Constrained -- value is always 0 or 1
int i;
//...
f( book * i );      // Randomly passes either 0 or i to f().
```

Eliminating the `*` right from **operator***() would yield an incorrect result in this case.

Listing 4.5. *random.hpp—* A Random-Number Data-Source Class

```
1    #ifndef __RANDOM_HPP
2    #define __RANDOM_HPP
3
4    #include <stdlib.h>        // contains RAND_MAX value & prototypes
5    #include <time.h>
6
7    class rand_num
8    {
9        static int instance;
10       int range;   // generated number in the range 0-range inclusive
11   public:
12
13       rand_num( int max_value = RAND_MAX-1 )
14       {
15           range = max_value + 1;
16           if( ++instance==1 )
17               srand( (unsigned) time(NULL) );
18       }
19
20       operator int()        // Convert from rand_num to int.
21       {
22           return rand() % range;  // shift into range if necessary
23       }
24
25       inline int operator/ (int right){ return (rand() % range) / right; }
26       inline int operator* (int right){ return (rand() % range) * right; }
27       inline int operator- (int right){ return (rand() % range) - right; }
28       inline int operator+ (int right){ return (rand() % range) + right; }
29   };
30
31   #ifdef RANDOM_COMPILE_METHODS
32   int rand_num::instance;
33   #endif RANDOM_COMPILE_METHODS
34   //-----------------------------------------------------------------------
35   #ifdef RANDOM_MAIN
36   #include <stdio.h>
37   void main( void )
38   {
39       rand_num constrained(1);    // constrained to value in range 0-1
40       rand_num rnum;
41       int    x, y;
42
43       x  = rnum ;       // An implicit rand-to-int conversion used to make
44       x += rnum ;       // the left operand match the right one in all
45       y = x * rnum ;    // three of these examples.
46       x = rnum * y ;    // Here, however, operator* must be used.
47
48       for( x = 10 ; --x >= 0 ; )   // print 10 random numbers
49           printf("%d ",  (int)rnum );
50       printf("\n");
51
```

→

```
Listing 4.5. continued...
52        for( x = 10 ; --x >= 0 ; )    // print 10 constrained random numbers
53            printf("%d ",  (int)constrained );
54        printf("\n");
55    }
56    #endif // RANDOM_MAIN
57    //-------------------------------------------------------------------------
58    #endif // __RANDOM_HPP
```

4.15 Accessing Two-Dimensional Types with operator()()

operator()()

There are two ways to access a multidimensional type in C++—the easy way and the right way. The easy way is to overload operator()()—the function-call operator.

In C++, a function name always evaluates to a function pointer, and the () operator can be applied to any function pointer to call the function. The situation is analogous to an array name and bracket operator. You can use the operator()() function to get control of the () operator when the left operand is something other than a function pointer. For example:

```
class egil
{
    int operator()(int first, long second);
    int operator()(double first);
}
//...
njal()
{
    egil viking;
    viking( 10, 20L );          // invoke egil::operator(int, long);
    viking( 3.0     );          // invoke egil::operator(double);
}
```

The operator()() function differs from other operator overload functions in that it takes a variable number of arguments, which are passed in the argument list as if you were using a normal function call.

You can use operator()() to access a two-dimensional-array element as follows:

```
int_matrix x( 10, 20 ) // A 10-row, 20-column matrix

x( 2, 3 ) = 0;          // modify row 2, column 3.
```

The class implementation looks like this:

```
class int_matrix
{
    int *ar;   // memory for 2-d array
    int nrows; // number of rows
    int ncols; // number of columns
public:
```

```
      int_matrix( int rows, int cols )
      {
        nrows = rows;
        ncols = cols;
        ar    = new int[ nrows * ncols ];
      }
      ~int_matrix(){ delete ar; }

      int &operator()(int r, int c);
      int &operator[](int row_index);
}
```

The `operator()()` function that accesses an array element looks like this:

```
int &int_matrix::operator()( int r, int c )
{
    if( !(0 <= r && r <= nrows) || !(0 <= c && c <= ncols) )
      fatal_error("array out of bounds");
    return *(ar + (r * ncols) + c);
}
```

The expression in the `return` statement figures out where the desired element is. The `*`, which would normally fetch the element itself, evaluates to a reference, not an object—a reference to the desired cell is returned rather than the cell's contents. The earlier

```
x( 2, 3 ) = 0;          // modify row 2, column 3.
```

is perfectly legal.

4.16 Auxiliary Classes

Another interesting use of classes is an *auxiliary class* that is used internally to do some operation, but is never used directly by an application program. This section presents two examples of how an auxiliary class might be used.

auxiliary class

4.16.1 Accessing Two-Dimensional Types with `operator[]()`

The main problem with using `operator()()` for two-dimensional array access is that a C program doesn't use parentheses to access array elements, and neither should C++. Using parentheses violates the "no surprises" rule. You really want to be able to say `x[2][3]`. Listing 4.6 demonstrates how to do it.

First, you must define an auxiliary class that represents a single row in the matrix. I've done this on lines 25 to 34 of Listing 4.6 with a `_row_ptr` class. (I've used a leading underscore because I don't want the user to even know that this class exists. The underscore moves `_row_ptr` into the ANSI name space that's reserved for compiler vendors.)

class row_ptr

The constructor for a `_row_ptr` just initializes the local row pointer (p) and the maximum column index (`ncols`) that is used later to do boundary checking. Since p is a pointer to a single row—a one-dimensional array of `int`—`operator[]` for the auxiliary class is easy—it's just like the `operator[]` for a one-dimensional array, returning a reference to the desired element.

private constructor   The constructor for a _row_ptr is **private**. Consequently, objects of this class cannot be created by an application program, only by member functions and friends. Since an int_matrix is a **friend** of a _row_ptr, then _row_ptr objects can (and will) be created by member functions of int_matrix.

Listing 4.6. *intmatrix.hpp*— Using Auxiliary Classes to Implement x[i][j]

```
1    #ifndef __INTMATRIX_HPP
2    #define __INTMATRIX_HPP
3
4    #include <stdio.h>
5    #include <stdlib.h>
6
7    class _row_ptr;
8    class int_matrix
9    {
10       int *ar;     // memory for 2-d array
11       int nrows;   // number of rows
12       int ncols;   // number of columns
13   public:
14
15       int_matrix( int rows, int cols )
16       {
17           nrows = rows;
18           ncols = cols;
19           ar    = new int[ nrows * ncols ];
20       }
21       ~int_matrix(){ delete ar; }
22       _row_ptr operator[](int row_index);
23   };
24
25   class _row_ptr
26   {
27       friend class int_matrix;
28       int *p;                      // pointer to desired row
29       int ncols;                   // maximum column index - 1
30
31       _row_ptr( int *r, int num_cols ):  p(r), ncols(num_cols) {}
32   public:
33       int &operator[](int index);
34   };
35
36   #endif // __INTMATRIX_HPP
37   //-------------------------------------------------------------------
38   #ifdef INTMATRIX_COMPILE_METHODS
39
40   _row_ptr int_matrix::operator[]( int row_index )
41   {
42       // This one is executed first to process the row index.
43
44       if( !(0 <= row_index && row_index < nrows) )
45       {
46           fprintf(stderr,"row index out of bounds (value=%d, max=%d)\n",
47                                                   row_index, nrows-1 );
```
➡

Listing 4.6. continued...

```
48              exit( 1 );
49          }
50
51          return _row_ptr( ar + (ncols * row_index), ncols );
52      }
53
54      int &_row_ptr::operator[](int col_index)
55      {
56          // This one is executed second to process the column index.
57
58          if( !(0 <= col_index && col_index < ncols) )
59          {
60              fprintf(stderr,"column index out of bounds (value=%d, max=%d)\n",
61                                              col_index, ncols-1 );
62              exit( 1 );
63          }
64
65          return p[col_index];
66      }
67
68      #endif // INTMATRIX_COMPILE_METHODS
69      //-------------------------------------------------------------------------
70      #ifdef INTMATRIX_TEST
71
72      #define NROW 10
73      #define NCOL  5
74
75      void main( void )
76      {
77          int_matrix x(NROW,NCOL);
78          int r, c;
79          int i = 0;
80
81          for( r = 0; r < NROW; ++r )
82              for( c = 0; c < NCOL; ++c )
83                  x[r][c] = i++;
84
85          for( r = 0; r < NROW; ++r )
86              for( c = 0; c < NCOL; ++c )
87                  printf("%2d%s", x[r][c], c==NCOL-1 ? "\n" : " " );
88
89          printf("\n");
90
91          x[0][NCOL] = 0;        // force an out-of-bounds error
92      }
93
94      #endif // INTMATRIX_TEST
```

You can see what I'm talking about by looking at int_matrix's **operator**[]()
on lines 40 to 52 of Listing 4.6. This function handles the leftmost set of brackets
in an expression like x[2][3]. The function checks for a valid row index, and

then creates (and returns) a _row_ptr object that points at the desired row (on line 51). The _row_ptr object is created by the cast operation.

Given

```
int_matrix x(20,30);   // A 20 X 30 matrix.
x[2][3] = 0;
```

the subexpression x[2] selects the third row of the array by calling int_matrix::**operator**[](2). This subroutine generates a temporary variable of type _row_ptr that contains (in its p field) the address of the first element of the third row.

The [3] is then applied to this temporary, not to the initial x, so _row_ptr::**operator**[](3) (on lines 54 to 66 of Listing 4.6) is called to process the [3]. It returns a reference to the fourth cell of the array (a reference to an **int**), which is then modified with the =0. (The **int** itself is modified.)

Looked at another way, the expression x[i][j] is translated by the compiler into

```
(  x.operator[](i)  ).operator[](j)
```

The left operator returns a _row_ptr object, so a dot is used to call the **operator**[]() function for that object.

Something like x[2]=2 (without the column index) is rejected by the compiler because x[2] evaluates to an object of type _row_ptr, and there is no defined assignment operation [no **operator**=() function] in the _row_ptr class. The compiler kicks out a hard error if the column index is missing.

4.16.2 A Virtual-Memory Paging System

A virtual-memory paging system provides another example of how auxiliary classes are useful. The idea is to be able to access a very large array that's actually stored in a disk file as if it were stored in memory. Array brackets are used to access array elements in the normal way.

class vchar: virtual array of char

The class presented here implements a virtual array of **char**. The array is dynamically sized—elements are effectively added as they are used—and the size is limited only by the amount of available disk space. An object is declared and used like this:

```
vchar a;        // virtual array of char

a[0]     = 10;
a[80000] = 20;
int i = a[0] + a[80000];
```

That is, you just access the virtual array with brackets, as if it were a normal in-memory array. The class definition takes care of all the details of managing the underlying disk file, accessing elements, and so forth.

The vchar implementation goes about things in a perhaps-too-simple way, but it makes an example complex enough to demonstrate the C++ -related problems. Each vchar object contains its own local buffer that's used to access a unique disk file, which is broken up into buffer-sized pages. When you request a specific cell (using notation like `vchar_obj[i]`) the system figures out which page contains the required element and reads it into the local buffer. If you modify the cell, the buffer is marked as "dirty," and the page will be flushed to disk as part of the read process when the current page is being replaced by another one.

The current class overloads the `[]` operator to access array elements, but it overloads it in an unobvious way. The obvious way is to overload `[]` to read the required page into the buffer and then return a reference to the required cell, much as if the cell were in memory to begin with. There are two problems with this approach. A simple expression like `a[i]=0` causes problems because the <u>real</u> array is on the disk, not in memory. That is, when you access `a[i]`, you are really accessing the *i*th element in the disk file. So, an expression like `a[i]` must generate an lvalue that references the disk element, not the copy in memory. The memory manager does the access by reading the block that contains the *i*th element from the disk to the local buffer, but it can't just return a reference to the position in memory where the *i*th element is found because the assignment would just modify the copy in memory, not the real cell on the disk.

The second problem is an assignment like `a[i]=a[j]`, where the two elements are on different pages in the disk file. The problem is that there's only one local buffer. When you read the page that contains the *i*th element, you'll by necessity overwrite the page that has the *j*th element and vice versa. You can't get them both into memory at once in order to do the assignment. Moreover, there's no guarantee that the expression to the right of the equal sign is evaluated before the one on the left—both are evaluated before the assignment operator is processed, but you don't know the order of evaluation. Consequently, you can't keep around the value of the most-recently-accessed element to use in situations like the current one. Both problems can be solved with an auxiliary class.

The `vchar` implementation is presented in Listing 4.7. My strategy is similar to that used for two-dimensional array access. The overloaded bracket operator does only part of an operation, generating a temporary variable of an auxiliary class to complete the operation. In an expression such as

```
vchar a;      // array of virtual characters
// ...
a[i]=a[j];
```

the bracket processing generates two temporary variables of type `vchar_aux`. The assignment is then done by a member function of `vchar_aux`, which can determine which operand is the left one and which is the right. Consequently, `vchar_aux::`**operator**`=()` can easily determine whether to flush the buffer because it knows that the `a[i]` access was on the left of the equal sign and that `a[j]` was on the right.

The `vchar` class definition, which starts on line 11 of Listing 4.7, concerns itself mainly with buffer management. The data fields are the buffer itself (`buf`), the page number of the disk file currently in the buffer (`page`), a `dirty` bit that tells the system that somebody has modified the contents of the buffer so that it will need to be flushed to disk before it can be overwritten when another page needs to be accessed, and a pointer to the `FILE` used for the disk buffer (`fd`).

operator[]()

auxiliary classes
and virtual arrays

vchar_aux

The vchar class has only three public functions. The constructor on line 21 of Listing 4.7 initializes page to a nonexistent page (-1) and dirty to zero. These values assure that a new page will be read on the first access, and that the initial buffer, which holds garbage, won't be flushed to disk before the page is read. The constructor also creates and opens a temporary file to be used for the disk buffer. The matching destructor on line 30 just closes the temporary file created by the constructor. Since the file is created by the ANSI tmpfile() function, it is deleted automatically when the file is closed or the program exits.

vchar::**operator**[]()   The only other public function is the **operator**[]() overload, declared on line 35 and defined on line 124. The **operator**[]() definition follows the vchar_aux definition because it calls the vchar_aux constructor. If **operator**[]() were defined on line 35, the compiler would give an error message that says that it cannot find any constructor for a vchar_aux (because it will not have seen the definition yet). All that the **operator**[]() function does is create a vchar_aux object initialized with the current index and a pointer to the vchar that holds the buffer. It does this with the following cast:

```
return vchar_aux( i, this );
```

private constructors   You'll notice that the vchar_aux constructor (on line 105 of Listing 4.7) is **private**— objects of class vchar_aux normally cannot be created by an application program or from another class. The vchar class is a **friend** of vchar_aux, however. (It's declared as such on line 95.) Consequently, vchar:: **operator**[]() can create a vchar_aux object.

While we're here...Though the vchar_aux constructor is **private**, the destructor (on line 108) must be **public**; otherwise, an object that was created by **operator**()[] couldn't be destroyed in the function that used the bracket operator. For example, in

```
int f( )
{
    vchar a;
    // ...
    return a[0];
}
```

the vchar::**operator**[] that is called implicitly by a[0] creates a vchar_aux object. But that object goes out of scope in f(), not in vchar::**operator**[]. Consequently, the destructor must be public or it cannot be called from f(). [f() could also be a **friend** of vchar_aux—but that's not really an acceptable solution. You can't modify the definition for vchar_aux every time you add a function that uses brackets to access a vchar object.]

vchar::cell()
vchar::change_cell()
The remainder of the vchar class consists of **private** member functions that manipulate the buffer. (Since the buffer is declared inside a vchar, it's only proper that the functions that manipulate it also be inside a vchar.) Two buffer-manipulation functions [cell(), and change_cell()] are all called from the vchar_aux member functions, so vchar_aux is declared as a friend on line 13 of Listing 4.7 to allow the access. All the functions are described in the comment starting on line 38.

Listing 4.7. *virtual.cpp*— A Simplified Virtual-Memory Manager

```
 1    #include <stdio.h>
 2    #include <stdlib.h>
 3    #include <iostream.h>
 4
 5    // Simplified virtual-array system. Each object has its own disk
 6    // file and buffer.
 7
 8    static const int Buf_size = 1024;
 9
10    class vchar_aux;
11    class vchar              // virtual-memory array of char
12    {
13        friend class vchar_aux; //
14
15        char buf[ Buf_size ]; // Local buffer to read pages into
16        long page;               // Page currently in memory
17        int  dirty;              // Page has been modified since read.
18        FILE *fd;                // File used for external buffer
19
20    public:
21        vchar() : page(-1), dirty(0) //
22        {
23            if( !(fd = tmpfile()) )
24            {
25                perror("can't open virtual-array temporary file\n");
26                exit( 1 );
27            }
28        }
29
30        ~vchar( void ) //
31        {
32            fclose( fd );    // close and delete temporary file.
33        }
34
35        inline vchar_aux operator[]( long i ); // found beneath vchar_aux
36                                              // definition, below.
37    private:
38        // Functions to do buffer manipulation. cell() and change_cell() are
39        // used by function in the vchar_aux class. Other functions are
40        // used internally.
41        //
42        // page_in            reads the specified page from the disk file.
43        // page_out           flushes the disk buffer to the current page,
44        //                    but only if the page has been modified (is
45        //                    dirty). Resets dirty to 0.
46        // load_required_page Load the page that holds the index-th element
47        //                    of the virtual array into memory, flushing the
48        //                    existing buffer to disk if necessary.
49        // cell               returns a reference to the cell in memory that
50        //                    holds the index'th array element.
51        // change_cell        works just like cell(), but sets the dirty bit.
52
```

➡

Listing 4.7. continued...

```
53        void page_in( long page )
54        {
55            fseek( fd, page * Buf_size, SEEK_SET );
56            fread( buf, sizeof(buf), 1, fd );
57        }
58
59        void page_out()
60        {
61            if( dirty )
62            {
63                fseek ( fd, page * Buf_size, SEEK_SET );
64                fwrite( buf, sizeof(buf), 1, fd );
65                dirty = 0;
66            }
67        }
68
69        void load_required_page( long index )
70        {
71            int page_needed = (int)( index / sizeof(buf));
72            if( page != page_needed )
73            {
74                page_out();
75                page_in ( page_needed );
76            }
77        }
78
79        char &cell(long index)
80        {
81            load_required_page( index );
82            return buf[ index % sizeof(buf) ];
83        }
84
85        char &change_cell( long index )
86        {
87            load_required_page( index );
88            dirty = 1;
89            return buf[ index % sizeof(buf) ];
90        }
91    };
92    //-------------------------------------------------------------------------
93    class vchar_aux
94    {
95        friend class vchar; //
96    private:
97        vchar *vobj;             // Virtual object being accessed
98        long index;              // Index in virtual object
99
100       // The vchar_aux constructor is private to restrict creation
101       // of an object to a vchar_aux or vchar member function.
102       // The destructor must be public otherwise the object cannot
103       // be destroyed when it goes out of scope.
104
```

➡

Listing 4.7. continued...

```
105          vchar_aux( long i, vchar *p ) : index(i), vobj(p) {} //
106
107     public:
108          ~vchar_aux() { vobj->page_out(); }
109
110          operator int ( void      ){ return vobj->cell( index )           ; }
111          int operator+( int right ){ return vobj->cell( index ) + right; }
112          int operator-( int right ){ return vobj->cell( index ) - right; }
113          int operator*( int right ){ return vobj->cell( index ) * right; }
114          int operator/( int right ){ return vobj->cell( index ) / right; }
115
116          int operator= (int right ){return vobj->change_cell(index)  = right;}
117          int operator+=(int right ){return vobj->change_cell(index) += right;}
118          int operator-=(int right ){return vobj->change_cell(index) -= right;}
119          int operator*=(int right ){return vobj->change_cell(index) *= right;}
120          int operator/=(int right ){return vobj->change_cell(index) /= right;}
121
122     };
123     //------------------------------------------------------------------------
124     inline vchar_aux vchar::operator[]( long i ) //
125     {
126          // This function must be down here to prevent Borland C++ from
127          // complaining about a missing constructor in the vchar_aux class.
128
129          return vchar_aux( i, this );
130     }
131     //------------------------------------------------------------------------
132     void main( void )
133     {
134          vchar virt_array;
135          int   i;
136
137          virt_array[0]    = 'x';
138          virt_array[4096] = virt_array[0];
139
140          printf("(%c) %x\n",(int)virt_array[0],    (int)virt_array[0] );
141          printf("(%c) %x\n",(int)virt_array[4096],(int)virt_array[4096]);
142
143          i= (   virt_array[ 1      ] = 1             ); cout << i << " ( 1)\n";
144          i= (   virt_array[ 70000 ] = 9             ); cout << i << " ( 9)\n";
145          i= (   virt_array[ 70000 ]+=virt_array[1] ); cout << i << " (10)\n";
146          i=     virt_array[ 70000 ];                   cout << i << " (10)\n";
147          i= 3 + virt_array[ 70000 ];                   cout << i << " (13)\n";
148          i=     virt_array[ 70000 ] + 5;               cout << i << " (15)\n";
149          i= (   virt_array[ 70000 ] += 2);             cout << i << " (12)\n";
150          i=     virt_array[ 70000 ];                   cout << i << " (12)\n";
151     }
```

Moving on to the vchar_aux class, in an expression like a[i]=0, the [i] invokes vchar::**operator**[](), which creates and returns a vchar_aux object that's initialized with an index of i and a vobj pointer that holds the address of a. The assignment is now done by vchar_aux::**operator**=(**char**), which starts on line 116 of Listing 4.7. The subroutine calls vchar::change_cell() to access the correct cell. vchar::change_cell() (which is on line 85) starts out by load-ing the page that contains the indexth element. Ideally, it will already be in the buffer, so the load_required_page() call will do nothing. It then sets the dirty bit—it couldn't do this before the load_required_page() call because that would force an unnecessary write operation. Finally, vchar::change_cell() computes the location of, and returns a reference to, the memory location occupied by the required cell. Control now passes back to vchar_aux:: **operator**=(), which assigns right to the cell returned from vchar::change_cell(). No buffer flush occurs because the next access could be to the same page, and you don't want to flush the buffer unnecessarily. Since the buffer is dirty, it will be flushed to the disk either when the system reads a new page into the buffer or when the vchar_aux object goes out of scope. (A flush is performed by the destructor on line 108.)

An expression like a[i]=a[j] works in much the same way, but there's an extra step. There is no vchar_aux::**operator**=(vchar_aux) function, so the vchar_aux-to-**char** conversion function on line 110 of Listing 4.7 is called to access the value of the right operand. This function loads the required page and then returns the contents of the required cell. Control now passes to vchar_aux::**operator**=(**char**), which loads the target page if necessary—it won't load if a[i] and a[j] are on the same page—and then proceeds as before.

This same vchar_aux-to-**char** conversion is used in expressions with non-vchar left operands (like **int** i=a[10]; or i+a[10]), but overloads of the other arithmetic operators (+, -, *, and /) are required for expressions like a[10]+i. The assignment forms of these operators also need overloads. These overloads all start on line 111 of Listing 4.7.

All this seems complicated, but it's actually doing a pretty complicated thing in a relatively easy-to-maintain way. For one thing, the application program that's using the vchar class is dramatically easier to maintain—it just accesses the vir-tual array as if it were a large dynamic array that can be arbitrarily large. The array size is effectively increased just by accessing a cell.

The current implementation could use some improvement, though. First, one buffer per object isn't the best way to do things. If you have lots of objects around, you'll also have lots of buffers. Moreover, the single buffer causes efficiency problems if you're accessing lots of very spread-out elements in the same array. You'll spend a lot of time flushing old buffers and reading new ones.

A more-realistic implementation would use a pool of buffers that are shared by all the objects. In this way, a very active object could have many buffers assigned to it, and a less active object could occasionally steal the least recently used buffer from a more active one.

Also, one disk file per object is also not a great idea because the files stay open for the life of the object. You can run out of FILE structures if you have a lot of

vchar::
load_required_page()

processing
a[i]=a[j] in
class vchar

improving**class**
vchar

virtual arrays in existence at once. The situation would be improved if one virtual-array file were shared by all of the objects. You'd need a pretty complex memory manager to handle this situation, though, and I didn't want to waste space with it here.[7]

Let me finish up by saying that this example is typical of a C++ class in that you do a lot of work to implement a simple thing. The class definition ends up seeming much too large and complicated for what it does. Occasionally, someone who realizes just how much work is involved in creating a class definition consigns C++ to the trash bin, thinking that creating a class is just too hard. There are two good answers to the criticism. First, you will use the class more often than you create it. Like any good library function, it's worth putting in a lot of work up front to make the function as robust as possible. A lot of the problems you may be having in understanding the code now just may be a lack of familiarity with the syntax of C++. Second, there's really no more work than there would be in doing the same thing in C; it's just that the work is hidden from you when you use the class. Don't think in terms of how complex the class is; think in terms of how easy it is to use the class in an application program.

4.17 Implementing Variant Records

The next example illustrates how you'd implement a Pascal-like variant record, in which the compiler keeps track of which field of a `union` is active as the union is modified.

The problem is usually solved in C by encapsulating the `union` into a structure along with a selector field that identifies the active field in the `union`:

```
struct variant
{
    int int_field_is_active;   /* selector */
    union                      /* contents */
    {
      int    i_val;
      double d_val;
    };
};
```

Keeping this selector updated correctly as the union is modified provides a constant maintenance problem. Moreover, it's an annoyance to have two different names for the same region of memory. Ideally, you'd have a variable (or field in a structure) with only one name, but whose type changes automatically depending on its contents. When you use the variable in an expression, it should evaluate as

automatic updating of `union`-field selector

---

[7] If you're interested, [Holub1] and [Holub2] describe more realistic systems. [Holub1] describes a one-buffer-per-object system that uses a shared file for all objects. [Holub2] uses a buffer pool that's shared by all objects. There is also a simple C++ implementation in [Holub1], but it doesn't use auxiliary classes so is less elegant (and more buggy) than the one presented here.

if it were declared as whatever type it actually is. (If it holds a `double`, it should act as if it were declared `double`, and so forth.)

You can do the foregoing in C++ with a special-purpose class. The principles are demonstrated in the `variant` class in Listing 4.8. A object of type `variant` can have an `int`, `long`, or `double` value. The value is set up automatically as part of the declaration:

```
variant a = 10;          // holds an int
variant b = 2L;          // holds a long
variant c = 3.0;         // holds a double
```

Thereafter, expressions that involve addition, subtraction, multiplication, and division can be executed with `variant` objects mixed freely with objects of type `int`, `long`, or `double`. When two variants are involved in an expression (like b+c), the smaller one (b) is scaled up to the current type of the larger one (c) and the result is a `variant` object whose type matches the larger operand. This way, if any of the `variant`s hold a `double` value, all arithmetic will be double-precision.

All of the relational operators are also supported, There is also a special implementation of `==` that lets you determine the type of the number actually stored in the record. You do this by comparing a `variant` object against one of the type identifiers defined in the enumerated type on line 29 of Listing 4.8. The possibilities are `id_int`, `id_long`, `id_double`. For example:

```
variant iv = 10;
variant dv = 10.0;

if( iv == id_int  ) // true,  iv holds an int
    ...
if( iv == id_long ) // false, iv doesn't hold a long
    ...
if( iv == dv )                // true, the values are the same
    ...
```

Casts to `double`, `long`, and `int` are supported so that you can access a `variant` object:

```
variant a =10;
printf("%d %ld %f\n", (int)a, (long)a, (double)a );
```

There's also a print function for debugging. It prints the object's value, its type, and an optional prefix string:

```
variant a = 10;

a.print();      // prints:  "(int) 10"
a.print("a="); // prints:   "a=(int) 10"
```

Since the function returns a reference to the printed object, it can be used in the middle of an expression for debugging purposes:

```
variant a = 10;                    // holds an int
variant b = 2L;                    // holds a long
variant c = 3.0;         // holds a double

c = (a * b).print("a*b") +c; // Print value of subexpression
                             // a*b as (a*b)+c is evaluated.
```

The `variant` type is implemented in Listing 4.8.

The listing introduces a new technique in declaring the `variant` class. Many of the operator-overload functions (such as all the relationals) require functions that are almost identical. The same goes for the constructors. It's a bad idea, though, to have eight or 10 almost identical subroutines floating around. It's difficult to maintain them because every time you change one, you'll have to change the others, too.

I've solved the problem by using the macro preprocessor to generate functions for me. Those parts of the functions that are different are passed into the macro as arguments. Taking the constructor-generation macro on line three as characteristic, the macro looks like this:

```
#define constructor( type )        \
           variant( type val ): \
                     v_##type( val ), i_am( id_##type ) {}
```

The invocation of

```
constructor( int )
```

on line 48 expands to

```
variant( int val ) : v_int( val ), i_am( id_int ) {}
```

The `type` argument becomes `int` in the expansion. The `##` concatenation operator is removed from the macro body after all substitutions are made, so `v_##type` is replaced by `v_##int` and the `##` is then removed, yielding `v_int`. The invocation of

```
constructor( long )
```

on line 49 expands to

```
variant( long val ) : v_long( val ), i_am( id_long ) {}
```

The `cast_to()` and `assignment()` macros defined on lines six and 17 of Listing 4.8 and used on lines 52 to 58 work in much the same way.

Some of the operator overloads are declared with the same procedure, but an operator is passed into the macro rather than a type name. Consequently, a macro must be used. (The earlier functions could have been implemented with a **template**. I didn't do so because I want to put the discussion of templates together in one place—in Chapter Six.) For example, the `_variant_plus_mult_rel()` macro invocations that start on line 172 of Listing 4.8 use the macro on lines 104 to 114 to create several operator overloads. An invocation of `_variant_plus-_mult_rel(!=, int)`, for example, generates an overload of **operator**`!=()` that returns an `int` value. The `op` argument to the macro is replaced by `!=` on expansion, and `type` is replaced by `int` in the same way.

Listing 4.8. *variant.cpp*— A Variant-Record Implementation

```
1      #include <stdio.h>
2
3      #define constructor( type ) \
4                      variant( type val ) : v_##type( val ), i_am(id_##type){}
5
6      #define cast_to( type ) operator type() const \
7                              { \
8                                  if( i_am == id_##type ) \
9                                      return v_##type; \
10                                 else \
11                                     return(i_am==id_int   )? (type)(v_int)   :\
12                                           (i_am==id_long   )? (type)(v_long  ):\
13                                           (i_am==id_double)? (type)(v_double):\
14                                                              (type) 0        ;\
15                             }
16
17     #define assignment( type ) \
18                             variant &operator=( type right ) \
19                             { \
20                                 i_am      = id_##type; \
21                                 v_##type = right; \
22                                 return *this; \
23                             }
24
25     // The variant_t type identifies variant-record fields. The members
26     // must be listed in increasing size. (eg. int is shorter than long,
27     // so id_int precedes id_long in the list.)
28
29     enum variant_t{ id_none, id_int, id_long, id_double };
30
31     class variant
32     {
33         variant_t i_am;       /* selector */
34         union                 /* contents */
35         {
36             int    v_int;
37             long   v_long;
38             double v_double;
39         };
40
41     public:
42         variant( void )           // default constructor
43         {
44             i_am = id_none;
45             v_double = 0.0;       // longest field in union
46         }
47
48         constructor( int    )     // create typed constructors with macro
49         constructor( long   )
50         constructor( double )
51
```

```
Listing 4.8. continued...
52      cast_to( int    )          // create cast-to-type with macro
53      cast_to( long   )
54      cast_to( double )
55
56      assignment( int    )       // create operator=() functions with macro
57      assignment( long   )
58      assignment( double )
59      variant &operator=( variant &right )
60      {
61          // Must supply this overload to avoid ambiguities. A simple
62          // structure copy is ideal, here, but "*this = right"
63          // is a recursive call to operator=() so can't be used.
64
65          i_am = right.i_am;
66          if(       i_am == id_int    ) v_int    = right.v_int;
67          else if( i_am == id_long   ) v_long   = right.v_long;
68          else if( i_am == id_double ) v_double = right.v_double;
69          return *this;
70      }
71
72      // There are two operator== functions. The first identifies
73      // the active type of the encapsulated union. For example,
74      // "x == id_double" is true if the internal union holds a double
75      // value.  The second operator== just compares values, doing any
76      // necessary casting internally.
77
78      int operator==( const variant_t what ) const { return i_am == what; }
79      int operator==( const variant &right ) const;
80      int operator!=( const variant &right ) const;
81      int operator<=( const variant &right ) const;
82      int operator>=( const variant &right ) const;
83      int operator< ( const variant &right ) const;
84      int operator> ( const variant &right ) const;
85
86      // Arithmetic operators need to be implemented as well;
87      // normal type conversions work here.
88
89      variant operator+( const variant &right ) const;
90      variant operator-( const variant &right ) const;
91      variant operator*( const variant &right ) const;
92      variant operator/( const variant &right ) const;
93
94      variant &print( const char *prefix = "" ) const;
95  };
96
97  #undef constructor      // don't need these any more
98  #undef cast_to
99  #undef assignment
100
101 // Note that a conditional (instead of if..return) in the following
102 // subroutine causes Borland C++ to generate bad code.
103 //
104 #define _variant_plus_mult_rel( op, type ) \
```

Listing 4.8. continued...

```
105   type variant::operator op ( const variant &right ) const \
106   {\
107       variant &large = ( i_am <= right.i_am ) ? right : *this ; \
108       variant &small = ( i_am <= right.i_am ) ? *this : right ; \
109       if(large.i_am==id_double) return type(
110                                       large.v_double op (double)(small));\
111       if(large.i_am==id_long  ) return type(large.v_long op (long)(small));\
112       if(large.i_am==id_int   ) return type(large.v_int  op (int )(small));\
113                                 return type(0);\
114   }
115
116   #define _variant_minus_div( op ) \
117   variant variant::operator op ( const variant &right ) const \
118   { \
119       return variant( \
120           (i_am <= right.i_am) ? \
121               ( \
122                   (right.i_am==id_double)?(double)*this op right.v_double: \
123                   (right.i_am==id_long  )?(long  )*this op right.v_long  : \
124                   (right.i_am==id_int   )?(int   )*this op right.v_int   :0\
125               ) \
126           : \
127               ( \
128                   (this->i_am==id_double) ? v_double op (double)right :    \
129                   (this->i_am==id_long  ) ? v_long   op (long )right :    \
130                   (this->i_am==id_int   ) ? v_int     op (int  )right : 0 \
131               ) \
132       ); \
133   }
134   //-----------------------------------------------------------------
135   // Everything above this point can be put into a .hpp file that is
136   // included in the current file.
137   //
138   // The remainder of the file contains the actual functions needed to
139   // implement the variant class. You can put each of these in a separate
140   // .cpp file as long as you include variant.hpp at the head of each
141   // of them. The macros, such as _variant_relational(), that generate
142   // the member functions, should all be placed in variant.hpp
143   // to facilitate this process.
144
145   variant &variant::print( const char *prefix ) const
146   {
147       // Note that this function can be applied to a subexpression
148       // provided that the subexpression is of type variant:
149       //   variant a, b, c, +d;
150       //
151       //   a = (b + c).print() +d
152       //
153       // The expression evaluates as if the .print() wasn't there,
154       // but the value of the intermediate temporary is printed.
155       //
156
```

Listing 4.8. continued...

```
157        printf("%s(%s) ", prefix, i_am == id_double ? "double":
158                                   i_am == id_long   ? "long  ":
159                                   i_am == id_int    ? "int   ": "undefined");
160        switch( i_am )
161        {
162        case id_double: printf("%f\n",  v_double ); break;
163        case id_long  : printf("%ld\n", v_long   ); break;
164        case id_int   : printf("%d\n",  v_int    ); break;
165        }
166        return *this;
167    }
168
169    // Generate overload functions by invoking earlier macros. Each of
170    // these macro invocations will expand to an entire function:
171
172    _variant_plus_mult_rel( !=, int      )
173    _variant_plus_mult_rel( <=, int      )
174    _variant_plus_mult_rel( >=, int      )
175    _variant_plus_mult_rel( < , int      )
176    _variant_plus_mult_rel( > , int      )
177    _variant_plus_mult_rel( + , variant  )
178    _variant_plus_mult_rel( * , variant  )
179    _variant_minus_div    ( -            )
180    _variant_minus_div    ( /            )
181
182    #ifdef VARIANT_MAIN      // A small main() to test the variant class
183    main()
184    {
185        variant dv = 1.0;
186        variant iv = 2;
187        variant lv = 3L;
188
189        printf("dv = %f\n",  (double)dv );
190        printf("iv = %d\n",  (int  )iv );
191        printf("lv = %ld\n", (long )lv );
192
193        dv = (dv * 3) /2;
194
195        printf("dv = %f\n",  (double)dv );
196
197        dv = 1.0;
198        dv = (dv * lv) / iv;
199
200        printf("dv = %f\n",  (double)dv );
201    }
202    #endif
```

Another interesting point is that the resulting function uses a reference variable (as compared to a reference argument)—a rare event, indeed. large and small (declared on lines 107 and 108 of Listing 4.8) are name aliases for whichever object holds the largest and smallest numbers. If one operand represents an int

reference variable

and the other represents a `double`, for example, `small` references the one that holds the `int` and `large` references the other one. Since the references must be initialized at run time because the values change from call to call, the compiler has to use anonymous pointers to implement the references. I could have implemented the function with pointers rather than references in order to make the mechanics more visible, as follows:

```
variant operator+( const variant &right )
{
    variant *large, *small;
    if( i_am <= right.i_am ){ large=&right; small = this;   }
    else                    { large= this;  small = &right; }

    return (large->i_am==id_double) ?
              variant( large->v_double + (double)(*small) ):
           (large->i_am==id_long  ) ?
              variant( large->v_long + (long)(*small) ):
           (large->i_am==id_int   ) ?
              variant(large->v_int +(int)(*small)): variant();
}
```

4.18 Overloading `new` and `delete`

Although they are not, strictly speaking, operators, the `new` and `delete` keywords can also be overloaded. As we've seen, `new` and `delete` statements do a lot more than allocate memory, and you cannot get control over this extra functionality. You can change the way that the memory management is done by `new` and `delete`, however.

I'll start with `new`. Normally, `new` returns `NULL` when it can't get enough memory for the requested object. You've probably noticed by now that most of my code is pretty nonchalant about checking for this value. The code just proceeds as if `new` succeeded in getting the memory.

I can do this because there are several ways of controlling the way that `new` handles an out-of-memory error and most of my code assumes that one or more of these mechanisms are in place.

The first possibilities are the `_new_handler` variable and `set_new_handler()` function. The `_new_handler` variable is a global function pointer, declared as follows:

_new_handler

```
void (*_new_handler)(void);
```

If this variable has a `NULL` value (the usual default), then `new` evaluates to `NULL` when it can't get memory. If `_new_handler` points at a function, then the function is called when `new` can't get memory. For example, this global-level definition in your program changes `new`'s behavior so that the program terminates when it can't get memory:

```
static void myhandler( void )
{
    printf(stderr, "Out of memory!\n" );
    exit(1);
}
void (*_new_handler)(void) = myhandler;
```

Note that if you don't modify _new_handler in a global-level definition—if you do it with an assignment within `main()`, for example—then your **new** handler won't be active when the global-level objects are created.

Some compilers don't allow a global-level definition, though. The problem usually lies in the compiler-vendor-supplied definition. For example, Zortech C++ defines _new_handler like this

```
void (*_new_handler)(void) = 0;
```

in its *new.cpp* file. The explicit =0 forces the foregoing to be a definition rather than a declaration. (Space is allocated in the load module.) Consequently, your redefinition is rejected by the linker because you can't have two explicitly initialized global variables with the same name. This rejection is particularly annoying since the default initialization value is zero regardless of whether you initialize it explicitly. If your compiler behaves like Zortech, you'll have to modify the library source code to eliminate the =0 and then replace the default library version of new() with your own to fix the problem.

If you want to change the out-of-memory behavior of **new** for a short time, a   `set_new_handler()`
function is provided that lets you install a temporary handler in a `signal()`-like fashion. The function, `set_new_handler()` returns the old handler and replaces it with a new one. Use it like this:

```
void temporary_handler( void ){ /*...*/ }
void (*old_handler)(void);

old_handler = set_new_handler( temporary_handler );
cls object *p = new cls; // use temporary handler;
set_new_handler( old_handler );
```

This mechanism can be used only locally because it must be called from a function, and all global-level objects will have been initialized at that juncture.

Another, more flexible approach is to overload the memory-allocation com-   **operator** new()
ponent of the **new** operator. Do it with a global-level operator-overload function like this:

```
#include <stdlib.h>    // for malloc() and size_t definitions
void *operator new(size_t size)
{
    void *p;
    if( !(p = malloc(size)) )
    {
        fprintf(stderr, "Out of memory!\n" );
        exit( 1 );
    }
    return p;
}
```

Applying the word "overload" to new is something of a misnomer, although it's commonly used in this way. First, new is not really an operator in the accepted sense of the word—it doesn't modify or manipulate any of the operands, for example. It's not possible to get complete control over what new does. The operator new() function controls only the memory-allocation component of what goes on when you use new. Implicit calls to the constructor, and so forth, are still performed automatically by the compiler, but your operator new() subroutine is called first to get the memory.

All overloads of operator new() must return a void* and take a size_t argument, much like malloc(). Your overload doesn't have to call malloc(), though—you can use your own memory manager instead. Also note that _new_handler and set_new_handler() work the way they do only because the default operator new() function—the one that comes with your compiler— supports them. You'll need to support _new_handler and set_new_handler() yourself if you replace the global-level operator new() function.

using new to construct objects in pre-allocated memory

You can provide more than one version of operator new() if you like. Your extra overloads need additional arguments, though, so they can be distinguished from the standard version. Most compilers come with just such an overload that lets you tell operator new() to use previously allocated memory instead of memory from the heap. It's used like this:

```
#include <new.h>
class xcls { ... };
static char buf[ sizeof (xcls) ]; // Enough memory to hold
                                  // an xcls object.

xcls *xp = new(buf) xcls; // Allocate xcls object into prev-
                          // iously declared memory rather
                          // than the heap. Returned pointer
                          // matches the 'buf' argument.
```

Note that the argument to the operator new() overload is attached to the new keyword. You can also specify a constructor argument. The following statement works like the previous one, but it calls a char* constructor for the xcls object rather than the default constructor:

```
xp = new(buf) xcls("string");
```

This version of new always returns its argument (buf here). It is a serious error to free the memory allocated by this form of new with a standard delete operation.

A **delete** xp doesn't know that the memory addressed by xp didn't come from the
heap, so it will try to pass buf to free() after calling the xcls destructor. It's as if
you had said **delete** buf. You must destroy the object before buf goes out of
scope, however, and you do so by calling the destructor explicitly. A fully qualified call such as the following is used for this purpose:

explicit destructor
call

```
xp->xcls::~xcls();
```

The call just executes the destructor function without deleting any memory. The
xp is required to supply a **this** pointer to the destructor, which has a **void** argument list. The xcls:: is required because the compiler treats the ~xcls in xp-
>~xcls() as a one's-complement operator applied to the object returned from a
cast operator and generates a syntax error because the resulting object cannot be a
structure field.

If your compiler doesn't support the foregoing version of **new**, you can implement the mechanism by providing a global-level overload of **operator new**()
that has an additional argument. The code looks like this

```
void *operator new( size_t size, void *existing_buf )
{
    return existing_buf;
}
```

The arguments following the **new** in a source-level statement are passed to the
new() subroutine as arguments following the size argument. You can add as
many arguments as you like using this mechanism. An overload like

```
void *operator new( size_t size, int a, int b, int c );
```

is invoked with a statement like the following:

```
int a, b, c;
cls *p = new(a,b,c) cls;
```

Note that, as is the case in any overload, the argument types in the call must match
the arguments in the definition to avoid ambiguity. You can have several three-
argument overloads of **new**() that take different argument types, for example.

new overloads are quite useful in several situations. The overload in Listing
4.9—for systems that support a UNIX-like alloca() function—lets you select
memory from either the stack or from dynamic memory (the heap). [This code
assumes that the compiler will indeed expand the code inline. The code won't
work as a real function because alloca() must use the calling subroutine's stack.]
You allocate from the stack like this:

allocate from stack,
new(STACK)
new(HEAP)

```
some_class *p1 = new( STACK ) some_class;
```

and from the dynamic-memory heap either like this:

```
some_class *p2 = new( HEAP ) some_class;
```

or like this

```
some_class *p3 = new some_class;
```

The (HEAP) is optional because two overloads of `operator new()` are supplied, one with an extra argument and one without.

Listing 4.9. *heap_new.cpp*— Allocate Memory from Stack or Heap

```
1    enum where_from { STACK, HEAP };
2
3    inline void *operator new( size_t size, where_from source )
4    {
5        int *p = where_from == STACK ? alloca( size + sizeof(int) )
6                                     : malloc( size + sizeof(int) ) ;
7        if( p )
8            *p++ = source;
9        return p;
10   }
11   void *operator new( size_t size )
12   {
13       int *p;
14       if( p = malloc( size + sizeof(int)) );
15           *p++ = HEAP;
16       return p;
17   }
```

an enumerated type is not an int

There are several things going on. First, a member of an enumerated type can be implicitly converted to `int`. Unlike C, a member of an enumerated type in C++ is not an `int`—it is a unique type. As a consequence, a `new` overload that takes a `where_from` argument does not conflict with an additional `new` overload that takes an `int` argument. For example, the following code implements two distinct overloads of `operator new()`:

```
enum etype { ENUM_MEM };
operator new( etype x ){/*...*/}
operator new( int   x ){/*...*/}
```

The call `new(ENUM_MEM)` uses the first version, a call of `new(0)` uses the second.[8]

overloading delete

The next issue is deletion. You can overload the `delete` operator if you like. There are two syntaxes. The first is

```
void operator delete( void *p ){ /*...*/ };
```

and in C++ 2.1, you can also use

```
void operator delete( void *p, size_t size ){ /*...*/ };
```

An overload that uses the second form is passed the size of the deleted object (in bytes). The problem is that these are the only two possibilities. Unlike `new()`, you

---

[8] A bug in Borland C++, version 2.0 does not handle this situation correctly. This version of the compiler incorrectly treats an enumerated-type object as an `int`.

cannot pass additional arguments to `delete`. A statement like `delete`(10) x is illegal.

The current `new` overload needs a special-purpose `delete`, though—memory allocated from the stack with an `alloca()` call cannot be passed to `free()`. The situation is handled by adding a `malloc()`-like header to the memory. The earlier `new` overload allocated size+`sizeof(int)` bytes and then put the source argument to `new()` into the header. The subsequent ++p increments the returned pointer beneath the header. A `delete` overload can now be provided to deallocate memory:

```
void operator delete( void *vp )
{
    int *p = (int*) vp; // convert type to simplify the code.

    if( p[-1] == HEAP )
        free(--p);
    else if( p[-1] != STACK )
    {
        fprintf(stderr, "Memory not from overloaded new\n");
        exit(1);
    }
}
```

This overload looks backward from the incoming pointer to see if a header is there, decrementing the pointer to pass it to `free()` in the case of HEAP memory. Two overloads of `new` were required (above) to ensure that a header is in place for all memory. The single `operator delete()` overload must handle all deletions, regardless of whether the memory came from the special-purpose `new`.

Here's a similar `new`/`delete` overload to allow access to both the near and far heaps in an 8086 mixed-model program:

allocate from far memory, `new`(FAR)

```
enum far_indicator  { FAR };

void far* operator new( size_t size, far_indicator )
{
    return farmalloc( size );
}

void operator delete( void far* p )
{
    farfree( p );
}
```

Get memory from the far heap like this:

```
char far* p = new(FAR) char[128];
// ...
delete p; // p is a far* so should get overloaded delete
```

I've used the Borland C++ memory-allocation system (but see footnote 8).

As another example, Listing 4.10 demonstrates how you can incorporate the run-time memory monitor from Chapter One into C++. As with the system in Chapter One, I'm using a `wrapper` layer to hold the debugging information. (It's

a debugging version of `new`

declared on line 11 of Listing 4.10.) The `new` overload logs a message to the monitor file on line 33 and then allocates enough memory for both the wrapper and the required object on line 35. The matching `delete` on line 57 logs a message and frees the memory. Finally, the macro on line 83 maps a statement like this

```
char *p = new int;
```

into

```
char *p = new( __FILE__, __LINE__ ) int;
```

Files that include *newdebug.h* will use the debugging version of `new` and files that don't use the standard version. All you need to do is remove the `#include` <newdebug.h> to switch from the debugging system to the standard one.

Listing 4.10. *newdebug.h*— A Debugging Memory Allocator

```
 1    #ifndef __NEWDEBUG_HPP
 2    #define __NEWDEBUG_HPP
 3
 4    #ifdef __NEWDEBUG_METHODS
 5    #include <stdlib.h>
 6    #include <stdio.h>
 7
 8    typedef long align;                         // worst-case alignment type
 9    #define MAGIC ( (align)0xabcd1234L )
10    //-----------------------------------------------------------------------
11    struct wrapper
12    {
13        int  line_number;
14        char *file_name;
15        align signature;
16    };
17
18    FILE *Logfile;
19    //-----------------------------------------------------------------------
20    void *operator new ( size_t size, char *file, int line )
21    {
22        wrapper *wp;
23
24        // Open the log file on the first call. Depending on
25        // exit() to close it.
26
27        if( !Logfile && !(Logfile = fopen("new.log", "w")) )
28        {
29            fprintf(stderr,"new: Can't open log file\n");
30            exit(1);
31        }
32
33        fprintf( Logfile, "%s: %d ", file, line );
34
35        if( wp = (wrapper *)malloc( sizeof(wrapper) + size ) )
36        {
37            wp->signature   = MAGIC;
38            wp->line_number = line;
```

→

Listing 4.10. continued...

```
39              wp->file_name  = file;
40
41              fprintf(Logfile,"(Allocating memory at %p)\n", wp );
42              ++wp;
43          }
44      else
45          {
46              fprintf( Logfile,"(Out of memory)\n" );
47
48  #        ifdef EXIT_ON_NO_MEMORY
49                  fprintf( stderr,"(Out of memory)\n" );
50                  exit( 1 );
51  #        endif
52          }
53
54      return (void *)wp;
55  }
56  //-------------------------------------------------------------------
57  void operator delete( void *p )
58  {
59      wrapper *wp = (wrapper *)p ;
60
61      if( !p )    // Null pointer okay, but print log message
62          fprintf(Logfile, "NULL pointer passed to delete\n");
63      else
64          {
65              --wp;
66              if( wp->signature != MAGIC )
67                  {
68                      fprintf(stderr,"Bad pointer passed to delete\n");
69                      exit( 1 );
70                  }
71              else
72                  {
73                      fprintf(Logfile,"%s: %d (Freeing memory at %p)\n",
74                                      wp->file_name, wp->line_number, wp );
75                      wp->signature = ~MAGIC;
76                      free(wp);
77                  }
78          }
79  }
80  #endif // __NEWDEBUG_METHODS
81  //-------------------------------------------------------------------
82  void *operator new ( size_t size, char *file, int line );
83  #define new new( __FILE__, __LINE__ )
84  //-------------------------------------------------------------------
85  #ifdef __NEWDEBUG_DEBUG
86
87  main()
88  {
89      char *p = new char[128];
90      delete p;
91  }
```

→

Listing 4.10. continued...

```
92
93   #endif  // __NEWDEBUG_DEBUG
94   #endif  // __NEWDEBUG_HPP
```

---

local new and delete overloads

You can also provide local instances of `operator new()` (and `delete`) for a specific class. There's an example in Listing 4.11. The problem that's solved here is the relative inefficiency of `malloc()` and `free()`. A program that uses too many calls to these functions pays an often significant run-time penalty. A program that uses a binary tree in an active fashion, adding and deleting many nodes over the life of the tree, can fall into the previous category if every tree node is allocated from `malloc()` and deallocated with `free()`.

A better strategy manages a local linked list of deleted nodes. That is, a delete operation adds the node to a free list rather than giving it to `free()`. A subsequent allocation operation calls `malloc()` only if there are no previously deleted nodes on the list; otherwise, it just unlinks and returns a free-list element. Only when the program is finished with the tree (when the last node is deleted) will the memory manager traverse the free list and pass all the elements to `free()`, one at a time.

The code in Listing 4.11 implements this strategy. The **static**, `free_list` field declared on line four is a head-of-free-list pointer that's shared by all instances of a `tree_node`. There's also an instance count maintained in `instance`, declared on the next line. The count is incremented on line ten (in the constructor). The matching decrement is in the destructor on line 16. When the count goes to zero, there are no active `tree_node` objects, and the entire free list is deleted.

The memory management is handled by local overloads of **new** and **delete** on lines 24 and 39 of Listing 4.11. The **delete** overload just links the deleted node to the head of the free list, using the `right` pointer as the next-element-in-list pointer. The **new** overload unlinks objects from the list if they're there; otherwise, it gets a new node from `malloc()`. Note that the local overloads use the scope operator to call the global-level **new** and **delete** on lines 20 and 32.

local new cannot create arrays

There are a few caveats of local **new** and **delete** overloads. First, they are used only to create and delete single objects of that class. They are never used to create arrays of objects, for example. This restriction is not a problem here because it's the nature of a tree to allocate nodes one at a time. In any event, using the global **new** rather than the local one doesn't cause serious problems because the global **delete** is also used to free the memory. You won't use the local free list, but the program will still work.

local operator new(), operator delete() static

Finally, local **new** and **delete** overloads are treated as **static** member functions—they can access only **static** data members of the current class. They have to work this way because they're called as part of the construction process before the constructor is called.

Listing 4.11. *treenode.cpp*— Local **new** and **delete** Overloads

```
 1   class tree_node
 2   {
 3       tree_node *left, *right;      // child pointers
 4       static tree_node *free_list;
 5       static int         instance;
 6
 7   public:
 8       tree_node( void )  .
 9       {
10           ++instance;
11           left = right = NULL;
12       }
13       ~tree_node( void )
14       {
15           tree_node *p;
16           if( --instance == 0 )           // deleted the last node
17               for( p = free_list; p ; )
18               {
19                   p = free_list->next;
20                   ::delete free_list;     // use global delete
21               }
22       }
23
24       operator new( size_t size )
25       {
26           void *p;
27           if( free_list )
28           {
29               p = free_list;
30               free_list = free_list->right;
31           }
32           else if( !(p = ::new char[size]) )  // use global new
33           {
34               fprintf(stderr, "No memory for tree_node\n");
35               exit( 1 );
36           }
37           return p;
38       }
39       operator delete( void *p );
40       {
41           p->right = free_list;
42           free_list = p;
43       }
44   };
45   tree_node *tree_node::free_list;
```

5

Derivation

Although all the examples in previous chapters are useful, the heart of C++ —and the part of the language that makes it object oriented—is derivation. You'll remember from Chapter One that the process of derivation is the process of adding fields to an existing structure to form a new structure. Taking the linked-list example from Chapter One as a case in point, you can create a useful general-purpose class without having any knowledge of how that class will be used. The linked list functions that manipulated `list` and `list_ele` structures in Chapter One were completely general purpose—they could manipulate all sorts of lists. They accomplished this feat, first by concentrating into the `list` and `list_ele` classes those components of list manipulation that are shared by all lists, and then by providing a group of functions that can manipulate those common components. This general-purpose list structure models a C++ *base class*.

base class

The list is customized to a specific application by making the general-purpose structure bigger—adding fields for a key, and so forth. The enlarged structure, of which the base class is a component, is the *derived class*. When a base-class function, which can access only those fields that are defined in the base-class structure, needs information about the derived class (as when it needs to compare the key fields in two derived-class objects) it calls a function that is supplied with the derived-class definition.

derived class

The advantages of this approach are characterized by the phrase *code reuse*, which means, simply, that the functions that manipulate base-class objects are reused in all derived-class objects. Once you solve a problem in the general case, you don't need to solve it again.

code reuse

One strength of C++ is the ability to do the foregoing with somewhat less work than is required in C, and this chapter describes the mechanics.

5.1 Relationships between Classes

Again, to review a bit, there are three possible relationships between classes. In a friend relationship, one class adds a capability to another as if the two classes were really a single, two-component class. This relationship was discussed earlier in the context of a linked-list class that was a friend of a list-element class. The second inter-class relationship is really an intra-class relationship—the case where an object of one class is a member of another class, such as an `employee_record` that has a `fixed` field representing the salary. The enclosed class (the `fixed` field) is called an *instance variable*. The third relationship is the derivation relationship, where one class is formed by extending the definition of another class to include additional fields or member functions. The original class is the *base class,* and the extended definition forms a *derived class.*

instance variable

base class, derived class

The tests to use for the last two relationships are the *has-a* and the *is-a* (or *kind-of*) test. If something "has an" attribute, then that attribute should be represented by a field or instance variable. If something "is a" kind of thing, then it derives from that thing.

has-a, is-a (kind-of)

Take, for example, an employee record which *has* a field of type `fixed` that represents the salary. An employee record *has* a `fixed` salary—it *is* not a salary. In this situation the `salary` field is an instance variable—an instance of the `fixed` class is used as a field in the `employee_record` class. You can represent this relationship as follows:

```
employee record:
    fixed  salary;
    fixed  deductions;
```

On the other hand, a group of employee records might be arranged in a linked list. In this case, an employee record *is* a linked-list element—an `employee_record` class should derive from a `list_ele` class. An employee record is a *kind of* list element—it has all the same attributes as a linked-list element. You can represent this relationship as follows:

```
list_ele:
```
```
employee record:
    fixed  salary;
    fixed  deductions;
```

The arrow points from the base to the derived class and represents the flow of inheritance. All objects of type `employee_record` effectively contain (inherit) all the public elements of a `list_ele`.

What if all employee records are not going to be members of linked lists? You will be wasting a lot of space carrying around fields used for linked-list management if you are not going to use these fields. Ideally, you want a vanilla `employee_record` and also an `employee_list_ele` that is an `employee_record` that can be put into a list. You represent this sort of inheritance relationship as follows:

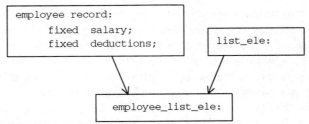

```
employee record:
      fixed   salary;
      fixed   deductions;
```

```
list_ele:
```

```
employee_list_ele:
```

multiple inheritance   This relationship is called *multiple inheritance*. The derived class (an `employee_list_ele`) has the characteristics (fields and functions) of both base classes (`employee_record` and `list_ele`). All functions that can manipulate an `employee_record` or a `list_ele` can also manipulate an `employee_list_ele`. The derived class is said to have multiple base classes. You can also declare a simple `employee_record` if you like, and it can be manipulated by `employee_record` functions. It cannot be put into a list, though.

But what if there is more than one type of employee? There will probably be one group of fields within an employee record that are required for all employees (`name`, `salary`, etc.). But there will be other fields that are used only by certain classes of employees. A salesperson's record might need a dollar-volume-of-sales field to figure commissions, for example. A manager's record might need a list of pointers to the employee records of each person in the manager's group. (You can use the earlier `employee_list_ele` class for this purpose.) You don't want several almost identical records in existence because they're too hard to maintain. Similarly, you don't want unused fields in a record. An object-oriented solution to this problem combines all common fields into common base classes, and the unique fields are divided among several derived classes. This way one group of subroutines can manipulate the common data in all the derived classes. The derivation hierarchy, which allows for two kinds of employee records that can (but don't have to) be in a linked list, is pictured in Figure 5.1.

This graph describes several potential structures. A simple `employee_record` is the first. The `manager` structure and the `salesperson` structure contain all the fields that are in an `employee_record` plus a few more. All of the subroutines that can manipulate an `employee_record` can also manipulate a `manager` and a `salesperson`. A `manager_list_ele` structure contains all the fields of a `manager` (including those from the `employee_record`), and the fields from a `list_ele` are added as well. A `salesperson_list_ele` contains all the fields in both a `salesperson` and a `list_ele`. Consequently, all functions that can manipulate either an `employee_record` or a `list_ele` can also manipulate a `manager_list_ele` or a `salesperson_list_ele`.

A similar example is a data-entry screen, which *is* a window, so a `data_entry` class should properly be derived from a `window` class. This way, all the window-management functions (move, resize, hide, etc.) could also manipulate data-entry screens. On the other hand, a common implementation of a `data_entry` object is a window that contains several subwindows, one for each field to be entered.

In this case, a data-entry screen *has* several fields, which are each instance variables of class `window` nested within the `data_entry` structure. So here's a case where an object both *is* a window and *has* windows as well. Not only does a `data_entry` structure derive from the `window` class, but it also contains instance variables of class `window`.

The point of all this is to minimize the amount of code that you have to write. Once you've created the `employee_record` class, all the **public** member functions of that class can be used to manipulate objects of any class that derives from an `employee_record`. You get this functionality simply by telling the compiler that some new class derives from an existing class. The base class, then, should hold all the fields that are needed by *all* of the derived class objects—the fields held in common.

Sometimes this last test (of commonality) can be used to decide whether to use derivation. Take, for example, a `window` class. You can derive a `red_window`, a `yellow_window`, and a `green_window` from a colorless `window` base class, but each of these derived classes would probably have a field (probably a **const** field, but a field nonetheless) that represented the color. Since this field is held in common in all the derived classes, then derivation is the wrong choice to make. You should have a `window` class with a `color` attribute—a field in a `window` that represents the color. You can then change the color with a `set_color()` member function.

Although derivation hierarchies are often arranged as trees, they actually form a *directed acyclic graph*, or *DAG*. A DAG is a tree in which a child can have multiple parents. No child ever points back up to an ancestor, though, so there are no cycles—circular paths through the tree. Some compilers detect derivation hierarchies that have cycles and refuse to process them; other compilers just hang when they encounter a cyclic class definition, so be careful.

directed acyclic graph, DAG

Figure 5.1. A Complex Class Hierarchy

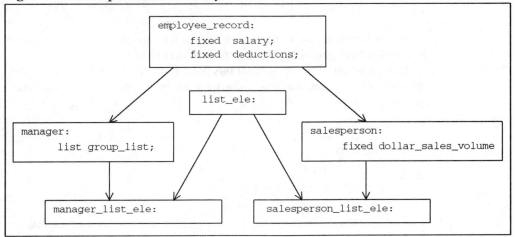

5.2 Instance Variables

objects of one class contained in another

Before jumping into derivation per se, it's useful to start out with a look at instance variables—contained objects. Instance variables are really half way between a simple class and a base/derived class. Here's an example:

```
class B
{
    b_private_data;
    b_private_funct();
public:
    b_public_data;
    b_public_funct();
};

class A
{
    int a_data;
    B b_obj;                // instance variable of class B
    a_private_funct();
public:
    a_public_funct();
};
```

instance variable not a base class

An instance variable is not the same as a base class because there's no inheritance relationship. The fact that class A contains a field of class B does not give functions that manipulate class B objects the ability to manipulate class A objects as well. Moreover, A's member functions can access only the **public** data and member functions of the class B object. The syntax for doing so is just like a nested structure in C:

```
A::a_public_funct()
{
    b_obj.b_public_funct();              // Here's one way
    this->b_obj.b_public_funct();        // Here's another
}
```

Since b_obj is here a **private** member of A, it (and its members) can be accessed only by member functions of A, just like a normal data field.

initializing instance variables

I've brought up instance variables at this point primarily because I want to discuss the way that they are initialized. Consider our employee record that contains a fixed field:

```
class employee
{
    string name;
    fixed  salary;
public:
    employee( char *name );
};
```

The most obvious way to initialize the salary field is from the body of a constructor, like this:

```
employee::employee( char *emp_name )
{
    fixed get_salary_from_database_for( char *name );

    salary = get_salary_from_database_for( emp_name );
    name   = emp_name;
}
```

The only problem is that there's more work going on than necessary. Since all fields in a `class` can be accessed from the constructor, it's imperative that the instance variables actually exist before the constructor is executed. That is, the constructors for all instance variables must be executed before the constructor for the current class is executed. In this way, member functions associated with the instance variable can safely be called from the current class's constructor.

In the current example, the compiler initializes the `name` and `salary` fields—before the constructor for class `employee` is executed—by using the default constructors for the `string` and `fixed` classes. It then overwrites the initial values of the `employee` and `salary` fields by calling the **operator=**() overloads from the `string` and `fixed` classes. The compiler also has to call `fixed::fixed(double)` to convert the right operand of the assignment to match the `fixed::operator=(fixed)` prototype. [`get_salary_from_database_for()` returns a **double**.]

This is a lot of work, of course. It's better to initialize the `fixed` field to the correct value to begin with, and you can do this with the member-initialization list that was discussed earlier in the context of **const** members of a class. The syntax is

member-
initialization list

```
double get_salary_from_database_for( name );

employee::employee( char *emp_name ) :
                    name    ( emp_name ),
                    salary ( get_salary_from_database_for(emp_name) ) {}
```

The `name(emp_name)` in the member-initialization list tells the compiler that it should use the `char*` constructor for the `string` object to initialize the `name` field, passing the constructor `emp_name` as its argument. Similarly, the `fixed` class's **double** constructor is used directly.

The member-initialization-list entry works much like the following declaration:

```
string employee( employee_name );
fixed  salary  ( get_salary_from_database_for(employee) ) {}
```

The

```
salary( get_salary_from_database_for(employee) )
```

in the member-initialization list is not a constructor call any more than the previous definition is a constructor call. It just tells the compiler "when you call the constructor for the `salary` field, use my argument to determine which constructor to use, and pass my argument to that constructor." Constructors for the instance variables are called in the order that the declarations appear in the **class** definition, and destructors are called in the opposite order. The ordering of the fields within the member-initialization list is immaterial.

The argument used in the member-initialization list can be of arbitrary complexity—it can include expressions involving function calls, objects of some class, constructor arguments, and so forth. You should try not to use the member-initialization list to initialize one member of the class from another member of the same class. Fields are guaranteed to be initialized in order of declaration, but the resulting code can be confusing. For example, this works:

```
class instance
{
public:
    instance( int x         ); // int constructor
    instance( instance &right ); // copy constructor
};

class containing
{
    instance first_b;
    instance second_b;
public:
    containing(): first_b(10), second_b( first_b ) {}
};
```

This does not (I've swapped the two instance declarations):

```
class containing
{
    instance second_b;
    instance first_b;
public:
    containing(): first_b(10), second_b( first_b ) {}
};
```

order of initialization of instance variables

Order of initialization is controlled by order of declaration, not by the order in which fields are listed in the member-initialization list. In the second example, first_b will not itself be initialized when it is used to initialize second_b. Unfortunately, most compilers accept the foregoing without so much as a whimper. Avoid the situation altogether by not using one field in a **class** or **struct** to initialize another. For example, the following modification to the code eliminates the problem:

```
class containing2
{
    instance second_b;
    instance first_b;
public:
    containing2(): first_b(10), second_b(10) {}
};
```

The initialization process is recursive. If an instance variable itself contains instance variables, the innermost classes are created first. The program in Listing 5.1 demonstrates the process. The output is presented in Table 5.1.

Listing 5.1. *instance.cpp*— Demonstrate Recursive Instance-Variable Initialization

```
 1    #include <stream.hpp>
 2
 3    class inner
 4    {
 5    public:
 6        inner()       { cout << "inner default constructor\n"; }
 7        inner(char *s){ cout << "inner char* constructor (" << s << ")\n"; }
 8    };
 9
10    class middle
11    {
12        inner x;
13    public:
14        middle()              {cout << "middle default constructor\n";          }
15        middle(char *s):x(s){cout << "middle char* constructor("<<s<<")\n";}
16    };
17
18    class outer
19    {
20        inner i;
21        inner j;
22        middle k;
23    public:
24        outer ()                   {cout<<"outer default constructor\n"; }
25        outer (char *s):j(s),k(s){cout<<"outer char* constructor ("<<s<<")\n"; }
26    };
27
28    main()
29    {
30        outer a;
31        cout << "--------------------------------\n" ;
32        outer b = "doo wha";
33    }
```

5.2.1 Object Copying and Instance Variables

There's one serious gotcha in the use of instance variables. The mechanism used for copying objects often does not work as you might expect. I'll demonstrate with an example.

By way of preparation, Listing 5.2 contains stripped-down versions of the string and fixed classes from earlier chapters. The string class has the full complement of constructors and an operator=() as well. As with the earlier string implementation, the actual string is stored in dynamic memory, allocated by the constructor and freed by the destructor. The copy constructor does a deep copy, allocating a new buffer for the object under construction and copying the source-object buffer's contents into the target object's newly allocated buffer. Similarly, string::operator=() frees the existing buffer and allocates a new one to hold the copy. A shallow copy (in which the source object's buf field is just copied into the destination object's buf field) won't work here because you

deep, shallow copy

Table 5.1. Output from Listing 5.1

Output	Comments
`inner `**`default`**` constructor`	i
`inner `**`default`**` constructor`	j
`inner `**`default`**` constructor`	the x in k
`middle `**`default`**` constructor`	k itself
`outer `**`default`**` constructor`	the a in main()
`inner `**`default`**` constructor`	i. The default constructor is used because there's no i(s) in the member initialization list on line 25 of Listing 5.1.
`inner `**`char*`**` constructor (doo wha)`	j
`inner `**`char*`**` constructor (doo wha)`	the x nested in k
`middle `**`char*`**` constructor (doo wha)`	the k itself
`outer `**`char*`**` constructor (doo wha)`	the b in main()

then would have two objects whose buf fields both addressed the same physical memory. Problems would arise when one of the objects went out of scope, freeing the shared buffer in the process, and leaving the other object pointing at garbage memory.

The stripped-down string class also provides an **operator char***() to allow easy access to the internal buf field. I discussed the problem with this approach in Chapter Three—it grants public access to private data, a practice that could cause difficulty if you store the pointer returned from **operator char***() in a global variable and then let the original string object go out of scope, thereby destroying the internal buffer and invalidating the global variable. I'm using the approach now because it's easy and I didn't want to complicate the example further than necessary.

Note that string::**operator char***() function modifies its behavior when DEBUG is defined so that it prints, not only the buffer's contents, but its location as well. We'll see why this extra information is useful in a moment.

The string class's **char*** constructor on line 11 of Listing 5.2 uses the default-argument mechanism to supply an empty string if the argument is missing. Since all of its arguments default to some value, the **char*** constructor is used as the default constructor as well.

The stripped-down fixed class at the bottom of Listing 5.2 is simpler than string. It stores a fixed-point number, initially a **double** value, but stored, scaled up by a factor of 100, in a **long**. The fixed class's **double** constructor also serves as the default constructor because its single argument defaults to zero. Note that the fixed class doesn't need a copy constructor or **operator**=() function because a C-style (shallow) structure copy—the mechanism used by the compiler when no alternative is provided—works fine in this case.

Listing 5.2. Stripped-Down String and Fixed Classes

```
 1   #include <string.h>
 2   #include <stdio.h>
 3   #include <stdlib.h>
 4
 5   #define DEBUG    // Activate debugging version of string::operator char*()
 6
 7   class string
 8   {
 9       char *buf;
10   public:
11       string ( const char *s = "" ){ buf = strdup(s);      }
12       string ( const string &r    ){ buf = strdup(r.buf); }
13       ~string( void                ){ free(buf);            }
14       string &operator=( const string &r )
15       {
16           free(buf);
17           buf = strdup( r.buf );
18           return *this;
19       }
20       operator char*() const
21       {
22           #ifdef DEBUG
23               static char debug_buf[128];
24               sprintf(debug_buf, "%s (@ 0x%p)", buf, buf );
25               return debug_buf;
26           #else
27               return buf;
28           #endif
29       }
30   };
31   //-----------------------------------------------------------------
32   class fixed
33   {
34       long num;
35   public:
36       fixed( double n = 0.0 ) { num = (long)(n * 100.0);      }
37       operator double() const { return (double)num / 100.0; }
38   };
```

Now let's put the foregoing classes to work. The simple implementation of the employee record in Listing 5.3 uses a **struct**.

Listing 5.4 holds a small main() to test the record. It declares an object (fred), initializes it, then tests the copy process with a second declaration (temp), initializing it from fred. Finally, it tests assignment with an explicit assignment of fred to temp.

The output from this test function seems okay at first glance, but it shows up a serious problem on closer examination. It looks like this:

Listing 5.3. An Employee Record

```
1   struct employee
2   {
3       string name;
4       fixed  salary;
5       int    part_time; // employee is a part-time employee
6   };
```

Listing 5.4. A Test Function for the Employee Record, struct Version

```
1   void emp_print( employee *p; )
2   {
3       printf( "Employee: %s\n", (char*)  p->name   );
4       printf( "Salary    %f\n", (double) p->salary );
5       printf( "part time %s\n", p->part_time ? "yes" : "no" );
6   }
7
8   void main()
9   {
10      employee fred;
11      fred.name      = "Flintstone, Fred";
12      fred.salary    = 20000.00;
13      fred.part_time = 0;
14
15      employee temp = fred;
16
17      printf("---------------------- fred:\n");
18      emp_print( &fred );
19      printf("---------------------- temp (initial):\n");
20      print( &temp );
21
22      temp = fred;
23      printf("---------------------- temp (after assignment):\n");
24      emp_print( &temp );
25  }
```

```
---------------------- fred:
Employee: Flintstone, Fred (@ 0x0C06)
Salary    20000.000000
part time no
---------------------- temp (initial):
Employee: Flintstone, Fred (@ 0x0C06)
Salary    20000.000000
part time no
---------------------- temp (after assignment):
Employee: Flintstone, Fred (@ 0x0C06)
Salary    20000.000000
part time no
```

The unexpected thing (at least to me) is the location field printed by the `string` class's debug-mode `operator char*()` function. The records look reasonable in all other respects—the copy operations seem to be working—but the `buf` fields of the `string` instance variables are all the same. That is, the `buf` contained within the `name` within `fred` has the same value as the `buf` contained within the `name` within `temp`—a shallow copy has been used for the `string` instance variables. The `string` class has both a copy constructor and an `operator=()` function (which would allocate new buffers), but neither were called.

This bug is particularly insidious because, if the location field weren't printed—and it would not normally be printed—everything would seem to be working properly. Also, note that a shallow copy is a reasonable action for the `salary` field because the `fixed` class contains no pointers. Consequently, your code could seem to work properly until you introduced a new field of some class that did contain pointers, and thus required a deep copy.

So, what's going on? As I said earlier, all objects that don't have copy constructors or `operator=()` functions are provided with versions of these functions by the compiler, and the supplied versions work just like a C structure copy works. Put another way, if a class doesn't have a copy constructor or `operator=()`, then a C-style structure copy is used to copy the object. There's more to it, though. Only the containing class is examined when the compiler determines how to copy an object. The existence of any copy constructors or `operator=()` functions within the instance variable are ignored—these member functions of the contained-class object are not called.

problems with compiler-supplied `operator=()`

So, let's try to fix the problem by turning `employee` into a real class rather than a simple `struct`. (I say "try" because the first attempt won't work, either.) The first attempt to redefine `employee` is shown in Listing 5.5. The data fields are now `private`, I've moved the `print()` function from the test routine into the class itself, and I've also added a constructor to set up the internal fields.

Note that I've used a member-initialization list on line 14 of Listing 5.5 to set up the instance-variable fields in order to avoid an unnecessary copy operation. Had I replaced the `name(emp_name)` in the list with a `name=emp_name` inside the body of the constructor, for example, the compiler would have initialized the `name` field with default constructor and then modified the field by calling `string::operator=()`. The `name(emp_name)` in the member-initialization list causes the compiler to initialize `name` to the correct value to begin with.

I've also provided a simple copy constructor and `operator=()` function at the bottom of the class.

A modified test `main()` looks like this:

```
void main()
{
    employee fred( "Flintstone, Fred", 20000.00, 0 );
    employee temp = fred;
```

Listing 5.5. employee Redefined as a Simple Class

```
1    class employee
2    {
3        string name;
4        fixed  salary;
5        int    part_time;
6    public:
7        void print()
8        {
9            printf( "Employee: %s\n", (char*)  name   );
10           printf( "Salary     %f\n", (double) salary );
11           printf( "part time %s\n", part_time ? "yes" : "no" );
12       }
13
14       employee( char *emp_name, double emp_salary, int emp_part_time )
15                                       : salary( emp_salary ),
16                                         name  ( emp_name   )
17       {
18           part_time = emp_part_time;
19       }
20
21       employee( void ) : salary(0.0), name(""), part_time(0) { }
22
23       employee( employee &r )
24       {
25           part_time = r.part_time;
26       }
27       operator=( employee &r )
28       {
29           part_time = r.part_time;
30       }
31   };
```

```
              printf("----------------------- fred:\n");
              fred.print();
              printf("----------------------- temp (initial):\n");
              temp.print();

              temp = fred;
              printf("----------------------- temp (after assignment):\n");
              temp.print();
          }
```

The output from this program is even more disturbing than in the last round, though. Here's what it looks like:

```
----------------------- fred:
Employee: Flintstone, Fred (@ 0x0C06)
Salary    20000.000000
part time no
```

```
----------------------- temp (initial):
Employee:  (@ 0x0C1C)
Salary     0.000000
part time no

----------------------- temp (after assignment):
Employee:  (@ 0x0C1C)
Salary     0.000000
part time no
```

The two copies now look nothing like the original `fred`. The problems with the modified version are caused by the presence of the copy constructor and `operator=()` functions that I just provided. The explicit functions replace the default compiler-generated functions, so no implicit shallow copying is performed. But the entire copy operation is now the responsibility of the new functions—the compiler does nothing at all, and the copy constructor and `operator=()` in Listing 5.5 aren't doing nearly enough work.

There are actually two problems. First, the modified copy constructor has no member-initialization list. When the compiler calls a constructor that has no member initialization list—and the copy constructor is a constructor—the compiler uses the default constructors of any instance variables to initialize the versions in the target object. That is, the `string` class's default constructor is used to initialize the `name` field in the copy because the `employee` class's copy constructor has no member-initialization list. Since the `string`-class's default constructor allocates an empty buffer, the `name` field in the copy is empty.

copy constructor member-initialization list

I've fixed this problem on line 23 of Listing 5.6 by adding a member-initialization list to the containing class's copy constructor. The `name(r.name)` chains to the instance variable's copy constructor—it causes the `string` copy constructor to be called, passing it `r.name`, when the compiler gets around to initializing the `name` field. (Instance variables are initialized in the order of declaration within the `class` statement—the ordering of the member-initialization list is immaterial.) I could also have put a `name=r.name` inside the copy constructor, but that would add an unnecessary inefficiency—the default constructor would be used to initialize the target field, then `string::operator=()` would be called to change the value to match `r.name`.

Note that the member-initialization list works even if the instance variable doesn't have an explicit copy constructor, as is the case with the `fixed salary` field. The compiler-generated constructor, which does a shallow copy, is called in this situation.

The second copying problem is similar to the previous one. The `operator=()` function works much like the copy constructor, but it copies into previously initialized memory. It must also explicitly copy all the fields from the source to the target object, though. Since the `operator=()` function is not a constructor, it can't have a member-initialization list, and it must use an explicit assignment to do its work. Put another way, an instance variable is treated just like a normal structure field once the construction process is complete. The instance variable is not copied to the target object unless it's copied explicitly—with an assignment in the class's `operator=()` function. I've fixed the problem in the current example by

containing class needs `operator=()`

Listing 5.6. A Working Employee-Record Class

```
1   class employee
2   {
3       string name;
4       fixed  salary;
5       int    part_time;
6   public:
7       void print()
8       {
9           printf( "Employee: %s\n", (char*)  name   );
10          printf( "Salary    %f\n", (double) salary );
11          printf( "part time %s\n", part_time ? "yes" : "no" );
12      }
13
14      employee( char *emp_name, double emp_salary, int emp_part_time )
15                                      : salary( emp_salary ),
16                                        name  ( emp_name   )
17      {
18          part_time = emp_part_time;
19      }
20
21      employee( void ) : salary(0.0), name(""), part_time(0) { }
22
23      employee( employee &r ) : name(r.name), salary(r.salary) //<- NEW
24      {
25          part_time = r.part_time;
26      }
27      employee &operator=( employee &r )
28      {
29          part_time = r.part_time;
30          name      = r.name;                 //<- NEW
31          salary    = r.salary;               //<- NEW
32          return *this;
33      }
34  };
```

adding assignments on lines 30 and 31 of Listing 5.6.

Note that the name-field assignment on line 30 of Listing 5.6 calls string::**operator**=() to do its work. The salary field assignment on the next line uses normal C-style structure copying because there is no fixed:: **operator**=() function.[1]

---

[1] Skipping ahead a bit, an explicit call to the **operator**=() function is also possible. It will look like this:

      string::**operator**=(r.name)

An explicit function call like the foregoing won't work if the instance class doesn't have an **operator**=() overload—as is the case with the salary field in the current example—so it's best to use an equals sign.

The two copying problems just described are major sources of grief even to experienced C++ programmers. Some newer compilers go part of the way towards solving the problem by always using the instance variable's copy constructor (if there is one) when copying the contained object as part of an initialization. That is, the copy constructors in these compilers implicitly chain to the copy constructors of all instance variables as if you had listed the instance-variable constructors in the member-initialization list. A compiler-generated copy constructor in a containing class will behave in the same way, changing to instance-variable copy constructors. Most compilers that do the foregoing do not extend the mechanism to assignment, however.

That the copy-constructor behavior described in the previous paragraph is not portable leads to a rule of thumb: **All classes that have instance variables should have a copy constructor that lists all of the instance variables in its member-initialization list.**

Unlike the copy constructor, a compiler-generated `operator=()` function never chains to the `operator=()` in the instance variable, even in compilers that support the extended copy mechanism just described. If the containing object has an `operator=()`, then this function must explicitly copy all the object's fields to the target object or the target object will have garbage in those fields. This behavior leads to a second rule of thumb: **All classes that have instance variables should have an `operator=()` function that explicitly copies all instance-variable fields to the target object.**

5.3 Inheritance and Derived Classes

An instance variable is in some ways a special case of derivation; that is, a base class is treated mechanically much like an instance variable is treated. It is effectively contained within the derived class, for example. The big difference is the inheritance process—a derived class inherits the `public` and `protected` members of the base class. An alternative declaration method is required to tell the compiler that a specific class is a base class rather than an instance variable. You couldn't, for example, just declare the base classes as fields of the derived class, as I had to do in the C examples in Chapter One, because a given class can have more than one base class. You can't declare two fields as both being the first field of a structure. (You can't use a `union` because both structures are active at the same time.)

I'll demonstrate the process with an example, yet another variation on the simplified linked-list class that I've used in previous chapters. The stripped-down versions of the `list` and `list_ele` base classes from Chapter Four are reproduced in Listing 5.7.

simplified list class

Again, the main point is that these functions can be written entirely in terms of base-class objects, without having to worry about what the actual list element is going to look like beyond what's in the `prev` and `next` pointers. Since all linked-list elements have `prev` and `next` pointers, these fields are put into the `list_ele` base class.

Listing 5.7. *striplist.cpp*— A Stripped-Down Linked-List Base Class

```
1    class list_ele
2    {
3        list_ele *next; // next list element
4        list_ele *prev; // previous list element
5    public:
6        static                    // static, so can be called w/o object.
7        init ( list_ele **headp )  // initialize head pointer in list class.
8        {
9            *headp = NULL;
10       }
11       insert( list_ele **headp )  // Insert current node into list at head.
12       {
13           prev   = NULL;
14           head   = *headp;
15           *headp = this;
16       }
17   };
18
19   class list
20   {
21       list_ele *head;
22   public:
23       list     (    void    ){ list_ele::init(&head); } // constructor
24       void add( list_ele *p ){ p->insert      (&head); } // add p to list
25   };
```

Now let's see how to do something useful with our list. Here's a new class that is essentially the `employee` class of the previous section, but with an addition:

```
class list_employee : public list_ele
{
    string name;
    fixed  salary;
public:
    employee( char *name );
};
```

The `: public list_ele` tells the compiler that `list_employee` derives from a `list_ele`. This means that all the characteristics of a `list_ele` are shared by a `list_employee`. All the functions that manipulate `list_ele` objects can also manipulate `list_employee` objects. All public fields and functions of the `list_ele` class can be treated as if they were declared inside a `list_employee`.

inheritance

(This last characteristic is *inheritance*.)

You can initialize and manipulate the `list_employee` in the normal way, just as if the base class weren't there, but you can now also put it into a list using the member functions of the `list` base class:

```
bedrock()
{
    list list_of_employees;
    list_of_employees.add( new
                        list_employee("Flintstone,Fred"));
}
```

The process can be simplified further by deriving a class from `list` that handles the mechanics of allocating space for a list element:

```
class employee_list : public list
{
public:
    void insert( char *name )
    {
        add( new list_employee( name ) );
    }
}
```

The `employee_list::insert()` function allocates memory for a list element using **new** and then inserts it into the list with a call to the base class's add-to-list function [`add()`]. Given the foregoing change, you can now modify `bedrock` to add an element to a list like this:

```
bedrock()
{
    employee_list  employees;              // list of employees
    employees.insert("Flintstone, Fred"); // add Fred to list
}
```

So, how does this all work? At the risk of repeating myself once too often, the derivation process extends the base-class (`list_ele`) definition by adding fields (the fields in `list_employee`) to it. The base class is effectively part of the derived class:

```
class list_ele  {  list_ele *next
                   list_ele *prev

                   string name;
                   fixed  salary;      }  class list_employee
```

derivation extends
base class

With the exception of constructors, destructors, and the **operator**=() function, all **public** and **protected** members (data and functions) in the base class are *inherited* by the derived class. This means that derived-class member functions can use **public** and **protected** data in the base class as if it were declared in the derived class. We saw this process earlier when `insert()` called `add()` to do its work—`add()` is a member of the base class that's called directly from a derived-class function.

public and **protected** members inherited

Nonmember functions can access base-class **public** data and functions in the same way, but they cannot access the **private** members. Here are all the possibilities:

```
class base
{
public:     int base_pub_f(), base_pub_data;
protected: int base_pro_f(), base_pro_data;
private:    int base_pri_f(), base_pri_data;
}

class derived : public base
{
    void goldilocks( void )
    {
      base_pub_f();             // okay
      base_pro_f();             // okay
      base_pri_f();             // ILLEGAL

      base_pub_data() = 0;      // okay
      base_pro_data() = 0;      // okay
      base_pri_data() = 0;      // ILLEGAL
    }
}

void rumpelstiltskin( void )
{
    derived d;

    d.base_pub_f();    // okay
    d.base_pro_f();    // ILLEGAL
    d.base_pri_f();    // ILLEGAL

    d.base_pub_data = 0; // okay
    d.base_pro_data = 0; // ILLEGAL
    d.base_pri_data = 0; // ILLEGAL
}
```

Since data members should always be **private**, it's really the member functions that are affected by the foregoing. Note that, as before, privacy does not grant invisibility. If you try to do any of the foregoing illegal operations, the resulting error message will probably be "you may not access this field" rather than "this field doesn't exist."

friendship not inherited

As a final inheritance issue, friendship is not inherited. If a base class has friends, the friend functions are not automatically made friends of the derived class. The derived class must explicitly grant friendship in this case. Given

```
class tom
{
    friend huck();
    //...
};

class becky : public tom
{
    //...
};
```

huck() **cannot** access becky's private members even though he's a friend of tom.

To do so, becky would have to grant friendship to huck() explicitly with a **friend** huck() definition.

In general, this inheritance issue causes no problems. A function that is a friend of a base class can manipulate derived-class objects without difficulty—it just won't be able to access the **private** members of the derived-class object. Offhand, I can think of no situation where a friend of the base class would need access to the derived-class component of the structure.

5.4 Type Conversion and Derived Classes

The next issue—type conversion from the derived to the base class—is perhaps more important than inheritance. A derived-class object effectively contains the base-class object within it. Similarly, the **this** pointer in a derived-class function is effectively the same as the **this** pointer in the base-class function. (Thinking back to the C analogy in Chapter One, the base class component of the derived-class object is at the top of the derived class—a pointer to one is also a pointer to the other.) Consequently, it's always safe to convert a derived-class object, reference, or pointer to a base-class object, reference, or pointer. It is this feature that gives you the ability to write base-class-level functions that can manipulate derived-class objects. The function is effectively manipulating the base-class component of the derived-class object. If the function takes a base-class object, reference, or pointer as an argument, then a derived-class object, reference, or pointer that's passed to that function is silently converted to the base class. We saw this process in action a moment ago when the add() function was declared like this

converting derived class to base class

```
class list
{
    //...
    void add( list_ele *p );
};
```

but is called with a pointer to an list_employee as its argument, not a list_ele pointer. The call looks like this:

```
list            list_of_employees;
list_employee *fred;

list_of_employees.add( fred );
```

Since an employee derives from a list_ele, fred is silently converted to a list_ele pointer when the function-call is processed. add(), then, manipulates the base-class component of the employee (the list_ele).

The same process applies to actual objects as well as pointers (and references). For example, the following code is perfectly legal:

```
list_employee   barney;
list_ele        duplicate_list_ele;

duplicate_list_ele = barney;
```

It copies the base-class component of the `list_employee` into the `list_ele` object. An `operator=()` function, if present in the `list_ele` structure, is used to do the copy; otherwise, C-style shallow copying is used. The source operand (`barney`) is, of course, not modified by this process.

can't use
base-class pointer
to traverse
derived-class array

It's important to note that the function that takes the base-class argument doesn't know or care that it's processing a derived-class object. Since the base-class object effectively resides at the top of the derived-class object, the `this` pointers are the same in both instances, and code that can manipulate a base-class object can also manipulate a derived-class object.

There's only one caveat. Since a base-class pointer can really point at a derived-class object, it's risky to use base-class pointers to traverse an array of objects. The following won't work:

```
class base                  { void print( void ); }
class derived : public base { int some_data;      };

base    *p;
derived array[10];

p = array;                      // works fine, no errors
for( i = 10; --i >= 0; )        // traverse array
    (p++)->print();             // no error, but doesn't work
```

The problem is that the compiler (at compile time) doesn't know that p actually points at a derived-class array (at run time). Consequently, the p++ increments p as if it were pointing at an object of class `base`.[2] Fix the problem by declaring p as a `derived*` rather than a `base*`.

5.5 Multiple Inheritance

multiple base
classes

Multiple base classes are also possible. For example, the following declarations let you create two kinds of employee records, one that can be in a list and a second that cannot. (I'm using the `employee` class from Listing 5.6 on page 230, which in turn uses the stripped-down `string` and `fixed` classes from Listing 5.2 on page 225.)

```
class employee_list_ele : public employee, public list_ele
{ /* no members */ };
```

----

[2] Skipping ahead a bit, once p is incorrectly incremented, the call to print() won't work either if print() is a virtual function. p must be pointing at a valid object or the compiler won't be able to find the virtual-function table.

An `employee_list_ele` inherits all the characteristics (public functions and data) of both base classes, and functions that manipulate objects of either base class can manipulate an `employee_list_ele` object as well. The `list` functions can manipulate `employee_list_ele` objects, for example. Since multiple base classes means that a derived class inherits fields from more than one class, this process is usually called *multiple inheritance*. An `employee` that is never placed in a list can be declared directly. An `employee_list_ele` is just like an `employee`, except that it can also be added to a list, so you declare an `employee_list_ele` if you want it in the list.

multiple inheritance

Note that the **public** must be repeated for the second base class in the `employee_list_ele` definition. Leaving it out is a serious problem that will be discussed in depth below.

Since the `employee_list_ele`—quite deliberately—has no elements in it, an `employee_list_ele` looks just like the earlier `employee_list` in memory and is manipulated in exactly the same way, but now you have the capability of declaring a simple `employee` that doesn't carry around unused linked-list fields.

Note that the compiler has to work a bit to do the derived-class-to-base-class conversion when there is more than one base class involved. Both base classes cannot be at the top of the structure. Nonetheless, the compiler must pass the base-class function a pointer to the correct base-class component of the derived-class structure. That is, the **this** pointer in the base-class function always holds the address of the correct base-class component of the derived-class object. The compiler does whatever is necessary to get that pointer set up correctly. When you have multiple base classes, part of the process of converting a derived-class object to a base-class object is figuring out where in the structure the base-class object is to be found, and then passing the address of the base-class component to the base-class function.

Occasionally situations can arise when you need to specify to which of several base classes a function belongs. You do this with the `::` operator. The syntax is *base_class*`::`*field_name*. Here's an example of when you'd use it. Say that you wanted a data structure that had the characteristics of both a tree and a linked list. The list is sorted by some criteria, and the tree is available when you need speedy random access. Here are the relevant class definitions:

ambiguity with multiple base classes, `::` operator

```
class tree{ public: add( tree_node *p ); }   // add node to tree
class list{ public: add( list_node *p ); }   // add node to list

class tree_list_node:  public tree_node, public list_node {/*...*/}

class tree_list: public tree, public list
{
    //...
}
```

Unfortunately, the writers of the `tree` and `list` class both—quite reasonably—chose to use `add()` as the name of the function that adds a new element to the data structure. The problem is that a simple call like the following won't work:

```
tree_list  list_of_things;
tree_list_node *p = new tree_list_node("Rubble, Barney");

list_of_things.add( p );
```

because the `tree_list` inherits the `add()` functions from both the `tree` and the
`list`. When you say `list_of_things.add()`, the compiler doesn't know which
base class's `add()` function to call. The `tree_list_node` argument can be converted to either base class, and the two `add()` functions have arguments that are
one or the other of the base classes.

In any event, you'd like to make insertions and deletions in your tree/list with a
single call that would manipulate both of the underlying data structures, so the best
solution to the foregoing is to add an `add()` function to the `tree_list` like this:

```
class tree_list: public tree, public list
{
    //...
public:
    add( tree_list_node *p )
    {
      tree::add( p );
      list::add( p );
    }
    //...
}
```

You use the `::` operator to tell the compiler which `add()` function to call.

**multiple, identical
base classes**

A related multiple-inheritance situation is not handled at all well by C++: the
problem of a node that must exist in two linked lists simultaneously. You can't
derive a class from the same base class twice. A declaration like the following is
guaranteed to create ambiguities:

```
class two_list: public list, public list {/*...*/};
```

The only solution is to encapsulate the base classes in an additional layer in order
to be able to specify which list is to be used at any given moment. Do it like this:

```
class list_one : public list {/*...*/}
class list_two : public list {/*...*/}

class two_list: public list_one, public list_two
{
    //...
public:
    add( two_list_node *p )
    {
      list_one::add( p );
      list_two::add( p );
    }
    //...
}
```

Note that you'll have to provide a member function in `two_list` for **every** public
function in `list` for this strategy to work.

5.5.1 Initialization and Copying under Derivation

Derived-class constructors are called much like the constructors for instance variables. The base-class constructors are called first, because the members of the base-class are available to the derived-class constructor. (The base class is the innermost one—it corresponds to the instance variable.) The compiler must ensure that the base class is initialized before it executes the derived-class constructor. If there are multiple base classes, they are called in the order that the base classes are listed in the `class` declaration.

The member-initialization list is pressed into service again, this time to pass arguments to the base-class constructors, even though the base class isn't, strictly speaking, a member. The only difference is that you use the base-class name rather than a field name. As with an instance variable, if a base class is not listed in a derived class's member-initialization list, then the base-class's default constructor is called when the derived class's constructor is used. For example:

member-initial-ization list

```
class employee
{
    employee( void     ){/*...*/}  // default constructor
    employee( char *name ){/*...*/}  // char* constructor
};

class list_emp_rec : public employee
{
    list_emp_rec(     void    )                    {/*...*/};
    list_emp_rec( char *name ): employee( name ) {/*...*/};
};
```

The default constructor for `list_emp_rec` has no member-initialization list, so the compiler uses the default constructor for both the base and derived class in a declaration like

```
list_emp_rec yazoo;
```

Since the `char*` constructor's member-initialization list does include the base class, specifying a `char*` argument, the base class's `char*` constructor is called when the derived-class's `char*` constructor is used. The following declaration calls the `char*` constructor in both the derived and base classes:

```
list_emp_rec yazoo = "yazoo" ;
```

If the member-initialization list of the derived-class `char*` constructor were missing, the base class's default constructor would be used rather than the `char*` constructor. As before, the constructor argument that's passed in the member-initialization list can be of arbitrary complexity—it can include expressions involving function calls, objects of some class, constructor argument, and so forth. It should not use a field from the current class, because that field is not initialized when the base-class constructor is called.

The one thing that you can't do in the member-initialization list of a derived class is initialize a `public` or `protected` data field in the base class, even though you could do this from the body of the constructor:

cannot access base-class data in derived-class initialization list

```
class string
{
protected:
    char *buf;
public:
    string(): buf( strdup("") ) {}; // legal, initializes
                                    // 'buf' to point at an
                                    // empty string.

    string( char *s ): buf( strdup(s) ){} // okay, copies s
                                          // into buf.
};
class numeric_string : public string // string that repre-
{                                     // sents a number
public:
    numeric_string() { buf = strdup("0") };     // okay
    numeric_string() : buf( strdup("0") ) {};  // ILLEGAL
};
```

This rule is necessary because the base class is initialized before the derived class. In the current example, the base class's default constructor is used because the numeric_string constructor does not list the base class in its member-initialization list. If the buf(strdup("0")) in the derived class's member initialization list was legal, then it would overwrite the pointer that was set up by the base-class constructor, and the memory that came from strdup("") would be lost.

The real problem is that the programmer has violated the black-box principle by using **protected** data. It would be much better to redefine the buf field as **private**, and then initialize the base-class object like this:

```
class numeric_string : public string
{
public:   numeric_string() : string("0"){};
};
```

copy construction
and operator=()
under derivation

The copy-construction process with respect to base classes has the same problems as instance variables — the default constructor is used to initialize each base class unless the compiler finds a member-initialization list. If a copy constructor is present at the lowest (most-derived) level, then the copy constructor is used at that level. Nonetheless, the default constructor is used for a base class unless the copy constructor has a member-initialization list that chains to the base class's copy constructor. This is the case even if the base class has a copy constructor. The chaining is not automatic.

operator=() is not
inherited

Similarly, base classes have the same problem with operator=() that instance variables had, but for a different reason: operator=() *is not inherited*. This rule means that an operator=() function in the base class is never called implicitly when you copy derived-class objects.

Listing 5.8 demonstrates both problems. (Again, the employee class is in Listing 5.6 on page 230, which in turn uses the stripped-down string and fixed classes from Listing 5.2 on page 225.) A salesper has all the characteristics of an employee, but adds a field to keep track of the total sales so that a commission can be determined.

Listing 5.8. Problems with Copying Under Inheritance

```
1    class salesper: public employee
2    {
3        fixed sales_volume;
4    public:
5        salesper( char *name, double salary, int part_time, double sales) :
6                            employee     (name,salary,part_time),
7                            sales_volume ( sales ) {}
8        void print( void )
9        {
10           employee::print();
11           printf( "Volume     %f\n", (double) sales_volume );
12       }
13   };
14
15   void main( void )
16   {
17       salesper willy( "Loman, Willy", 5000.00, 1, 1000.00 );
18       willy.print();
19
20       printf("----------------------- initialized:\n");
21       salesper tmp = willy;
22       tmp.print();
23
24       printf("----------------------- assigned:\n");
25       tmp = willy;
26       tmp.print();
27   }
```

The following output is generated when the program is run:

```
Employee: Loman, Willy (@ 0x0B88)
Salary    5000.000000
part time yes
Volume    1000.000000
----------------------- initialized:
Employee: Loman, Willy (@ 0x0B88)
Salary    5000.000000
part time yes
Volume    1000.000000
----------------------- assigned:
Employee: Loman, Willy (@ 0x0B88)
Salary    5000.000000
part time yes
Volume    1000.000000
```

As was the case in the instance-variable situation, shallow copying is used in both the initialization and the assignment because the `salesper` class has neither a copy constructor nor an `operator=()` function. The `salesper` class does not inherit `operator=()` from the base class.

As before, adding incomplete versions of the constructor and assignment overload just make matters worse. For example, the following additions to the `salesper` class:

```
class salesper: public employee
{
    fixed sales_volume;
    // ...
public:
    salesper( salesper &r ) : sales_volume(r.sales_volume){}
    salesper &operator=( salesper &r )
    {
      sales_volume=r.sales_volume;
      return *this;
    }
};
```

cause the following output to be generated:

```
Employee: Loman, Willy (@ 0x0BF6)
Salary     5000.000000
part time yes
Volume     1000.000000
----------------------- initialized:
Employee:  (@ 0x0C08)
Salary     0.000000
part time no
Volume     1000.000000
----------------------- assigned:
Employee:  (@ 0x0C08)
Salary     0.000000
part time no
Volume     1000.000000
```

The base class is, again, being treated much like an instance variable here. There's no member-initialization list in the copy constructor and the `operator=()` function doesn't do anything about the base-class component of the target object. As a result, the `employee` class's default constructor is used by the initialization, and a C-style shallow copy is used for the assignment.

Both problems are really fixed by adding a little more code, though the mechanics vary a bit from the instance-variable solution. The copy constructor must be modified to chain to the base class as follows:

```
salesman( salesman &r ): sales_volume(r.sales_volume),
                   employee( r ) {}              //<-NEW
```

Note that the `employee` base class doesn't have a constructor with a `salesper` argument. The `employee(r)` works nonetheless because `employee` does have a copy constructor (with an `employee&` argument), and a derived-class object can always be converted to the base class. Consequently, the derived-class object (`r`) is converted to its `employee` base class and passed to `employee`'s copy constructor.

The fix continues with a new version of the assignment overload:

```
salesper &operator=( salesper &r )
{
    sales_volume=r.sales_volume;
    *((employee*)this) = r;        // <- NEW
    return *this;
}
```

The weird-looking code is required here because the application programmer shouldn't have to know whether the base class has an `operator=()` function. An explicit call like `employee::operator=(r)` probably won't be accepted by the compiler if there is no explicit `operator=()` function defined in the `employee` class. On the other hand, `*((employee*)this)` = r works whether or not the base class has an `operator=()` function—C-style structure copying is used if the function is missing. The `(employee*)` converts `this`—which is a pointer to a `salesper` in the current context—to a pointer to an `employee`—the base class. The `*` on the left then converts the pointer to an actual object. That is, it evaluates to the structure that comprises the base class. The `=r` is then used to select the `operator=()` function. You could do the same thing like this:

calling base-class
operator=(),
((base)**this**)=r;

```
employee *ep;

ep  = (employee *) this; // get base-class component
*ep = r;                 // assign
```

As was the case earlier, r is silently converted from the derived to the base class to make the types match. The foregoing behavior leads to two more rules of thumb:
- **All derived classes should have a copy constructor that chains to the copy constructors of all base classes in their member-initialization lists.**
- **All derived classes should have an** `operator=()` **function that chains to the base-class** `operator=()` **with an expression like** `(*(base*)this)=src.`

The second rule means that your derived class must supply an `operator=()` even if a C-like shallow copy is okay at the derived-class level—the shallow copy might not be okay at the base-class level.

It's worth noting that there are occasional situations where the foregoing behavior is reasonable. Take, for example, a linked-list element like the `list_employee` I used earlier. If you copy an `employee` that's part of a list, you don't actually want to copy the `list_ele` fields; otherwise, you'll end up attempting to put both elements in the same position in the list, which clearly won't work. Ideally, the `list_ele` component of the copy should be initialized by the default constructor to a pristine state—only the `employee` component of the structure should be copied. This way the copy won't be in the list, although you could insert it later if you wanted to.

lack of base-class
copying occasion-
ally correct

To finish up the subject of functions that are not inherited, most books say "the constructor, destructor, and `operator=()` function are not inherited," but this statement actually clouds the issue, so I didn't use it earlier.

We've already seen what goes on with respect to the `operator=()` function. The constructor situation is a bit different. Each base class in a derivation is initialized by its own constructor, and the derived class is initialized with its own

constructor for each level is used at that level. This behavior is evinced even if a
derived class has no constructors at all. The default constructors are used in those
levels at which they exist.

The only way to specify anything other than a default constructor in a base
class is through a member-initialization list in some derived-class constructor. If
there are no derived-class constructors, there are no such member-initialization
lists. This code does not work:

```
class base                        { base( int ); };
class derived : public base{ /*...*/        }; //no constructor

fred()
{
    derived x=10;   // ERROR, no derived-class int constructor
}
```

There's no way to invoke a base-class constructor other than the default one unless
the derived class itself has a constructor and that constructor has a member-
initialization list that specifies the desired base-class constructor. You can fix the
previous situation by providing a derived-class constructor that chains to the base-
class constructor as follows:

```
class base                        { base    ( int x );              };
class derived : public base{ derived( int x ): base(x) {} };

fred()
{
    derived x = 10;   // okay, invokes base-class constructor
                      // via the derived-class constructor.
}
```

5.7 Nested Classes

There are several scoping issues at work in class definitions. The first can be a
source of real confusion. In C, one **struct** definition may be nested inside
another, but the nesting does not limit the scope of the nested class to the enclosing
class. That is, a nested-class definition is effectively a global-level definition.
There's no difference between

```
struct outer
{
    struct inner { /*...*/ };
    struct inner fred;
};
```

and

```
struct inner { /*...*/              };
struct outer { struct inner fred; };
```

Older C++ compilers support exactly the same system. If inner has a member
function, it is declared outside the class declaration as follows, regardless of which

form of declaration is used:

```
void inner::f()
{
}
```

I prefer this nonnested form because it describes the real situation more clearly.

Newer versions of C++ modify the foregoing mechanism to support true nested **struct** or **class** definitions. I'll describe the mechanics momentarily, but frankly, this new "feature" usually causes more problems than it solves, primarily in the realm of portability. If you need your code to port to older C++ (or to C) compilers, you should *always* use the nonnested declaration syntax just described.

Newer compilers treat a nested declaration like the one in Listing 5.9 as a true nested declaration. Various ways of accessing the nested structure are also shown in Listing 5.9. Note the double :: used on line 18 to declare a member function of the inner class. Also note the :: used on line 32 to declare a stand-alone inner structure. (This last construction is legal only if the inner class is public.)

One of the big problems with the nested-class system is that nested definitions cannot be used as a Pascal-like scoping mechanism. An inner structure cannot call member functions or access the member data of the structure within which it's nested. The following code is illegal, whether or not nested structure definitions are supported, but for different reasons:

double :: references nested-class member

```
class outer
{
    int x;
    class inner
    {
        int y;
        f(){ x = y; }    // ILLEGAL (x undefined)
    }
    fred;
};
```

By the old rules, the inner class is really a global-level definition. Consequently, it has no access to the data in the outer class. By the new rules, x is really **this**->x, and **this** is a pointer to the inner class when inside inner::f(). There is no inner::x field, and there's no way to convert **this** to an outer pointer, so the statement is illegal.

One place where nested definitions are truly useful is an enumerated type nested inside a class definition. Consider this fragment from a file class:

enum as class member

```
class file
{
public:
    file(char *name);
    enum open_mode { read, write, append };
    //...
    open( open_mode mode );
};
```

The nested **enum** effectively limits the scope of the read, write, and append constants to the class, unlike a macro, which would have global scope. This way, you

Listing 5.9. Nested Class Definitions

```
1    class outer_cls
2    {
3        int x;
4    public:
5        class inner_cls
6        {
7        public:
8            void inner_f(void);
9        }
10       inner_obj;
11       void outer_f(void);
12   };
13   void outer_cls::outer_f(void)
14   {
15       inner_f();             // ILLEGAL, must have an object
16       inner_obj.inner_f(); // okay if inner_obj is public
17   }
18   void outer_cls::inner_cls::inner_f(void)
19   {
20       outer_f();   // ILLEGAL, translates to "this->outer_f()" and "this"
21                    // is a "inner_cls" pointer, not an "outer_cls" pointer.
22       x = 0;       // ILLEGAL for the same reason.
23   }
24
25   void main( void )
26   {
27       outer_cls o;
28       o.outer_f();              // okay
29       o.inner_obj.inner_f();    // okay if public
30
31       inner_cls i;              // ILLEGAL, not a global-level definition.
32       outer_cls::inner_cls i; // Okay if outer_cls::inner_cls is public.
33       i.inner_f();              // Okay if inner_cls is public.
34   }
```

don't have to worry about your symbolic-constant names conflicting with other definitions hidden in *.h* files. You access the enumerated constants as follows:

```
file a_file("name");        // declare a file
a_file.open( file::read ); // open file for reading
```

5.7 Class Scope

class forms scope relative to member function

A class does form a scope with respect to a member function. That is, if a class has a member (function or data) with the same name as a global function or variable, the class member takes precedence over the global while inside the member function. Similarly, a member function's local variables take precedence over the fields in class, and variables declared within a compound statement within the function take precedence over the local variables in the normal way. Finally, a derived class forms a scope with respect to its base classes. This last rule means that a member (function or data) of the derived class is used in a derived-class function, even if the base class has a member (function or data) with the same name. The nested scopes are summarized by the diagram in Figure 5.2.

derived class forms
scope relative to
base class

Figure 5.2. Class Scope Levels

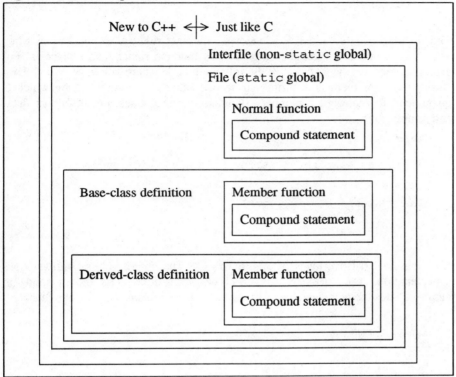

In general, the scope rules just described work in your favor. They save you from needing to know what a base-class definition looks like in order to derive a class from it. It doesn't matter if your derived class uses a name that's also used in the base class—base-class functions use the base-class object and derived-class functions use the derived-class object. The situation is analogous to `static` global variables in two different modules of the same program, but which happen to have the same name.

In terms of inheritance, the derived class wins when a base and derived class both have functions or data with the same name. You can use the `::` operator to specify the base-class version, however. Here's the syntax:

```
class base                     { public: f(); }
class derived : public base { public: f(); }

alphonso()
{
    derived d;
    d.f();                 // call derived::f();
    d.base::f();           // calls base::f();
}
```

shadowing
problems when
adding overloads

The one place where the derived-shadows-base-class rule causes problems is when
you want to add an overload to a base-class function rather than replace it. For
example, consider the situation in the following code where you have two string
classes. One of them is a normal string; the other is a numeric string which is
guaranteed to represent a number. (Numeric-string classes are useful for data-
entry applications.)

```
class string
{
    string operator+( string &right );  // concatenate
};

class numeric_string : public string
{
    int operator+( numeric_string &right );     // add
};
```

Both classes have overloads of operator+(). The string-class overload does
concatenation. The numeric_string-class overload converts the operands to
numbers, adds them, and evaluates to the sum. The problem surfaces like this:

```
string          s1,  s2;
numeric_string ns1, ns2;
int             i;

s2 = ns1 +  s1; // ERROR
i  = ns1 + ns2; // add
```

There is a problem only if you want the currently erroneous statement to concatenate the strings rather than kick out an error. If you want to look at the
numeric_string as an entirely new type that has no connection to the base class,
the error is desirable.

The foregoing code would work fine if the operator+() overload in the
numeric_string weren't there—the numeric_string class would inherit
operator+(string) so that the strings would be concatenated by this function.

The code won't work as it stands, however, because there is a version of
operator+() in the numeric string. This version shadows all the versions in the
base class—it does not add an overload. The statement ns1+s1 is rejected because
the compiler won't find a version of operator+(string) to match the expression. It cannot convert a base-class object to the derived-class object (only the
other way around).

If you want to allow concatenation of a normal string to numeric string, you
must redefine numeric_string to include a string overload as well as the

`numeric_string` overload of `operator+()`:

```
class numeric_string : public string
{
    int    operator+( numeric_string &right );  // add
    string operator+(            string &right )  // concatenate
    {
        return string::operator+( right );
    }
};
```

This second overload is just an `inline` alias for a base-class function call, so there's no run-time penalty. There is a maintenance problem, though, since all the base-class versions of the function must be duplicated in the derived class in order to simulate inheritance.

The final scoping issue is a class that is defined locally to a function:

classes declared local to a function

```
sigmund()
{
    int id;
    class super_ego
    {
        void ego( void ){ /* body */ }
    };
}
```

Locally defined classes like this are not very useful in practice. Their scope is indeed limited to the function, but there are many implementation difficulties.

To start out, class member functions must be defined in the class definition itself. If `ego()` did not have a body, for example, you'd have to define it outside the class declaration with a definition like

local class member functions must be **inline**

```
super_ego::ego(){...}
```

There's no place that this definition can go, though. You can't put it outside the **class** `super_ego` definition but inside `sigmund()` because nested function definitions are not permitted in C++ any more than they are in C. You can't put the definition at the global level—outside of `sigmund()`—because the definition for `super_ego` is out of scope at that point, so the compiler rejects `super_ego::ego()` because `super_ego` is undefined.

The next problem is really a different side of the earlier one. Since you can't have nested function definitions, a local-class member function must be treated as if it were a global-level function. Consequently, it may not access local variables in the enclosing function. For example, `super_ego::ego()` may not access `id` in the current example. If a global variable called `id` existed, `super_ego::ego()` would be able to access it, but this would just add to the confusion because you'd probably expect the local variable to be used.

local classes cannot access local variables

The final scoping issue is a useful one (for a change). Class members are in scope for the entire class definition. This means that the position of a declaration within a class definition is unimportant. In the following code, for example, it doesn't matter that the `archetypes` definition follows its use:

members are in scope for entire definition

```
class carl()
{
private:     daemon(){ archetypes = 0; }
protected:  int archetypes;
}
```

This relaxed ordering of fields is particularly useful when you want to put all the
`public` data and functions together in one part of the definition and all the
`private` data and functions together in another. The `private` functions can freely
access the `public` data and functions, even if these `public` fields are declared
beneath the `private` function in the class declaration.

5.8 Inheritance and `new` and `delete` Overloads

In addition to the shadowing problems mentioned earlier, inheritance sometimes
affects local overloads `new` and `delete`. The first issue is that a local overload of
`new` is inherited by derived classes. That's why the size argument is necessary.
Consider this code:

```
#include <stdio.h>
#include <stdlib.h>

class base
{
    char some_data[16];
public:
    void *operator new ( size_t size )
    {
        void *p = malloc( size );
        printf("new(%d)=%p\n", size, p );
        return p;
    }
    void operator delete ( void *p )
    {
        printf("delete %p\n", p );
        free(p);
    }
};

class derived : public base { char some_more_data [16]; };

void main( void )
{
    base  *p = new base;
    base *dp = new derived;
    delete p;
    delete dp;
}
```

The foregoing code prints

```
new(16)=0786    (16 is size of a base-class object)
new(32)=079A    (32 is size of a derived-class object)
delete 0786
delete 079A
```

The foregoing behavior generally works in your favor. If, for example, you over-load new to create tree nodes, as was the case in the last chapter, then your over-load is used for all kinds of tree nodes that derive from the tree_node base class.

Multiple inheritance can cause problems, though. You'll have a compile-time ambiguity if more than one base class has a new overload. For example:

problems with
operator new(),
operator delete()
under multiple
inheritance

```cpp
#include <stdlib.h>
#include <stdio.h>

class base1
{
public:
    void *operator new ( size_t size )
    {
        printf( "base1::new\n" );
        return ::new char[ size ];
    }
    void operator delete( void *p )
    {
        printf( "base1::delete\n" );
        ::delete p;
    }
};

class base2
{
public:
    void *operator new ( size_t size )
    {
        printf( "base2::new\n" );
        return ::new char[ size ];
    }
    void operator delete( void *p )
    {
        printf( "base2::delete\n" );
        ::delete p;
    }
};

class der : public base1, public base2
{
    int some_data;
};
```

```
int main()
{
    der *p = new der;      // AMBIGUOUS (which new?)
    delete p;              // AMBIGUOUS (which delete?)

    der *p2 = base1::new der;   // Might be okay, but
    base1::delete p2;           //    depends on compiler
}
```

The compiler doesn't know which base class's **new** or **delete** overload to use to manage the memory for a derived-class object. One solution to this problem is discussed in the following section, but it works only in some situations. In general, it's best if only one base class has a **new** or **delete** overload in a multiple-inheritance situation.

5.9 Virtual Base Classes

The foregoing example demonstrates a situation where the normal way in which base classes are implemented under multiple inheritance causes problems. If more than one base class has a function that's called from the derived class, the compiler can't determine which version of the function to use.

Here's another example of this problem. Say you have a window base class from which you derive pop_up and pull_down classes like this:

```
class window                      { move();        }
class pop_up:     public window   { display();     }
class pull_down:  public window   { display();     }
```

The idea is that the pop_up and pull_down classes add special-purpose display functions to a basic window class. You then create a menu class by deriving it from both a pop_up and a pull_down in order to allow a menu to use either display method:

```
class menu : public pop_up, public pull_down {/*...*/}
```

The resulting data structure is shown in Figure 5.3. There are two problems. Since a window is a member of both a pop_up and pull_down, there are two windows in the resulting menu.

unwanted windows   This multiplicity of windows causes several problems. First, you really don't want two windows around—you're deriving from pop_up and pull_down to get the display functions, not to get a second window. The double window causes a conflict every time you want to use an inherited function. For example:

```
menu m;
m.move(); // ERROR pop_up::move() or pull_down::move()?
```

This is a particular annoyance because the two "conflicting" functions are really the same function. Nonetheless, you won't be able to use inheritance to access any of the window class's functions. You'll have to provide a disambiguating function in the menu class for every window function that you intend to use, like this:

Figure 5.3. A menu Object

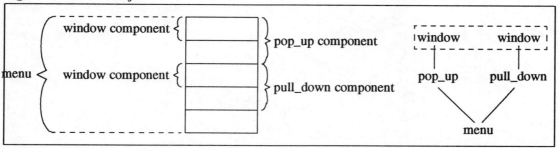

```
class menu : public pop_up, public pull_down
{
public:
    move(){ pop_up::move(); }
}
```

The second, equally serious, problem is that you'll probably end up with two windows on the screen, one on top of the other. The constructor for window is called twice when you create a menu, once for each window base class. If the constructor draws the window, you'll have two windows.

Similar problems are caused in other situations. Say, for example, you have a node class that contains the common functions and data that are needed by both a linked-list element and a node in a binary tree: You'd do it like this:

```
class node             { /*...*/ };
class list_ele : public node { add(); };
class tree_ele : public node { add(); };
```

Now you want a data structure that can be either a tree element or a linked-list element:

```
class emp_rec: public list_ele, public tree_ele
{
    add()
    {
      list_ele::add();
      tree_ele::add();
    }
};
```

The resulting data structure is in Figure 5.4.

An emp_rec can be in both a tree and a linked list simultaneously because it contains two node components, one for use by in a tree and one for use in a linked list. We can't use inheritance because we want to call the add() functions from both data structures when asked to add an element to the combined tree-list structure in order to keep the two data structures synchronized, hence the add function in the emp_rec class. The ambiguity issues discussed earlier are immaterial in the current example.

node in both
tree and list

Figure 5.4. Record That Can Simultaneously Be in a Tree and a List

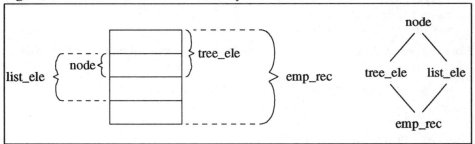

But what if you want the `emp_rec` to be in either a list or a tree, but not in both at the same time? Keeping two `node` structures around in this situation is a waste of memory. The problem is solved by making the duplicate base class (the `node`) a **virtual** base class in both of the classes that derive directly from it. The syntax looks like this:

```
class node                              { /*...*/ };
class list_ele: virtual public node     { /*...*/ };
class tree_ele: virtual public node     { /*...*/ };
class emp_rec : public list_ele, public tree_ele { /*...*/ };
```

The resulting data structure is pictured in Figure 5.5.

Figure 5.5. Record That Can Be Alternately in a Tree or List

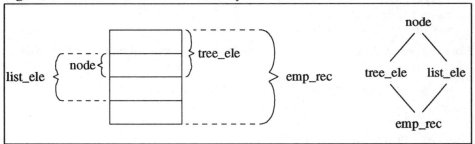

There is now only one copy of a `node` in the `emp_rec`. Functions in the `list_ele` and `tree_ele` that access fields in a `node` now both manipulate the same `node` component of the derived class, so the `emp_rec` can't be in both data structures simultaneously.

derivations with
both **virtual** and
non-**virtual** base
classes

If a derivation contains both **virtual** and non-**virtual** instances of a base class, one instance is created for all **virtual** classes combined, and several additional instances are also created, one for each non-**virtual** base class. Also note that the compiler will have to work pretty hard (and do pretty tricky things) to ensure that pointers to the correct base class are passed to base-class functions. It will have to change the value of **this**, for example, when a derived-class function calls a base-class function.

The construction of an object containing `virtual` base classes works much like the construction of a normal derived class. The constructor for the `virtual` base class is called only once, though. There is one additional difference: at any given derivation level, all the `virtual` base classes are constructed first (in order of declaration) and then the non-`virtual` base classes are constructed (in order of declaration). This behavior shouldn't cause problems as long as the classes don't interact with one another—as is proper.

constructing objects containing `virtual` base classes

In general, `virtual` base classes are a mixed blessing. They are handy in situations like the ones just discussed, but there is a serious maintenance problem—discussed momentarily—that can overwhelm the advantages. Sometimes, you can dispense with the `virtual` in the base class with no loss in functionality. The tree-list, for example, works equally well whether or not a `node` is a `virtual` base class, but you have a bit more storage overhead.

problems with `virtual` base classes

The maintenance problem I just mentioned is the initialization process. Normally, the member-initialization list of a derived class can initialize its own data members and functions in the immediate base class only. The compiler starts with the most-base class[3] and works its way down to the most-derived class, calling each constructor in turn. The member-initialization list is used at each level to determine which base-class constructor to call. The advantage to this system is that a class needs to know only about the classes immediately above it in the hierarchy; a class needs to know only about its immediate base class.

Unfortunately, this process cannot be used when there are `virtual` base classes in the hierarchy. For example, in the earlier `tree_list` class, should the compiler use the member-initialization list in the `tree_ele` to initialize the `node` or should it use the initialization list in the `list_ele`? It can't use both and the two lists might be completely different.

The answer to the foregoing question is "neither." When `virtual` base classes are present in a derivation hierarchy, the member-initialization list of the constructor for the most-derived class is used, and this constructor must initialize all elements above it in the hierarchy—all the way up to the top. All other member-initialization lists in the hierarchy are ignored. In the `tree_list` example, the member-initialization list for a `emp_rec` must specify constructor arguments for the `tree_ele`, the `list_ele`, and the `node`. The member-initialization lists in the `tree_ele` or `list_ele` class are ignored. In a complicated class hierarchy, there could be 20 or more classes to initialize from the most-derived class.

This situation is really untenable. It violates the most important precept of object-oriented programming, that the classes be black boxes. A change made at

---

[3] Since a node on any given branch of the DAG that represents a class hierarchy can't point back up at any of its ancestors, descendants must all be either beneath the node or at the same level on the current branch of the DAG. Consequently, one (and only one) of the nodes in the system will represent the "most-derived" class—the class that has the maximum number of ancestors along any one path to the root. The `most-base` class is the base class closest to the top of the hierarchy—the root in a tree-style DAG. Since the hierarchy can have more than one root, there can be more than one most-base class, in which case the order of declaration determines what gets initialized first.

any level of the hierarchy with `virtual` base classes could conceivably ripple down the entire hierarchy instead of being contained to one class and its immediate descendants.

There's only one real solution to the problem: **all construction should be done using default constructors when `virtual` base classes are used.** This way, there won't be any member-initialization lists used anywhere in the hierarchy, and we're back to the black-box model.

virtual base classes
usually not needed

The foregoing problems are made more palatable once you realize that virtual base classes hardly ever need to be used in practice. The window-class problem, for example, suffers more from design deficiencies than a from a need for virtual base classes. The problem lies in the decision that a `pop_up` and a `pull_down` *are* `window`s (thereby indicating inheritance). A much better choice would be to say that a `window` *has a* display methodology that can be changed from pop-up to pull-down with a message like `win.display_as(window::pop_up)`. A `menu` can now derive from `window` using single inheritance.

A similar situation arises in the case of the `node` class, but here it's more a matter of dogmatic Smalltalk-ism getting in the way of good design. A hard-core Smalltalker will say that redundant code is evil, even if the redundant code is only a few lines long, and that you should always use derivation to eliminate the redundancy. This attitude is wrong headed at best. There are only two reasons to justify a common `node` base class: (1) there is a reasonable amount of common functionality implemented in the common base class, or (2) you need to write a function that manipulates a generic `node` without having any knowledge of the derived class. Case (1) doesn't hold here because the only possible common functionality is memory management (local overloads of `new` and `delete`), but this is easily done with a global-level, but `static` function:

```
static void *node_alloc( size_t s ){/*...*/}

class tree_ele{ public: void *operator new(size_t s)
                            { return node_alloc(s); }
             }
class list_ele{ public: void *operator new(size_t s)
                            { return node_alloc(s); }
             }
```

The duplicate code is easily hidden in a class template (discussed in Chapter Six).[4] Similarly, case (2) above, should it ever come up, is easily handled with a function template (discussed in Chapter Two). Its also worth noting that making `node` a virtual base class of `tree_ele` and `list_ele` precludes an `emp_rec` from ever simultaneously being a member of both a tree and list.

---

[4] Skipping ahead a bit, the argument that at common `object` class (which would probably be implemented as a virtual base class) is needed to implement a Smalltalk-like "collection" also doesn't hold water—template-based container classes are a better solution in C++.

Polymorphism and Virtual Functions

Saving the best for last, virtual functions are one of the truly worthwhile features of C++. It is virtual functions that let you write a truly general-purpose base class that can be customized for a specific application simply by deriving a second class from it.

This mechanism is called *polymorphism*, which you'll remember from Chapter One, is the ability of two different classes to recognize the same message but perhaps handle the message in different ways. In practical terms, the `circle` and `line` classes, which both derive from a `shape` class, have `draw()` subroutines that handle "draw yourself" messages. Just as a polymorphic bee differentiates into a "queen" and a "drone" adult form, the `shape` base class differentiates into two adult forms—the `circle` and `line`. Both of these "adult forms" recognize a `draw()` message, but they process it in different ways, one by drawing a circle and the other by drawing a line.

polymorphism

6.1 Virtual Functions at the Implementation Level

I'll start discussing polymorphism by describing one way that it could be implemented.

The compiler normally keeps an internal list of member functions. When you use the member function, the compiler inserts a call to that function directly into the output code. This process is *static* (or *early*) *binding*.

static (or early) binding

Virtual functions are handled differently, though. You'll remember from Chapter One that a *virtual function* is a derived-class function that is called from a base-class function through a pointer stored in the base-class component of a derived-class object. Different derived classes can provide different functions to the base class, but the function pointer is at the same place in the base class. Consequently, you can write a base-class function that defers some of the processing to a function that is supplied by the derived class. It calls the virtual function

virtual function

indirectly through the pointer when it needs some piece of information that can be provided only by the derived class.

virtual-function table (vtable, vtab)

In order to save space, the C++ compiler typically isolates the virtual-function pointers into an array called the *virtual-function table* (often abbreviated as *vtable* or *vtab*). Every object carries around a pointer to the table rather than pointers to all the virtual functions, thereby making the class only a little larger (by the size of one pointer).

Figure 6.1 shows the situation for a simple class that has three virtual functions: the compiler allocates space for the virtual-function-table pointer in addition to the space needed for the data fields. You are never given direct access to this pointer, but it's there nonetheless. A `sizeof` statement for a structure with virtual functions usually yields a number somewhat larger than the size you'd expect by adding together the sizes of the fields. Your program thinks that only the shaded region of the structure has been allocated.

Figure 6.1. Virtual Functions in C++

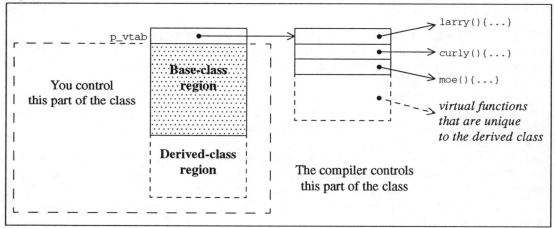

declaring virtual functions

dynamic (late) binding

You declare a virtual member function by adding the `virtual` keyword to the function declaration in a manner similar to a storage class. This keyword tells the compiler to make a slot for the function in its table. The compiler stores the index of the table element associated with a virtual function in its symbol table. When the function is accessed, the compiler generates an indirect function call through the table, using the previously stored index to figure out which function to call. This process is *dynamic* (or *late*) *binding*.

For example, the compiler might translate this definition

```
class stooge
{
    int stooge_data;
public:
    void          stooge (void); // constructor
    virtual int larry (void);
    virtual int curly (void);
    virtual int moe   (void);
    int           fang  (void);
};

void stooge::stooge (void){ /*...*/ }
int   stooge::larry  (void){ /*...*/ }
int   stooge::curly  (void){ /*...*/ }
int   stooge::moe    (void){ /*...*/ }
int   stooge::fang   (void){ /*...*/ }
```

into the following class definition and virtual-function-table declaration:

```
typedef (*funct_ptr)();
void stooge__stooge (void){ /*...*/ } // stooge-class
int   stooge__larry  (void){ /*...*/ } // functions
int   stooge__curly  (void){ /*...*/ }
int   stooge__moe    (void){ /*...*/ }
int   stooge__fang   (void){ /*...*/ }

funct_ptr virtual_stooge[3] =  // virtual-function table
{                              // for stooge class
    stooge__larry,
    stooge__curly,
    stooge__moe
};

struct class_stooge     // data component of stooge class
{
    funct_ptr *vtab;
    int stooge_data;
};
```

Since the constructor [stooge__stooge()] and fang() aren't virtual, there's no slot for them in the table. A stooge definition in the input file such as the following one

```
stooge s;
```

generates the following output:

```
struct class_stooge s;  // allocate space
stooge_stooge( &s );    // call constructor, &s is the
                        // implicit "this" pointer
s.vtab = virtual_stooge; // initialize virtual-function-
                         // table pointer
```

The object's virtual-function-table pointer is initialized when the object is created—at run time. That's another difference between **new** and malloc()—**new** must both call the constructor and set up the virtual-function-table pointer; `mal-loc()` does neither.

static binding

Function calls are handled in two ways. A call to the nonvirtual `fang()` that looks like this

```
s.fang();
```

is translated in the output into a direct call like this:

```
stooge__fang( &s );
```

dynamic binding

Again, this is static binding. The `&s` is the **this** pointer. A call to a virtual function like `curly()` that looks like this in the input

```
s.curly();
```

is treated differently—it's accessed indirectly through the virtual-function table by the following output:

```
(* s.vtab[1])( &s );
```

If you derive a class from `stooge` like this

```
class commie_stooge: public stooge
{
    int commie_data;
    commie_stooge( void );
public:
    virtual int vladimir();
    virtual int curly    (); /* local curly */
};

    commie_stooge::commie_stooge(void){ /*...*/ };
int commie_stooge::vladimir       (void){ /*...*/ };
int commie_stooge::curly          (void){ /*...*/ };
```

the compiler generates another class definition and virtual-function table for the derived class. It looks like this:

```
void commie_stooge__commie_stooge(){/*...*/};
int  commie_stooge__vladimir      (){/*...*/};
int  commie_stooge__curly         (){/*...*/}; //local curly
struct class_commie_stooge
{
    funct_ptr *vtab;     // compiler maintains this region
    int stooge_data;  // base-class component of struct
    int commie_data;  // derived-class component of struct
};

funct_ptr virtual_commie_stooge[3] =
{
    stooge__larry,
    commie_stooge__curly,
    stooge__moe,
    commie_stooge__vladimir
};
```

The virtual-function table in the derived class looks much like the one in the base class, but the original `curly` pointer is replaced by a pointer to the `commie_stooge` version of curly.

A derived class can also define virtual functions that are not defined in the base class as the case with `vladimir()`. Typically, the pointers to the derived class's unique virtual functions are just tacked onto the end of the base-class's virtual-function table, as is the case here.[1]

It's important to note that the member functions from the base class appear in the derived class's table, and that they appear in the same order as in the base-class's table. Similarly, the base class's data fields also appear in the derived class, and in the same order as they were found in the base class. Finally, the virtual-function-table pointer is found in the same place in both structures. Consequently, base-class code can manipulate the base-class component of a derived-class object without difficulty. The base-class function doesn't even know that it's pointing at a derived-class object.

Say, for example, you declare a pointer to a `stooge` and initialize it to point at the derived class as follows:

```
stooge *p = new commie_stooge;
```

The compiler will initialize the `vtab` pointer in the resulting structure to address `commie_stooge`'s virtual-function table. The earlier **new** statement is effectively handled like this:

```
stooge *p = malloc( sizeof(commie_stooge) );
stooge__stooge( p );                // base-class constructor
commie_stooge__commie_stooge( p ); // derived-class    "
p.vtab=virtual_commie_stooge;       // virtual-funct-tab ptr.
```

Note that the `vtab` pointer is initialized to the derived-class's virtual-function table because a derived-class object is specified to **new**. p, though, is a base-class pointer, and a call to p->curly() generates the same code that it did earlier:

```
(* s.vtab[1] )();
```

This code called `stooge`'s version of `curly` in the earlier example because the virtual-function-table pointer addressed `stooge`'s table. Now, though, the same code calls `commie_stooge`'s version of `curly()` because `commie_stooge`'s virtual-function table is active.

As a final issue, the compiler knows about only those virtual functions that are members of the class that's used to access the function. p, for example, was a base-class pointer, so the compiler knows only about the virtual functions declared in the base class. As in C, the compiler doesn't know what p is really pointing at—it just assumes that it is pointing at the right thing. A p->vladimir() is

base class doesn't know about functions introduced in derived class

---

[1] Since the compiler will need several such tables if several classes derive from a common base class, the compiler might also give the derived class its own virtual-function-table pointer, but it's conceptually easier to think of one big table.

illegal in the current example because p is a pointer to a stooge, not a commie_stooge—there is no vladimir() member function in a stooge. In other words, a base class doesn't know about virtual functions that are introduced beneath it in the hierarchy. Consequently, these lower-level functions cannot be accessed via a pointer to a base-class object, only by a derived-class pointer.

6.2 Virtual Functions: Basic Use

use virtual functions
to tell base class
about derived class

Looking at the foregoing process at a higher level, a base class that knows that it needs information that only the derived class can provide handles the situation by declaring a virtual function and then using that virtual function wherever it needs the information. Later on, when you create the derived class, you'll also create a virtual function for the base class to call. Thereafter, whenever a derived-class object is manipulated by a base-class function, the base-class function's call to the virtual function will actually call the derived-class's version.

list-class virtual
functions

Let's look at how virtual functions are used in practice. The linked-list class that I've been using as an example has a print_list() function that prints the entire list. A class definition that shows the relevant code is presented in Listing 6.1. The subroutine of interest is list::print_list() on line 18. It traverses the list one element at a time, calling each list element's print() function on line 22, effectively sending a "print yourself" message to the element. The element-level print function is declared **virtual** in the list_ele class on line eight. The **virtual** keyword effectively says "make a slot in your virtual-function table for this function and initialize it to point at the current function." At a higher level, the **virtual** in the base-class definition is asking the derived class to "provide me with a function that has the following interface."

This process is the one place in C++ where a minor shift in thinking is required. When a base class specifies a virtual function, it is effectively reaching into the derived class and pulling a derived-class function up to its level—a sort of reverse inheritance in which the parent gets a function from a child. When it calls the virtual function, it is calling the derived-class function.

Listing 6.2 demonstrates how the foregoing is used. The program declares an employee record on lines one to 13. Since an emp_rec derives from a list_ele, it can be manipulated by all the linked-list functions as if it were a list_ele. The derived class also provides a version of print() on line nine of Listing 6.2. When the compiler finds a derived-class function that has the same signature as a **virtual** base-class function (when it matches the base-class declaration exactly), it replaces the original virtual-function-table pointer entry with the address of the derived-class function—it pulls the derived-class function up to its own level. (The **virtual** keyword is actually optional in the derived class, although it provides good documentation.) In the current case, emp_rec::print() has the same signature as list_ele::print(), so the compiler replaces the print() pointer in the base class's part of the virtual-function table with a pointer to emp_rec::print().

Looking back up at the call on line 22 of Listing 6.1, even though the p in p->print() is a base-class pointer, p is actually pointing at a derived-class object

Listing 6.1. *list3.cpp*— A Linked-List Class with a Print-List Function

```
 1    class list;        // resolve forward reference for friend
 2                       // definition in class list_ele, below
 3    class list_ele
 4    {
 5        friend class list;
 6        list_ele    *next;
 7    protected:
 8        virtual void print( void )
 9        {
10            printf( "*** unprintable list element ***\n" );
11        };
12    };
13
14    class list
15    {
16        list_ele *head;      // head-of-list pointer
17    public:
18        print_list()
19        {
20            list_ele *p;
21            for( p = head; p ; p = p->next )
22                p->print();
23        }
24        //...
25        add()( list_ele *p ){ /* add p to the list */ }
26    };
```

when a list is traversed. It is the actual object that controls what happens, not the pointer declaration. The **virtual** definition of print() means that when p actually points at a derived-class object, the derived-class's version of print() is called. If p were pointing at a base-class object, the base-class version of print() would be called. If p were pointing at an object of some class other than emp_rec that also derived from list_ele, then that other class's version of print() would be called.

None of this would be the case if print() were not virtual. In the non-virtual case, because p is declared as a pointer to a base-class object, p->print() would always call the base-class version of print(), regardless of what p actually pointed at.

Returning to the current example, a list is created and a few emp_recs are added to the list on lines 17 to 21 of Listing 6.2. The list is then printed with the employees.print() call on line 23. We just saw how this function traverses the list, calling each element's print() function in turn. The base-class function uses a list_ele pointer (a base-class pointer) to traverse the list, but since print() is declared **virtual**, when p actually points at an emp_rec, emp_rec()::print() is called to print an element rather than list_ele::print().

The virtual-function mechanism has let me write a general-purpose function that prints a list of emp_rec structures without having to have any knowledge of

Listing 6.2. *prntdemo.c*— Demonstrate the Print-List Function

```
1    struct emp_rec : public list_ele
2    {
3        char name[32];
4        emp_rec( char *employee )    // constructor
5        {
6            strncpy( name, employee, sizeof(name) );
7        }
8
9        virtual void print( void ) // matches virtual function in list_ele
10       {
11           printf( "%s\n", name );
12       }
13   };
14
15   main()
16   {
17       list employees;
18
19       employees.add( new emp_rec( "Jobs, Steven"     ) );
20       employees.add( new emp_rec( "Scully, Jonathon" ) );
21       employees.add( new emp_rec( "Gates, William"   ) );
22
23       employees.print_list();        /* print list of all employees */
24   }
```

what an emp_rec actually looks like. That knowledge is provided at run time by means of a virtual-function call.

shape-**class virtual functions**

Moving on to a more complex example that introduces a few new language features, I've implemented a classic method of representing drawing elements in an object-oriented system: a shape class holds data common to all drawing elements, and several classes that derive from shape represent various concrete drawing elements like circles, lines, and so forth. A set of general-purpose drawing-manipulation functions can then be written to manipulate shapes, and these same functions will also be able to manipulate objects of classes that derive from shape. The code presented here shows how to implement this system in a real graphics environment (the one supplied with Borland C++), but the problems that are addressed in the implementation aren't compiler-specific.

grengine.h, **struct** point

The first file of interest is *grengine.h* (for "graphics engine"—MS-DOS allows only eight characters in a file name) in Listing 6.3. The **struct** point on lines 26 to 48 represents a point on the graphics plane and is used to pass coordinates to the various drawing functions. I've put the x field into a union with col (and y into a union with row) so that you can use either (y,x) or (col,row) to specify coordinates.

Since there are only two data components to a point (the x and y coordinates), and since it's reasonable both to access and to modify both coordinates directly, I've chosen to implement a point as a normal **struct**—in which direct access to the fields is possible—rather than a **class** with private members.

The one possible reason for accessing the `point` fields through member functions is to verify that a point is legal in the current graphics environment before allowing the modification. The problem is graphics-environment initialization, which might not happen until after several global-level points are created—the boundaries of the screen won't be known until the environment is initialized, though. Provision is made for verifying a point's correctness—you can call `point::ok()`, defined on line 40 of Listing 6.3 and used like this:

`point::ok()`

```
point pt( 100, 200 );

if( pt.ok() )
    // then it's in bounds
```

`point::ok()` returns garbage if the graphics system is uninitialized.

The other `point` function of interest is `point::close_to` on line 42, which compares a given point with the current point and returns true if they're close to one another. I've also provided a constructor (on line 38 of Listing 6.3) so that you can create a point on the fly with an expression like `point(y,x)`—a cast that evaluates to an initialized `point` structure.

`point::close_to`

The other data structure in Listing 6.3 is the `graphics_engine` (declared on lines five to 22, with the function definitions immediately following). This class serves three purposes. First of all, it simplifies initialization of the graphics environment by concentrating the initialization code into its constructor. This way, the graphics environment is initialized automatically when the program boots, provided that you declare a global-level `graphics_engine` object. This declaration is made impossible to avoid by putting it into the `.h` file, on line 57 of Listing 6.3. This line compiles, but only when `GRAPHICS_ENGINE_ALLOC` is defined (the `#ifdef` is on line 50). I created a `graphics_engine` object (called `Graphics`) by renaming the file to `grengine.cpp` and compiling with

`graphics_engine`

automatic graphics-environment initialization via constructor

```
bcc -DGRAPHICS_ENGINE_ALLOC grengine.cpp
```

The `-D` switch creates an implicit `#define` for `GRAPHICS_ENGINE_ALLOC` so that the definition is compiled. The non-`inline` member functions of the `graphics_engine` class are compiled at the same time. I then put the resulting object file into a library and change the file name back to `grengine.h`, which I include everywhere that I need to use the engine. The object is called in from the library if the `Graphic` object is used anywhere in the code, as will be the case if you draw a circle with a call to `Graphic.circle()`, for example. Calling in the `Graphic` object from the library guarantees initialization of the graphics environment before `main()` is executed because the constructor does this initialization.

The only difficulty with this approach is that, in the unlikely event of a graphics function being called as part of a global-level initialization, the environment will not have been initialized.

The second thing you get from the `graphics_engine` class is the isolation of the mechanics of the Borland graphics system from the rest of the program. Only `graphics_engine` functions are permitted to call the Borland functions. (Like a FILE, there's nothing in the language stopping an application program from calling a Borland function directly other than the good sense of the programmer. You

use class to isolate nonstandard library functions from application

Listing 6.3. grengine.h

```
 1   #ifndef __GRENGINE_H      // make multiple-inclusion harmless
 2   #define __GRENGINE_H
 3   //-----------------------------------------------------------------
 4   struct point;             // defined below
 5   class graphics_engine
 6   {
 7       int maxx, maxy;
 8       int color;            // Current drawing color
 9
10   public:
11       graphics_engine ( void );
12       ~graphics_engine( void );
13
14       point_ok( int x, int y )
15       {
16           return (0 <= x && x <= maxx) && (0 <= y && y <= maxy);
17       }
18
19       void circle ( const point &center, int    radius,     int dcolor );
20       void line   ( const point &pt1,    const point &pt2, int dcolor );
21
22   };
23   extern graphics_engine Graphic; // An extern declaration for normal
24                                   //  files. The definition is below.
25   //-----------------------------------------------------------------
26   struct point // Represents a point, not worth implementing as a class.
27   {
28       static const int slop;
29       union{               // This way you can use either row or y to
30           int row;         // fetch the vertical coordinate, whichever
31           int y;           // strikes your fancy.
32       };
33       union {
34           int col;
35           int x;
36       };
37       point( const point &s            ) : y(  s.y   ), x(  s.x   ){}
38       point( int row_or_y, int col_or_x ) : y(row_or_y), x(col_or_x){}
39
40       ok( void ){ return Graphic.point_ok(x,y); }
41
42       int close_to( point &pt )
43       {
44           // Return true if pt is in the vicinity of the current point
45           return    ( (x - slop) <= pt.x && pt.x <= (x + slop) )
46                  && ( (y - slop) <= pt.y && pt.y <= (y + slop) );
47       }
48   };
49   //-----------------------------------------------------------------
50   #ifdef GRAPHICS_ENGINE_ALLOC
51
```

➡

Listing 6.3. continued...

```
52    #include <stdio.h>
53    #include <stdlib.h>
54    #include <conio.h>
55    #include <graphics.h>    // Definitions for Borland Graphics Functions
56
57    graphics_engine Graphic;        // Create the object
58    const int point::slop = 5;      // five pixels of slop in a point
59
60    graphics_engine::graphics_engine(void)
61    {
62        // Initialize graphics system. This code is taken directly
63        // from the Borland C++ manual.
64
65        // request auto detection
66        int gdriver = DETECT, gmode, errorcode;
67
68        // initialize graphics and local variables
69        initgraph(&gdriver, &gmode, "/util/tc/bgi");
70
71        /* read result of initialization */
72        errorcode = graphresult();
73        if (errorcode != grOk)  // an error occurred
74        {
75            printf("Graphics error: %s\n", grapherrormsg(errorcode));
76            printf("Press any key to halt:");
77            getch();
78            exit(1); // terminate with an error code
79        }
80
81        maxx = getmaxx();  // Load into structure to avoid making subroutine
82        maxy = getmaxy();  // calls later on. These numbers won't change
83                           // after initialization.
84        color= getcolor(); // This does change, set the initial value to the
85                           // current value.
86    }
87
88    graphics_engine::~graphics_engine( void )
89    {
90        closegraph();
91    }
92
93    void graphics_engine::circle(const point &center, int radius, int dcolor)
94    {
95        if( color != dcolor )
96            ::setcolor( dcolor );
97        ::circle( center.x, center.y, radius );  // Call Borland function
98    }
99
100   void graphics_engine::line(const point &pt1,const point &pt2, int dcolor)
101   {
102       if( color != dcolor )
103           ::setcolor( dcolor );
104       ::line( pt1.x, pt1.y, pt2.x, pt2.y );
```

➡

Listing 6.3. continued...

```
105     }
106
107     #endif // GRAPHICS_ENGINE_ALLOC
108     #endif // __GRENGINE_H
```

---

don't have to do so, though, so you probably won't.) This way, all you need to do to change the graphics environment is change the `graphics_engine` definition and recompile. That's the purpose of the small member functions like `circle()`, declared on line 19 and defined on line 93 of Listing 6.3. The application program calls `Graphic.circle()` to draw a circle, and this function calls Borland's `circle()` function in turn. Note the `::` scope operator that's used on line 97 to prevent `circle()` from calling itself recursively. The scope operator specifies the global-level (Borland) function.

The third advantage to the engine approach is that Borland has used several names (like `circle` and `line`) that I want to use elsewhere as class names. These names are all defined in *<graphics.h>*, so I can't `#include` this file anywhere that uses `circle` or `line` for some other purpose. Since the `#include` `<graphics.h>` is placed inside the `#ifdef` GRAPHICS_ENGINE_ALLOC (on line 55 of Listing 6.3), it is used to compile the `graphics_engine` member functions, but won't be called in anywhere else in the program because the Borland functions aren't called anywhere else in the program. Consequently, the Borland names are freed up for my own use.

The `shape` class itself is defined in Listing 6.4. A `shape` holds information that's needed to manage a generic shape—all real shapes (like `circle` and `line`) derive from `shape`. You never create an object of class `shape`, though. You create only derived-class objects like `circles` and `lines` that represent concrete shapes.

abstract base class
The `shape`, then, is an *abstract base class* because a concrete instance of it never exists.

The `=0` in the definition on line 19 of Listing 6.4 handles a situation that often arises when virtual functions are used. A virtual function must appear in the base class, even if it doesn't do anything there. Here, for example, a `print()` function in a `shape` has no meaning—what would it print? Think of the base-class definition as a place holder in the virtual-function table. Remember, the compiler doesn't know that a base-class pointer is actually pointing at a derived-class object. It just goes to some offset in a table and calls a function. Consequently, there must be a slot in the table for that function, and the **virtual** keyword is what gets you the slot.

pure virtual
functions
The `=0` in the definition on line 19 of Listing 6.4 tells the compiler that this is a *pure virtual function.* A pure virtual function has an entry carved out for it in the virtual-function table, but the entry is not initialized. Consequently, classes that contain pure virtual functions are forced to be abstract classes—the compiler won't let you declare an object of any **class** that contains a pure-virtual-function definition. This is the only way of preventing you from inadvertently calling the function through an uninitialized pointer.

Of course, you can declare pointers or references to abstract base classes—that's the whole reason they exist, so you can write a function that uses base-class pointers to manipulate derived-class objects.

In order to declare an actual object, you must derive a class from the abstract `shape` in which concrete versions of the pure virtual functions are defined. The compiler fills the empty slots in the base-class's virtual-function table by picking up the addresses of the derived-class functions. For example, the `circle` class on line 22 of Listing 6.4 derives from the abstract `shape` class, and since it defines `draw()` on line 29, you can declare a `circle`. The `draw()` function draws the shape represented by the `circle` object on the screen. (Let's hope it draws a circle.) The `line` class on line 35 of Listing 6.4, also derives from `shape` and also provides a version of `draw()`. This version draws a line, however.

You must redefine all of a base class's pure virtual functions in all classes that derive from the base class. If you don't want to provide an actual function at the derived-class level, you can redefine the function as pure by putting an `=0` in place of the function body in the derived-class's redefinition. The derived class is then also an abstract class, so the compiler won't let you declare derived-class objects, either. You must derive a class from the derived class and either declare real functions at that level or defer to yet another derivation level with another `=0`.

must redefine all base-class pure virtual functions in derived class

Listing 6.4. *Classes—* `shape`, `circle`, and `line`

```
1    #ifndef __SHAPE_H
2    #define __SHAPE_H
3
4    #include <stdio.h>
5    #include <stdlib.h>
6    #include <conio.h>
7    #include <cpp/grengine.h>   // graphics engine.
8    //------------------------------------------------------------
9    class shape
10   {
11       int color;
12   protected:
13       shape ( void ) : color( RED ) {};
14       virtual ~shape(){}
15   public:
16       void set_color( int newcolor ){ color = newcolor; }
17       int  get_color(    void       ){ return color;    }
18
19       virtual void draw( void ) const = 0;
20   };
21   //------------------------------------------------------------
22   class circle : public shape
23   {
24       point center;
25       int   radius;
26   public:
27       circle( const point &c, int r ) : center( c ), radius( r )  {}
28       virtual ~circle( void )                                     {}
29       virtual void draw( void ) const
```

Listing 6.4. continued...

```
30        {
31              Graphic.circle( center, radius, get_color() );
32        }
33    };
34    //-------------------------------------------------------------------------
35    class line : public shape
36    {
37        point  pt1;
38        point  pt2;
39
40    public:
41        line( const point &start, const point &end ): pt1(start), pt2(end){}
42        virtual ~line(){}
43        virtual void draw( void ) const
44        {
45              Graphic.line( pt1, pt2, get_color() );
46        }
47    };
48    //-------------------------------------------------------------------------
49    #ifdef TEST_SHAPE
50
51    void main( void )
52    {
53        line   l( point(0,0),    point(200,200)); // Use cast to create
54        circle c( point(100,100), 50           ); // point on the fly.
55        shape *p;
56
57        l.set_color( RED ); // Draw the line in red
58        c.set_color( RED );
59        l.draw();                    // draw shapes directly
60        c.draw();
61        getch();
62
63        p = &l;                              // redraw polymorphically in a
64        p->set_color( LIGHTGRAY ); // different color.
65        p->draw();
66
67        p = &c;
68        p->set_color( LIGHTGRAY );
69        p->draw();
70
71        getch();
72    }
73
74    #endif // TEST_SHAPE
75    #endif // __SHAPE_H
```

virtual destructors   Note that all the classes in Listing 6.4 provide virtual destructors, so derived-class destructors are called when objects are destroyed through base-class pointers. (I'll discuss this matter further in the next section—so don't worry about it if the foregoing sentence isn't crystal clear.) These destructors are not pure, though, because

I don't want to force the derived class to have a destructor if it doesn't need one. A definition like **virtual** ~shape(){} creates a slot for the destructor in shape's virtual-function table and initializes the slot to point at a function comprised entirely of a single **return** statement. The overhead of calling such a minimal function is trivial and the added flexibility of the resulting class is well worth the overhead.

Having now done all the work (whew!), you can see how the class is used in the small test routine on lines 51 to 72 of Listing 6.4. A line extending from (0,0) to (200,200) is declared on line 53, a circle with center (100,100) and radius 50 is declared on line 54.

The two shapes are drawn on lines 59 and 60 of Listing 6.4 with direct calls to the derived-class draw() functions. The code on lines 63 to 69 demonstrates how virtual functions are used to do the same thing. Each object is assigned in turn to a shape pointer, and then drawn. My point is that the compiler doesn't know what sort of shape it's pointing to, but it does know that all shape objects have a draw() capability, so can be displayed as shown.

Now, take this example a step further by representing an entire drawing as a linked list of shapes. You can do this by making circle and line classes that can also be list elements. The class hierarchy is pictured in Figure 6.1 and the new classes look like this:[2]

```
class list_circle : public list_ele, public circle
{
    list_circle( const point &c, int r ) : circle( c, r ){}
    print(){ draw() };
}

class list_line : public list_ele, public line
{
    list_line( const point &start, const point &end ) :
                                        line( start, end ){}
    print(){ draw() };
}
```

They each have two members. First, a constructor is needed so that you can chain to the constructor in the shape base class. If that constructor were not present, the compiler would try to call the default constructor in the base class, and would fail because there is no default constructor in either the circle or line base class. The print() function in each class provides a real function to use for the virtual function in the list_ele base class. It both cases, print() calls the draw() function that it gets from either circle or line.

---

[2] I won't introduce class (as compared to function) templates for a few pages yet, but a class template would be better than two almost identical class definitions if you could use default constructors from the base class—you can't do that, here, though.

Figure 6.2. A Linked-List Drawing Element

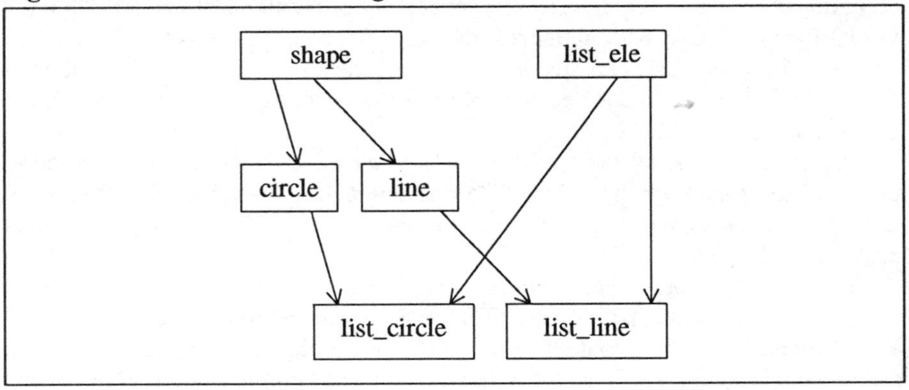

You can now create a two-element drawing, and print it, like this:

```
main()
{
    list_ele *p;
    list  drawing;
    drawing.add( new list_line  ( point( 0, 0), point(10,20) ) )
    drawing.add( new list_circle( point(10,10), 5            ) )
    drawing.print();
}
```

inheritance vs.
polymorphism

Inheritance is used to call the `draw()` function and polymorphism (calling virtual functions) is used to call the `print()` subroutine. The compiler goes up the inheritance graph to a `circle` or `line` to find a `draw()` function, so this is inheritance at work. For example, `draw()` is inherited by `list_line::print()`. On the other hand, `list_line::print()` is called by `list::print()` to print a list element because there's a **virtual** version of `print()` in the `list_ele` base class, and `list::print()` calls that virtual function. Because `print()` is virtual, the base class picks up the derived-class's function to actually do the work, and the derived-class's function calls the inherited `draw()` function.

bridge class,
multiple inheritance

This last example—which used a derived class as a bridge that connects a function in one base class to a virtual-function table in a second base class—is pretty useful in C++, where you tend to have a flat class hierarchy. Listing 6.5 summarizes the process. Note that the declared object in `main()` is the `bridge`— the derived class—but the functions that are actually called are the members of `uses` (which are inherited by `bridge`). The `supplies` class has a more passive role. It is just supplying functions that are specified as virtual in the `uses` class and linked to `uses` via the `bridge` class.

There is a small penalty to pay. Even though the bridge function (`bridge::vfunct()`) would normally be **inline**, it will have to be expanded by the compiler to a real function because the compiler needs a pointer to put into the virtual-function table. You have the overhead of an extra function call as a consequence. On the plus side, `supplies::vfunct()` is **inline** and will stay that way, so there won't be two levels of function, only one.

Listing 6.5. *bridge.cpp*— A Bridge Class

```
1    #include <stdio.h>
2
3    class uses
4    {
5    public:
6        virtual void vfunct( void ) = 0;
7        void uses_vfunct( void ){ vfunct(); }
8    };
9
10   class supplies
11   {
12   public:
13       void vfunct( void ){ printf("in supplies::vfunct()\n"); }
14   };
15
16   class bridge : public uses, public supplies
17   {
18       virtual void vfunct( void ){ supplies::vfunct(); };
19   };
20
21   main()
22   {
23       bridge  b;
24       b.uses_vfunct();
25   }
```

If you don't need to create drawing elements that are not also potential linked-list elements, you can reorganize the earlier hierarchy to the system shown in Figure 6.3 so that all drawing elements can be list elements. This system has the advantage of easier maintenance because you don't need to create list_circle and list_line classes that do nothing but chain to the circle and line base-class functions. A drawing element always carries around the extra fields that are needed for list maintenance, however.

an alternative organization

Figure 6.3. Another Linked-List Drawing Element

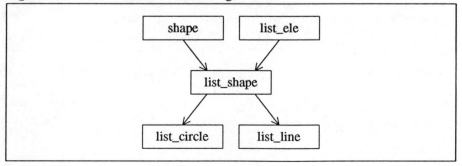

The class definitions for this new system are given in Listing 6.6. At the application level, these classes are used just like the earlier classes were used—the test `main()` at the bottom of Listing 6.6 looks just like the earlier one. The internal definitions of the classes are different, though. Note that the `list_shape` definition on line 14 needs to have one member in addition to the **virtual** destructor: a redeclaration of the pure `draw()` function from the `shape` base class. You must redefine all pure functions in derived classes. Since a concrete `draw()` function makes no more sense here than it did in a `shape`, I've redefined it as pure in the derived class as well. Also note that the class definitions are considerably simplified by the exclusive use of default constructors at the base-class level. If this were not the case, `list_shape` would have to have a full complement of constructors that chained to the base-class (`shape` and `list_ele`) constructors.

Listing 6.6. *shape2.cpp*— An Alternate `shape` Hierarchy

```
 1    class shape
 2    {
 3        int color;
 4    protected:
 5        shape ( void ) : color( RED ) {};
 6        virtual ~shape( void ){};
 7    public:
 8        void set_color( int newcolor ){ color = newcolor; }
 9        int  get_color(    void      ){ return color;      }
10
11        virtual void draw( void ) const = 0;
12    };
13    //------------------------------------------------------------
14    class list_shape : public shape, public list_ele
15    {
16        virtual void draw( void ) const = 0;
17        virtual ~list_shape( void ){};
18    }
19    //------------------------------------------------------------
20    class list_circle : public list_shape
21    {
22        point  center;
23        int    radius;
24    public:
25        circle( const point &c, int r ) : center( c ), radius( r ) {}
26        virtual ~circle(){}
27        void draw( void ) const
28        {
29            Graphic.circle( center.x, center.y, radius, get_color() );
30        }
31    };
32    //------------------------------------------------------------
33    class list_line : public list_shape
34    {
35        point  pt1;
36        point  pt2;
37    public:
```

➡

```
    Listing 6.6. continued...
38        line(const point &start, const point &end): pt1(start), pt2(end) {}
39        virtual ~line(){}
40        void draw( void ) const
41        {
42            Graphic.line( pt1.x, pt1.y, pt2.x, pt2.y, get_color() );
43        }
44    };
45    //-------------------------------------------------------------------
46    #ifdef TEST_LIST_SHAPE
47
48    main()
49    {
50        list_ele *p;
51        list  drawing;
52
53        drawing.add( new list_line  ( point( 0, 0), point(10,20) ) )
54        drawing.add( new list_circle( point(10,10), 5            ) )
55        drawing.print();
56    }
57    #endif
```

6.3 When to Use Virtual Functions

We've now seen how to use polymorphism (virtual functions) in a general sense. You use virtual functions when you know generally what all objects of a class should be able to do (print, rotate, invert, and so forth), but want to leave the details of the implementation for specific subclasses. There are a host of little issues and rules that need to be discussed in the remainder of the chapter, though.

First and foremost, **do not make a function `virtual` unless you want the derived class to be able to get control of it.** I've seen some books recommend that you should just make everything `virtual` in order to avoid confusion—but that's simply not good advice. If a base-class function is declared `virtual`, the derived class can get control of the function simply by providing a function with the same name. When the base-class function calls the virtual function, it will really be calling the derived-class's version, not its own. Effectively, this means that the base class cannot expect any virtual function to behave in a predictable way. If you set up this situation in all member functions of the class, one member function of the class could hardly ever call another function because it would have no idea what the called member function would do.

virtual gives derived class control over function

The same situation comes up in older K&R C compilers when you use a library-function name for one of your own functions. For example, a non-ANSI-conforming C compiler's version of `fopen()` might call `open()` to open the file at the low level. If you provide a function called `open()`, yours will be linked rather than the library version, and `fopen()` will not work correctly. It's sometimes desirable to redefine `open()`, however. (Say that you were porting the code to a diskless environment where the files were actually I/O ports.) In this case you want to redefine `open()` and you want `fopen()` to use your redefined version. This last situation is the equivalent of declaring the function as **virtual**. Do not declare the function **virtual** unless you want the derived class to be able to redefine what that function does.

If the base-class function is not virtual, then the derived class can inadvertently use a function name from the base class without ill effects; the derived-class version will be used by derived-class member functions and the base-class version will be used by base-class member functions.

In general, **a base class should make virtual only those subroutines that need knowledge of the derived class to do their work.** Similarly, **virtual functions should provide the base class with information about the derived class, but should never manipulate base-class data.** This way, you can write a general-purpose method in the base class that can manipulate all derived-class objects, and you can write the derived-class function without having to know too much about the internal workings of the base class. The base-class method calls the virtual function only when it needs some derived-class-relative operation to be performed. Base-class workhorse functions and functions that manipulate private data should never be declared **virtual**. (There's no sense in it—the derived class can't provide its own version of this function because it can't get at the data).

6.4 Static Binding and Virtual Functions

virtual functions
sometimes bound
statically

Though the whole point of virtual functions is to access them through the table of pointers, virtual-function calls are sometimes resolved statically (to an actual function call) rather than dynamically (to an indirect call through the virtual-function table). There are three such situations:

virtual function
invoked via object,
not pointer

• A **public** virtual function call is resolved statically when it is invoked explicitly through an object rather than a pointer or reference.

```
class base                { virtual f(){/*...*/} };
class derived : public base {         f(){/*...*/} };

base a, *p;
a.f();              // not virtual, calls base-class version
p = new base;
p->f();             // virtual, calls base-class version
p = new derived;
p->f();             // virtual, calls derived-class version
                    // because p points at derived-class object.
```

This situation does not arise when some member function calls a virtual function because you're accessing the virtual function through the implicit **this** pointer, not through an explicit object.

explicit :: operator

• A virtual function is resolved statically when it is called with an explicit scope operator, even if a pointer or reference is used. Given the earlier definitions

```
p->base::f(); // not virtual, calls base-class version
```

- A virtual function is resolved statically when called from a base-class constructor. Given these definitions

```
class base
{
    virtual void f(){ printf("in base f()\n"); }
    base(){ f(); }
};
class derived : public base
{
    virtual void f(){  printf("in derived f()\n"); }
    derived(){}
};
```

the string "in base f()" is printed whenever you create a base-class or a derived-class object. The derived-class version of f() is never called from the base-class constructor—only the base-class version is called. This behavior is really mandated by the construction process. The derived-class object doesn't exist when the base-class constructor is called. Consequently, the base-class constructor can't use the derived-class function because the derived-class function may be using uninitialized derived-class data.

6.5 Problems with a Default `virtual` in Derived Classes

The next problem surfaces if you manipulate objects with base-class pointers in some situations and derived-class pointers in others. I mentioned earlier that the `virtual` storage class in the derived-class version is not required, though it provides good documentation so should be used. There's another reason to use it, though. The virtuality of a function is determined by whether that function is declared `virtual` in the class, a pointer or reference to which is being used to access the object. This rule can yield surprising results. Consider this code:[3]

```
class A    { public: virtual void f(){ printf("A"); } };
class B:A { public:        void f(){ printf("B"); } };
class C:B { public:        void f(){ printf("C"); } };

void main()
{
    A *ap = new A; // Works as expected:
    ap->f();        //          Calls A::f()
    ap = new B;
    ap->f();        //          Calls B::f()
    ap = new C;
    ap->f();        //          Calls C::f()
```

---

[3] Some compilers require a cast in the assignments: ap=(A*)new B rather than ap=new B, for example.

```
B *bp = new B;
bp->f();          //                Calls B::f()

bp = new C;   // Doesn't work as expected: calls B::f()
bp->f();      // because p is a B pointer and f()
              // isn't declared virtual in B.
}
```

The problem is the attempted call of `C::f()` through a B pointer at the bottom of
`main()`. Some compilers actually work correctly in this situation—they actually
call `C::f()` through the B pointer. Most compilers call `B::f()`, though. Because
`f()` is not declared **virtual** in the **class** B definition, the `b->f()` call is statically bound to `B::f()` at compile time. It's best to use the **virtual** keyword at
every derivation level to avoid these sorts of problems.

derived class can
change protection
level of a virtual
function

The protection level of the virtual function works in a similar way. It's okay to
make protection level of a virtual function more restrictive in a derived class than
it was in the base class, but the protection level is controlled by the class of the
pointer or reference through which the virtual member is accessed:

```
class B                { public:  virtual void f(){} };
class D:  public B{ private:  virtual void f(){}  };

class DD: public D{ g(){f();} }; // ILLEGAL, f() is
                                 //          private in B
B *bp = new D;
bp->f();          // okay, pointer type controls protection
                  // level and f() is public in class B
D  *dp = new D;
dp->f();          // Illegal, it's private in class D
```

You can't make the protection level less restrictive, though. This is illegal:

```
class B                { private:  virtual void f(){} };
class D: public B { public:  virtual void f(){} }; // ILLEGAL
```

If it weren't, you would be able to get at any private member simply by deriving a
class.

6.6 Virtual Constructors and Destructors

constructors can't
be **virtual**

The next issue is constructors and destructors. Constructors can't be **virtual**
because they are used during the construction process, but the virtual-function
table isn't available until after this process is complete.

destructors can and
should be **virtual**

Destructors are another matter. Not only can they be declared **virtual**, they
should be declared **virtual**, as they were in the earlier shape example. Think of
it this way: The compiler always modifies your supplied destructor code by tacking calls to the base-class destructors onto the end of your destructor subroutine. If
you call the base-class destructor explicitly (with a function call rather than letting
the compiler do it automatically), only the one function is executed. If you call a
derived-class destructor explicitly, it is executed and then the base-class destructor
is executed as well. That's because the derived-class destructor actually calls the
base-class destructor. Note that the derived class is destroyed first, then the

base class is destroyed—the opposite order of construction. This is always the case, destructors are called in the opposite order of construction.

Consider what happens when a destructor is not virtual:

```
class base                    { public:  base()    {/*...*/}
                                          ~base()   {/*...*/} };
class derived : public base{ public:  derived (){/*...*/}
                                          ~derived (){/*...*/} };

base *p;
p = new derived; // Call constructor in base() and derived().
delete p;        // Call base::~base() only because p is a
                 // base*. derived::~derived() isn't called.
```

Fix the problem like this:

```
class base                    { public:     base()    {/*...*/}
                                   virtual ~base()    {/*...*/}};
class derived: public base { public:     derived(){/*...*/}
                                   virtual ~derived(){/*...*/}};
base *p;
p = new derived ; // Call base() and derived() constructors
delete p;         // Call derived::~derived() because p
                  // points at a derived-class object and
                  // the destructor is virtual. derived::
                  // ~derived() then calls base::~base.
```

The same problem comes up if you add a delete_list() function to a list class like the ones we've been looking at. For example, the lack of a virtual destructor in the list_ele definition in Listing 6.7 causes problems.

Listing 6.7. A List-Element Definition

```
1    class list; // resolve forward reference for friend def. in list_ele
2    class list_ele
3    {
4        friend class list;
5        list_ele    *next;
6    protected:
7        list_ele *successor( void ){ return next; }
8        //...
9    };
```

The following `delete_list()` function won't work properly:

```
class list
{
    list_ele *head;    // head-of-list pointer
    //...
public:
    void delete_list( void ) // Delete all list elements
    {
      list_ele *p, *cur;
      for( p = head; p ; )
      {
          cur = p;
          p   = p->successor();
          delete cur;    // ERROR, calls list_ele destructor
      }                  // only. The derived-class
    }                    // destructor is not called.
}
```

The list element is actually an object of a class that derives from `list_ele`. Nonetheless, the list element is deleted through a `list_ele` pointer, so the `list_ele` class's destructor is called. (Since the current implementation of `list_ele` doesn't have a destructor, the compiler supplies one that does nothing.) The destructor for the derived-class object is not called.

Fix the problem by redefining the `list_ele` destructor as follows:

```
class list_ele
{
    friend class list;
    list_ele    *next;

public:
    virtual ~list_ele( void ){ /*...*/ }        // <-- NEW
};
```

The main thing the destructor definition is doing is creating a slot in the virtual-function table for the derived class to fill. The destructor has an empty body (rather then being declared pure) so that the derived class doesn't have to provide a destructor if it doesn't need one.

As a final comment on the issue of virtual destructors, I just mentioned that the compiler creates a destructor if a class doesn't have one. Moreover, the compiler-generated destructor includes code to chain to the base-class destructors. The utility of this default (one of the few such defaults that actually do something reasonable) is demonstrated in the following code. Class c does not have a destructor. Nonetheless, the destructors for a and b are both called when the c object is destroyed through an a pointer at the bottom of main. This action takes place because the compiler creates a destructor for c that calls the base-class destructor.

```
#include <stdio.h>

class a
{
public:
    virtual ~a(){ printf("~a()\n"); }
};

class b : public a
{
public:
    virtual ~b(){ printf("~b()\n"); }
};

class c : public b { };

void main()
{
    a *ap = new c;
    delete ap;
}
```

Note that the foregoing code would not work if a's destructor were not declared
virtual—only the a destructor would be called were this the case.

6.7 Agreement between Base and Derived-Class Definitions

The redefinition of a virtual function in the derived class must match the definition
in the base class exactly (name, argument types, return value). If the two definitions do not have the same signature, the new definition shadows the old one and
you have the situation described earlier. The code in Listing 6.8 demonstrates the
problem.

virtual-function
redefinition must
match base-class
definition

This signatures-must-match rule can lead to a thorny but soluble problem.
Here's the list_ele again, but this time I've added an **operator**==() function
for comparing two objects that derive from list_ele. The list_ele::**operator**==() function is declared pure—it has an =0 in the definition instead of a
body—because the key fields that will be compared are in the derived class. There
is no way to write a meaningful base-class version.

```
class list_ele
{
    friend list;
    list_ele *next;
public:
    virtual int operator== ( const list_ele &x ) const = 0;
};
```

This function can be used to implement a list::find() function that searches
for a match of a derived-class object in the list. The == in the following code
evaluates to a call to list_ele::**operator**==() because the operands (*p and
this_obj) match the definition in the list_ele class. Because list_ele::

Listing 6.8. *shadow.cpp*— Demonstrate Function Shadowing

```
1   #include <stdio.h>
2
3   class A            { public: virtual void f(     ){ printf("A::f()" ); }};
4   class B:public A { public: virtual void f(int x){ printf("B::f(x)"); }};
5   class C:public B { public: virtual void f(     ){ printf("C::f()" ); }};
6
7   main()
8   {
9       A *ap;
10      B *bp;
11      C *cp;
12
13      ap = new A;
14      ap->f();    printf( "<--should be A::f()\n" );
15
16      ap = new B;
17      ap->f(10);  // ERROR: f(10) is a member of B, but ap is a
18                  // pointer to an a. Since A doesn't have a
19                  // version of f() that takes arguments, this call
20                  // generates a "not a member function" error.
21
22      ap->f();    printf( "<--should be A::f()\n" );
23
24      ap = new C;
25      ap->f();    printf( "<--should be C::f()\n" );
26
27      bp = new B;
28      bp->f(10);  printf( "<--should be B::f()\n" );
29
30      bp = new C;
31      bp->f(10);  printf( "<--should be B::f()\n" );
32
33      bp->f();    // ERROR: same problem as before, but in
34                  // reverse. The f() in B shadows the one
35                  // in A. So you can't get at the one in A
36                  // through a B pointer.
37      cp = new C;
38      cp->f();    printf( "<--should be C::f()\n" );
39  }
```

`operator==()` is virtual, the derived class's version of `operator==()` is used when p points at a derived-class object.

```
class list
{
    list_ele *first;   // Head of NULL-terminated linked list
public:
    list_ele *find( list_ele &this_obj )
    {
        list_ele *p;
        for( p = first; p && !(*p == this_obj) ; p = p->next )
            ;
        return p;
    }

    void add( list_ele *p ){ /* add *p to list */ }
};
```

Now let's implement a list of records that have an integer key by introducing an
int_ele class that derives from list_ele. Since operator==() compares two
int_ele objects, the first attempt to define it might look like this:

```
class int_ele : public list_ele
{
    int i;       // key
public:
    int_ele( int init_i ){ i = init_i; }
    virtual int operator== (const int_ele &x) const // ERROR
    {
        return( i == x.i );
    }
}
```

You can create a list, add a few elements, and search for one of them like this:

```
main()
{
    list the_list;
    int_list *p;

    the_list.add( new int_list(1) );
    the_list.add( new int_list(5) );
    the_list.add( new int_list(6) );

    if( p = the_list.find( new int_list(5) ) ) // find 5
        delete p;                              // and delete it.
}
```

Unfortunately, the foregoing code won't work. The problem is that int_ele::
operator==() takes an int_ele reference as its argument, not a list_ele as is
required by list_ele::operator==(). Consequently, the compiler will not
pick up int_ele::operator==() to use for the virtual function in list_ele—
the redefinition shadows the base-class definition, it doesn't provide a virtual overload. Since list_ele::operator==() is pure, the compiler at least gives an
error message (on the order of "no function in derived class to match virtual function in base class") in this situation. If list_ele::operator==() were not
pure—if it had a body that printed an error message, for example—you wouldn't

A nonmatching redefinition shadows base-class virtual function get a compile-time error; rather, `list::find()` would call `list_ele::` **`operator==()`** instead of `int_list::` **`operator==()`**, and a run-time error would be printed.

How, then, do you go about providing a derived-class overload? You need to provide an **`operator==()`** definition that matches the base-class definition exactly, like this:

```
class int_ele : public list_ele
{
    int i;      // key

public:
    int_ele( int init_i ){ i = init_i; }

    virtual int operator== ( const list_ele &x ) const
    {
       return( i ==   ((int_ele *) &x)->i );
    }
}
```

The **`operator==()`** takes a base-class reference argument (`list_ele &x`), not a reference to a derived-class object, as was the case earlier. Consequently, it matches the **virtual** definition in the base-class exactly and `list::find()` will use `int_list::`**`operator==()`** to compare elements when the list is made up of `int_lists`.

downcasting (-casting a base-class object to a derived-class object)There's now a new problem, though. `int_ele::`**`operator==()`** is really passed an `int_ele`, not a `list_ele` as you would believe from the argument definition. Consequently, you must tell the compiler to treat the incoming object as an `int_ele` rather than a `list_ele`. This is done by *downcasting*—converting the incoming base-class pointer into a derived-class pointer—with the cast `((int_ele *)&x)->i`, which works as follows: x is a reference to an `list_ele`, so `&x` is the address of that element—a pointer to a `list_ele`. The `(int_ele*)` converts that pointer to an `int_ele` pointer, and the `->i` gets the i field from the `int_ele`. There's one caveat: some compilers will not permit the foregoing conversion from the derived to the base class if the base class is **virtual**—another reason not to use virtual base classes (described in Section 5.9 on page 253) if you can avoid them.

6.8 Implementing a `typeof()` Function

The foregoing solution to the signatures-must-match problem introduces whole new vistas of potential difficulties. It happens to work because the list is homogeneous—all of the list elements are `int_ele` objects. But what if the list is heterogeneous, containing objects of two or more types? This is the case in the earlier list of drawing elements, for example. The comparison function can't blithely assume that the incoming right operand is of the same type as itself, as is the case now. The solution is to introduce a `typeof(x)` member function that evaluates true when its operand is of the same type as the current object. **`operator==()`** can use this function to determine whether the right operand is of the same type as `*this`. This operator is provided as a primitive in many object-oriented languages, but you have to do some work to get it in C++.

You can use two approaches (as before, the easy way and the right way). I'll start with the easy way. Modify the `list_ele` definition to hold an `i_am` field and `typeof` function like this:

safe downcasting, using a flag

```
class list_ele
{
    int i_am;
protected:
    int typeof( list_ele &right )
    {
      return i_am == right.i_am ;
    }
    list_ele( int what_i_am ) : i_am( what_i_am ) {}
}
```

The `list_ele` constructor initializes `i_am` from its argument.

Use the field by introducing an enumerated type to describe the various possibilities:

```
enum concrete_shapes { CIRCLE, LINE };
```

and then use these values to initialize the `i_am` field in the base class. The **operator==()** function can now use `typeof()` to see if the incoming argument is a circle:

```
class list_circle : public circle, public list_ele
{
public:
    list_circle(point center, int radius) :
                    circle   ( center, radius ),
                    list_ele ( CIRCLE )  // i_am = CIRCLE
                    {}

    int operator==( list_ele &right )
    {
      // Chain to base-class operator== function if types match;
      // otherwise return 0.

      return typeof(right) ? circle::operator==(right) : 0;
    }
}
```

There are two major problems with this approach. First, you'll have to modify the enumerated type every time you add a new shape, and this violates the precept that you shouldn't have to modify existing code to introduce a new type into the system. Second, in a large program that's being written by several people, all of those people will have to coordinate the values that they use to identify their own classes. For example, if 1 represents a member of the `circle` class, it can't be used elsewhere to identify any other class.

Both of these problems can be solved with only minor modifications to the earlier code. First of all, you must change the definition for `list_ele:i_am` to a pointer and change the constructor to reflect the new type:

safe downcasting, using a pointer to a **static** data member

```
class list_ele
{
protected:
    int *i_am;                                  // <--added *
    int typeof( list_ele &right )
    {
        return i_am == right.i_am ;
    }
    list_ele(int *what_i_am): i_am(what_i_am){} // <--added *
}
```

Everything else stays the same at this level. Next, you have to modify the
derived-class code to use pointers rather than an enumerated type. In order to get a
unique value for each derived class, you must use the address of a **static** member
of the class like this:

```
class list_circle : public circle, public list_ele
{
    static int me;                      // <-- NEW
public:
    list_circle(point center, int radius) :
            circle   (center, radius),
            list_ele ( &me )       // <-- NEW, pass address
            {}

    int operator==( list_ele &right )
    {
      return ( typeof(right) ) ? circle::operator==( right ) : 0 ;
    }
}
```

You can take the address of the **static** member with an ampersand in the normal
way because it's at a fixed memory location. Every instance of the class uses the
same **static** variable for the field rather than putting the field inside the object.
You can't take the address of a non-**static** class member[4] because a **struct** field
doesn't have an address in the normal sense (or rather, the field has a different physical address in every object).

The new version of typeof() works just like the old version, but it doesn't
have either of the earlier problems. The **static** members for all classes are at
different addresses by definition so they form unique identifiers, and an enumerated
type is no longer needed to provide the type identifiers.

Let me finish this example with another minor critique of the language. To my
mind, a type_of x function (and a matching kind_of x that evaluates true if x
shares a base class with the current object) is so basic to object orientation that it
really should be a language primitive. I imagine that it wasn't implemented
because the steps that I just went through would still have to be done. It's just that

missing typeof **and**
kindof operators

---

[4] Actually, you can, but I don't want to discuss how to do it yet. You need to do a lot more than just
use an ampersand, though.

the compiler would do the work rather than you. If a class doesn't need a `typeof` operator, it's not reasonable to both increase the size of the object (by adding the `i_am` field) and slow down object creation (by initializing that field) to implement an unused operation. I actually agree with this reasoning, but also feel that you could have the best of both worlds by introducing `kindof` and `typeof` keywords into the language. Only those classes that use the `typeof` or `kindof` operators in a member function would have code added to their constructors and an implicit field added to the structure to support the operation.

There are two small loose ends to tie up before leaving the topic of virtual functions. First, like constructors, `new` and `delete` overloads cannot be **virtual**. Second, friends cannot be virtual because they aren't member functions.

> **operator new()**,
> **operator delete()**
> can't be **virtual**

6.9 A Few More Implementation Issues

There are a few more virtual-function implementation details that you should know about before leaving the topic.

Making a function virtual introduces a normally insignificant run-time penalty because all calls to the function have to be done indirectly through the virtual-function table. There is sometimes a significant code-size penalty, however. First, you can have as many as one virtual-function table per class per module. The compiler has no way of knowing whether a class is used in more than one module, so it must generate a `static` declaration of a class's virtual-function table in every module in which that class is used. The table is effectively initialized as part of the declaration—at compile time. A smart linker will detect duplicate definitions for a table and eliminate all but one of them, but not all linkers are so smart.

> virtual-function
> code-size penalties

> duplicate
> virtual-function
> tables

Next, virtual functions can not be `inline` because you need a pointer to them. The same logic applied earlier to table definitions applies to virtual functions that are declared in the body of a class definition but forced out of line by their virtuality. A `static` version of the function might have to be expanded in every module in which an object of that class is used. The functions are expanded as `static` functions to avoid linker conflicts, but that creates another problem. Since the virtual-function table entry is initialized at compile time to address a `static` function, all the identical out-of-lined functions will evaluate to different addresses in the various tables. Therefore, it is more difficult for a linker to tell that the tables are identical because they will actually hold different addresses. If the linker isn't smart enough to handle this situation, every module that uses an object of a class could conceivably hold a virtual-function table for that class as well as a complete set of out-of-lined `static` functions for that class. In general, virtual functions should not be declared `inline`.

> virtual functions are
> never **inline**

To make matters worse, all virtual functions must be called into the final program—whether or not they are actually used—because there's a pointer to them in the virtual-function table. Nonvirtual functions work like C functions; they are linked only if they are used.

There's one final implementation issue that's worth mentioning. Because the virtual-function-table pointer changes its value from execution to execution, you cannot write an object on a disk in binary form, terminate the program, restart the

> persistance

program, and then reinitialize the data from the disk. This property of an object—
to be able to maintain its value between program invocations—is called *persis-
tance*.

The problem here is that a simple binary write flushes the current execution's
virtual-function-table pointer to the disk along with the current object. When you
try to read the information back, however, you'll read the previous version's
virtual-function-table pointer, not the current one.

One solution to the problem is shown in Listing 6.9. (The same techniques can
be used to read and flush configuration information to and from the disk.) The constructor for the class initializes the object by reading data from the disk. It opens
the file on line 15 when the first object is created and then reads the data one field
at a time. [You can simplify the read by encapsulating all the data fields into a
nested structure, but this complicates all other access to the data. Since `fread()` is
a buffered function, there is little or no speed benefit.]

The destructor rewinds the input file on line 26 the first time an object is destroyed. (I'm assuming that the entire disk file is transferred into active objects, the
objects are used in some way, and then all objects are destroyed at once.) The data
fields are then flushed to the disk, and the file is closed after the last object is
flushed.

The advantage to this approach is obvious—disk reads and writes are done
automatically without the programmer having to do anything. There are
difficulties, though. For example, it's up to the application to determine the order
in which objects are flushed to disk. Since objects are destroyed in the opposite
order of creation for any given scoping level, the file could end up flipped upside
down. You also have to make sure that all disk objects are destroyed (they might
not be if they're allocated by `new`). Otherwise, they won't be flushed to disk when
the program terminates.

6.10 Private Base Classes

I've delayed the discussion of `private` base classes until now because the only
time that I've ever used them in my own code is when virtual functions have also
been involved. A `private` base class is declared either by omitting the `public`
keyword from the base-class list in a derived-class declaration or by replacing the
`public` with `private`. Both `base1` and `base2` are private in the following declaration:

```
class derived : base1, private base2 {/*...*/}
```

Be careful with this syntax, the `public` and `private` keywords don't work like a
storage class. They don't cross a comma. In the following definition the first base
class is `public` and second one is `private`:

```
class fred: public public_base_class, private_base_class {...}
```

It's best to explicitly declare every base class as `public` or `private`, both for
documentation purposes and to avoid these sorts of problems.

Listing 6.9. *diskinit.cpp*— Initialization from Disk

```
1   class some_class
2   {
3       static FILE       *disk_file;
4       static const char *disk_filename;
5       static int        instance_count;
6       static int        ndestroyed;
7
8       int    data1;
9       long   data2;
10      double data3;
11
12      some_class( void )
13      {
14          if( ++instance_count == 1
15                      && !(disk_file = fopen(disk_filename,"rw")) )
16          {
17              perror( disk_filename );
18              exit(1);
19          }
20          fread( &data1, sizeof(int),    1, disk_file );
21          fread( &data2, sizeof(long),   1, disk_file );
22          fread( &data3, sizeof(double), 1, disk_file );
23      }
24      virtual ~some_class( void )
25      {
26          if( ndestroyed++ == 0 )
27              rewind( disk_file );
28
29          fwrite( &data1, sizeof(int),    1, disk_file );
30          fwrite( &data2, sizeof(long),   1, disk_file );
31          fwrite( &data3, sizeof(double), 1, disk_file );
32
33          if( instance_count-- == 1 )
34              fclose( disk_file );
35      }
36  };
37
38  FILE       *some_class::disk_file      = NULL;
39  const char *some_class::disk_file_name = "program.dbf";
40  int         some_class::instance_count = 0;
41  int         some_class::ndestroyed     = 0;
```

differences between
public and **private**
base classes

Private base classes exist in a twilight zone somewhere between a real base class and an instance variable. They really are base classes in that they can pick up virtual functions from the derived class and the derived class can inherit **public** and **protected** functions and data from them. In all other respects, though, they are treated as a **private** instance variable of the derived class:

- A derived class is never implicitly converted to a private base class. You cannot, for example, pass a derived-class object to a function that expects a base-class argument if the base class is **private**. You cannot assign a derived-class object, pointer, or reference to a private base-class object, pointer, or reference. Only a `public` one can be converted in this way.

- The `public` and `protected` members of a `private` base class are treated as `private` members of the derived class. That is, classes that derive from the derived class do not inherit functions from the private base class and the base class cannot pick up virtual functions from them unless the second-level derived class is declared as a `friend`.

`private` `editor` class   I'll demonstrate what `private` base classes are good for with an example. One of the classes that I use regularly is an `editor` class—a general-purpose editing engine that can be used in virtually any environment. It is customized for an environment by deriving a class from it. A much simplified version of the class—which can edit a single line of text—is shown in Listing 6.10. The editor takes a simple set of commands, listed in Table 6.1.

Table 6.1. Editor Commands

Ctrl-E	Move to end of line.
Ctrl-H	Perform destructive backspace.
Ctrl-I	Add spaces until the cursor column is an even multiple of eight.
Ctrl-L	Move left one character.
Ctrl-N	Enter insert mode.
Ctrl-O	Enter overwrite mode.
Ctrl-R	Move right one character.
Ctrl-S	Move to start of line.
Ctrl-W	Move to next word.
Ctrl-X	Clear entire line and reset cursor to start of line.
all others	Either overwrite or insert the character at the current cursor position and move cursor to the right one notch. Use *Ctrl-N* and *Ctrl-O* to control whether characters are inserted or overwritten.

The editor is a general-purpose tool. It will work in any environment. I'll demonstrate how to customize it by using the Borland C++ interface to the IBM-PC screen. You can just as easily make the editor work in a windowing system of some sort or customize it for an ANSI terminal, though. This flexibility is achieved by deferring decisions about how to do hardware-related things. The editor calls `virtual` member functions to move the cursor, output a character, and so forth. The editor is customized by deriving a class from it in which the functions that are needed by the editor are supplied. You can derive several classes from an `editor` to support various environments. Since a single program can have instances of more than one of these derived classes, it's also possible to have a program that can edit in several environments simultaneously. For example, one editor could use an IBM-PC's keyboard and screen and a second editor in the same program could talk to an ANSI terminal via a serial port. Moreover, even though there are multiple derived classes, there's only one editor base class, so the code that is doing the editing is not duplicated in the derived class. The program is thereby made both smaller and easier to maintain.

The current example implements a line editor for the IBM-PC environment using the derivation hierarchy pictured in Figure 6.4. There's only one true derivation—a line_editor *is* an editor. On the other hand, a line_editor *has* a text buffer (of class buffer) and it *has* a screen manager (of class ibm_pc), so these two subclasses are implemented as instance variables.

editor **class hierarchy**

Figure 6.4. An Editor Derivation

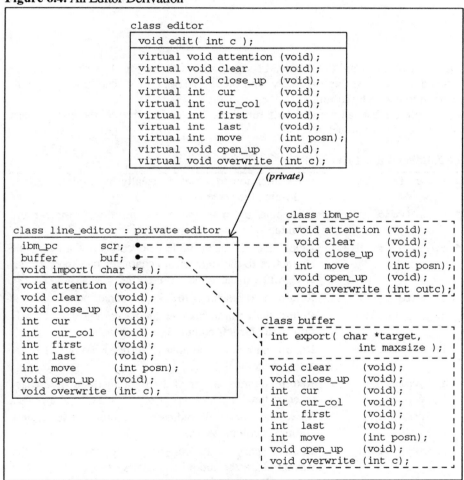

The editor's low-level workhorse functions are specified by the **virtual** definitions in the editor class (in the bottom part of the box that represents an editor in Figure 6.4. These functions are all provided by the line_editor derived class. They are all bridge functions that just provide access to the buffer and ibm_pc components of the class, though. For example, the close_up() function which deletes the character under the cursor by moving all characters to the right of the cursor one space to the left, is implemented as follows in line_editor:

bridge class

```
class line_editor : private editor
{
    buffer  buf;
    ibm_pc  scr;

    void close_up(void)
    {
      buf.close_up();
      scr.close_up();
    }
    //...
}
```

In order to close up a character, line_editor::close_up() is called from the the editor. It closes up the buffer with the buf.close_up() call, then adjusts the screen to match by calling scr.close_up().

Table 6.2 lists all the **virtual** functions that are required by the editor class and describes what they must do.

Table 6.2. Editor Virtual Functions

void attention(**void**)	Draw attention to yourself, usually by ringing the bell or flashing the screen.
void clear(**void**)	Clear line and reset the cursor position to the far-left column.
void close_up(**void**)	Delete the character under the cursor by moving all characters to the right of the character one space to the left. Add a space at the far left.
int cur(**void**)	Return the character at the current cursor position.
int cur_col(**void**)	Return the column number of the current cursor position. (The far-left column is column zero.)
int first(**void**)	Return the column number of leftmost nonwhite character on the line.
int last(**void**)	Return column number of the rightmost nonwhite character on the line.
int move(**int** posn)	Move the cursor to indicated column. (The far-left column is column zero.)
void open_up(**void**)	Insert a space at the current position by moving the current character and all characters to its right over one notch. The cursor remains at the original position, under the space.
void overwrite(**int** c)	Overwrite the character at current cursor position with c. Do not move the cursor.

Using the
line_editor **class,**
editor::edit()
editor::import()

The editor is used in a somewhat circuitous fashion by the derived-class object (the line_editor in Figure 6.4). A line is edited by getting characters from the input and sending them to the `editor::edit()` function, as is done in the following slightly simplified version of the `line_editor` class's `import()` function:

```
void line_editor::import( char *s )
{
    int c;
    edit( 'X'-'@' ); // Send Ctrl-X to editor to clear buffer

    while( (c = getch()) != '\n' && c != '\r' )
      edit( c );

    buf.export( s, size ); // Copy internal buffer to s.
}
```

This function gets a stream of characters from the input [`getch()` is Borland's unbuffered keyboard-input function] and relays them to the editor with successive `edit()` calls. These characters are either added to an internal buffer maintained by the editor object, or are treated as commands that tell the editor how to modify the buffer. The buffer is copied to `s` with an `export()` call when an end of line is found.

Inheritance is used here to call `edit()` which is a member of the `editor` base class, not the derived (`line_editor`) class. `edit()`, in turn, uses polymorphism to call the derived-class functions that do the work. That is, `edit()` calls virtual functions that are provided in the derived class whose function calls `edit()`. For example, the line buffer used by the editor is actually declared locally in the `line_editor` class (as the `buf` field) A buffer is cleared by a `line_editor` somewhat indirectly. The `editor` class calls a local virtual function to clear the buffer as follows:

```
class editor
{
    //...
    virtual void clear( void ) = 0;

    edit( int c )   // Send CTRL-X to edit to clear screen
    {
        //...
        if( c ==  'X'-'@') // CTRL-X
            clear
        //...
    }
}
```

That virtual function is supplied by the derived class as follows

```
class line_editor : private editor
{
    buffer buf;
public:
    void line_editor::clear(void)
    {
      buf.clear();
      //...
    }
}
```

and this supplied function does the real work by calling `buffer::clear()`.

editor

The `editor` class itself is in Listing 6.10. The class doesn't have much to it, consisting mainly of virtual-function definitions. In order to force an `editor` to be an abstract class, these are all pure virtual functions. The important thing is that there are no **public** functions. The editor functions can be called only from a derived-class object. No public-level object can access them. Similarly, there are no functions in the program that manipulate editors—an `editor` object is never passed to a function.

This behavior should be beginning to seem familiar. A **private** instance variable acts in the same way. An `editor` cannot be an instance variable inside the `line_editor` class because it needs to use polymorphism to pick up virtual functions. Consequently, it must be a base class, but it is a **private** base class, thereby restricting access as if it were a **private** instance variable.

Listing 6.10. *editor.cpp*— A General-Purpose Line-Editor Class

```
1   #ifndef __EDITOR_H
2   #define __EDITOR_H
3
4   class editor
5   {
6       int insert_mode;        // If true, character writes push characters
7                               // to the right over a notch to make room.
8   public:
9       editor() : insert_mode(1) {}
10
11  protected:
12      void edit( int c );                     // interface to edit engine
13
14      virtual void attention(void)    = 0; // draw attention to yourself.
15      virtual void close_up(void)     = 0; // delete current cursor char
16                                           // and close up line.
17      virtual void open_up(void)      = 0; // insert a space at the current
18                                           // position by moving current
19                                           // character and all characters
20                                           // to right over a notch. cursor
21                                           // remains under space.
22      virtual int cur( void )         = 0; // return character at current
23                                           // cursor position.
24      virtual void overwrite( int c )= 0; // overwrite character at current
25                                           // position with c.
26      virtual void clear( void )      = 0; // clear line, cursor to column 0
```

Listing 6.10. continued...

```
27          virtual int   move( int posn )   = 0; // move to column (left=0)
28          virtual int   cur_col( void )     = 0; // return current column (left=0)
29          virtual int   last( void )        = 0; // return column of last nonwhite
30                                                 // character on line
31          virtual int   first( void )       =0;  // return column of first non-
32                                                 // white character on line
33      };
34      //--------------------------------------------------------------------
35      #ifdef EDITOR_COMPILE_METHODS
36      #include <ctype.h>
37
38      #define CTRL(c)  ((c)-'@')              // CTRL('A') evaluates to Ctrl-A, etc.
39                                             // This macro, unfortunately, can't be
40                                             // a virtual function because it's
41                                             // used in a switch and Borland won't
42                                             // accept it.
43      void editor::edit( int c )
44      {
45          switch( c )
46          {
47          case CTRL('H'):                 // Destructive Backspace
48              if( !move( cur_col()-1 ) )
49                  attention();
50              else
51                  close_up();
52              break;
53
54          case CTRL('L'):                 // Move left one character
55              if( !move( cur_col()-1 ) )
56                  attention();
57              break;
58
59          case CTRL('R'):                 // move right one character
60              move( cur_col() + 1 );
61              break;
62
63          case CTRL('E'):                 // move to end of line
64              move( last() );
65              break;
66
67          case CTRL('S'):                 // move to start of line
68              move( first() );
69              break;
70
71          case CTRL('W'):                 // move to next word
72              while( !isspace(cur()) && cur_col() < last() )
73                  move( cur_col()+1 );
74              while( isspace(cur()) && cur_col() < last() )
75                  move( cur_col()+1 );
76              break;
77
```

➡

Listing 6.10. continued...

```
 78         case CTRL('I'):                    // expand to 8-character tabstop
 79             do
 80             {
 81                 open_up();
 82                 if( !move( cur_col() + 1 ) )
 83                     break;
 84             }
 85             while( cur_col() % 8 );
 86             break;
 87
 88         case CTRL('N'):                    // Enter insert mode
 89             insert_mode = 1;
 90             break;
 91
 92         case CTRL('O'):                    // Enter overwrite mode
 93             insert_mode = 0;
 94             break;
 95
 96         case CTRL('X'):                    // Clear line & reset cursor
 97             clear();
 98             break;
 99
100         default:
101             if( insert_mode )
102                 open_up();
103             overwrite( c );
104             move( cur_col() + 1 );
105             break;
106         }
107     }
108
109     #undef CTRL      // don't need this any more
110
111     #endif // EDITOR_COMPILE_METHODS
112     #endif // __EDITOR_H
```

Though the previous point is the whole reason for bringing up the editor example at this juncture, it's instructive to continue and look at the rest of the implementation. The only function that does any work at the editor level is edit(), on line 43 of Listing 6.10, and it's doing most of its work vicariously through virtual functions. The **default** case at the bottom of the subroutine, for example, inserts a character by calling the virtual open_up() function to make room for the new character, the virtual overwrite() call prints the character, and the virtual move() call moves the cursor one notch. The other cases work in a similar manner.

buffer class

The buffer class in Listing 6.11 supplies some of the functions that will ultimately be called by the editor. This class manages a simple one-dimensional text buffer, allowing simple editing operations on it. A buffer is not a string, which is a more general-purpose data structure. A buffer's intended purpose is to allow

internal manipulation of a buffer only. Consequently, there are no operator overloads except for `operator=()` on line 29 of Listing 6.11. (There's also a copy
constructor just above it. Also note that the destructor on line 25 is declared virtual so that the `buffer` can be used safely as a base class.) Overloads that support
string operations (like comparison, concatenation, and so forth) are better done in a
`string` class that derives from `buffer`.

An alternate way of implementing a `buffer` would be to flip things around:
create a more general-purpose `string` class and then derive `buffer` from it to add
editing capability to the `string`. I opted for the current approach primarily to simplify things by removing unnecessary functionality. That is, it's possible for a
class to be *too* general-purpose—to do considerably more than is needed in a particular application—and this overabundance of functionality can cause as many
maintenance problems as the reverse situation—when there's no generality at all. I
opted for simplicity.

Most of the functions in Listing 6.11 are self-explanatory. Note the `export()`   `buffer::export()`
function on line 61 that copies the internal buffer into an external array of **char**.
You can use this function to access the internally maintained buffer without any
side effects that would be caused by giving direct access to the `buf` field.

Listing 6.11. *buffer.h*— A One-Dimensional Text-Buffer Class

```
 1   #ifndef __BUFFER_H
 2   #define __BUFFER_H
 3
 4   #include <ctype.h>
 5   #include <mem.h>
 6   #include <string.h>
 7   #include <stdlib.h>
 8
 9   class buffer
10   {
11       char *buf;
12       int  size;          // Size of array pointed to by buf.
13       char *cursor;       // Points at current character.
14       char *end;          // Pointer to last element of buf, makes
15                           // out-of-bounds checking a little more
16                           // efficient.
17       void init( int sz ) // Initialize data fields.
18       {
19           cursor = buf = new char[size = sz];
20           end    = buf + (size - 1);
21       }
22
23   public:
24       buffer( int sz )          { init(sz);    }
25       virtual ~buffer( void  ) { delete buf; }
26       buffer( buffer &s )       { init(s.size); memcpy( buf, s.buf, size );}
27       void clear( void )        { memset( cursor = buf, ' ', size ); }
28
```

Listing 6.11. continued. . .

```
29        buffer &operator=( buffer &s )
30        {
31            delete buf;
32            init( s.size );
33            memcpy( buf, s.buf, size );
34            return *this;
35        }
36
37      int   cur        ( void ) { return *cursor;        }
38      void overwrite ( int c ) { *cursor = c;          }
39      int   cur_col    ( void ) { return cursor - buf;  }
40      void close_up  ( void )
41        {                              // Delete current character and close up
42            if( cursor >= end )
43                return;
44            memmove( cursor, cursor+1, end-cursor );
45            *end = ' ';
46        }
47      void open_up (void)
48        {                              // insert a space at current character
49            if( cursor >= end )
50                return;
51            memmove( cursor+1, cursor, end-cursor );
52            *cursor = ' ';
53        }
54
55      int move ( int posn );
56      int last ( void    );
57      int first( void    );
58
59      int min(int a, int b){ return a < b ? a : b ; }
60
61      int export( char *target, int max_size )
62        {
63            // Export the current line, truncating all white space
64            // on the right of the line. Return false if line was
65            // truncated (line len > max_size-1 characters) or blank.
66
67            int need = last() + 2; // +1 converts index to size, then 2nd
68                                   // +1 provides space for '\0\.
69            int used = min(need, max_size);
70
71            if( used == 2 && isspace(*buf) )        // blank line
72                --used;
73
74            strncpy( target, buf, used-1 );
75            target[used-1] = '\0';
76            return( used == need );
77        }
78    };
79    //-----------------------------------------------------------------
80    #ifdef BUFFER_COMPILE_METHODS
81    int buffer::move( int posn )
```

Listing 6.11. continued. . .

```
82   {
83         // Move internal cursor position to desired position.
84         // return true on success, false if the target position
85         // is not in the buffer.
86
87         int rval = 0;
88         cursor = buf + posn;
89         if            ( cursor > end ) cursor = end;
90         else if       ( cursor < buf ) cursor = buf;
91         else                           rval  = 1;
92         return rval;
93   }
94
95   int buffer::last( void )
96   {
97         // return the index of the rightmost nonwhite character
98
99         char *p, *last;
100        for( p = last = buf; *p && p < end; ++p )
101            if( !isspace(*p) )
102                last = p;
103
104        return( last - buf );
105  }
106
107  int buffer::first( void )
108  {
109        // return the index of the leftmost nonwhite character
110
111        char *p;
112        for( p = buf; isspace(*p) && p < end ; ++p )
113            ;
114        return p - buf;
115  }
116  #endif //  BUFFER_COMPILE_METHODS
117  #endif //  __BUFFER_H
```

The ibm_pc class in Listing 6.12 is a simple screen manager for the IBM-PC.   ibm_pc **class**
It uses Borland C++'s screen-interface functions—isolating them into a single
class to make porting to another compiler or video environment easier. I've used a
separate class, rather than extending the graphics_engine class presented earlier, because these are all text-mode functions. The two classes could probably be
combined, but then you run into the too-much-complexity problem, again.

Since I never expect ibm_pc to be anything except an instance variable, I've
not added support for derivation. There is no virtual destructor, copy constructor,
or operator=() function, for example. I don't expect that an ibm_pc object will
ever be copied, but if it is, C-style structure copying will work fine—there are no
pointer members in ibm_pc.

Listing 6.12. *ibm_pc.h* — IBM-PC Screen Manager Class

```
1   #ifndef __IBM_PC_H
2   #define __IBM_PC_H
3
4   #include <conio.h>
5   #include <stdio.h>
6   #include <stdlib.h>
7
8   class ibm_pc
9   {
10  private:
11      int width;
12
13  public:
14      ibm_pc()
15      {
16          text_info t;
17          gettextinfo( &t );
18          width = t.screenwidth -1;
19          clear();
20      }
21
22      void clear      (void){ move(0); clreol(); } // clear line
23      int  getkey     (void){ return getch();    } // direct keyboard input
24      void attention (void){ putchar('\a');      } // ring bell
25
26      void open_up (void)
27      {
28          int x = wherex();
29          int y = wherey();
30          movetext(x, y, width -1, y, x+1, y );
31          overwrite(' ');
32      }
33
34      void close_up (void)
35      {
36          int x = wherex();
37          int y = wherey();
38          movetext (x+1, y, width -1, y, x, y);
39          gotoxy   (width, y);
40          overwrite(' ' );
41          gotoxy   (x, y);
42      }
43
44      int  move(int posn)
45      {
46          if( posn < 0 || posn >= width )
47              return 0;
48          else
49          {
50              gotoxy( posn+1, wherey() ); // Borland cursor 1==leftmost col
51              return 1;
52          }
```

➡

Listing 6.12. continued. . .

```
53        }
54
55        void overwrite( int outc )
56        {
57            int c;
58            gettext( wherex(), wherey(), wherex(), wherey(), &c );
59            c = (c & ~0xff) | outc ;
60            puttext( wherex(), wherey(), wherex(), wherey(), &c );
61        }
62    };
63    #endif // __IBM_PC_H
```

The final class in the system is the `line_editor` class that actually derives from `editor`, linking the editor to the functions provided in the `buffer` and `ibm_pc` classes. It's in Listing 6.13. There is a small sample `main()` on line 46 of Listing 6.13 that demonstrates how to use the class—it's pretty straightforward. You declare a `line_editor` object and then extract a sequence of lines from it with a call to the `import()` function: `line_editor` **class**

```
char buf[ SIZE ];
line_editor ed( buf );   // declare an editor
ed.import( buf );        // get a line
```

You can also mimic the stream I/O system with the following shift overload

```
line_editor &operator>>( line_editor &left, char *right )
{
    left.import( right );
    return left;
}
```

and then input two successive input lines like this:

```
char str1[ LINE_MAX ];
char str2[ LINE_MAX ];
line_editor keyboard( LINE_MAX );
keyboard >> str1 >> str2 ;
```

Listing 6.13. *leditor.h*— Line-Editor Class

```
1    #ifndef __LEDITOR_H
2    #define __LEDITOR_H
3
4    #include "buffer.h"
5    #include "ibmscr.h"
6
7    class line_editor : private editor
8    {
9        buffer   buf;
10       ibm_pc   scr;
11       int      size;
12
```

Listing 6.13. continued. . .

```
13   public:
14       line_editor( int max_size ) : size(max_size), buf(max_size) {}
15       void import( char *s );
16
17   private:
18       virtual void clear      (void)  {buf.clear();      scr.clear();      }
19       virtual void close_up   (void)  {buf.close_up();   scr.close_up();   }
20       virtual void open_up    (void)  {buf.open_up();    scr.open_up();    }
21       virtual void overwrite (int c) {buf.overwrite(c); scr.overwrite(c);}
22
23       virtual int move(int posn){return buf.move(posn) && scr.move(posn);}
24
25       virtual void attention (void) { scr.attention();      }
26       virtual int cur        (void) { return buf.cur();      }
27       virtual int cur_col    (void) { return buf.cur_col(); }
28       virtual int last       (void) { return buf.last();     }
29       virtual int first      (void) { return buf.first();    }
30   };
31   //-----------------------------------------------------------------
32   #ifdef LEDITOR_COMPILE_METHODS
33
34   void line_editor::import( char *s )
35   {
36       int c;
37       edit( 'X'-'@' ); // Ctrl-X clears buffer
38       while( (c = scr.getkey()) != '\n' && c != '\r' )
39           edit( c );
40       buf.export(s, size); // export buffer to application at end of line
41   }
42
43   #endif LEDITOR_COMPILE_METHODS
44   //-----------------------------------------------------------------
45   #ifdef LEDITOR_TEST
46   void main( void )
47   {
48       char buf[40];
49       line_editor ed( sizeof(buf) );       // create a line editor for buf
50
51       ed.import( buf );                    // import a line from the editor
52       printf("\n<%s>\n", buf );            // print it.
53
54       ed.import( buf );                    // import another line
55       printf("\n<%s>\n", buf );            // print it.
56   }
57   #endif // LEDITOR_TEST
58   #endif // __LEDITOR_H
```

loosing privacy
through multiple
inheritance

There is one loose end to tie up before finishing with `private` base classes. If there is a `public` path from the base class to the derived class, then the base class is `public`, even if there is also a `private` path. Here's an example:

```
class A                          { public: int x; }
class B: public  A               { public: ... }
class C: private A               { public: ... }
class D: public B, public C      { public: ... }

D derived;
derived.x = 0;
```

Members of an ancestor can be accessed provided there is a public path from the ancestor to the current class, even if other paths have more restricted access.

6.11 Member Pointers

Member pointers do not, strictly speaking, have anything to do with derivation. They are useful, however, for doing derivation-like things without actually deriving a class. That's why I'm presenting them in this chapter. I'll start off by solving a problem with derivation, and then demonstrate how to do the same thing with member pointers.

Listing 6.14 shows a simplified version of the int_array class we looked at a few chapters back.

Listing 6.14. *intarray.cpp*— A Simplified int_array Class

```
 1   class int_array
 2   {
 3       int *buf;
 4       int size;
 5   public:
 6       int getsize      ( void     ){ return size;             }
 7       int_array        ( int sz   ){ buf = new int[size = sz]; }
 8       ~int_array       ( void     ){ delete buf;              }
 9       int &operator[] ( int index ){ return buf[index];       }
10   };
```

The int_array is a very basic type, though. There are other data structures that are based on arrays, but treat them in specialized ways. For example, Listing 6.15 shows how to implement a stack class based on the array class. A queue can be implemented in much the same way—the code is presented in Listing 6.16.

Derivation is really the correct choice in the current situation because the int_stack class adds several capabilities to the int_array class that were not there previously. **Derivation, when used properly, adds capabilities to an existing class.** *(use derivation to add capabilities)*

But what if instead of adding capabilities, you are just changing the way that existing features are used? For example, you can use a linked list to implement an array of int by deriving an int_ele from a list_ele: *(array-of-int implemented as list)*

Listing 6.15. *arrstack.cpp*— An `int_stack` Class

```
 1    class int_stack : public int_array
 2    {
 3        int stack_ptr;
 4    public:
 5        int_stack(int size): int_array(size), stack_ptr(size) {}
 6
 7        int  full ( void  ){ return stack_ptr <= 0;           }
 8        int  empty( void  ){ return stack_ptr == getsize();   }
 9        void push ( int x ){ if( !full() )
10                                     // call int_array::operator[]()
11                                     // function. Could also use
12                                     // (*this)[ --stack_ptr ] = x, but
13                                     // that seems even harder to read.
14
15                                     operator[]( --stack_ptr ) = x ;
16                             }
17        int pop( void )      { if( !empty() )
18                                     return operator[]( stack_ptr++ );
19                             }
20    }
```

```
            int_ele : public list_ele
            {
                int key;
                operator int()  { return key; }
                int_ele( int i ){ key = i;      }
            }
```

You don't need a copy constructor, `operator=()`, and so forth, because C-style structure copying works fine. The conversion operators also handle the vast majority of arithmetic situations. For example, if you say

```
            int_ele x;
            x = 10;
```

the compiler uses the **int** constructor to transform 10 into an `int_ele` and then uses C-style structure copying to do the assignment.

The advantage to a linked-list versus an array approach is that a linked list's size is limited only by the amount of available memory. Consequently, a `stack` that's built from a `list` will never fill up. Moreover, the `list` functions are not tied into a specific array-element type, as is the case with the `int_array`. Lists can be lists of any object that derives from a `list_ele`. A stack that's implemented from a list is equally flexible.

Turning our attention to the `list` for a moment, a reasonable implementation will have at least two insertion functions and two deletion functions—add and delete from the list head, and add and delete from the list tail. This way the list can be maintained as a queue, a stack, or an arbitrary list. Adding an add-in-sorted-order function lets you maintain a sorted list. It traverses the list from head to tail until it finds an element whose key is larger than the element to insert, and then

Listing 6.16. *arrqueue.cpp*— An int_queue **Class**

```
1    class int_queue : public int_array
2    {
3        int head;
4        int tail;
5    public:
6        int_stack( int size ) : int_array(size), head(0), tail(0)  ;
7
8        int  empty( void  ){ return head == tail; }
9        int  full ( void  ){ return (head == 0 && tail == getsize()-1)
10                                    || (head == tail-1 );
11                           }
12       void enqueue(int x){ if( !full() )
13                            {
14                                   operator[]( tail ) = x ;
15                                   tail = ++tail % getsize();
16                            }
17                          }
18       int dequeue( void ){ if( !empty() )
19                            {
20                                   int rval = operator[]( head );
21                                   head = ++head % getsize();
22                                   return rval;
23                            }
24                          }
25   }
```

inserts the new element to the left of the existing element. Leaving aside the implementation mechanics, here's what the list class definition would look like:

```
class list
{
private;
    list_ele *head, *tail;
    int is_sorted;     // list is in sorted order.
    sort();            // sorts the list; used to add_sort()
                       // to a previously unsorted list.
    // ...
public:
    add_head(list_ele *p); // add *p to the head of the list
    add_tail(list_ele *p); // add *p to the tail of the list
    add_sort(list_ele *p); // add *p in a sorted position

    list_ele *remove_head(void); // remove (and return) the
                                 // head-of-list object
    list_ele *remove_tail(void); // ditto, but tail object.
    // ...
};
```

There's no code-size penalty for having this many member functions in the class. Just because the list class has several insert and delete functions does not mean that all of the code for these functions will end up in the final program. Unless the functions are `virtual` (which they are not) the linker will call in only those functions that are actually used, provided that the functions were compiled separately—one function per file.

You can argue—reasonably—that this general-purpose list class is nonetheless too complex. A better solution is to implement an abstract `list` class that has no insertion and deletion functions at all, requiring the derived class to implement stacks, queues, and sorted lists:

```
class list
{
protected;
    list_ele *head, *tail;
    virtual void      add    (list_ele *p) =0;
    virtual list_ele *remove ( void     ) =0;
}

class sorted_list : public list
{
private:
    int is_sorted;            // List is in sorted order.
    sort();                   // Sort the list if you do an add_sort(
                              // to a previously unsorted list.
public:
    void add(list_ele *p);    // Add element in sorted order
    list_ele *remove( void ); // remove smallest element from head
}

class queue : public list
{
public:
    void add(list_ele *p);    // Add to head of list
    list_ele *remove( void ); // remove from tail of list
}

class stack : public list
{
public:
    void add(list_ele *p);    // Add to head of list
    list_ele *remove( void ); // remove from head of list
}
```

There's one big problem with this approach. You might not want to use the `list` in a consistent way throughout its life. For example, inserting previously sorted elements into a `sorted_list` is a very expensive operation because the insertion function will have to traverse the entire list with every insertion in order to add an element to the end. You can get around this specific problem by checking the value of the tail element before traversing, but the average-case behavior of a straight insertion sort is not great [it's $O((n^2-n)/4)$]. You'd be much better off inserting the elements into a queue, sorting the queue if necessary, and then transforming the queue into a sorted list so that subsequent insertions will be in order.

You can define conversions from `queue` to `sorted_list`, and so forth, to do this transformation, but now you'll have a tremendous amount of complexity—

much more than was the case with the original, more general `list` implementation. Moreover, these conversions will, by necessity, involve copying the list because the conversion must be implemented by constructors or overloaded cast operators.

So a better approach is to have a general-purpose `list` whose default maintenance mechanism can be changed with subroutine calls like the following ones:

```
become_queue();
become_stack();
become_sorted();
```

A single `insert()` and `remove()` function will be supported, but `insert()` will behave in a different way when the list is a sorted list than it will when the list is a queue.

There are two ways to do the foregoing. The first is to use a `what_i_am` field and a switch. An implementation is presented in Listing 6.17.

changing default-maintenance mechanism with a switch

The main problem is the unnecessary code and maintenance complications caused by the **switch** statements and enumerated types. A better solution redefines the `add()` and `remove()` functions to call the required list-manipulation function through a pointer whose contents are modified by the `become` functions. This solution effectively does explicitly what the compiler does for you when a function is declared **virtual**.

There's one difficulty, though. You cannot take the address of a field in a **class**, and the list-manipulation functions are fields. The easiest way to see the problem is to look at a normal data member. The following is illegal:

changing default-maintenance mechanism with member-function pointers

```
class fred { public: int x; };
int *p = &fred::x;                        // ILLEGAL
```

The problem is that `fred::x` isn't at any one address—it's at a different address in each object. There's nothing to stop you from doing the following:

```
class fred { public: int x; };
fred a_c_object;
int *p = & a_c_object.x ;
```

But `p` holds the address of a specific `x` field—it is not a general-purpose pointer that lets you access the `x` field of any arbitrary object of class `fred`.

The same restriction applies to functions. The following is illegal:

```
class fred { public: int f(void); };
int (*pfi)(void) = fred::f;   // ILLEGAL
```

The difficulty is not that `f()` is going to move around (which it won't), but that a call through `pfi` must be handled in one of two ways, depending on whether `f()` is **virtual**. An extra implicit level of indirection is required for the **virtual** functions. This behavior is different from that of a normal function pointer, which always calls the function in the same way with only one level of indirection.

pointers to virtual member functions

None of the foregoing applies to **static** class members because they do have addresses. I used a pointer to a **static** member in the earlier `typeof()` implementation, but you probably didn't notice anything special because the code works as expected. Here's the syntax:

member pointers not needed for **static** members

Listing 6.17. *list5.cpp*— A General-Purpose List

```
1    enum list_type { QUEUE, STACK, SORTED };
2    class list
3    {
4        list_type what_i_am ;
5        sort();                         // sort the list.
6        add_head(list_ele *p);          // Add *p to the head of the list
7        add_tail(list_ele *p);          // Add *p to the tail of the list
8        add_sort(list_ele *p);          // Add *p in a sorted position
9        list_ele *remove_head(void);// Remove & return the head-of-list obj
10       list_ele *remove_tail(void);// Remove & return the tail-of-list obj
11       // ...
12   public:
13       void become_sorted(void) {  if( what_i_am != SORTED )
14                                       if( (what_i_am = what) == SORTED )
15                                           sort();
16                                 }
17       void become_queue(void)   {   what_i_am = QUEUE;   }
18       void become_stack(void)   {   what_i_am = STACK;   }
19       void add( list_ele *p )
20       {
21           switch( what_i_am )
22           {
23           case SORTED:     add_sort(p); break;
24           case STACK:
25           case QUEUE:      add_tail(p); break;
26           }
27       }
28       list_ele *remove( void )
29       {
30           switch( what_i_am )
31           {
32           case STACK:      return remove_tail();
33           case SORTED:
34           case QUEUE:      return remove_head();
35           }
36       }
37   }
```

```
struct beanie {  static int x;
                 void cecil( void )
                 {
                     int *p = &x; // address of x field.
                     *p = 0;      // modify x.
                 }
              };
int beanie::x;
```

```
void bullwinkle( void )
{
    beanie::x = 0;           // modify x directly
    int *p   = &beanie::x;   // modify x through pointer
    *p       = 0;
}
```

Returning to the problem of non-**static** member pointers, rather than provide a mechanism for handling only the oddball case of an indirect virtual-function call—so that you can use normal function pointers on nonvirtual functions—all class members must be accessed indirectly using an entirely new syntax. The best way to demonstrate the syntax is with a member-data pointer, even though a member-data pointer is rarely (if ever) used in practice.

member-data
pointers

You have to use a two step process to declare a member pointer, and the syntax is rather weird. A declaration like

```
class fred { ... int i; ... };
int  fred::* pi_fred;
```

creates a pointer to an **int** member of the fred class. The operator is fred::*, which means "pointer to an element of fred." Member pointers must be attached to specific classes in this way.

class_name::*

The pointer is now initialized like this:

```
pi_fred = &fred::i ;
```

This syntax is very misleading, and to my mind is a syntactic bug in the language. The & usually means "address of." Here, though, it means nothing of the sort. The i field of a fred doesn't have an address unless there's a specific object involved. The earlier assignment loads pi_fred with the offset from the base of the structure to the the i field, not with its address.

&class_name::field

Since the member pointer effectively holds only an offset, you also need a base address for a real object to use it. The syntax is like this:

```
fred Flintstone;               // Declare a fred object
fred *MacMurry = &Flintstone;  // and a pointer to a fred.

Flintstone.*pi_fred = 10; // Put 10 into the int-sized field
                          // whose offset is in pi_fred.
MacMurry->*pi_fred = 10;  // ditto but via pointer.
```

The .* and ->* are operators are used to access the members. You may be thinking that the introduction of two new operators is superfluous, and you'd be right. The compiler knows perfectly well that pi_fred is a member pointer because it's declared as such. There is absolutely no theoretical reason why the compiler can't process the . and -> operators in a special way when the right operand is a member pointer rather than a field name. Nonetheless, you <u>must</u> use the special .* or ->* operators. You cannot use a normal . or ->.

.* ->*

Moving on to member-function pointers, the same syntax is used as is used for variables. Listing 6.18 shows a redefinition of the general-purpose list class that uses member-function pointers rather than switches and enumerated types. The declaration

member-function
pointers

```
           void (list::* p_add)( list_ele *p );
```

on line two creates a pointer to a member function of a list. Figure 6.5 demonstrates how to break up the declaration.

Listing 6.18. The `list` Class Redefined to Use Member Pointers

```
1    class list
2    {   void        (list::* p_add    )(list_ele *p);
3        list_ele *(list::* p_remove)(void          );
4
5        list(): p_add(list::add_tail), p_remove(list::remove_head) {}
6    public:
7        void become_sorted(void) {  if( p_add != fred::sorted )
8                                          sort();
9                                     p_add    = list::add_sort;
10                                    p_remove = list::remove_head;   }
11       void become_queue(void)  {  p_add    = list::add_tail;
12                                    p_remove = list::remove_head;   }
13       void become_stack(void)  {  p_add    = list::add_tail;
14                                    p_remove = list::remove_tail;   }
15
16       void      add  ( list_ele *p ){ this->*p_add( p );           }
17       list_ele *remove(    void   ){ return this->*p_remove();     }
18   }
```

Figure 6.5. Parsing a Pointer to Member Function Declaration

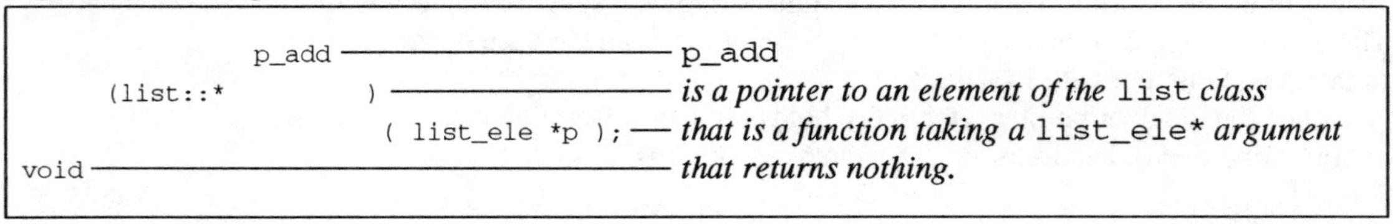

The second declaration

```
           list_ele *(list::* p_remove)(void);
```

also creates a pointer (named `p_remove`) to a list member function. The function
returns a `list_ele*` and takes no arguments. The pointers are initialized so that
the default behavior of a `list` mimics a queue. The `become` functions in the earlier declaration modify the member-function pointers to address the correct function for the list type. The `add()` and `remove()` functions are **inline** aliases for
indirect function calls.

As you can see, the revised definition is both smaller and more efficient than
the earlier enumerated-type-and-**switch** solution. There is no more overhead than
there would be in a virtual-function solution. There's still a lot of complexity,
though, and member pointers are not very well understood by many C++ programmers. In general, you should restrict their use to only those situations where
derivation cannot do the job—where you need to modify the existing behavior of a

class rather than adding new behavior, which is more properly done with derivation.

6.12 Container Classes and Templates

Although derivation is the primary means of customizing a class definition to a specific application, it can't always do the job. C++ provides an alternative to derivation—a *class template*—that can handle situations in which you cannot use derivation. A class template works much like a function template (described in Chapter Two), letting you generate multiple versions of a class definition, each customized to an explicit application. Derivation lets you add fields to an existing structure; templates let you change the type definition of an existing field within the structure.

class template

Class templates are typically used to implement a kind of class called a *container class*—a class that is intended only to hold instances of another class. I'll demonstrate the mechanism with a simple example—an array-of-objects container—and will bring up the subject again in the next chapter, where I can discuss container classes in a more realistic context. But first, the syntax.

container class

Consider the problem of creating a general-purpose array type as compared to a specific array such as the `intarray` used in previous chapters. Listing 6.19 shows a definition for a specialized array type that supports boundary checking on array indexes by overloading the bracket operator. The main problem is that this class can support arrays of only one type. To implement an array of `char` pointers, for example, I'd have to create an almost identical `class` definition with a different class name and with `char*` replacing `int` in the statements on lines six, nine, and in the return value on line 12 of Listing 6.19.

You really don't want to maintain a large body of almost identical subroutines, though. One not-very-elegant solution is to create an array-class-generation macro much like the `min()`-generation macro discussed in Chapter Two. I've done this at the top of Listing 6.20. A few invocations at the bottom of the listing demonstrate how to use the macro. For example, the macro invocation on line 28 of Listing 6.20 creates an array-of-`int` class called `arrayofint`. It passes the `int` type to the macro, which expands it in the class name on line five of Listing 6.20 (using the `##` concatenation macro) and on lines seven, ten, 11, and 14 as well. The resulting class definition will look exactly like the definition in Listing 6.19. Invoking `arrayof(long)` does much the same thing, but a class called `arrayoflong` that implements arrays of `long` integers is generated.

class-generation macro

Although the macro solution in Listing 6.20 does work, the syntax is awkward and the code is hard to debug. (Error messages generated by bugs in the class definition will all be called out for the line on which the macro is expanded, for example.) It's also easy to run out of macro-expansion space when the macros get this large.

A better solution is to use the `template` mechanism. A simple `template` variant of the array class is shown in Listing 6.21. As was the case with function templates, the `template` statement on line four binds to the immediately following declaration—in this case the `class` array declaration. The template's `type`

Listing 6.19. *arrayofi.cpp*— An Array-of-`int` Class

```
1    #include <stdio.h>
2    #include <stdlib.h>
3
4    class arrayofint
5    {
6        int   *p;
7        int   size;
8    public:
9        arrayofint  ( int sz ){ p = new int[size = sz];        }
10       ~arrayofint  (    void ){ delete p;                      }
11       numele       (    void ){ return size;                  }
12       int &operator[]( int index )
13       {
14           if( !(0 <= index && index < size) )
15           {
16               fprintf(stderr, "Array out of bounds\n");
17               exit(1);
18           }
19           return p[index];
20       }
21   };
22
23   void main( void )
24   {
25       int i;
26       arrayofint ai( 10 );            // 10 element array of int
27
28       for( i = 0; i < ai.numele(); ++i )
29           ai[ i ] = i ;
30
31       for( i = 0; i < ai.numele(); ++i )
32           printf("%d ", ai[ i ] );
33       printf("\n");
34   }
```

argument is used in the class definition on lines seven, ten, and 14. When the compiler encounters a declaration like the one on line 28, it matches the actual types in the angle-bracketed list with the ones in the **template** statement. It then expands the template into a class definition, replacing all references to the **template**-argument type with the explicit type in the declaration. In the current example, the **class** type in the **template** definition on line four of Listing 6.21 is matched by the `int` on line 28. When the compiler expands the template into a class definition, it replaces all of the types with `int`.

class keyword in
template statement

There's a certain amount of unnecessary confusion caused by the use of **class** in the **template** statement. Stroustrup should really have introduced a `type` keyword for this purpose. When you see **class** in a template statement like

        template <class fred>

the **class** really means that the `fred` argument to the template is a type specifier

Listing 6.20. *arraymac.cpp*— An Array-Class-Generation Macro

```
1   #include <stdio.h>
2   #include <stdlib.h>
3
4   #define arrayof( type )                                      \
5       class arrayof##type                                      \
6       {                                                        \
7           type  *p;                                            \
8           int   size;                                          \
9       public:                                                  \
10          arrayof##type ( int sz ){ p = new type[size=sz]; } \
11          ~arrayof##type(   void ){ delete p;             } \
12          numele        (   void ){ return size;          } \
13                                                               \
14          type &operator[]( int index )                        \
15          {                                                    \
16              if( !(0 <= index && index < size) )              \
17              {                                                \
18                  fprintf(stderr, "Array out of bounds\n");    \
19                  exit(1);                                     \
20              }                                                \
21              return p[index];                                 \
22                                                               \
23          }                                                    \
24      }
25
26  // Generate class definitions for various arrays:
27
28  arrayof(int  );            // generate definition for arrayofint type //
29  arrayof(long );            // generate definition for arrayoflong type
30
31  typedef char *charptr;   // generate definition for arrayofcharptr type
32  arrayof(charptr);
33
34  void main( void )
35  {
36      int i;
37      arrayoflong ai( 10 );         // 10 element array of int
38
39      for( i = 0; i < ai.numele(); ++i )
40          ai[ i ] = (long)i ;
41
42      for( i = 0; i < ai.numele(); ++i )
43          printf("%ld ", ai[ i ] );
44      printf("\n");
45  }
```

(an abstract declarator, to be more exact). It does not mean that fred must be a user-defined class or anything else of the sort. The fred argument to the template specifies an incoming type. When you specify a real type in the template expansion such as the array<int>, the compiler effectively creates a **typedef** whose name (`fred`) is fetched from the template statement and whose declaration (`int`) is fetched from the `array<int>`. It then uses that **typedef** when expanding the template.

Moving back to the template-expansion process, a second declaration in which the template-argument types differ from the first causes the compiler to expand the class template a second time. There will now be two different class definitions in existence, and two sets of method subroutines as well. For example, a declaration that reuses the template, but with a different argument, such as

```
array<char*> acp( 100 ); // 100 element array of char ptrs.
```

makes the compiler generate a new class definition, but this time with **char*** replacing `type` in the expansion and with a new set of methods that process character-pointer array elements. (The amount of code that can be generated by template expansions is sometimes significant since all of the method functions are expanded in addition to the class definition itself. I'll discuss this problem further in the next chapter.)

complex type arguments to a template

The `type` argument to a template can be arbitrarily complex. Here's a definition for an array of pointers to functions that take a `long` argument and return an `int`:

```
array<int(*)(long)> pfi_array( 16 );
```

The replacement mechanism is more like a **typedef** than a simple macro replacement. The `array` definition can take class arguments, too. This one creates an array of `string` objects:

```
class string { /*...*/ };

array<string> string_array( 16 );
```

nested template expansions

Finally, template expansions can nest. Here, for example, is a definition that creates an array of `int` arrays:

```
array< array<int> >   array_of_int_arrays(10);
```

In this last example, you can access the individual elements with normal C-style array indexing. A statement like

```
array_of_int_arrays[2][3] = 0;
```

works fine. The `[2]` uses the **operator**`[]()` function to return a reference to an entire `array<int>`, the fourth element of which is then referenced with the `[3]` using the **operator**`[]()` from the original template expansion. That is, there are two separate **operator**`[]()` functions used here—one was created by the `array<int>` and the second by the `array<array<int>>`.

nested template constructor problems, non-type template arguments

There is one problem with `array<array<int>>`. The earlier

```
array< array<int> >   array_of_int_arrays(10);
```

created a 10-element array of `array<int>` objects by passing 10 to the `array` constructor, which is declared on line ten of Listing 6.21. The interior arrays (the `array<int>`s) must be created with the default constructor (on the next line of the listing) because they do not have names to which you can attach a constructor

Listing 6.21. *arraytem.cpp*— An Array-Class Template

```
 1    #include <stdio.h>
 2    #include <stdlib.h>
 3
 4    template <class type>
 5    class array
 6    {
 7        type   *p;
 8        int    size;
 9    public:
10        array  ( int sz ){ p = new type[size = sz ]; }
11        array  ( void  ){ p = new type[size = 100]; }
12        ~array (    void ){ delete [sz]p; } /* delete sz-element array */
13        numele (    void ){ return size;   }
14        type &operator[]( int index )
15        {
16            if( !(0 <= index && index < size) )
17            {
18                fprintf(stderr, "Array out of bounds\n");
19                exit(1);
20            }
21            return p[index];
22        }
23    };
24
25    void main( void )
26    {
27        int i;
28        array<int> ai( 10 );            // 10 element array of int called ai
29
30        for( i = 0; i < ai.numele(); ++i )
31            ai[ i ] = i ;
32
33        for( i = 0; i < ai.numele(); ++i )
34            printf("%d ", ai[ i ] );
35        printf("\n");
36    }
```

argument. Consequently, the earlier declaration created a 10-element array of default-sized 100-element arrays.

You may not want the interior arrays to be the default size, though. C++ handles this situation by letting you use normal arguments as well as `class` arguments in a class template. Listing 6.22 demonstrates how to use the mechanism. I've modified the earlier definition by adding an `int` sz to the `template` statement on line seven of Listing 6.22, which now looks like this:

```
template <class array_type, int sz>
```

Look at the `template` statement as an analog to a function argument list. This list says that the template is passed two arguments; the first specifies a type of some sort (that's what the `class` means) and the second argument is an `int`. In the current example, a declaration like array<int,10> causes the compiler to expand the array template, using int everywhere that array_type is found in the template class and using 10 everywhere that sz is found. The only restriction is that non-class arguments to templates must be constants. Something like array<int,i> is not permitted, but this should be okay:

```
const int i = 10;
array<int,i>  ar;
```

I've made use of this mechanism in Listing 6.22 to pass a size into the constructor. I've removed the original int constructor and modified the default constructor to the one on line 13 of Listing 6.22. The new version gets the array size from the template rather than using a constant for the default size. You can declare a 10-element array of int like this:

```
array<int,10>  ten_ints;
```

and you can declare a 10-element array of 5-element-int arrays like this:

```
array< array<int,5> ,10>  fifty_ints;
```

The syntax leaves a lot to be desired, but the functionality is quite useful.

Listing 6.22. *array.h*— An Improved Array-Class-Generation Macro

```
1   #ifndef __ARRAY_HPP
2   #define __ARRAY_HPP
3
4   #include <stdio.h>
5   #include <stdlib.h>
6
7   template <class array_type, int sz>
8   class array
9   {
10      array_type  *p;
11      int     size;
12  public:
13      array  ( void ){ p = new array_type[size = sz ]; }
14      ~array ( void ){ delete p;              }
15      numele ( void ){ return size;           }
16      array_type &operator[]( int index )
17      {
18          if( !(0 <= index && index < size) )
19          {
20              fprintf(stderr, "Array out of bounds\n");
21              exit(1);
22          }
23          return p[index];
24      }
25  };
26  #endif // __ARRAY_HPP
27  //------------------------------------------------------------------------
28  #ifdef ARRAY_MAIN
29
```

➡

Listing 6.22. continued...

```
30    #define NROW   5
31    #define NCOL   10
32
33    void main( void )
34    {
35        array< array<int,NCOL>, NROW> x;   // like:  int x[NROW][NCOL];
36                                           // but with boundary checking
37        int r, c;
38        int i = 0;
39
40        for( r = 0; r < NROW; ++r )
41            for( c = 0; c < NCOL; ++c )
42                x[r][c] = i++;
43
44        for( r = 0; r < NROW; ++r )
45            for( c = 0; c < NCOL; ++c )
46                printf("%2d%s", x[r][c], c==NCOL-1 ? "\n" : " " );
47
48        printf("\n");
49
50        x[0][NCOL] = 0;        // force an out-of-bounds error
51    }
52    #endif // ARRAY_MAIN
```

A template class (a class that is created by expanding a template) can be used in derivation without difficulty. For example, you can use the following to create a stack-of-int class:

template classes under derivation

```
class intstack : array<int>
{
    // ...
}
```

You cannot use a class template in this way, though. (A "class template" is an unexpanded template; don't confuse this with a "template class"—an expanded template.) The following is illegal:

class template vs. template class

```
class stack : array
{
    //...
}
```

You can get around the problem by making the derived class a template, too. There's an example in Listing 6.23. The `stack` class derives from the `array` class in Listing 6.22, and its declaration is also a class template rather than a normal declaration. The `type` and `sz` arguments from the `template` statement on line eight are used on line nine to specify the exact definition of the base class. Given a declaration like

```
stack <char*,93>
```

the compiler expands the first line of the `stack` template to

```
class stack : public array<char*,93>
```

by replacing the type with **char*** and the sz with 93. This relaying of the template information to the base class means that the template for the base class might have to be expanded every time the template for the derived class is expanded— along with versions of the member functions from both classes for each expansion. You can create a vast amount of code in this way if you're not careful.

Listing 6.23. *stack.h*— A stack Template

```
 1   #ifndef __STACK_HPP
 2   #define __STACK_HPP
 3
 4   #include <stdio.h>
 5   #include <stdlib.h>
 6   #include "array.h"
 7
 8   template <class type, int sz>
 9   class stack : public array<type,sz>
10   {
11       int stack_ptr;
12   public:
13       stack( void ) : stack_ptr( sz ){}
14
15       int  full  ( void ){ return stack_ptr <= 0;        }
16       int  empty ( void ){ return stack_ptr == numele();  }
17
18       void push ( type &x );
19       type &pop ( void );
20   }
21   #endif // __STACK_HPP
22   //------------------------------------------------------------
23   #ifdef STACK_COMPILE_METHODS
24
25   template <class type, int sz>
26   void stack<type,sz>::push ( type &x )
27   {
28       if( !full() )
29           operator[]( --stack_ptr ) = x ;
30   }
31   //------------------------------------------------------------
32   template <class type, int sz>
33   type &stack<type,sz>::pop( void )
34   {
35       static type garbage;
36
37       if( !empty() )
38           return operator[]( stack_ptr++ );
39        else
40           return garbage;
41   }
42
```

```
Listing 6.23. continued...
43    #endif // STACK_COMPILE_METHODS
44    //--------------------------------------------------------------
45    #ifdef STACK_MAIN
46
47    void main( void )
48    {
49        stack<int,10>    intstack;  // stack of ten ints
50        int i;
51
52        for( i = intstack.numele(); --i >= 0 ; )
53            intstack.push( i );
54
55        printf("should print: 9 8 7 6 5 4 3 2 1 0 ---> ");
56        while( !intstack.empty() )
57            printf("%d ", intstack.pop() );
58        printf("\n");
59    }
60
61    #endif // STACK_MAIN
```

There are a few additional peccadillos in the declaration syntax. You need to use an overwordy syntax to declare the member-function declarations on lines 23 to 43 for several reasons. First, member functions of a class template are not functions at all. They are themselves templates that are expanded when the class template is expanded. Consequently, each member-function template must be prefixed by a `template` statement that matches the one for the class definition. The process is analogous to the `template` statement used in a normal function template like the ones described in Chapter Two. You'll find these `template` statements on lines 25 and 32 of Listing 6.23.

template-class member functions are function templates

The function names are also peculiar looking. Taking the push() function as characteristic, it looks like this:

naming template-class member functions

```
void stack<type,sz>::push ( type &x  )
```

The <type,sz> must match the arguments from the original class template, also. You have to say stack<type,sz>:: rather than a simple stack:: to handle the situation shown in Listing 6.24. Put simply, you can have several class templates that use the same class name but have different `template` statements attached to them. Since the `template` statement is effectively part of the class definition, you are really creating separate classes in this situation.

Frankly, I think that this practice doesn't lead to very manageable code and should be avoided at all costs. **Class template names should be unique, even if the attached `template` statements would be sufficient to differentiate them.** If the practice were made illegal, the member-function `template` statements and <...> in the function name would be unnecessary. Nonetheless, since multiple templates with the same class name are legal, you need to use the wordy syntax described earlier.

Listing 6.24. Why You Need <..> in Template-Member-Function Expansions

```
1    template <type t>
2    class flipper { int f(void);  };          // This is the flipper<t> class
3
4    template <type t>                           // And here is its f() function
5    int flipper<t>::f(void){ /*...*/ }
6
7    template <type t, int s>
8    class flipper { int f(void)  };            // This is the flipper<t,s> class
9
10   template <type t, int s>                    // And here is its f() function
11   int flipper<t,s>::f(void){ /*...*/ }
12
13   rin_tin_tin()
14   {
15       flipper<int> x;      // expand the flipper<t> template to create a
16                            // flipper<int> class and allocate an instance of
17                            // it called x. The expansion expands the
18                            // flipper<t>::f() template into a
19                            // flipper<int>::f() function
20
21       flipper<int,10> y; // expand the flipper<t,s> template to create a
22                            // flipper<int,10> class and allocate an instance
23                            // of it called y. The expansion expands the
24                            // flipper<t,s>::f() template into a
25                            // flipper<int,10>::f() function
26
27       x.f();               // Call the function  flipper<int>::f() that was
28                            // created when expanding the flipper<t> template.
29
30       y.f();               // Call the function  flipper<int,10>::f() that was
31                            // created when expanding the flipper<t,s> template.
32   }
```

special-purpose
versions of class
templates

There is another related issue. As was the case in a normal function template, you can also provide explicit overloads of both a template-class and a template-class member function. I'll demonstrate the issue with a linked-list element:

```
class list_ele { /*...*/ };          // A generic linked-list-
                                     // element abstract class

template <class t>                   // Use templates to create
class link : public list_ele         // lists of int, char*, etc.
{
    t key;
public:
    // ...
    int operator==( list_ele &r );
};
```

The operator==() function looks like this, and needs some explanation:

```
template <class t>
int link<t>::operator==( list_ele &r )
{
    printf("<t>operator==\n");
    return key == ((link<t> *) &r )->key;
}
```

First, it's a template function, so it needs a preceding **template** statement. Next, you cannot cast into a link pointer. There is no such thing as a link—only those classes that are created by expanding the link template exist. That is, a declaration like

```
link<int> x;
```

causes the link template to be expanded into a class called link<int>. The template is itself not a class, so you can't have a pointer to it. Consequently, the **return** statement at the end of **operator**==() must use a cast like (link<t> *) to convert the address of the incoming right operand to a pointer to the current expansion of the link class. You cannot use (link *) for this purpose.

The main problem is a list element that happens to be a character pointer, declared as follows:

```
link <char*>      clink;
```

The normal link<t>::**operator**==() function won't work in this situation because it will compare the two addresses, not do a lexicographic comparison. You take care of this situation with a special-purpose version of **operator**== that is declared like this:

```
int link<char*>::operator==( list_ele &r )
{
    printf("<char*>operator==\n");
    return strcmp( key,   ((link<char*> *)&r )->key );
}
```

As with a normal function template, the compiler uses the explicit version that you provide rather than a version that it creates by expanding a template.

There's one final small issue that concerns template-class member functions. The <...> is part of the class name, not the function name. The only time that this is likely to cause confusion is in the constructor and destructor functions, which share the class name. The correct syntax is

<...> part of
template-class
name

```
template <type t>
class whatever
{
    whatever( int x );
    ~whatever( void );
};
template <type t>  whatever<t>::  whatever( int x ){/*...*/}
template <type t>  whatever<t>::  ~whatever( int x ){/*...*/}
```

The class that contains the function is specified by the whatever<t>::. The whatever that follows the :: is the function name, not the class name, so it doesn't require the <t>.

An Example Class Library

The book goes full circle by finishing up with an example: a C++ implementation of the linked-list library from Chapter One. Though this class library is really quite small, it can serve as the basis of a much larger one. Along the way, I'll discuss not only the implementation details but also the design decisions that I had to make, and why I made the ones that I did.

I've taken a two-step approach here. The first part of the chapter describes how to use the classes, going into low-level implementation details only when necessary to describe how the classes work. The second part of the chapter describes these low-level implementation details. There is by necessity some overlap between the two halves. If you are the sort of person that gets more from looking at code than prose, you may want to skip ahead to the implementation section and then turn back to the start of the chapter to see how the classes are used.

7.1 Using the Collection Classes

collection defined

A generic "collection" is a group of related data, stored in no particular order. The concept is something like a set—you can add members to a collection, remove members, test for membership, merge sets together, and so forth, but operations that imply some sort of ordering are not supported. Unlike an array, a member of a `collection` has no relative position. Since a raw collection is not too useful, you need to derive various kinds of collections to get any work done. The current library provides three kinds of collections: stacks, queues, and arrays.

I'll demonstrate how these classes are used by describing the public interface to the various classes involved and presenting a few simple examples. The current library provides two ways to do things—one way that uses templates and one that does not. The template solution is dramatically simpler to use than the nontemplate version, so I'll discuss it first.

7.1.1 The Collection Template Classes

The easiest set of collection classes to use are the ones created by expanding one of the various templates provided in the library definition. These classes are all collections of some sort (they all derive from the `collection` class). The supported classes are listed in Table 7.1.

```
collection
templates:
array_c<cls>
stack_c<cls>
queue_c<cls>
array<t> stack<t>
queue<t>
```

Table 7.1. Collection-Class Templates

Template name	Defined in	Description
array_c<cls>	array.hpp	An array of class `cls` objects
stack_c<cls>	stack.hpp	A stack of class `cls` objects
queue_c<cls>	queue.hpp	A queue of class `cls` objects
array<type>	array.hpp	An array of type `type` variables
stack<type>	stack.hpp	A stack of type `type` variables
queue<type>	queue.hpp	A queue of type `type` variables
iterator_c<cls>	listnode.hpp	an iterator for all of the `<cls>` templates
iterator<type>	listnode.hpp	An iterator for all of the `<type>` templates

The _c templates (the first four templates in Table 7.1) are used for class objects; the other forms are for basic types like **int**, **long**, **short**, and so forth. For example, you can declare various collections that hold objects of class `string` as follows:

declaring template collections

```
class string { /*...*/ };

stack_c<string>  str_stack;   // stack of strings
queue_c<string>  str_queue;   // queue of strings
array_c<string>  str_array;   // array of strings
```

Collections of basic types such as **int** are done like this:

```
stack<int>    int_stack;     // stack of ints
queue<long>   long_queue;    // queue of long ints
array<char*>  charptr_array; // array of character pointers.
```

(I'll look at the two iterators in a moment.) It's not a compiler error to use the `stack`, `queue`, and `array` templates for class objects, but you won't be able to access any of the object's member functions or data if you do. You'll get hard errors from the compiler if you try to use the _c templates for basic types like **int**, though.

You can use the objects I just declared in a straightforward manner. Table 7.2 summarizes the operations that are unique to each of the three types. (There are also a set of operations that can be used on any sort of collection, including the template classes discussed here. Using these additional functions requires some knowledge of the internal workings of the classes, though, so I'll discuss these operations below.) All three kinds of collections are dynamically sized—a stack is made larger by pushing elements, for example. There's no upper limit on size of a stack, queue, or array beyond the amount of available memory. The same goes for arrays; when you access an array element, the array is expanded, if necessary, to include that element. Stacks and queues shrink as elements are popped and dequeued. This is not the case in arrays, however. Once it is made larger by accessing an element, it stays that size until the array is destroyed, either when the array goes out of scope or when a pointer to an array is passed to `delete`.

Table 7.2. Operations Unique to Collection Subclasses

Classes	Operations	Description
stack<type> and stack_c<cls>	s.push(x) x = s.pop()	Push object x onto the stack. Pop an object from the stack.
queue<type> and queue_c<cls>	q.enqueue(x) x = q.dequeue()	Enqueue object x. Dequeue an object.
array<type> and array_c<cls>	a[i] = x; x = a[i];	a[i] evaluates to a reference to the contained object (the type or cls object) within the *i*th array element. The array is made larger if it doesn't have *i* elements.

Using the template collections

Listing 7.1 holds a few examples of the functions in Table 7.2. Copy construction and assignment are supported on all the template-generated types, so statements like the following are all supported:

```
stack<int> int_stack, int_stack2;   // Two stacks of ints.
queue<int> int_queue;               // A queue of ints.

int_stack.push( 1 );   // Push a few elements on the stack.
int_stack.push( 2 );
int_stack.push( 3 );

stack<int> int_stack3 = int_stack;   // Copy one stack to
int_stack2 = int_stack;              // another stack.

int_queue = int_stack;   // Copy all elements from a stack
                         // to a queue.
```

I'll present further sample uses of these various template classes below, where I discuss their internal workings.

Listing 7.1. Using the Stack, Queue, and Array Templates

```
1   stack_c<string> str_stack;        // A stack of class-string objects.
2   str_stack.push( "a string" );     // Push a string onto the stack. Uses
3                                      // the char* constructor in the string
4                                      // to do initialization.
5   string x = str_stack.pop();       // Pop it off again.
6
7   array_c<string> str_array;        // An array of class-string objects.
8   str_array[0] = "zero";            // Uses string::operator=(char*)
9   str_array[1] = "one";
10  printf("%s\n", (char*) str_array[0] );  // Print array element, use
11                                    // string::operator char*() to
12                                    // convert.
13
14  array<char*>    charptr_array;         // An array of char pointers
15  charptr_array[0  ]= "zero" ;
16  charptr_array[100]= "one hundred"; // Expands array size to 101 elements
17                                     // array[1] to array[99] exist, but
18                                     // their contents are undefined.
19  char *p = charptr_array[100] + 1;  // Points at the first 'n' in "one
20                                     // hundred". charptr_array[i]
21                                     // evaluates to a char* because
22                                     // this an array<char*>.
23
24  queue<long> long_queue;                // A queue of long ints.
25  long_queue.enqueue( 0L );              // Enqueue a few elements.
26  long_queue.enqueue( 1L );
27  printf("%ld", long_queue.dequeue() );  // Dequeue and print the elements.
28  printf("%ld", long_queue.dequeue() );
```

7.1.2 The collection-Class Hierarchy

Though the template classes from the last section are by far the easiest ways to use the collection classes, they cannot be used in every situation. Sometimes you just need more control over the mechanics of an operation than is available through the template definition; sometimes you don't have a compiler that supports templates. (Many compilers that claim to be C++ version 2.1 compatible do not support templates— check your documentation.) Consequently, it's important to look one level down and examine the classes and functions that the various templates use to do their work. In order to do this, we need a little more in-depth knowledge of how the various classes actually work.

Figure 7.1 shows the class hierarchy for the collection library. The solid lines indicate derivation, pointing from the base to the derived class. The dashed lines indicate friendship, pointing from the granting class to the friend class. The class in a dashed box is one that's used internally by the class system, but you'll never create an object of that class yourself.

collection-class
hierarchy

The collection class (at the top left of the figure) provides the basic functionality of a collection—functions like "add an element," that are used by all sorts of collections. The classes that derive from collection refine the basic idea

Figure 7.1. The Class Hierarchy

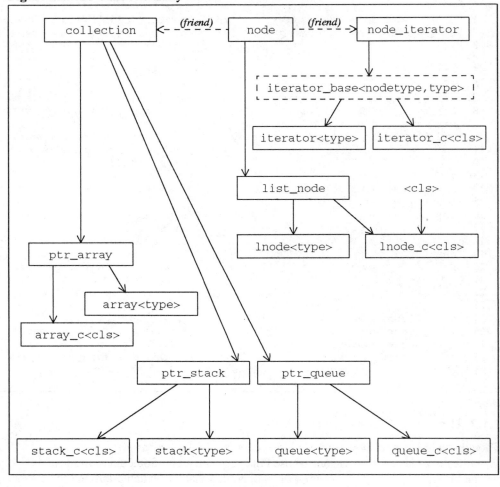

of a collection by adding specialized functions like "push" and "pop" (in the case of a stack type).

The `node` and `list_node` classes work in concert with the `collection` classes. The member functions of `collection` all manipulate `node`s, and the `node` supplies various functions that are used by the `collection` to do that manipulation.

For example, the `node` class has a virtual "insert yourself into collection" function that's called by `collection::insert()` to put a new element into a collection. The `node` class is an abstract class, though—you cannot create instances of it—and the "insert yourself into collection" function in the node is pure, it has no function body. You must derive a class from `node` and the knowledge about how the collection members are actually organized is encapsulated in this derived class. In the current situation, the members of the `list_node` class manipulate a linked list, so the collection members are organized into a linked list. When a `collection` method calls the `node`'s virtual "insert yourself into collection" function, it picks up the real function from the `list_node` class, which inserts the current node into a linked list.

The advantage of this approach is twofold. First, all information and knowledge about how to manipulate collection elements is concentrated in one place—in the `list_node` class. Maintenance is simplified as a consequence.

The second advantage is the opposite side of the same coin: the internal organization of the data structure used to hold the collection elements is completely hidden from the `collection` class itself. Consequently, you can change the internal organization of a collection without affecting any of the `collection` functions themselves. You just modify the class that derives from `node` to maintain the collection members in a different way. For example, the current implementation treats collection elements as linked-list elements because functions in the `list_node` class manage a linked list. A `list_node`'s "insert yourself into collection" function is treated by the `list_node` object as an "insert yourself into a linked list" request. It is a simple matter to change this internal behavior by providing a `tree_node` class that also derives from `node`, but which interprets a call to "insert yourself into collection" as an "insert yourself into a tree" request. A `hash_node` class that derives from `node` would interpret a similar request as an "insert yourself into a hash table" request. You have to do a little more work to get this separation of high-level (`collection`) and low-level (`list_node`) functionality, but the ultimate maintenance benefits are nontrivial.

Unfortunately, the separation between the `collection` class and the class that provides the member-manipulation methods cannot be total because there can be more than one collection in existence at a time. Some mechanism is needed to tell the `node` functions which collection to manipulate. Consequently, a `collection` object contains two pointers—ostensibly head-of-list and tail-of-list pointers—the addresses of which are passed to the functions like "insert yourself into collection." It's up to the "insert yourself into collection" to decide what to do with these pointers, though. The `list_node`'s version of "insert yourself into collection" indeed treats them as head- and tail-of-list pointers. A `tree_node` might use one to point to the tree's root and the other to point at the tree element with the smallest value. A `hash_node` might use one to point at the hash table and not use the other at all.

`collection::head`
`collection::tail`

Since the classes that derive from `node` contain the functions that actually define how the collection elements are manipulated, all collection members must be of a class that derives from `node`. (The `node` doesn't have to be an immediate base class of the collection member—it usually isn't, but `node` must be an ancestor of the collection member in the class hierarchy.)

Leaving aside the class templates for a moment, the concept of a `collection` is modified by deriving array, stack, and queue classes from it. There are various flavors of all three data structures, but treated collectively, they add various ways of ordering the list to the idea of a collection. A `stack` has a top and bottom, for example, and a `queue` has a head and a tail, an array element has an index. You use the derived types to declare collections that have the desired characteristics.

arrays, stacks, and queues

Since these classes derive from `collection`, they inherit all the functionality of a collection. A `collection`'s test-for-membership function, for example, can also be used to see if an object is in a stack or queue. By the same token, all functions that manipulate collections can also manipulate stacks and queues.

7.1.3 The `lnode<type>` and `lnode_c<cls>` Templates

Declaring collection
members with
template container
classes

The first order of business in creating a collection of any sort is declaring objects that can be collection members. The simplest way to create such an object is with the `lnode<type>` template, which is used to declare collection members that are of a basic type—`int`, `long`, `char*`, and so forth—anything that you could declare in C. The members of a collection of `int`s, for example, can be declared like this:

```
lnode<int>  mem1;                    // uninitialized
lnode<int>  mem2 = 10;               // initialization okay
lnode<int> *p1 = new lnode<int>;     // uninitialized
lnode<int> *p2 = new lnode<int>(10); // class-style init.
```

The `stack<type>`, `queue<type>`, and `array<type>` templates discussed earlier all use the `lnode<type>` templates to allocate collection members. (The `stack_c<cls>`, `queue_c<cls>`, and `array_c<cls>` use the `lnode_c<cls>` templates, discussed below.)

lnode<type>

The `lnode<type>` template creates a container class that contains a `type` object within it. You'd do it like this if you were doing it by hand:

```
class lnode_int : public list_node
{
    int contained_object;
    //...
};
```

There's only one restriction for types declared in this way: the contained object (the `int`) must have defined operations for `<` and `==`. This restriction is satisfied by all the basic types, but might not be satisfied by a user-supplied class. Since the `lnode<type>` should not be used with class objects, the restriction is really a non-issue in practice.

conversions
between lnode<*t*>
and *t*

Conversions to and from the contained type (`int`) and the containing type `lnode<int>` are automatically defined (so `mem1=10` and `i=10+mem1` are both legal). You can also use a cast to the contained type to force a conversion:

```
int i = (int)mem1 + 10;
```

cannot call member
functions of object
contained in
lnode<t>

The main problem with an `lnode<type>`—and the reason it can't be used for class objects—is that no member functions of the contained object can be called—not even operator overloads. Say, for example, you wanted a collection of `fixed` objects, which define overloads of the + operator. You cannot do this:

```
lnode<fixed> f1 = 1.0;      // okay
lnode<fixed> f2 = 2.0;      // okay
lnode<fixed> f3;            // okay
f3 = f1 + f2;               // ILLEGAL:
                            //    no lnode<fixed>::operator+()
f1.some_member_of_fixed();  // ILLEGAL:
                            //    can't call member function.
```

You can use a cast to get the last two lines to work

```
f3 = (fixed)f1 + f2;
(fixed(f1)).some_member_of_fixed();
```

but that's too much work and it's ugly.

Since these restrictions are really unacceptable, a second template is provided for situations where the collection's members are objects of a class of some sort— the `lnode_c<cls>` template. The `cls` in an `lnode_c` is a public base class, not an instance variable. You'd declare it more or less like this if you were doing it by hand:

<code>lnode_c<cls></code>

```
class lnode_c_cls: public list_node, public cls
{
    //...
}
```

All public functions and data from the `cls` class are inherited by objects of class `lnode_c<cls>`. An object of class `lnode_c<fixed>` has all the characteristics of class `fixed`—it can be treated just like a simple `fixed` object—but can be a member of a collection as well. In addition, `lnode_c<type>` provides conversions from `lnode_c<type>` to `type` and vice versa. [It provides a `lnode(type)` constructor and an **operator** `type()` function.] Consequently, casts are available to force a conversion when necessary. The following code works fine:

```
lnode_c<fixed> f1 = 1.0;
lnode_c<fixed> f2 = 2.0;
lnode_c<fixed> f3;
f3 = f1 + f2;
f1.some_member_();
```

In evaluating `f3=f1+f2`, the `lnode_c<fixed>` class defines a conversion from `lnode_c<fixed>` to `fixed` and the `fixed::`**operator**+`(fixed)` function is inherited by `lnode_c<fixed>` from the `fixed` class. The compiler uses the first function to convert the `f2` in `f1+f2`, to `fixed`. It then uses the inherited `fixed::`**operator**+`()` to do the addition. Finally, the assignment is processed using two functions. First, another `lnode_c<fixed>`-supplied conversion—this one from `fixed` to `lnode_c<fixed>`— converts covert the `fixed` temporary that results from the addition back to `lnode<fixed>`. Then `lnode<fixed>::` **operator**=`()` is called to do the assignment. The whole process can be expressed as

```
// f3 = f1 + f2 ==
f3.operator=(   f1.(operator lnode<fixed>)
                (
                        f1->operator+( f2.(operator fixed)() )
                )
            );
```

where **operator**+() is inherited from the fixed class and all other functions are provided by lnode<fixed>.

cannot use basic type in lnode_c<t>

There are two caveats in using the lnode_c<cls> template. Since you can't derive a class from a basic type like **int**, you can't legally expand an lnode_c<**int**> template because the compiler would effectively be trying to process the following illegal code:

```
class lnode_c_int: public list_node, public int {/*.../*}
```

To my mind, this behavior is really an inconsistency in the language. For purposes of derivation, the basic types should be treated as predefined classes with public operator overloads and constructors, thereby rendering the lnode versus lnode_c distinction unnecessary. The language doesn't work this way, though.

copying lnode<t> **and** lnode_c<cls> **objects**

The second caveat applies to both the lnode<type> and lnode_c<type> templates. Both implementations take the conservative approach and use copying for initialization, assignment, and converting from type to lnode<type> or cls to lnode_c<cls> (and vice versa). There are implicit copy-constructor calls when you copy a class object out of an lnode_c(), for example. In general, the copying is the correct approach. The overhead of copying is trivial for an **int**, for example, and guarantees integrity of the data. The extra overhead can be quite high if the objects are large—if you have a collection of linked lists, for example.

the contained() **function**

A contained() member function is available in both the lnode<type> and lnode_c<cls> to allow direct access to the contained variable when you need it, thereby avoiding the copies that are otherwise present at the expense of slightly more cluttered code. The contained() function returns a reference to the contained variable (in the case of an lnode) or to the base-class object (in the case of an lnode_c). For example, the following code adds one to the **int** object that's contained in the lnode.

```
lnode<int> x;
x.contained() += 1;
```

A simple x+=1 is illegal because there's no **operator**+=() in the lnode template.

For consistency's sake, the following code does the same for the fixed object:

```
lnode_c<fixed> ff;
ff.contained() += 1;
```

You don't really need the contained() function in this last case, though, because lnode_c<fixed> inherits **operator**+=() from fixed. A simple ff += 1 would work fine. On the other hand, the code

```
fixed fix_obj;
lnode_c<fixed> lnode_fix_obj;
    ...
fix_obj = lnode_fix_obj;
```

works, but probably involves two copy operations. A conversion from
lnode_c<fixed> to fixed must be used to convert the right operand—the function that's handling the = is fixed::**operator**=(fixed)—and that conversion
uses the copy constructor to return a copy of the contained object. The
fixed::**operator**=() function then uses a second copy into the target object.
The same situation applies when you use a cast. The following code works just
like the previous code—it just makes explicit the previously implicit conversion:

```
fix_obj = (fixed)lnode_fix_obj;
```

You can easily avoid the first copy as follows, though:

```
fix_obj = lnode_fix_obj.contained();
```

7.1.4 The node and list_node **Classes**

Explicit derivation is the alternative to the implicit derivation used in the
lnode<type> and lnode_c<cls> templates. The templates just provide an easy
way to derive classes from list_node—the derivation process is hidden from you
inside the template class definition, but the derivation is still there.

Using explicit derivation is a bit more complicated than using a template, but it
has advantages—you have finer control over object manipulation, and you can
program around both problems mentioned at the end of the previous section, for
example. Moreover, derivation is the only avenue open to you if your compiler
doesn't support templates.

All members of a collection must derive from some sort of node. The node is
an abstract class composed primarily of definitions for pure virtual functions that
the collection class needs to go about its work. You must derive a class from
node to provide definitions for real low-level functions that the collection class
can use, and then further derive individual list elements from that derived class.
I've done the first-level derivation for you, providing a list_node class that
derives from node, which uses linked lists to manage the collection elements. You
can create a collection member by deriving a class from list_node.

collection members must derive from node

I've done this derivation for a relatively simple case of a collection of **ints** in
Listing 7.2. You can create a few int_nodes and manipulate them as follows:

```
int_node ten = 10;
int_node zero;
int i = ten;        // operator int() converts int_node to int
i = 5 + ten;        // ditto
i = (int)ten + 5;   // use cast to extract int value of left
                    // operand because there's no int_node::
                    // operator+(int)
```

The **int** key is defined on line three of Listing 7.2, and the constructors and
operator int() functions on lines six to ten take care of conversions from an
int to an int_node and vice versa. The default constructor on line six initializes

the `int` to zero. Note that `operator int()` returns the *value* of the contained `int`. A second function, `contained()` on line 11 of Listing 7.2, lets you access the `int` itself. It returns a reference to the `key` field rather than its value. The advantage of this approach (as compared to simply making the `key` field public) is that access to a private field through a function can be monitored when debugging—direct access of the field cannot. The code is easier to maintain as a consequence.

Two overloads of `operator=()` are provided on lines 14 and 15 of Listing 7.2. The first takes care of assignment of an `int` to an `int_node`. The second takes care of assignment of one `int_node` to another. This second `operator=()` wouldn't seem necessary because the compiler-supplied `operator=()` (which does a C-style structure copy) would do the job. A compiler-supplied `operator=()` doesn't chain to the base-class `operator=()` as I'm doing on line 16, though. I haven't overloaded the other arithmetic operators, so you must use a cast in arithmetic expressions. It's an easy matter to add operator overloads, though.

Listing 7.2. *intstack.cpp*— An Integer Collection Element

```
 1   class int_node : public list_node
 2   {
 3       int key;
 4       static int me;
 5   public:
 6       int_node ( void       ): key(0)                { settype(&me); }
 7       int_node ( int i       ): key(i)               { settype(&me); }
 8       int_node ( int_node &r ): list_node(r), key(0) { settype(&me); }
 9
10       operator int   ( void ){ return key; }
11       int &contained ( void ){ return key; }
12
13       virtual void print ( FILE *stream ){ fprintf( stream, "%d", key ); }
14       int_node operator= (  int r       ){ key = r; }
15       int_node operator= (  int_node &r ){ key = r.key;
16                                            *(list_node*)this = r;
17                                          }
18       virtual node *clone( void ) const
19       {
20           return new int_node( key );
21       }
22       virtual int  operator< ( const node &r )
23       {
24           return typeof(r) ? key < ((int_node *) &r)->key : 0 ;
25       }
26       virtual int  operator== ( const node &r )
27       {
28           return typeof(r) ? key == ((int_node *) &r)->key : 0 ;
29       }
30   };
```

The remainder of the int_node-class definition provides versions of various virtual functions that are required by the list_node base class. These functions are summarized in Table 7.3, 7.4, and 7.5 along with a few list_node functions that the derived-class can use for other purposes.

Table 7.3. Interface between list_node and Derived Class: Supplied Functions

Base-class (node) functions used only by derived class	
void settype(**void** *type_id);	Called from the derived-class constructor. The argument must be the address of a **static** data member of the derived class.
int typeof(**const** node &r);	For use in comparison functions, etc. Passed a reference to any object that derives from node, evaluates true if the incoming object is of the same derived class as the current object.
int delete_ok();	The node class supports version of **new** and **delete** that is used to allocate space for all single node objects as well as objects of any class that derives from node. If delete_ok returns true, then the node came from the local **new**. Otherwise, it was allocated by a normal definition, it came from the global-level **new**, or it is part of an array.

Table 7.4. Interface between list_node and Derived Class: Required Functions

Virtual functions that must be supplied by derived class	
node *clone(**void**) **const**;	Return a pointer to an exact copy of the current object. Memory for the copy must come from **new**. That is, all data elements from the current object should be copied to the returned object. Use a deep copy.
int operator ==(**const** node &r) **const**;	Return true if the current object's key matches the key in r.

All classes that derive from list_node must provide versions of clone() and operator==(). The functions listed in Table 7.5 are optional.

Of particular interest are the settype() and typeof() functions provided by the node base class. These functions let you support heterogeneous collections by allowing a specific derived class to identify objects of the same derived class as itself. settype() is called from the constructors (on lines six to eight of Listing 7.2) to initialize an identifier field contained in the node base class. settype() is passed the address of a local static **int**. Having done this initialization, typeof() can be used as it is in the relational-operator overloads on lines 24 and 28 of

int_node::
settype(),
int_node::
typeof()

Table 7.5. Interface between `list_node` and Derived Class: Optional Functions

Virtual functions that may be supplied by derived class	
`int operator< (const node &r) const;`	Return true if the key in the current object is less than the key in `r`. This function is optional because a less-than test is not always meaningful. The < operator evaluates to zero (false) if you don't provide an overload. You can't call `collection::sort()` (discussed below) unless `operator<()` is defined.
`void print ( FILE *stream ) const;`	Print the object to the indicated output stream.
`char *sprint(char *buf, int maxbuf)` `const;`	Print the object into the `char` array addressed by `buf`; `buf` contains `maxbuf` characters.

Listing 7.2 to see if the incoming right operand, which must be defined as a `node*` in order to match the prototype in the base class, is really pointing at an `int_node`. Remember that the argument definitions for the virtual functions must match the base-class function definition exactly, thus the elaborate cast that's used to convert the incoming `node` argument to an `int_node` to extract the key on lines 24 and 28 of Listing 7.2. The incoming object is of the same derived class as the current object—an `int_node`—if `typeof()` returns true; otherwise, the incoming object is not an `int_node`. (It's either a simple `node` or an object of some derived class other than `int_node`.)

7.1.5 The `collection` Class

Having created an object that can be put into a collection, we can now move on to the `collection` class itself. All these functions are also available to classes that derive from `collection`, including the stack, queue, and array template classes discussed earlier. This section describes the public interface to the collection class in depth, and Tables 7.6, 7.7, and 7.8 present capsule summaries.

allocating collections

A collection is created with a simple declaration, like this:

```
collection  c1;
collection  *cp = new collection;
```

You can also initialize from an existing collection like this:

```
collection  c2 = c1;
collection  *cp2 = new collection(c1);
```

Note that the copy constructor does a deep copy, which copies all the members of the source collection into the new object. This copy can be a quite expensive operation, so should be used with care: avoid passing collections to functions by value or returning collections by value, even though both operations are supported. Use pointers and references instead.

insertion in a collection

A basic `collection` manages pointers to objects that derive from `node`. That is, you insert an object into the collection by passing a function a pointer to a `node`

Table 7.6. The Public Interface to a `collection`: Operator Overloads

`collection &operator=` `( const collection &src );`	Delete existing members of current collection, then overwrite current collection with copy of `src`.
`collection &operator+=` `( const collection &src );`	Concatenate copy of the `src` collection to the current collection.
`collection operator+` `( const collection &src ) const;`	Evaluates to a new collection that holds the concatenation of the `src` and current collections. Neither operand is modified.

Table 7.7. The Public Interface to a `collection`: Member Manipulation

`collection &grab` `( collection &src );`	Transfers all members of the `src` collection to the current collection. The `src` collection is empty after the operation is performed. [cf. **operator**+=()]
`virtual void insert` `( node *collection_element );`	Insert a new element into the collection using the default insertion method for the current object.
`node *remove` `( node *collection_element );`	Remove the member addressed by `collection_element` from the collection. Returns the argument, but does not delete the memory for the removed node.
`virtual node *remove(void)`	Remove the default member from the collection.
`node *replace` `( node *this_one, node *with_this );`	Remove the member addressed by `this_one` from the collection and insert `with_this` in its place. Returns the left argument, but does not delete the memory used by the replaced node.
`void clear(void);`	Removes all members from the current collection.
`int sort(void);`	Sort the collection by some criteria defined by the node.

of some sort. Here are a few examples:

```
int_node x = 100;
c1.insert( &x );

lnode<int> y = 200;
c1.insert( &y );
```

Table 7.8. The Public Interface to a `collection`: Status Functions

`node *find` `( const node &matching ) const;`	Returns a pointer to the collection member whose key matches that of the node addressed by the `matching` argument or NULL if there is none.
`node *start( void ) const`	Return pointer to the oldest (least recently added) member of the collection. Used to initialize iterator (see below).
`node *end( void ) const`	Return pointer to the newest (most recently added) member of the collection. Used to initialize iterator (see below).
`int size( void ) const`	Evaluates to the number of members in the collection.
`int empty( void ) const`	Evaluates true if the collection has no members, false otherwise.
`void print` `( FILE *stream) const;`	Prints all members in the current collection. Prints an error message if the members don't define print functions.

```
c1.insert( new int_node  (1) );
c1.insert( new lnode<int>(2) );
```

collection-element allocation, local new and delete

As you can see, the memory for the inserted objects can be declared in the normal way, or can come from `new`, though allocation via `new` is preferable because the `collection`'s destructor automatically deletes the memory associated with all collection elements when it goes out of scope. It tries to detect whether the memory came from `new` and does not pass explicitly declared collection members (such as x, above) to `delete`, but the algorithm used for this purpose (discussed below) is not foolproof. It's safest to remove all such nondynamic objects from the collection before the collection goes out of scope—I'll discuss how to remove elements in a moment.

Since the memory for the collection elements are discarded automatically along with the collection, code such as the following is in error. The memory used for the `node` will be passed to `delete` twice, once explicitly and once when the `collection` goes out of scope.

```
{
    collection c1;
    int_node *p = new int_node(10);
    c1.insert( p );
    delete p;
}
```

Again, error-processing code in the `node` class's local overloads of `new` and `delete` try to detect this situation and not permit the second `delete`, but the second `delete` is a run-time, not a compile-time, error, and so should be avoided.

Since the local overloads of **new** and **delete** are not used on arrays, the following code always causes problems:

don't allocate arrays
of collection
elements

```
roger()
{
    collection c1;
    int_node *p = new int_node[2];
    c1.insert( &p[0] );
    c1.insert( &p[1] );
}
```

Again, the local memory-management system tries to detect this situation and call
out a run-time error if it finds something wrong, but it might not always be able to
do so. It's best to explicitly remove and delete all list elements that are not allocated one at a time from **new**:

```
honey_bunny()
{
    collection c1;
    int_node *p = new int_node[2];
    c1.insert( &p[0] );
    c1.insert( &p[1] );
    // ...
    c1.remove( &p[0] ); // remove nodes from list before
    c1.remove( &p[1] ); // collection goes out of scope.
    delete p;
}
```

The next problem shows up when the collection is declared at a scoping level different from that of its members. Consider this situation:

declare elements at
inner or same level
as collection

```
collection global_col;
ikklebickle()
{
    int_node local_node;
    global_col.insert( &local_node );
}
```

The local int_node goes out of scope when you exit the enclosing function and is
destroyed at that time. The collection doesn't know that the node has been destroyed, however, so the pointer internal to the collection addresses garbage
memory. Using **new** to get new collection members solves the problem here, too,
at the cost of a little extra overhead for the allocation. My advice is to go ahead
and use explicitly declared objects if it makes sense in a particular application, but
be careful when you do so and document the code to indicate the potential problems.

The int_node is a container class because it contains the actual collection
member. The class generated from the lnode<type> template is also a container
for similar reasons. This container-class organization has its own set of problems:
access to the contained object is difficult because it is encapsulated within the containing structure. For example:

problems with
container classes

```
class base { public: f(); }
class contain_base
{
    base x;
    operator base ()
    {
        return x;    // return uses copy constructor
    }
};
contain_base mem;
mem.f();                // Illegal
mem.x.f();              // Illegal if x is private
( base(mem).f();        // Legal, but requires a copy.
```

The same situation applies in the template class:

```
class base { public: f(); }
lnode<base> mem;
mem.f();                // ILLEGAL
(base(mem)).f()         // okay, but copies base component of y
```

Using multiple base classes (or using the lnode_c<cls> template, which declares cls as a base class rather than a contained object) solves the problem:

```
class member : public list_node, public base {};
member mem;
mem.f();                    // fine

lnode_c<base> mem2;
mem2.f();                   // fine
```

collection::insert()
is virtual

Moving back to collection::insert(), this function is declared **virtual**, so the actual insertion mechanism can vary from derived class to derived class. The intention is that a derived class will modify the behavior of insert() so that it makes sense in the context of that class—queue<type>::insert() performs an enqueue operation, for example, and stack<type>::insert() does a push. [collection::insert() actually does an enqueue—it has to do something—but that's immaterial to the behavior of a raw collection in which ordering is not important by definition.]

The insert() method can be radically different from any of the supplied-classes' versions. Say, for example, that you introduced a sorted_list type in which the members were guaranteed to be in sorted order. You can do this by creating a sort_node to use in place of a list_node and then introduce an add-yourself-in-sorted-order function to the sort_node. The collection::insert() function goes about its work by calling a list_node() method, passing it the message "insert yourself into the list that has this head pointer and this tail pointer." The two pointers are stored in the collection object, and their addresses are passed to the node's add-yourself-to-collection function. Changing the behavior of the node's add-yourself function changes the internal behavior of the collection, but does not affect the collection functions in any other way. You do not have to modify any member functions of class collection.

In the current situation, a call to `collection::insert(p)` causes the `node` addressed by `p` to be put into the list in sorted order if that `node` is really a derived-class object of type `sort_node`. If `p` addresses a `list_node`, then the object is inserted at the head of the list in the normal way.

Two status functions are provided that are helpful in collection maintenance. The `size()` function returns the number of members in the collection and `empty()` returns true only when the collection has no members. Use them like this:

collection-status

```
collection x;
i = x.size ();    // number of members currently in collection
i = x.empty();    // true if collection has no members.
```

There is also a test-for-membership function—`collection::find()`. `find()` is passed a pointer to an object of some class that derives from `node`. It then searches the collection looking for a member that matches the one passed in as an argument. That is, the incoming `node` must be of the same derived class as the collection member. The derived-class **operator**`=()` function does the comparison. `find()` returns a pointer to the matching node if it finds a collection member with the same key. Here's an example:

finding collection
members (testing
for membership)
collection::find()

```
int_node x = 10;
int_node *p;
collection c;

c.insert( &x );   // insert x into the collection

if( p = c.find( int_node(10) ) )
    // found it
```

I've used a cast in the `find()` call to create a matching node for `find()` to use as a template, but could also have used a declared variable—like this:

```
int_node matches_this;

matches_this = 10;
p = c.find( matches_this );
```

The latter approach is preferable if you're doing a lot of searching—it saves you the overhead of creating and deleting many `int_node` objects just to get a node to compare against the list node.

The only potential difficulty is that all versions of `find()`—including the template versions—return a pointer to the matching `node`, not the contained object. For example, in the code

```
collection c;
int_node ele(10);
node *p;

c.insert( &ele );   // Insert element that holds 10
    //...
p = (int_node*) c.find( &ele ); // See if the node is in
                                // the collection.
```

`collection::find()` returns a `node` pointer, not an `int_node` pointer. The returned pointer really points at an `int_node`, but there's no way for a collection-class function to know this—thus the cast to `int_node*` to the left of the `find()` call. Moreover, p holds the address of an `int_node` that contains the **int** field, not to the **int** itself. You must extract the **int** with another cast if you intend to use it:

```
printf("%d", (int) * (int_node*) c.find( &ele ) );
```

The * to the left of the `(int_node*)` cast converts the `int_node` pointer to an actual `int_node`. The (**int**) cast then extracts the **int** itself—it's really an implicit call to int_node::**operator int**(), which returns the value of the contained **int**.

If you are using `find()` only to test for membership, the return value is a non-issue. `find()` returns false (NULL) when it can't find a match and true (a pointer of some sort) when it does find a match—just treat the return value as a Boolean quantity.

The `find()` interface is simplified somewhat by the various templates, which provide versions of the `find()` function that hide the mechanics of declaring a second object to use for the search criteria. You still need a cast to access the object contained within the collection member, but the code is much simpler than that in the previous examples. Here's how it works:

```
queue<int> q;
node       *p;

q.enqueue( 10 );
//...
if( p = find(10) )
    printf("found %d\n", (int)(*p) )    // note cast and *
```

collection::
remove()

The main purpose of the find function, in addition to testing for membership, is removing members from a collection when you don't know the members' address. The actual removal is done with a call to `collection::remove()`. Removing explicitly declared objects is easy:

```
collection c;
int_node    x = 100;
int_node    *p = new int_node(10);

c.insert( &x );
c.insert( p );
  //...
c.remove( &x );
c.remove( p );
delete p;    // An explicit delete is required; remove()
             // doesn't delete the memory, it just removes
             // the node from the collection.
```

If you don't have the address, you need to use find() to get it. Here's an example for a stack<**int**>.

```
stack<int> s;
s.push(10);
  //...
s.remove( s.find(10) );
```

There are two versions of remove() available. The one just described removes an explicit member from the collection. There is also a remove-default-member function—remove() with no arguments. This is a virtual function, so the actual removal mechanism can vary from derived class to derived class. That is remove()—with no arguments—defines the default removal mechanism for the current collection type: pop for a stack, dequeue for a queue, and so forth. For example:

```
stack<int> s;
queue<int> q;
//...
int i = s.remove(); // pops an item (removes from tail)
int j = q.remove(); // dequeues an item (removes from head)
s = q;              // overwrite stack with queue elements
i = s.remove();     // pop an item.
```

The default remove() in a raw collection removes the oldest (least-recently inserted) member. The default remove() in an array removes ar[0].

Note that remove() returns a pointer to the removed node—it does not discard the memory, though. You must do that with an explicit **delete** operation.

Two functions are provided to get access to the two ends of the collection—both for use in a remove() call and for initializing an iterator (discussed below): The start() function returns the address of the first node in the collection and the end() function returns the address of the last node. Table 7.9 lists the ways that the "start" and "end" objects are to be interpreted for the various collection types.

The final member-removal function is collection::clear()—a c.clear() call removes (and discards the memory used by) all members of the collection c.

Three operators have been overloaded for all collection types: =, +=, and +. The = and += operators both copy items from the right-operand collection to the left-operand collection. The = operator discards all members of the left-operand

remove all elements, clear() collection:: operator=() **and** collection:: operator+()

Table 7.9. Interpreting the `start()` and `end()` and `remove()` Functions

Data structure	Sample declaration	Function call	Gets the following item
Collection	`collection c;`	`c.start()`	Least-recently added
		`c.end()`	Most recently added
		`c.remove()`	Least recently added
Stack	`stack<int> s;`	`s.start()`	Bottom of stack
		`s.end()`	Top of stack
		`s.remove()`	Top of stack
Queue	`queue<int> q;`	`q.start()`	Head of queue
		`q.end()`	Tail of queue
		`q.remove()`	Head of queue
Array	`array<int> a;`	`a.start()`	`a[0]`
		`a.end()`	`a[` *largest index* `]`
		`a.remove()`	`a[0]`

collection before it does the copy. Both operators transfer items from any sort of collection to any other sort—from stacks to stacks, stacks to queues, queues to arrays, and so forth. The transfer algorithm traverses the source collection, starting with the `start()` element and inserting members into the target list using the left operand's `insert()` function—`push()` if the left operand is a stack, `enqueue()` if it's a queue, and so forth.

collection::
grab()

A second transfer function, `grab()` is also provided. It's used as follows:

```
collection src, dst;
//...
dst.grab( src );
```

All the members of the `src` collection are transferred to the `dst` collection. Unlike the `=` and `+=` operators, this actual operation of `grab()` is controlled by the class that derives from `node`. In the case of a `list_node`, the members of the source collection are just grafted onto the end of the target collection. A different node type (such as a `tree_node`), might work differently (incorporating the nodes into the tree in their appropriate places). The source collection is empty after another collection grabs its members.

collection::
operator+()

The third overloaded operator is addition (+). This operator creates a third collection that holds the concatenation of the operands. This code

```
collection a, b, c;
// ...
c = (a + b);
```

is essentially the same as the following code:

```
collection a, b, c, t0;
// ...
t0  = a;
t0 += b;
c  = t0;
```

The final collection member function of interest is sort()—a call to c.sort() sorts the members of the collection c. After the sort, c.start() yields a pointer to the smallest element; c.end() gives you a pointer to the largest.

<code>collection::
sort()</code>

7.1.6 Refining and Simplifying the collection Interface

Three refinements of a basic collection are provided for you in the current library. These are the ptr_stack, ptr_queue, and ptr_array classes from which the stack, queue, and array templates are built. You can use these classes directly in situations where templates aren't convenient (or available). They let you manipulate the collection as a stack, queue, or array of pointers to node-based objects.

<code>ptr_stack,
ptr_queue, and
ptr_array classes</code>

The ptr_stack class works just like a collection, but it also defines push(p) and pop() operations that let you push objects of any class that derives from node onto a stack and pop them off again. The insert(p) and remove() operations have also been modified in the ptr_stack class to do pushes and pops.

The ptr_queue class is a collection expanded to include an enqueue(p) and dequeue() operation. [A queue defines the default behavior of a collection, so no modifications need to be made to insert(p) and remove() in the case of the ptr_queue class.]

Finally, the ptr_array class is a collection expanded to let you use the bracket operator to access collection members.

I'll use the ptr_stack class to demonstrate how both the ptr_stack and ptr_queue classes are used.

<code>ptr_stack and
ptr_queue</code>

Though inserting a member into a raw collection is a relatively straightforward process, there is some overhead that you'd rather the user not have to worry about. For example, the following code inserts an int_node into a collection, removes it, and deletes the memory:

```
collection c;
int i = 10;
node *p;

c.insert( new int_node( i ) );

p = c.remove( c.find( i ) );
delete p;
```

A better implementation would hide these details from you. Here's a possibility:

```
int_collection c;
c.insert( 10 );
c.remove( 10 );
```

Further customization is also possible. You can provide an int_stack class that manipulates the collection of **int** members as a stack and supports operations such as the following ones:

```
int_stack c;

c.push( 10 );
i = c.pop();
```

You can provide the extra levels of customization by deriving various classes from collection. Listing 7.3 shows a simple implementation of an int_stack. The ptr_stack class at the top of the listing is a simplified version of the one provided in the library. It provides a copy constructor and **operator**=() function that just chains to the base-class versions. These are needed, even though there are no data elements in **class** ptr_stack itself, to ensure that the base-class version gets called when a derived-class object is copied. The ptr_stack class in Listing 7.3 also redefines how the default collection::remove(**void**) works—the ptr_stack version removes from the end rather than the start of the list, thereby modifying remove() to do a pop rather than a dequeue operation. The ptr_stack class also provides push() and pop() functions.

Listing 7.3. intstack.cpp

```
31    #include <string.h>
32    #include "collect.hpp"
33
34    class ptr_stack : public collection
35    {
36    public:
37        ptr_stack( void           ): collection(    ){}
38        ptr_stack(ptr_stack &src): collection(src){} // Chain to base-class
39                                                      // copy constructor.
40        ptr_stack &operator=( ptr_stack &right )
41        {
42            *(collection *)this = right;    // Chain to base-class function
43            return *this;
44        }
45
46        node *remove(    void    ){ return collection::remove( end() ); }
47        void  push ( node *ele ){ insert( ele );                        }
48        node *pop   (    void    ){ return remove();                    }
49    };
50
51    class int_stack : public ptr_stack
52    {
53    public:
54        void push( int i ){ ptr_stack::push( new int_node(i) );   }
55        int  pop ( void  ){ int_node *p = (int_node *)ptr_stack::pop();
56                            int          i = (int) *p;
57                            delete    p;
58                            return    i;
59                          }
60        void print( FILE *stream )
61        {
62            node_iterator it = start;
```

➡

Listing 7.3. continued. . .

```
63              while( it )
64                  fprintf( stream, (it++)->key );
65          }
66  };
67  //------------------------------------------------------------------
68  #ifdef __INTSTACK_MAIN
69  int main( int, char ** )
70  {
71      int_stack s;
72
73      s.push( 1 );
74      s.push( 2 );
75      s.push( 3 );
76      s.push( 4 );
77
78      while( !s.empty() )
79      {
80          printf( "Got %d, stack is: ", s.pop() );
81          s.print( stdout );
82          printf("\n");
83      }
84      return 0;
85  }
86  #endif // __INTSTACK_MAIN
```

The `ptr_stack` class, like a `collection`, is still generic in nature. It can manipu-   `ptr_stack`
late any sort of object that derives from `node` by being passed pointers to that
object. You still need to create the nodes explicitly, though—like this:

```
ptr_stack  a_stack;
a_stack.push( new int_node(10) );

node *p = a_stack.pop();
delete p;
```

The `int_stack` definition starting on line 51 of Listing 7.3 simplifies this inter-   `int_stack`
face by customizing the generic `ptr_stack` to a stack of `int_node` objects. In
particular, it takes over the work of allocating and deallocating individual nodes
by redefining the way that `push()` and `pop()` work so that you can say

```
int_stack istack;
istack.push(10);

int i = istack.pop();
```

`int_stack::push()` (on line 54 of Listing 7.3) redefines push to create an   `int_stack::push()`
`int_node` and initialize it from `int` argument to `push()`. Note how
`int_stack::push()` uses the `ptr_stack::push()` base-class function to do the
actual work. The whole point of using derivation here is to refine an existing
type—you should never duplicate code from a base-class function in a derived-
class function.

`int_stack::pop()` on lines 55 to 59 of Listing 7.3 undoes the work of the push() redefinition. The base-class function `ptr_stack::pop()` is called to pop an `int_node` object, which is then discarded. The integer value stored in the `int_node` needs to be remembered in order to **delete** the object safely. Trying to extract this value from the node after the **delete** call would be risky at best—it would most likely work only sometimes, and be a difficult bug to track down. Never try to access **delete**d memory.

The only differences, in terms of use, between the `ptr_stack` and `ptr_queue` classes are the replacement of push() and pop() with enqueue() and dequeue().

The `ptr_array` class is a bit different, though. First, as with the two array templates, the collection size is expanded automatically simply by accessing an element—an array-out-of-bounds condition is impossible: negative array indexes are treated as references to ar[0] and you'll get a hard run-time error if there isn't enough memory to expand the array to the size required to access the ith element.

There are two difficulties. First of all `ptr_array` is an abstract class—it contains a pure virtual function called new_object() that new_object() must be supplied by you. This function allocates and returns a pointer to a new array element, which must be of a class that ultimately derives from node. Here, for example, is an `int_array` class that provides this function:

```
class int_node   : public node { /*...*/ }
class int_array : public ptr_array
{
public:
    node *new_object(){ return new int_node(0); }
};
```

The next difficulty is that the overloaded bracket operator returns a pointer to the desired element—a pointer to a node. This means that the return value from the [] operation almost always needs to be cast in order to be used. The following code demonstrates the mechanics:

```
int_array ar;
*(int_node *)ar[0] = 1;   // Uses int_node::operator=(int)
                          // to do the assignment.
```

The cast to do a simple access is even worse:

```
int i = (int) *(int_node *)ar[0] // Uses int_node::operator
                                 // int() to extract value.
```

Fortunately, this horrific code can be easily hidden by adding an operator[]() overload to the `int_array` class. A redefined version looks like this:

```
struct int_array : public ptr_array
{
    node *new_object(){ return new int_node(0); }
    int &operator[]( int i )
    {
        return ( (int_node*)( ptr_array::operator[](i)) )
                                              ->contained();
    }
};
```

All I'm doing is moving the (int_node*) cast into int_array::**operator**[]()
so it doesn't have to be used by the application program. The ptr_array::
operator[](i) calls the base-class version of **operator**[] to prevent recursion.
The (int_node*) cast comes next, then the contained **int** is extracted. I'm using
int_node::contained() to access the enclosed **int** instead of the cast to **int**
used in the earlier examples. The **int** cast just extracts the value from the
int_node; contained() returns a reference to the enclosed **int**. Using a reference lets you use an array element on the left of an equals sign.

Having done the foregoing, we can simplify the earlier code to the following:

```
int_array ar;
ar[0] = 1;
int i = ar[0];
```

There's one caveat. The pointer returned from ptr_array::**operator**[] can be
passed to collection::remove() without causing any problems. The value that
comes back from int_array::**operator**[]() and from the **operator**[] overloads in the two array templates does cause problems, though. For example:

```
ptr_array par;
remove( par[0] );          // okay

int_array  iar;
array<int> iar_templ;

remove( &iar[0] );         // ERROR: &iar[0] is address of
remove( &iar_templ[0] ); //         contained int, not of the
                         //         enclosing list_node.

remove( (*(ptr_array*)(&iar))[0] ); // Looks awful,
                                    //         but it works.
```

All of these bracket overloads return references to the the contained object, not to
the containing, node-based class. It's an error to pass a pointer to the contained
object—which probably won't derive from node—to remove().

You can avoid this difficulty by extending the int_array definition (and the
class templates discussed below) to provide a version of remove() that worked
correctly, but removing an element from an array is not a common operation. Consequently, I've opted to simplify things by omitting a function that isn't likely to
be used.

7.1.7 Iterators

iterator

An *iterator* is an auxiliary class that's used to traverse the members of another class in some sort of order. In the current case, the iterator traverses a collection, visiting each member in turn. Although the collection class could have an iterator function that returns pointers to successive collection members on successive calls, this strategy would require a collection to have a field that holds the address of the return value from the most recent iterator-function call. Since you don't need to iterate through all collections, you don't want to unnecessarily increase the size of a collection object by carrying around this field whether or not you use it, so I've split the iteration functionality into an auxiliary class. A separate iterator class also lets you have several simultaneous iterations, each working through the collection elements at a different rate.

Three kinds of iterators are available:

iterator_c<cls>

iterator_c<cls> Iterate through a stack_c<cls>, queue_c<cls>, or array_c<cls> object.

iterator<type>

iterator<type> Iterate through a stack<type>, queue<type>, or array-<type> object.

node_iterator

node_iterator Iterate through a generic collection of objects that derive from node.

As with the earlier templates, the iterator templates are easier to use than the generic node_iterator class. Here's an example of iterating through an array<**int**> using an iterator<**int**>:

```
array<int>    ar;
iterator<int> it;
ar[0] = 0;
ar[1] = 1;
ar[2] = 2;

for( it = ar.start(); it ; printf("%d\n", *it++) ) // forward
    ;

for( it = ar.end(); it ; printf("%d\n", *it-- ) ) // backward
    ;

class cls { public: f(); }
array_c<cls> ar;          // array of cls objects.
// ...
for( iterator_c<cls> it = ar.start(); it ; ++it )  // forward
{
    it->f();    // Call public member of current object.
    (*it).f();  // You can do the same thing this way.
}
```

node::start(), node::end()

The iterator is initialized with a node pointer—I've used start() and end() to get the pointers here. You could also use find()—or use the address of explicitly declared node—if you wanted to start the iteration in the middle of the collection. You can do the initialization as part of the declaration, but it's more often done with an assignment. The ++ and -- operators advance or decrement the iterator to the next or previous element. These operators work in unsurprising ways:

it++	Evaluates to the address of the current node, then advances iterator
++it	Advances iterator, then evaluates to the address of the node
it-- --it	Like ++ but moves the iterator toward the start of the list

The * operator translates the address returned from ++ or -- into a reference to the contained object—in the current case, the int in the lnode<int> that holds a collection member.

The generic node iterator is only slightly more complicated to use. Here's an example:

```
gabba_gabba_hey
{
    collection c;
    int_node *p;
    c.insert( new int_node(1) );
    c.insert( new int_node(2) );
    c.insert( new int_node(3) );
    node_iterator it = c.start;   // initialize in declaration
    while( it )
    {
        p = (int_node *) it++ ;   // The ++ gets ptr to object
        printf("%d\n", (int)*p ); // The * converts from
                                  // pointer to object; operator
                              // int() extracts the field.
    }
}
```

The main difference between the generic iterator and the iterator generated from a template is that you have to use casts to access the current object.

7.2 Implementing the collection Class

I'll start the discussion of how all the foregoing is implemented with the collection class, the definition of which starts in *collect.cpp*—Listing 7.4.

collect.cpp

7.2.1 Preprocessor Directives

A few things appear in not only the current file but in most of the other files discussed in the current chapter as well. The first is the use of preprocessor directives to control compilation. As with many of the class definitions presented earlier, an

__COLLECT_HPP

```
#ifndef __COLLECT_HPP
#define __COLLECT_HPP
```

and matching

```
#endif // __COLLECT_HPP
```

appear at the very top and bottom of the file so that multiple inclusion of

COLLECTION_COMPILE-
_METHODS

collect.hpp is not a problem. The macro name is the file name with a couple leading underscores appended and an underscore replacing the dot.

I've put the method-function definitions (the actual function bodies, not just the prototypes) in the *.h* file as well. The code is bracketed by an

#ifdef __COLLECTION_COMPILE_METHODS

and a matching **#endif**. I compile the *.hpp* file once, using Borland C++'s *-P* and *-DCOLLECTION_COMPILE_METHODS* command-line switches, and put the resulting object module into a library. The *-P* switch says to do a C++ compile even though the file name ends in *.h*—the compiler normally does a C++ compiler only if the file ends in *.cpp*. The *-D* switch tells the compiler to implicitly **#define** COLLECTION_COMPILE_METHODS as if a macro definition were found in the file.

COLLECT_MAIN

At the bottom of the file I've included a simple main() that tests the classes defined in the current file. The main() subroutine is surrounded with an

#ifdef __COLLECT_MAIN

and matching **#endif** that I can enable with another *-D* command-line switch when I want to test the class definitions. I generally include a test main() in a library file so that when I need to make a change or fix a bug, I have a test subroutine already in place and don't have to make one up.

collection classes,
source-file
organization

A final organizational note is also in order. I generally put method-function definitions into *.h* files only when the methods are small and there is a relatively small number of them. The main advantage of this approach is that the class definition is in the same file as the function bodies—debugging and maintenance are both simplified by putting everything in one place. The main disadvantage is that all of the method functions are in a single source module, so even if only a few of them are actually used, they could all be called into the final program by the linker (depending on how dumb your linker is). Unless your linker can selectively pick out of an object module only those functions that are actually used by a program, you should put the large member functions into their own source files, compile the files independently, and then put them into the library independently. (Each file must **#include** the *.h* file that holds the class definition.)

In the current example class library, I've put class definitions and methods into the same file more to simplify the discussion than anything else. You can make a good case for breaking up some of these files into smaller units.

7.2.2 The collection **Definition**

collection class

The collection class definition starts on line eight of Listing 7.4. The initial comment on line ten is an important part of the class definition. Though an actual **friend** definition is in the granting class, it's important to know to which classes friendship is granted because changes in the granting class often affect code in the current class. The comment spells out the friend relationship.

collection:: head,
collection:: tail

The data components of a collection object are defined next. The nel field holds the number of elements currently in the collection. The head and tail pointers ostensibly point at the head and tail of a linked list used to manage the collection members. I say "ostensibly" because these pointers are never manipulated directly by a collection member function; rather, their addresses or contents are passed to various node functions that do the actual manipulation. This way each collection object can have a unique set of pointers, but the details of manipulation are concentrated in one place—the node class. This organization gives you the ability to change the way that members are stored—from a linked list to a tree, for example—without affecting the actual collection class at all. The details will become more clear when I discuss the node, below.

Listing 7.4. *collect.hpp*— The collection Class Definition

```
1    #ifndef __COLLECT_HPP
2    #define __COLLECT_HPP
3
4    #include <stdio.h>
5    #include <stdlib.h>
6    #include "node.hpp"
7
8    class collection
9    {
10       // collection is a friend of class node
11
12   private:
13       node *head; // head-of-list pointer, NULL if list empty
14       node *tail; // tail-of-list pointer, Initialized to NULL.
15       int   nel;  // number of elements
16
17   public:
18       collection() : nel(0), head(NULL), tail(NULL) {}
19       collection( const collection &src ): nel(0), head(NULL), tail(NULL)
20       {
21           *this += src; // use operator+= to copy.
22       }
23       virtual ~collection ( void );
24
25       node *start( void ) const { return !head? NULL : head->first(tail);}
26       node *end  ( void ) const { return !head? NULL : head->last (tail);}
27       int       size ( void ) const { return nel;  } // number of elements
28       int       empty ( void ) const { return !nel; }
29       void      clear ( void )        { this->collection::~collection(); }
30
31       inline int    sort   ( void                          );
32              void   print  ( FILE *stream                  ) const ;
33              node  *find   ( const node &matching           ) const ;
34              node  *remove ( node *collection_element    );
35       virtual node  *remove ( void                          );
36              node  *replace( node *existing, node *with_this );
37       virtual void   insert ( node *collection_element    );
38
39       collection &operator=  ( const collection &src );
40       collection &operator+= ( const collection &src );
41       collection operator+   ( const collection &src ) const ;
42       collection &grab       ( collection &src        );
```

Listing 7.4. continued...

```
43    };
44
45    inline int collection::sort( void )
46    {
47        // Since the collection doesn't actually know how the nodes are
48        // organized, it can't do the sorting itself. Defer to a
49        // node-level function that's passed the addresses of the head and
50        // tail pointers. Refuses to sort (and returns false) if the list
51        // is too small, is already sorted, or can't be sorted because of
52        // an incompatible node type. Returns true on success.
53
54        return !(head && nel > 1 && !head->is_sorted()) ? 0 :
55                        ((head = head->sort( &tail, &nel )) != NULL);
56    }
```

---

collection::
collection()

The collection's collection() constructors and destructor come next, on lines 18 and 19 of Listing 7.4. Both constructors initialize the pointer fields to NULL and nel to zero to indicate an empty list, using the member-initialization list for this purpose. The copy constructor on line 19 goes on to call the **operator**+=() function to copy elements from the source list to the initially empty current list. Since the member-initialization list is processed before the constructor body, the **operator**+=() call is adding elements to an empty—not an uninitialized—list.

collection::-
~collection()

The destructor, on line 23, comes next. It is declared **virtual** so that a base-class pointer that addresses a derived-class object can be used to destroy both the derived-class and base-class components of the object. Otherwise, code like

```
collection *p;
p = new stack<int>;
// ...
delete p;
```

wouldn't work—only the base-class (collection) destructor would be called.

The collection definition continues on line 25 of Listing 7.4 with a handful of small **inline** functions. The first two, start() and end(), demonstrate what I was talking about a moment ago when I said that collection member functions don't access head and tail directly. Taking start() as characteristic, if the head pointer is NULL, the collection is empty by definition, so collection::start() can safely return NULL to indicate this condition. If head is not NULL, the list is not empty, but there's no telling whether head actually points at the starting member of the collection. If the collection members are stored as a tree, for example, the head pointer could be the tree's root and the start() member the leftmost leaf in the tree, a pointer to which is not stored in the collection object. The problem is resolved by deferring to the node class, which knows how the members are organized. The call head->first(tail) in collection::start() calls node::first() to find the start member. The function can access both the head and tail pointers—head is available inside node::first() as **this** (the value of **this** inside node::first() is the same as the value of head in the calling expression `head->first(tail)`; `tail` is passed explicitly as a function argument. The `node::first()` function then uses the information in the `head` and `tail` pointers to get the head- and tail-of-list pointers.

In the current system, `node::first(tail)` returns **this** and `node::last(tail)` returns its argument. Both functions are **inline** [as are `start()` and `end()`], so there is no overhead incurred by what looks like multiple subroutine calls. The compiler just makes substitutions as if nested macros are involved. For example, the call

```
stack<int> s;
//...
it = s.start();
```

is effectively replaced with the code

```
it = s.head
```

Moving on to the `size()` and `empty()` functions on lines 27 and 28 of Listing 7.4: these are examples of simple "access" functions, which provide read-only access to otherwise private data fields—in this case the number-of-elements field. The `clear()` function on line 29 is a little more interesting. It clears the current collection (deletes all members) with an explicit call to the `collection`'s destructor. This subroutine just calls the destructor function; it does not free the memory used for the `collection` itself. Only the memory for the members is freed. Memory for the `collection` object itself isn't freed until the object goes out of scope or is passed to **delete**.

<code>collection::
size(),
collection::
empty()</code>

The next definition of interest is `sort()` (on line 31 of Listing 7.4). This function is declared **inline**, and then defined later on in the current file (on line 45) because the largish comment in the function definition would clutter up the class definition. In general, I'm reluctant to put the body of a function into a class definition unless it's at most two lines long. I've found that putting larger function bodies into class definitions tends to make the class definition itself too hard to read because it gets too large. It's true that putting the function body into the **class** definition makes it **inline** by default, but just because a language has a feature doesn't mean that you have to use it, and not using it here gives you more readable code.

<code>collection::
sort()</code>

The remainder of Listing 7.4 holds prototypes for the other `collection` member functions, whose definitions start in Listing 7.5, which holds the destructor. The destructor is also isolated from the mechanics of node manipulation, as was the case with `collection::start()` discussed earlier. The **while** loop executes as many times as there are elements in the list. The call to `head->first()` gets a pointer to the first list element, which is then passed an "unlink yourself from the list" message in the guise of the call to `node::unlink()` on the next line. This unlink operation moves a new node into the first position, so the earlier call to `first()` returns a pointer to the next node to delete when it's called again in the next loop iteration.

The call to `node::delete_ok()` on line 66 tries to discover a potentially illegal delete before passing the node to **delete** on line 69. The `node` class has its own local versions of **new** and **delete** that are used to allocate individual list

<code>node::delete_ok()</code>

nodes. These versions are discussed below, but they use the memory-validation technique discussed earlier in the book to check for valid **delete** operations— node::**new**() allocates a little more memory than necessary from the global **new** and uses that extra memory as a header at the top of the memory block. node::**new**() puts a magic number into that header and then returns a pointer to the area just beneath the header. node::free() decrements the incoming pointer and checks to see if the magic number is in place before doing the free operation. node::delete_ok() returns true if it finds a magic number where it expects one, false if it doesn't. If node::delete_ok() returns false, you are guaranteed that the memory did not come from node::**new**(). There is a small possibility that a node did not come from node::**new**() but the memory above the node just happens to contain the magic number, in which case node::delete_ok() will return a false positive—it will think that the memory came from node::**new**() when it didn't. This behavior is acceptable because the documentation says that nodes must either come from node::**new**() or be removed from the collection object before the collection goes out of scope. Consequently, the test on line 66 is really backup error checking in case you forget to pull suspect nodes out of the collection. It's meant to catch errors that would otherwise go undetected, not to provide a foolproof way to put a node into a collection with no thought as to how that node was allocated.

Listing 7.5. *collect.hpp*— The collection Class—The Destructor

```
57   #ifdef __COLLECTION_COMPILE_METHODS
58
59   collection::~collection( void )
60   {
61       node *p;
62       while( --nel >= 0 )              // remove and delete all elements
63       {
64           p = head->first(tail);
65           p->unlink( &head, &tail );  // shifts new node into first posn
66           if( head->delete_ok() )     // Try to detect bad deletes.
67           {
68               D( printf("Deleting dynamic node @%p\n", head ); )
69               delete p;
70           }
71       }
72       nel = 0;
73   }
```

collection::
print()

The next group of functions (in Listing 7.6) take care of list traversal. The first function, print(), prints or otherwise displays all members of the collection. It calls node::print()—a virtual function—to do the printing. If a class that derives from node is printable, all it need do is provide a void print(FILE *) function to allow collection::print() to do its job. The default definition for node::print()—the one actually in the node class— prints an error message so collection::print() works, though it does nothing useful, if the class that derives from node isn't printable.

The traversal mechanism used in collection::print() is different than the one used in the destructor. The head->first(tail) call is still used to get the pointer to the first node in the list, but now p->succ() is used to get the successor to the node addressed by p rather than using the left shift implicit in deleting the first node in the list. In the current linked-list implementation, node::succ() just returns the next-element-of-list pointer that's stored in the list_node structure. A tree-based node would behave much differently, though, probably returning the in-order successor.

Listing 7.6. *collect.hpp*— The collection Class—Traversal

```
74    void collection::print( FILE *stream ) const
75    {
76        node *p;
77        D( fprintf(stream,"head=%p, tail=%p, nel=%d, elements:\n", \
78                                          head, tail, nel ); )
79        for( p = head->first(tail); p ; p = p->succ() )
80            p->print( stream );
81    }
82    //---------------------------------------------------------------------
83    node *collection::find( const node &matching ) const
84    {
85        node *p;
86        for( p = head->first(tail); p ; p = p->srch_succ( matching ) )
87            if( *p == matching )
88                return p;
89        return NULL;
90    }
```

The find() function, also in Listing 7.6, traverses the list looking for a node whose key matches the one passed into find() as an argument. There are two new developments. First of all, p->srch_succ() is called rather than p->succ(). You need two successor functions because the order in which you visit members of a data structure can be different from the order in which you visit members when searching. The ordering doesn't vary with the linked list—you always search from front to back of the list in linear order. A tree behaves differently, though. The normal succ() function would probably just do an in-order traversal of the tree. The srch_succ() function would start at the root of the tree and work its way down a single path to a leaf. The first traversal method would yield a linear average-case search time in a tree. (It takes, on average, $N/2$ comparisons to find a node in the list, where N is the number of tree elements.) The second method yields a more preferable logarithmic search time in a tree. (It takes on the order of $\log_2 N$ comparisons.) In the current linked-list implementation, succ() and search_succ() are identical.

The next group of subroutines — insert(), remove(), and replace() in Listing 7.7 — insert, remove, and replace members from the collection. In all

collection::find()

node::srch_succ()
node::succ()

collection::insert(), collection::remove(), collection::replace()

cases, the actual work is deferred to an "insert yourself into the list," "delete your-self from list," or "replace yourself with this node" function that's provided by the node, not here. The relevant calls are on lines 95, 108, and 119 of Listing 7.7. All three functions are passed the addresses of the head and tail fields so that they can handle insertions or deletions of a node addressed by these pointers (i.e., at the head or tail of the list).

Listing 7.7. *collect.hpp*— The collection Class—Insertion and Removal

```
91   void collection::insert( node *collection_element )
92   {
93       if( collection_element )
94       {
95           collection_element->link( &head, &tail );
96           ++nel;
97       }
98   }
99   //--------------------------------------------------------------------
100  node *collection::remove( node *p )
101  {
102      // Remove arbitrary link addressed by 'p'.
103      // col.remove( col.find(pattern) ) is okay--it returns NULL if
104      // pattern is not found.
105
106      if( p )
107      {
108          p->unlink( &head, &tail );
109          --nel;
110      }
111      return p;
112  }
113  //--------------------------------------------------------------------
114  node *collection::replace( node *this_one, node *with_this )
115  {
116      // Pull "this_one" out of the list and put with_this into its place.
117
118      if( this_one && with_this )
119          this_one->replace( &head, &tail, with_this );
120      return this_one;
121  }
122  // - - - - - - - - - - - - - - - - - - - - - - - - - - - - - - - - - -
123  /*virtual*/ node *collection::remove( void )
124  {
125      return remove( head->first(tail) );   // call collection::remove()
126  }
```

Listing 7.8 holds the next group of functions—those that concatenate collections or transfer members from one collection to another. The first of these is opera-tor+=() at the top of the listing. This function makes a copy of the source list by traversing it one element at a time, calling node::clone() on line 135 to get duplicates of the source members. node::clone() is a virtual function that's provided by the derived class, more or less like this:

```
class node                    {virtual void node( void )= 0;}
class list_node: public node {virtual void node( void )= 0;}
class int_node : public list_node
{
    int i;
public:
    int_node(int_node &right): list_node(right), i(right.i){}
private:
    void clone(void){ return new int_node(*this); }
}
```

The **new** call in the int_node class creates a derived-class object that holds a copy of the current object, using the int_node's copy constructor for this purpose. This roundabout duplication is necessary in order to get a duplicate of the derived-class data. A **new** node(*p) in collection::**operator**+=() would yield a copy of only the base-class component of the structure. The duplicate nodes are linked into the current list one at a time on line 136 of Listing 7.8.

The grab() function on line 146 of Listing 7.8 goes about things differently—it uses node::mergeto() to move the source list into the current object—in fact, grab is little more than an alias for a call to mergeto().

List merging is relegated to a node member function because the organization of the list is controlled by the node and the amount of work required for a merge operation can vary radically with the data structure actually used for the list. The merge process for two linked lists is simple and efficient—the subroutine adjusts the pointers in the last element of the source list to point at the first element of the target list; the process is repeated with the previous-element pointer at the head of the concatenated list; and finally the tail pointer in the collection is adjusted to point at the new end of list. Merging two trees (or two sorted lists) in an efficient manner is a more-complicated process because each new element must go in its proper place in the tree (or sorted list).

I could have simplified the design, at the cost of efficiency, by eliminating the mergeto() function and modifying grab() to work much like **operator**+=. Here's grab() modified to use a one-element-at-a-time strategy:

```
node *p, *next;
for( p = src.head->first(tail); p ; p = next )
{
    next = p->succ();
    p->unlink( &src.head, &src.tail );
    p->link  ( &head,     &tail     );
}
```

Even in a linked-list implementation, each of those removals and each insertion involves the manipulation of two or three pointers. By moving the merge process into the node class, I can optimize the operation for the data structure actually used.

I've compromised by not using the same strategy in operator+=() that I used in grab() to merge lists—not deferring the actual work to a node member

collection::
grab()

node::mergeto()

collection::
operator+=()

Listing 7.8. *collect.hpp*— The `collection` Class—Concatenation and Assignment

```
127   collection &collection::operator+=( const collection &src ) // Deep copy
128   {
129       // Merge the src list into the current list. The source list is not
130       // modified.
131
132       node *p, *duplicate;
133       for( p = src.head->first(tail); p ; p = p->succ() )
134       {
135           duplicate = p->clone();
136           duplicate->link( &head, &tail );
137           ++nel;
138       }
139       return *this;
140   }
141   //------------------------------------------------------------------------
142   collection &collection::grab( collection &src )
143   {
144       // Like +=, but transfers all elements from src to current list.
145
146       head->mergeto( &head, &tail, &src.head, &src.tail );
147       nel     = src.nel;
148       src.nel = 0;
149       return *this;
150   }
151   //------------------------------------------------------------------------
152   collection &collection::operator=( const collection &src ) // Deep copy
153   {
154       this->collection::~collection();    // Clear existing list if any.
155       *this += src;                        // Call operator+= to do the copy
156       return *this;
157   }
158   //------------------------------------------------------------------------
159   collection collection::operator+( const collection &src ) const
160   {
161       collection col = *this; // copy constructor duplicates current list
162       col += src;             // add src elements with operator+=().
163       return col;
164   }
165   #endif // __COLLECTION_COMPILE_METHODS
```

function. My reasoning is that the efficiency gains are not nearly so high in `operator+=()` as they are in `grab()` because the source list must be copied rather than being bodily transferred from one `collection` to another. Consequently, I opted for the more maintainable approach. Modifying `operator+=()` to use a node workhorse function is a reasonable change, though.

collection::
operator=(),
collection::
operator+()

The `operator=()` and `operator+()` functions in Listing 7.8 just call `operator+=()` to do their work, in the first case clearing the existing list and then adding the source list, and in the second case by creating a copy of the current list and adding the source list to it. The remainder of `collect.hpp` is the small test module in Listing 7.9.

Listing 7.9. *collect.hpp*— The collection **Class—Test Routines**

```
166   #ifdef __COLLECT_MAIN
167
168   #include <string.h>
169   #include "listnode.cpp"
170
171   struct ele : public list_node
172   {
173       char *key;
174   public:
175       ele( char *s    ) :                        key(s) {}
176       ele( ele &right ) : list_nodew(right),  key(s) {}
177
178       virtual void print( FILE *stream )
179       {
180           list_node::print( stream );
181           printf("key=%s\n", key );
182       }
183       virtual node *clone( void ) const
184       {
185           return new ele( *this );
186       }
187       virtual void clonefrom( const node *src )
188       {
189           if( !typeof(src) )
190           {
191               fprintf( stderr, "Illegal clone-from operation\n");
192               exit( 0 );
193           }
194           key = ( (ele *)src )->key;
195           return this;
196       }
197       virtual int  operator< ( const node &r )
198       {
199           const ele *p = (const ele *)( &r );
200           return( !typeof(r) ? 0 : (strcmp(key, p->key) < 0) );
201       }
202       virtual int  operator== ( const node &r )
203       {
204           const ele *p = (const ele *)( &r );
205           return( !typeof(r) ? 0 : (strcmp(key, p->key) == 0) );
206       }
207   };
208   //------------------------------------------------------------------------
209   int main( int, char ** )
210   {
211       collection x;
212
213       ele  first  =          "first  (static )"  ;
214       ele  second =          "second (static )"  ;
215       ele *third  = new ele("third  (dynamic)" );
216       ele *fourth = new ele("fourth (dynamic)" );
```

Listing 7.9. continued...

```
217
218        x.insert( &first  );
219        x.insert( &second );
220        x.insert( third   );
221        x.insert( fourth  );
222
223        printf("\nx is:\n");
224        node_iterator xi;
225        for(xi = x.start(); xi;  ++xi )        // test iterator
226            xi->print( stdout );
227
228        printf("\ny=x, y is::\n");
229        collection y = x;    // test copy constructor
230        y.print( stdout );
231
232        printf("\n\n");
233
234        if( !x.remove( x.find( ele("third  (dynamic)"))) )
235            printf("could not find and remove third element:");
236        else
237        {
238            printf("successfully removed third element. List is:\n");
239            x.print(stdout);
240            printf("\n");
241        }
242
243        printf("restore x with x=y\n");
244        x = y;        // test assignment by restoring original list
245        x.print(stdout);
246
247        y.clear();
248        y.insert( new ele("doo")   );
249        y.insert( new ele("wha")   );
250        y.insert( new ele("ditty") );
251
252        (x+y).print( stdout );
253
254        return 0;
255    }
256    #endif // __COLLECT_MAIN
257    #endif // __COLLECT_HPP
```

7.3 Implementing the node **Class**

The node class is the second class that composes a collection. That is, the node
and collection classes are so closely coupled that they are conceptually part of
the same class—one collection object and several node objects work in concert
to implement a single conceptual collection.

The node definition begins in Listing 7.10. For the most part, a node is a collection of virtual functions that are called by the collection methods and provided by the class that derives from node—I'll look at these functions in depth later on when I derive a class from node.

Some work is done in the node itself, though. The first of the two data fields in the node (me, declared on line 19 of Listing 7.10) is used for derived-class identification. This field holds a unique identifier for each derived class; the identifier is supplied by the derived-class object. The derived-class object does this by calling settype() (declared on line 23 of Listing 7.10). Typically, me is initialized to hold the address of a local **static** field of the derived class. Since the variable is **static**, all instances of the derived class share it, so its address can serve as a class identifier.

You need a settype() function because a base-class constructor cannot pick up a virtual function from a derived-class object during initialization. In an ideal world, the node constructor would set up the me field by calling a derived-class function that returned the address of a local **static** variable—it would call a virtual "identify yourself" function that's provided by the derived class. Unfortunately, a base-class constructor can't call derived-class virtual functions because the base class is created first—the derived-class object won't exist when the base-class constructor is executed. The only reasonable solution, then, is to provide a **protected** base-class function that's called from the derived-class constructor to finish the initialization of the base-class component of the object. The int_node class presented at the beginning of the chapter did it like this:

```
class int_node : public list_node
{
    int key;
    static int me;
public:
    int_node( int i    ):              key(i){settype(&me);}
    int_node( void     ):              key(0){settype(&me);}
    int_node(int_node &r):list_node(r), key(0){settype(&me);}
    // ...
    virtual int operator==( const node &right ) const;
}
```

The main problem with this mechanism is the ease with which you can forget to call a base-class function [settype()] from a derived-class constructor—something you don't do very often.

Once the me field is set with a call to settype() a derived-class object can use typeof() (declared on line 25 of Listing 7.10) to see if a node of some sort— usually a second derived-class object addressed via a base-class pointer—is of the same derived class as the current object. The int_node::**operator**==() function, for example, is a concrete version of a pure virtual function in the node base class. int_node::**operator**==() must take a node reference as its argument in order to match the base-class definition exactly, but it can validly compare itself against another object only if that object is of the same derived class as itself. Here's how it looks:

node::me

node:: settype()

node:: typeof()

```
        virtual int int_node::operator==( const node &right ) const
        '{
            return !typeof(right) ? 0 : key - ((int_node*)&right)->key;
        }
```

If `typeof(right)` returns true, then `right` is of the same derived class as the current object—they're both `int_nodes`. In this case, the address of `right` can be safely cast into an `int_node` pointer in order to extract the `key` field.

Listing 7.10. *node.hpp*— The `node` Class

```
 1    #ifndef __NODE_HPP
 2    #define __NODE_HPP
 3
 4    #include <stdio.h>
 5    #include <stdlib.h>
 6
 7    #ifdef DEBUG              // If debug is defined, then D(printf("..."));
 8    #define D(x) x           // expands to its argument---printf("...");
 9    #else                    // otherwise, D(printf("...")); expands to an
10    #define D(x)             // empty string, effectively disappearing from
11    #endif // DEBUG          // the input.
12
13    typedef long align;      // worst-case alignment type for current machine
14    class node
15    {
16        friend class collection;
17        friend class node_iterator;
18
19        void            *me;        // Used by typeof().
20        static const align magic;   // Used for memory management by public
21                                    // overloads of new and delete.
22    protected:
23        void  settype( void *type_id )        { me = type_id;       }
24    public:
25        int   typeof ( const node &r ) const { return me == r.me; }
26
27        virtual ~node()                                        {}
28        node ( void                         ) : me ( NULL)     {}
29        node ( const node &right            ) : me ( right.me) {}
30        node &operator= ( const node &right ) { me = right.me; return *this;}
31
32        void *operator new      ( size_t size    );
33        void  operator delete   ( void *p        );
34        int             delete_ok ( void         );
35
36        virtual node *clone    ( void                    ) const = 0;
37        virtual void print     ( FILE *stream            ) const = 0;
38        virtual int  operator==( const node &right        ) const = 0;
39        virtual int  operator< ( const node & /*right*/ ) const {return 0;}
40
41    private: // called by both iterator and collection
42
```

```
Listing 7.10. continued...
43        virtual node *pred       ( void                              ) const = 0;
44        virtual node *succ       ( void                              ) const = 0;
45
46    private: // for use by collection --- provided by derived class
47
48        ------------------------------------------------------------------|
49        virtual void replace    (node **head, node **tail, node *with_this)=0;
50        virtual void link       (node **head, node **tail    )       = 0;
51        virtual void unlink     (node **head, node **tail    )       = 0;
52        virtual node *srch_succ(const node &looking_for       ) const = 0;
53        virtual node *sort      (node **tail, int *nel        )       = 0;
54        virtual int  is_sorted  (void                         ) const = 0;
55        virtual node *first     (node *tail                   ) const = 0;
56        virtual node *last      (node *tail                   ) const = 0;
57
58        virtual void mergeto( const node * *const dst_head,
59                                    node * *const dst_tail,
60                                    node * *const src_head,
61                              const node * *const src_tail ) = 0;
62
63    };
```

The me field is copied from the right operand by both the copy constructor and the assignment overload on lines 29 and 30 of Listing 7.10. The default constructor on the previous line initializes me to NULL—so all derived classes that omit the set-type() call from their constructors will be considered equivalent.

Note that operator<() on line 39 of Listing 7.10 is declared **virtual**, but is not pure—it has a body that returns false. The default function body gives the derived class the option of not providing an **operator**<() if the less-than operation doesn't make sense in the derived-class's context. You won't be able to sort collections made up of this sort of object, but there are no other difficulties. The derived class must provide an **operator**==() for use by collection::find(), however.

node:: operator<()

The remainder of the actual functions in the node class are devoted to memory management. The node provides local overloads of **new** and **delete** that are used not only to allocate basic nodes but also to allocate objects of all classes that derive from node as well. This is just simple inheritance in action—the derived class inherits the **new** and **delete** overloads from node in the normal way. The size argument gives **new**() the size of the derived-class object when it allocates a derived-class object. [**new**() could use **sizeof**(*this) if all it allocated were base-class objects.]

node::

The current implementations of **new** and **delete** just do data validation, using a header containing a magic number for this purpose. I didn't implement the linked-list strategy for maintaining a free list of deleted nodes, as was described in Chapter Four, for two reasons. First, there's no guarantee in a general-purpose implementation that collection nodes will be freed up often enough that the memory used for the nodes won't just be lost if they aren't sent to free().

Second, `new` and **delete** manage derived-class objects as well as simple `nodes`, so a free list of recyclable nodes will contain objects of several different sizes. Searching this list at allocation time for a node that's the correct size is not much better than calling `malloc()`—there's little performance benefit for the extra work. Neither of the foregoing were problems in the example in Chapter Four because trees are typically used in different ways than general-purpose collections—I could assume that the application made only one tree at a time, that the tree would be used dynamically for a short while, and that the entire tree would be destroyed periodically. No such assumptions are safe in the current context.

The local overloads of `new` and **delete** are here primarily to solve a problem in both C and C++. When a collection goes out of scope, it frees all memory used for the members. This behavior is fine (even desirable) when the individual collection members are allocated by `new`, but if the elements are just declared instead of being dynamically allocated, they will be incorrectly sent to **delete**. They'll also be destroyed twice, once by **delete** and once when they go out of scope.

node:: delete_ok()

The problem is solved with a local new/delete overload that puts a wrapper that holds a magic number—a signature—around the memory. The `delete_ok()` member function returns true only if it finds the magic number in place, and this function is called in turn by the destructor [and by `collection::clear()`, which is an inline alias for a destructor call] before it tries to delete a list element.

There is a small chance that a nondynamic list element will have a magic number in the right place, but it's unlikely. In any event, I'm assuming that all normal list elements come from `new`—always the case when you use the templates discussed earlier. Consequently, this mechanism is really a backup, error-detection mechanism. If you allocate list elements from the stack or directly from the global-level `new`, you must remove the nodes from the list before allowing the list to go out of scope.

Implementations of the local `new` and **delete** are in Listing 7.11. The `new` overload allocates space for a new `node`, but it treats the memory as an array of `align`'s (`align` is declared, above, on line 13 of Listing 7.10) rather than an array of **char**—more on this in a moment. The statement on line 71 of Listing 7.11 adjusts the incoming size to be in align-sized chunks rather than bytes. The global `new` is then used to get enough memory for both the object and an additional `align` object to hold the signature. A magic number is assigned to the top of the memory block, thereby marking the block as valid, and a pointer to the region just beneath the magic number is returned to the application.

The magic number itself is declared, above, on line 66 of Listing 7.10 and defined, below, on line 66 of Listing 7.11. It's a local **private** field, so access is restricted to the `node` methods. It's also a **static const**, however, so the compiler does not have to allocate memory for it. In the worst-case scenario, the compiler will allocate space for a single `align` object that's shared by all instances of `node`. `node::magic` is initialized to its own address, a convenient unique number, when defined on line 66 of Listing 7.11. If all node-like memory managers in the system use the same strategy, then they will all use different magic numbers and avoid any potential magic-number conflicts.

The memory is treated as an array of align objects by node::new() in order to ensure that the increment on line 77 of Listing 7.11 results in a value that is a valid address of any sort of object. I'll demonstrate the problem with an example that won't work. Say that the worst-case alignment type in a machine is a 4-byte long and the compiler for that machine supports a 2-byte int. That is, a variable of type long must be at an address that is an even multiple of four, ints must be at addresses that are even multiples of two, and there are no restrictions at all on the address of a char. These limitations are imposed by the hardware in order to make memory access more efficient, so you just have to work with them.

alignment
in memory
management

Now consider this simplified version of our memory allocator.

```
void *allocate( int size )
{
    int *p = malloc( sizeof(int) + size );
    *p++ = magic_number;
    return p;
}

fred( )
{
    long *lp = (long *) allocate( sizeof(long) );
    *lp = 0L; // HARDWARE (ALIGNMENT) ERROR!
}
```

The malloc() call in allocate() returns a pointer that can address any sort of object. It must satisfy the worst-case alignment restriction imposed by the hardware, so in the current situation, the returned address must be an even multiple of four. Otherwise, you couldn't use malloc() to get an array of longs. p, however, is a two-byte int pointer, so the increment on the next line adds two to p. p is no longer a valid address for a long because it's no longer an even multiple of four. Consequently, allocate() returns an address that is valid for a two-byte int, but is not valid for a four-byte long. The subsequent assignment generates a hardware error that will either terminate the current process or crash the machine, depending on your operating system.

The node::operator new() function avoids the problem by always incrementing the pointer in even multiples of the worst-case-alignment-type size. It accomplishes this feat by declaring the pointer to memory as an align pointer, with align typedef'd as a worst-case alignment type.

The next function of interest is delete_ok(), on line 81 of Listing 7.11. This function checks for a valid, locally allocated node by treating the incoming pointer as addressing the second element of an array of align objects. It examines the previous element with a [-1], returning false if the current node wasn't allocated by the local new. A false value from delete_ok() is always safe—the indicated node did not come from the local new. A true value from delete_ok() is probably safe—it is unlikely but possible that a node that lives on the stack happens to be preceded by a long that holds the magic number, in which case delete_ok() will return a false positive.

The final function in Listing 7.11 is node::operator delete() on line 86. It backs up the incoming pointer, checks for the magic number, and deletes the

Listing 7.11. *node.hpp*— Local Overloads of `new` and `delete`

```
64    //------------------------------------------------------------------------
65    #ifdef __NODE_COMPILE_METHODS
66    const align node::magic = (align)( &node::magic ); // unique number
67
68    void *node::operator new( size_t size )
69    {
70        align *p;
71        size = (size / sizeof(align)) + ((size % sizeof(align)) != 0);
72        if( !(p = ::new align[size + 1] ))              // +1 for the header
73        {
74            fprintf(stderr, "new node: No memory for list element." );
75            exit( 1 );
76        }
77        *p++ = magic;  // Initialize the signature and advance past it
78        return p;      // return pointer to area beneath signature.
79    }
80    //------------------------------------------------------------------------
81    int node::delete_ok( void )
82    {
83        return ((align *)this)[-1] == magic;
84    }
85    //------------------------------------------------------------------------
86    void node::operator delete( void *ip )
87    {
88        align *p = (align *) ip;     // cleans up the code a bit
89        if( *--p != magic )
90            D( fprintf(stderr, "node::delete(): Nondynamic node found\n") );
91        else
92        {
93            *p = ~*p; // Make sure that the != magic succeeds in the case
94            delete p; // of multiple deletes on the same memory, then delete.
95        }
96    }
97    #endif // __NODE_COMPILE_METHODS
```

node if the number is there. Note the assignment on line 93, which ensures that an error is detected if the same pointer is passed to `delete` twice in succession.

7.4 Implementing the `node_iterator` Class

The next class of interest is the `node_iterator` class in Listing 7.12. Since a `node_iterator` has no non-**inline** member functions, it's declared in the same file as the `node` so you can include one file to get both declarations.

The `node_iterator` has one data member, `current`, which holds the address of the most recently visited node. `current` is set to NULL if you declare an iterator without initialization, as in the following declaration:

```
node_iterator it;
```

You'll need to initialize this uninitialized iterator explicitly (with a pointer to a collection member) as follows:

```
collection col;
// ... add some members
for( it = col.start(); it ; ++it )
    it->print();
```

Alternatively, you can initialize the iterator as part of the declaration:

```
foo( collection col )
{
    node_iterator it = col.start();
    while( it )
      (it++)->print();
}
```

The `current` field is set back to `NULL` when you go off either end of the list in the process of traversal, so it must be reinitialized with an assignment if you want to traverse the list again. This approach lets you use `current` as an at-end-of-list marker.

An alternate strategy would have `current` stick at one end or another. A `++` operation wouldn't go past the end of the list, for example. An extra field is needed to keep track of whether you're at end of list, however, and this approach is generally more complicated. In most of my applications, at least, an iterator that stuck at the end of the list would serve no useful purpose because I'd just have to reinitialize it to the start of the list at the next iteration anyway.

The `operator int()` function on line 114 of Listing 7.12 is used to test for the end-of-list condition. For example, the test component in a `for` loop such as

testing for end of list, - `node_iterator:: operator int()`

```
for( it = col.start(); it ; ++it )
    ...
```

implicitly invokes `operator int()`, which evaluates to zero when there are no more elements to examine—when `current()` is `NULL`.

The iterator is advanced with the overloads of `++` and `--` on lines 116 to 137 of Listing 7.12. Remember that the postincrement forms (the two functions with dummy arguments) are available only in C++ version 2.1 or later. Note that all of these functions use either `node::pred()` or `node::succ()` to get to the next collection member. Consequently, changing the way that `node` organizes a list does not affect the `node_iterator()` class at all.

`node::pred()`, `node::succ()`

The `++` and `--` operators all evaluate to pointers to either the current `node` or the previous one, depending on whether the "pre" or "post" version of the operator was used. In the case of the earlier examples, `node` had a virtual `print()` function, so a statement like `(it++)->print()` is reasonable. `operator++()` returns a `node` pointer that is then used as the left operand of a `->` to access a member function. Accessing a field in a derived-class object is a bit trickier, and requires a cast:

Listing 7.12. *node.hpp*— The `node_iterator` **Class**

```
 98   class node_iterator
 99   {
100       // friend of class node;
101
102       node    *current;
103   public:
104       node_iterator(        void      ): current ( NULL  ) {}
105       node_iterator( node *first    ): current ( first ) {}
106       node_iterator &operator=( node *here )
107       {
108           // called with return value from collection::start() or
109           // collection::end() as its argument.
110
111           current = here;
112           return *this;
113       }
114       operator int(void){ return current != NULL; } // true at end of list
115
116       node *operator++( /* prefix */ )
117       {
118           return current = current ? current->succ(): NULL;
119       }
120       node *operator--( /* prefix */ )
121       {
122           return current = current ? current->pred(): NULL;
123       }
124       node *operator++(int /* postfix */ )     // the argument isn't used
125       {                                        // so don't name it.
126           node *ret_value = current;
127           if( current )
128               current = current->succ();
129           return ret_value;
130       }
131       node *operator--(int /* postfix */ )
132       {
133           node *ret_value = current;
134           if( current )
135               current = current->pred();
136           return ret_value;
137       }
138
139       node *operator-> (void){ return current;  }
140       node &operator*  (void){ return *current; }
141   };
142   #endif __NODE_HPP
```

```
int_stack stk;    // really a collection of int_nodes
stk.push(1);      // creates and initializes an int_node,
stk.push(2);      //                          then pushes it
stk.push(3);
```

```
node_iterator it = stk.start();
while( it )
    printf("%d\n",  ((int_node *)(it++))->key );
```

I've gotten around this rather ugly code by generating iterators for specific types from templates, as was discussed a few sections back. I'll discuss the template implementations shortly.

The two remaining iterator functions are `operator->()` and `operator*()` on lines 139 and 140 of Listing 7.12. They let you access the current object without advancing the iterator. `operator->()` returns a pointer to the current object and `operator*()` returns a reference to the current object.

Note that C++ has pretty restrictive rules about how `operator->()` can be overloaded. In particular, it is treated as a *unary* operator whose operand is to its left. It must return a pointer to an object of some sort, so the thing to the right of the `->` in an expression must specify a field in the object. Given the class

`operator->()`

```
class cls { public int eye; }
```

`x->eye` is treated as `(x.operator->())->eye`. This restriction effectively limits overloads of `->` to applications like the current one—`operator->()` just isn't useful in other contexts.

The `operator*()` overload on line 140 of Listing 7.12 isn't nearly so weird. Although `operator*()` could, in theory, do anything, it's used here in a reasonable way to get access to the current object. That is, if you look at the iterator as a pointer-like thing—`it++` is an analog for a pointer increment and `(int)it` is much like testing for a NULL pointer, for example—then it makes sense that `*` evaluates to the addressed object—the `node` to which the iterator points. Supporting a `*` operation also yields a useful symmetry—the two operations `it->field` and `(*it).field` are treated identically because `->` returns a pointer and `*` returns a reference to the same thing.

Though `(*it).field` isn't likely to come up very often, `*it` is useful when you need to call a function that takes a `node` argument (as compared to a node-pointer argument) or if you need to return a `node` from a function. Given iterator `it;`, an `f(*it)` passes the actual node to `f()`, either by value or by reference, depending on how `f()` defines its argument. Similarly, a `g(&*f)` passes the address of the current node to `g()`.

The following global-level overload of the `[]` demonstrates the utility of the `*` operator. It uses array brackets to access collection elements. The algorithm (which is rather simplistic—a better one is presented at the end of the chapter) traverses the collection using an iterator, counting members as it goes. It returns a pointer to the *index*-th node or NULL if there is no such node. The `return` statement at the end of the subroutine uses the `*` operator to extract a reference to the current member from the iterator. The `&` then gets the address of that element:

```
node *operator[](collection *col, int index)
{
    if( index >= col.size() )
        return NULL;

    iterator it = col.start();
    for( cur_index = -1; ++cur_index < index ; ++it )
        ;
    return &(*it);          // return address of current object
}
```

One useful addition to the iterator that I haven't implemented is a `rewind()` function that returns the iterator to the state it was in when it was initialized most recently. This function is useful if you want to pass an iterator without wanting to pass the object to iterate as well:

```
sid()
{
    collection col;
    iterator it;
    // ...
    nancy( it = col.start() );
}

void nancy( iterator &it )
{
    while( it )                    // traverse the list
        (it++)->print();

    it.rewind();                   // rewind to initial member.
    while( it )                    // traverse it again.
        (it++)->print();
}
```

You can add a `rewind()` by introducing a second pointer field to the iterator that's set to the same value as `current` in the constructor and `operator=()` functions, but isn't modified by the increment or decrement operators. `rewind()` just sets `current` to the value of this second pointer. I chose not to implement the feature because it isn't that useful and would double the size of a `node_iterator` object.

7.5 Implementing the `list_node` Class

Slouching gradually toward the real world, our next step is to customize the `node` so that the collection members are organized into some sort of real data structure—in the current implementation, a linked list. The `list_node` class's *raison d'être* is to provide real versions of the various virtual collection-member-manipulation functions called from the `collection` class. I'll discuss these one at a time in a moment. The `list_node` class definition is given in Listing 7.13. Only two data members are present in every `list_node`: `next` points at the next linked-list element and `prev` at the previous one. (`head` and `tail` are **static**, and so won't be in the object itself—I'll look at how they're used in a moment.) The constructors on lines 19 and 20 of Listing 7.13 set the `prev` and `next` pointers to `NULL` to indicate that the `list_node` isn't in a list yet.

The `operator=()` function on the next line doesn't modify `head` or `tail`, though. [It does chain to the base class's **`operator=()`** with the `*(node *)`**`this`** `= right` statement, but doesn't modify anything in the `list_node` component of the object.] There is actually a somewhat thorny problem being solved here. There are three approaches to take when copying one `list_node` to another. The approach to avoid at any cost is to copy the pointers from the source to the target node. The problem is shown in Figure 7.2—the copy effectively forms a new head of list, but the copy is not really in the list because nothing points at it. Bad things happen if the list is then deleted or otherwise modified through the copied node.

`list_node::`
`operator=()`

Figure 7.2. Introducing a False Head-of-List Pointer

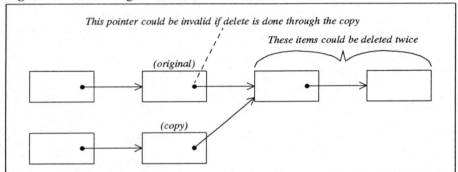

This pointer could be invalid if delete is done through the copy

These items could be deleted twice

(original)

(copy)

There are two additional possibilities. The first leaves the `prev` and `next` pointers of both lists untouched. The problem with the don't-touch-it approach is that any implicit ordering in the target list—if it's sorted, for example—is lost after the copy. The only way to handle this situation is to remove the target node from its list if it's in one, do the copy, and then reinsert the node into the list using the proper insertion criteria.

This procedure would mess up the ordering in an array, though, and in any event, there's no easy way for the `list_node` to know the ordering criteria used by the application program. A possible solution to this problem is to disallow an assignment when the target node is already in a list, thereby forcing application writers to worry about the sorted-list problem. They would have to explicitly remove the target node from the collection before doing the assignment. This approach would be pretty annoying when manipulating lists used as arrays, though.

The second approach handles the situation where both the source and target nodes are already in lists. You'll copy the application area—defined by the class that derives from `list_node`—but you won't modify the `list_node` component of the object at all, so both lists will remain intact. This is the only approach that works when you copy one `array`-class member to a second array, which is why I've used it.

The destructor on line 26 of Listing 7.13 also deals with a thorny list-pointer problem. You don't want to destroy an active list element—one that's still in a list.

`list_node::`

Consequently, the destructor complains when it detects this condition, examining the prev and next pointers to see if the node is part of a list. The remove-from-list function that I'll discuss shortly sets these pointers to NULL.

virtual destructors   Note that the destructor is **virtual**, as it was with the base-class destructor, so that destruction of a derived-class object through a base-class pointer works as expected.

Listing 7.13. *listnode.hpp*— The list_node Class

```
1    #ifndef __LISTNODE_HPP
2    #define __LISTNODE_HPP
3    #include <stdio.h>
4    #include <stdlib.h>
5    #include "node.hpp"
6
7    class list_node : public node
8    {
9    private:                    // true private stuff---for internal use only
10       list_node *next;        // next list element.
11       list_node *prev;        // previous list element.
12
13       static list_node *tail;                     // variables and functions
14       static list_node *head;                     // used for sorting.
15       void        tree_traverse( list_node *root );
16       list_node  *tree_insert  ( list_node *root, list_node *p );
17
18   public:
19       list_node( void               ): next(NULL), prev(NULL)          {}
20       list_node( const list_node &r): next(NULL), prev(NULL), node(r) {}
21       list_node &operator=( const list_node &right )
22       {
23           *(node *)this = right; // call node::operator=() if there is one
24           return *this;
25       }
26       virtual ~list_node()
27       {
28           if( next || prev )  // node is still in a list---hard error
29           {
30               fprintf(stderr,"Can't destroy active collection element\n");
31               exit( 1 );
32           }
33       }
34
35   private:         // definitions of virtual functions required by the
36                    // base class and are provided by the current class:
37
38       virtual node *first    (node * /*tail*/) const {return (node*)this;}
39       virtual node *last     (node *   tail  ) const {return tail;      }
40       virtual node *pred     (void            ) const {return prev;      }
41       virtual node *succ     (void            ) const {return next;      }
42       virtual node *srch_succ(const node &    ) const {return next;      }
43
```

➡

Listing 7.13. continued...

```
44        virtual void replace    ( node **head, node **tail, node *with_this);
45        virtual void link        ( node **head, node **tail      );
46        virtual void unlink      ( node **head, node **tail      );
47        virtual node *sort       ( node **tail, int  *num_ele_p );
48        virtual int  is_sorted ( void                        ) const;
49
50        virtual void mergeto (const node * *const dst_h,
51                                     node * *const dst_t,
52                                     node * *const src_h,
53                               const node * *const src_t );
54
55                    // base-class functions that must be provided
56                    // by classes that derive from list_node:
57
58   private: virtual node *clone     (void               ) const = 0;
59   public:  virtual int  operator==(const node &r     ) const = 0;
60
61                    // base-class functions that can be provided
62                    // by classes that derive from list_node:
63   public:
64        virtual void  list_node::print ( FILE * D(stream) ) const
65        {
66            D( fprintf(stream, "%s list_node(@%p): prev=%p, next=%p ",     \
67                                delete_ok() ? "dynamic" : "static " , \
68                                this, prev, next);                          )
69        }
70        virtual char *list_node::sprint( char *buf, int D(maxbuf) ) const
71        {
72            *buf = '\0';
73            D( if( maxbuf > 70 ) )  // 70 == length of string printed by:
74            D(     sprintf(buf, "%clist_node(@%p): prev=%p, next=%p ",    \
75                                delete_ok() ? ' ' : '*', \
76                                this, prev, next);             )
77            return buf;
78        }
79   };
```

The various functions on lines 38 to 42 of Listing 7.13 are small enough to be `inline`. The first functions are called as follows from the collection class to get the head- and tail-of-list pointers:

`list_node::
first(),
list_node::last()`

```
class collection
{
    node *head;        // Head-of-list pointer
    node *tail;        // Tail-of-list pointer
    //...
    start(){ return head->first( tail ); }
    end  (){ return head->last ( tail ); }
};
```

Again, this extra level of function calling takes care of the situation where the nodes are organized as a complex data structure like a tree rather than as a simple linked list. The collection object's head pointer might address the tree's root, for example. In the current simple situation, the functions just return the incoming pointers. The head-of-list pointer is passed implicitly to both functions as this [because the functions are called via head-> —the p in p->f() is always accessible as this inside the called function]. Note that first() and last() are both inline functions, so there's no run-time overhead in calling them. You get a lot of flexibility with no penalty.

list_node::pred(), list_node::succ()

The predecessor and successor functions on the next three lines are more straightforward. They just return the value of the current node's prev or next field, as appropriate.

list_node:: print(), list_node:: sprint()

The only other functions defined in the list_node definition itself are print() and sprint() on lines 64 and 70 of Listing 7.13. The D() macro and its arguments are effectively removed from the source code when DEBUG is not #defined. Use these functions for debugging. print prints the contents of the private portions of the object to the indicated stream; sprint() outputs to a buffer. These functions are here primarily as a convenience for the derived class. If the derived class supports a print() operation, for example, it can print the base-class component of the object by chaining to the base class's (list_node's) print() function.

list_node:: link(), list_node:: unlink(),, list_node:: replace()

The list_node functions continue in Listing 7.14 with link(), unlink(),, and replace() which respectively add an element, remove an element, and replace an element. The main complication is that these functions must be passed the addresses of the head and tail pointers in the collection object— they're passed pointers to node pointers. This way they can treat the collection object's head and tail pointers much as they would static global variables, modifying fields in the collection object as necessary. You can't put these fields into the node because one head and one tail pointer are shared by all nodes in the list. You can't make them static members of a node because you then could have only one collection in the program.

list_node:: mergeto()

The only other complication is in mergeto() (on line 131 of Listing 7.14), which moves all elements from one list to another. This function must be passed node** arguments to match the virtual function definition in the node class. Since these arguments really hold the addresses of list_node pointers, they must be downcast into list_node** (i.e. converted from the base class to the derived class) to be used. You don't need the cast in the other functions because all the conversions there go from list_node pointers to node pointers, and silent conversion from the derived to the base class is always permitted.

downcast

sorting collections, list_node:: sort()

The last set of functions in the listnode class concern themselves with sorting the list. They are all to be found in Listing 7.15. There are several ways to sort linked lists.[1] The method I've used takes advantage of the fact that a list_node

---

[1] There's a nice QuickSort implementation for linked lists that's a good alternative to the current method in [CGaz].

Listing 7.14. *listnode.hpp* — Linking and Unlinking

```
80    #ifdef __LISTNODE_COMPILE_METHODS
81    //----------------------------------------------------------------------
82    void list_node::link( node **headp, node **tailp )
83    {
84        // Default link-yourself-into-list routine, links to tail of list
85
86        list_node *tail = (list_node *) *tailp;
87        if( !*headp )                          // list is empty
88        {
89            *headp     = this;
90            this->prev = NULL;
91        }
92        else if( tail )
93        {
94            tail->next = this;
95            this->prev = tail;
96        }
97        else
98        {
99            fprintf(stderr,"INTERNAL ERROR list_node::link(), no tail\n");
100           exit( 1 );
101       }
102       this->next = NULL;
103       *tailp     = this;
104   }
105   //----------------------------------------------------------------------
106   void list_node::unlink( node **headp, node **tailp )
107   {
108       // remove the current node (the one addressed by this) from the list.
109
110       if( prev             ) prev->next = next;
111       if( next             ) next->prev = prev;
112       if( *headp == this ) *headp      = next;
113       if( *tailp == this ) *tailp      = prev;
114
115       prev = next = NULL; // mark node as "not in a list" (see destructor)
116   }
117   //----------------------------------------------------------------------
118   void list_node::replace( node **head, node **tail, node *with_this )
119   {
120       // Replace current node (pointed to by this) "with_this" node.
121
122       list_node *with = (list_node *)with_this;    // avoid messy casts
123
124       if( *head == this    ) *head = with_this;
125       if( *tail == this    ) *tail = with_this;
126       if( with->prev = prev ) prev->next = with;
127       if( with->next = next ) next->prev = with;
128       prev = next = NULL; // mark current node as not in list
129   }
130   //----------------------------------------------------------------------
131   void list_node::mergeto(const node * *const dst_h,
```

→

```
Listing 7.14. continued. . .

132                                        node * *const dst_t,
133                                        node * *const src_h,
134                           const node * *const src_t )
135    {
136        // Move all elements of src list to end of dst list;
137        // both lists can be empty, but neither list has to be empty.
138
139        if( (* (list_node **) dst_t )->tail = *(list_node **)src_h )
140        {
141            (      *(list_node **)src_h )->prev = *(list_node **)dst_t;
142            (      *(list_node **)dst_t )      = *(list_node **)src_t;
143            if( ! *(list_node **)dst_h )
144                *(list_node **)dst_h = *(list_node **)src_h;
145            *src_t = *src_h = NULL;
146        }
147        // else src list is empty--nothing to do.
148    }
```

list_node::
tree_insert()

contains two pointers. The sorting algorithm in sort yanks the nodes off the list, one node at a time, and inserts the nodes into a binary tree, using the tree_insert() function for this purpose. The prev field in the list_node is pressed into service as the left-child pointer and the next field as the right-child pointer. The tree is then traversed in order by tree_traverse(), removing the nodes one at a time and reinserting them into the list in order.

The only difficulty with this approach is that the final traversal is done recursively, so there's a possibility of a run-time stack overflow if you try to sort an already sorted list. (The "tree" constructed from the linked list will *be* a linked list in this case; recursively traversing a linked list requires as many recursion levels as there are list elements.) The is_sorted() function at the top of Listing 7.15 addresses this problem by letting the calling routine know whether the list is already sorted before bothering to resort it. You could actually solve the problem, rather than just detecting it, by going to a more sophisticated tree structure like an AVL or right-threaded binary tree.

list_node::
is_sorted()

The two **static** data members of the list_node (list_node::head and list_node:tail, declared in the **class** definition and defined at the top of Listing 7.15) are used in the sorting process to keep track of the head and tail of the new list as it's constructed. These fields can be **static** because they're used only during the sorting process and are reinitialized at the beginning of every sort.

7.6 Implementing the lnode<type> Template

The next stage in the evolution of the collection is to make the listnode a bit more tractable, developing two class templates that generate the most common classes that would normally derive from list_node. The first of these is the lnode<type> template in Listing 7.16. An lnode is a classic *container class*—a class that exists only to contain an object of some sort. For example, an

container class

Listing 7.15. *listnode.hpp*— Sorting Functions

```
149    list_node *list_node::tail ;      // Head and tail of sorted list.
150    list_node *list_node::head ;
151    //------------------------------------------------------------------
152    int list_node::is_sorted( void ) const
153    {
154        // Checks for a sortable list---a list that is not already in order.
155
156        const list_node *p;
157        for( p = this; p && p->next ; p = p->next )
158            if( !( *p < *(p->next) || *p == *(p->next) ))
159                return 0;
160        return 1;
161    }
162    //------------------------------------------------------------------
163    node *list_node::sort( node **tailp, int *num_ele_p )
164    {
165        // Called from collection::sort()  with:
166        //    head = head->sort( &tail, &nel );
167        // num_ele_p points at the number of elements in the initial list.
168        // The sorted list could be smaller because duplicate elements are
169        // deleted as part of the sorting process.
170        //
171        // Sort the list. The list is taken apart, turned into a tree,
172        // and then reassembled in sorted order. Reassembling is done
173        // using a recursive tree-traversal algorithm, so sorting a sorted
174        // list might end up with a stack overflow. Be careful. Once the
175        // list is sorted, insertions are replaced in their proper position
176        // in the list. The "next" field is used as the right-child pointer,
177        // the "prev" field is the left-child pointer. Duplicate nodes are
178        // discarded if they exist.
179
180        list_node *nextp, *p, *root;
181
182        root       = this;            // Make a tree with one node in it
183        p          = root->next;
184        root->next = root->prev = NULL;
185
186        for(; p ; p = nextp )
187        {
188            nextp = p->next;
189            if( p = tree_insert( root, p ) ) // Destroys all pointers in p
190            {
191                // Then p is a duplicate node, set prev and next pointers
192                // to NULL so that delete will believe that the duplicate
193                // node has been removed from the list, then get rid of it.
194
195                p->next = p->prev = NULL;
196                delete( p );
197                --*num_ele_p;
198            }
199        }
200        tail = head = NULL;
```

Listing 7.15. continued. . .

```
201        tree_traverse( root );      // Traverse the tree, reinserting the nodes
202
203        tail->next = NULL;          // Mark ends of list
204        head->prev = NULL;
205        *tailp = (node*)tail;       // Set new end of list in collection
206        return   (node*)head;       // Return new start of list to collection
207    }
208    //-----------------------------------------------------------------------
209    list_node *list_node::tree_insert( list_node *root, list_node *p )
210    {
211        // Insert p into a nonempty tree. Returns p (and doesn't insert it)
212        // if it matches a node that's already in the tree; otherwise
213        // returns NULL. Uses prev as the left-child pointer, next as the
214        // right-child pointer.
215
216        list_node **parent; // pointer to next or prev field of parent node.
217
218        while( root )           // executes at least once
219        {
220            if(      *root == *p ){ return p;                                  }
221            else if(*root < *p  ){ parent = &root->next; root = root->next;}
222            else /* *root > *p */{ parent = &root->prev; root = root->prev;}
223        }
224
225        *parent = p;
226        p->prev = p->next = NULL;
227        return NULL;
228    }
229    //-----------------------------------------------------------------------
230    void list_node::tree_traverse( list_node *root )
231    {
232        // Traverse a nonempty tree, transferring all elements back to the
233        // linked list.
234
235        list_node *right;
236        if( root->prev )                    // if there is a left child
237            tree_traverse( root->prev );
238
239        // When we return here, entire left subtree has been deleted (moved
240        // from the tree back into the linked list). Remember the right-
241        // subtree pointer so that the current node can be inserted
242        // --insert() overwrites the prev and next pointers--then
243        // process the right subtree.
244
245        right = root->next;     // remember right-child pointer.
246
247        if( !tail )             // Add to end of list,
248            head = root;        // this is first insertion, remember new head
249        else
250            tail->next = root; // add to end of existing list
251
```

Listing 7.15. continued...

```
252         tail = root;
253
254         if( right )                 // traverse right subtree.
255             tree_traverse( right );
256     }
257 #endif  // __LISTNODE_COMPILE_METHODS
```

`lnode<int>` object contains an `int`. An `lnode<string>` contains an object of class `string`. The contained-object's type is passed into the class template at declaration time and the compiler generates a class by expanding the template, changing various types within the template definition to match the ones specified in the template-class declaration. For example, when you declare an `lnode<int>`, the compiler expands the `lnode` template to create the `lnode<int>` class (think of the `int` as part of the class name), replacing all occurrences of `type` in the **class** `lnode` declaration with `int`. Similarly, the `type key` on line 261 of Listing 7.16 (which declares the contained object) is replaced by `int key` in the expansion. The matching definition on line 304 of Listing 7.16 is expanded to `int lnode<int>::id`, thereby creating an `int` member of class `lnode<int>`.

The **class** `lnode` definition provides versions of all the various functions required in a class that derives from `list_node`, but these functions are customized to the contained object's type. For example, a cast-to-contained-type operation is defined on line 266 of Listing 7.16 with the statement

```
operator type( void ) const { return key; }
```

In the case of `lnode<int>`, the declaration is mapped to

```
operator int( void ) const { return key; }
```

The other common sort of statement you'll see in the `lnode` definition is a cast (or creation of) an object of the template class. For example, the `clone()` function on line 264 of Listing 7.16 creates a new object of the current class (of the template class) with the following code:

(margin note: cast to template class)

```
new lnode<type>( key );
```

In an `lnode<int>` expansion, the compiler swaps the `type` with `int`, so the expanded code looks like this:

```
new lnode<int>( key );
```

(Remember, `lnode<int>` is the class name.) This code creates a new `lnode<int>` object, calling the constructor on line 277 of Listing 7.16 to initialize the memory.

You can find a similar construction in the copy-constructor definition on line 275 of Listing 7.16, which looks like this:

Listing 7.16. *listnode.hpp*— The lnode<type> Template

```
258    template <class type>                    // type must have < and == defined
259    class lnode : public list_node
260    {
261        type key;
262        static int id;                       // identifier for typeof operation
263
264        virtual node *clone( void ) const { return new lnode<type>( key ); }
265    public:
266        operator type  ( void ) const { return key; } // extract key field
267        type &contained( void )        { return key; }
268
269        // Need copy constructor and operator= to copy the contained object.
270        // I'm deliberately using the default list_node constructor for
271        // the base-class component because I don't want the copy to be in
272        // the list. The operator=() function in the list_node also clears
273        // the prev and next pointers, so I call it from lnode::operator=().
274
275        lnode( const lnode<type> &obj ) : key( obj.key ){ settype(&id); }
276        lnode(        void         )                    { settype(&id); }
277        lnode( const type &obj      ) : key(   obj  ){ settype(&id); }
278
279        lnode<type> &operator=( const lnode<type> &right )
280        {
281            // Handles code like this:  lnode<int> a, b;
282            //                          a = b;
283
284            *((list_node *)this) = right;    // calls list_node::operator=()
285            key = right.key;                 // calls <type>::operator=()
286            return *this;
287        }
288        lnode<type> &operator=( const type &right )
289        {                                   // handles code like this:
290            key = right;                    // lnode<int> x, int y;
291            return *this;                   // x = y;
292        }
293        virtual int  operator< ( const node &r ) const
294        {
295            return typeof(r) ? key < ((lnode<type> *) &r)->key : 0;
296        }
297        virtual int  operator== ( const node &r ) const
298        {
299            return typeof(r) ? key == ((lnode<type> *) &r)->key : 0;
300        }
301    };
302
303    template <class type>
304    int lnode<type>::id;                      // identifier for typeof operation
```

```
                    lnode( const lnode<type> &obj ) : key( obj.key )
                    {
                        settype(&id);
```

```
}
```

The expanded constructor definition in the lnode<**int**> class takes an argument called obj of type reference-to-lnode<**int**>. The constructor then chains to the contained object's constructor in the memory initialization list.

Also of interest is the cast to the derived class in the **operator**<() and **operator**==() functions on lines 295 and 299 of Listing 7.16. The cast looks like ((lnode<type>*)&r) — cast the address of r into a pointer to an lnode of the current type.

There are a couple of design issues to discuss in addition to the implementation details just covered. First, you could eliminate the lnode template class entirely by making the list_node class a template and adding a field for the contained object to list_node. Although this change seems to simplify the code, it causes the compiler to generate a tremendous amount of unnecessary code. Remember, when the compiler expands a class template, not only does it redefine the **struct**-like component of the class, changing the declared types of various fields as specified by the **template** statement, but it also creates new versions of all the member functions. The list_node class contains a nontrivial amount of non-**inline** functions, and were this class a template, versions of every one of these functions would be created every time the template is expanded. A very large amount of unnecessary code would result as a consequence.

lnode<type> design issues

I've solved the problem by deriving the template class from the list_node. In this way the generated template classes inherit the various list_node functions rather than generating new versions of them. Only one version of each list_node function will exist in the final code. **In general, it's best to put into a normal base class all functions that don't use objects (or have arguments) of a type that is specified in a template statement. You then derive the template class from this base class.** In this way the functions that don't need to be customized by template expansion are just inherited in the normal way, and those that do need to be customized are created by the compiler as necessary.

The next design issue is the print() function. You can't put a simple function in the template class that prints an lnode<type> object, because you have no idea what type is going to be. There are several solutions to this problem.

lnode<t>:: print()

The first solution requires the contained object to have a function called print() that can be called from the template class like this:

```
void lnode<type>::print( FILE *fp ) { obj.print( fp ); }
```

The main problem is that simple objects (like an **int**) do not naturally carry print function with them. The earlier code will create a compiler error in an lnode<**int**> definition because the generated code would effectively be

```
int obj;
//...
obj.print(fp);
```

You can't print an **int** in this way.

The next solution adds a pointer-to-print-function argument to the constructor. This is not a great solution because it adds complexity to all declarations and won't

let you get an array of collections from new (since the array elements must be initialized with the default constructor). Here's a sample declaration to demonstrate
the process:

```
template <class t>
class lnode : public list_node
{
    t key;
    void (*prnt_funct)(t);
public:
    lnode()                          { prnt_funct = NULL;      }
    lnode( void (*printptr)(t) ){ prnt_funct = printptr; }
    print(){ if( prnt_funct) prnt_funct(key);
             else             printf("UNPRINTABLE ELEMENT\n }");
}

pint( int &x ){ printf("%d ", x ); }

lnode<int>  x(pint);
ar = new lnode<int>[10];   // array of ten lnode<int>s

x.print();        // okay, prints the "key" field's value
ar[0].print();    // Prints "UNPRINTABLE ELEMENT"
```

You can get around this problem by adding a print-function argument to the
template—probably the best solution if you want to guarantee that all objects have
a print function:

```
template <class t, void (*printptr)(t &x)>
class lnode : public list_node
{
    t key;
    void (*prnt_funct)(t x);
public:
    stack(){ prnt_funct = printptr; }
    print(){ prnt_funct(key);       }
}

pint( int &x ){ printf("%d ", x ); }
lnode<int,pint>  x;
new lnode<int,pint>  ar[10];

x.print(stdout);        // okay
ar[0].print(stdout);    // okay
```

Moving the function pointer from the constructor-argument list to the template-
argument list hasn't done much to improve the too-much-complexity problem,
though.

Other solutions are also possible (you can derive the template class from a
class that contains a print function, passing this second class into the lnode template as an argument, for example), but none of them are really satisfactory, which
leads us to the solution used here: Don't worry about it—use an iterator to print an
entire collection rather than collection::print().

7.7 Implementing `lnode_c<type>`

The other `node`-related template is the `lnode_c<cls>` template in Listing 7.17. This template definition is almost identical to the `lnode<type>` definition that I just discussed. The only real difference is that the contained object is defined as a base class on line 306 rather than as an instance variable—a field within the class. Making the contained object a base class gives a user of the generated class access to all public functions in the contained object. The following code demonstrates the problem:

```
class some_class { public: f(){ /*...*/ } };

lnode<some_class>      container_obj;
lnode_c<some_class>    base_obj;

base_obj.f();           // okay
container_obj.f();      // ILLEGAL, 'f()' is not a member of
                        // lnode<some_class>. It is a member of
                        // container_obj.key, but this field is
                        // private, so cannot be accessed
```

Other differences are best described by comparing the functions in Listing 7.16 with the similarly named functions in Listing 7.17.

7.8 Implementing `iterator<type>` and `iterator_c<cls>`

The final `node`-related templates are the two iterators, `iterator<type>` and `iterator_c<cls>`. As with `lnode<type>` and `lnode_c<cls>`, the two definitions are almost identical. Similarly, the iterator templates customize the `node_iterator` class to make it easier to use with a specific `node` type.

In order to minimize the amount of duplicate code in the iterator definitions, I've created a template class from which the two iterators derive. The application program is never intended to create objects of this base class directly, but the class simplifies program maintenance by concentrating common functions into a single base class. In this way the two real template classes won't have a large amount of almost identical code.

internal template used to minimize redundant code

The common base-class template—`iterator_base<nodetype,type>`—is presented in Listing 7.18. It is passed both the type of the contained object (`int`, `string`, etc.) and the node type (`lnode<int>`, `lnode_c<string>`, etc.) and uses this information to customize versions of the various increment and decrement operators and the `operator*()` function. There's no overload of `operator->()` at this level because this function is used only in an `iterator_c` object—the `iterator_base` template provides functions used in both a simple `iterator` and an `iterator_c`.

iterator_base<n,t>

Since there's no reason for an application ever to create an `iterator_base` object, the constructors are `protected`, effectively making a direct declaration of an `iterator_base` object illegal. You can declare objects that derive from `iterator_base` without difficulty. You could also prevent direct declaration of an object by creating a bogus pure virtual function (one with an `=0` in place of the

protected constructor

Listing 7.17. *listnode.hpp*— The `lnode_c<cls>` Template

```
305   template <class cls>                        // t must have < and == defined
306   class lnode_c : public list_node, public cls
307   {
308       static int id;                          // identifier for typeof operation
309
310       node *clone( void ) const
311       {
312           lnode_c<cls> *p = new lnode_c<cls>( *this );
313           return p;
314       }
315   public:
316       lnode_c( const lnode_c<cls> &obj ) : list_node(obj), cls(obj)
317       {
318           settype(&id);
319       }
320       lnode_c(     void          )                    { settype(&id); }
321       lnode_c( const cls &obj ): cls(obj) { settype(&id); }
322
323       cls &contained(void){ return *(cls *)this; } // return reference to
324                                                     // the base-class obj.
325
326       lnode_c<cls> &operator=( const lnode_c<cls> &right )
327       {
328           *((list_node *)this) = right;          // list_node::operator=()
329           *((cls        *)this) = right;          // cls::operator=()
330           return *this;
331       }
332
333       lnode_c<cls> &operator=( const cls &right ) //      lnode_c<cls> x;
334       {                                           //      x = cls_obj;
335           *((cls*)this) = right;                  // call cls::operator=()
336       }
337       virtual int  operator< ( const node &r ) const
338       {
339           return typeof(r) ? cls::operator<( *(const lnode_c<cls> *)&r ):0;
340       }
341       virtual int  operator== ( const node &r ) const
342       {
343           return typeof(r) ? cls::operator==( *(const lnode_c<cls> *)&r):0;
344       }
345   };
346
347   template <class cls>
348   int lnode_c<cls>::id;                    // identifier for typeof operation
```

function body) in `iterator_base()`, thereby making `iterator_base` an official abstract class. That's a pretty messy solution, though. It requires the base class to create a virtual-function overload with an empty body—a seemingly meaningless task. Moreover, it creates an unnecessary slot in the virtual-function table.

The main difference between the current template and the earlier
node_iterator class is that where node_iterator functions return pointers and
references to nodes—to entire list elements—the template functions return
pointers and references to the object contained within that node—to the int in an
lnode<**int**> or the string in an lnode_c<string>. Taking the **operator**++()
overload on line 358 as characteristic, the code on lines 360 and 361 of Listing
7.18 looks like this:

```
nodetype *p = (nodetype *) node_iterator::operator++();
return p ? &(p->contained()) : NULL;
```

The first line calls the base-class (node_iterator) function to both increment the
iterator and get a pointer to the appropriate list element. The **return** statement
returns a pointer to the contained object or NULL if there is no such object.

The one exception to the foregoing behavior is operator*() on line 378 of
Listing 7.18. Since this function returns a reference to the contained object (as
compared to a pointer), it can't return NULL on error. It gets around this problem
by returning a reference to the **static** garbage field (declared on line 352 and
defined on line 386 of Listing 7.18) when an error is detected. There's no explicit
constructor for this field, so it will be initialized by the default constructor if the
contained object is a class object. Its value is undefined in the case of a basic type
like a lnode<int>. Application programmers must make sure that an iterator is
not at the end of a list when they use the * operator. Something like the following
does the job:

Margin note: iterator_base:: operator()*

```
iterator<int> it;
// ..
for(; it; ++it )
    (*it).print();
```

Replacing the **for** statement with an **if**(it) also works fine. The garbage field
is declared static in an attempt to waste as little memory as possible.

The iterator_base template is used by the templates in Listings 7.19 and
7.20 to create classes used directly by applications. When you create an
iterator<**int**>, for example, the compiler automatically creates an
iterator_base <lnode<**int**>, **int**> because the iterator class—at the top
of Listing 7.19—derives from iterator_base <lnode<type>, type>. The
int in the iterator<**int**> declaration corresponds to type in the template definition in Listing 7.19. Consequently, the type in iterator_base <lnode<type>,
type> is replaced by iterator_base <lnode<**int**>, **int**>. If no such class
exists, the compiler creates one by expanding the template in Listing 7.18.

The iterator_c template in Listing 7.20 does much the same thing, but it
derives from iterator_base <lnode_c<cls>, cls>, thereby creating an
iterator_base class with a different node type (lnode_c rather than lnode).
The two templates are otherwise almost identical, inheriting most of their functions from the common base class.

Margin note: iterator_c

Listing 7.18. *listnode.hpp*— The `iterator_base<nodetype,type>` Template

```
349     template <class nodetype, class type>
350     class iterator_base : public node_iterator
351     {
352         static type garbage;
353     protected:
354         iterator_base(    void        ): node_iterator(        ) {}
355         iterator_base( node *first ): node_iterator( first ) {}
356
357     public:
358         type *operator++( /* prefix */ )
359         {
360             nodetype *p = (nodetype *) node_iterator::operator++();
361             return p ? &(p->contained()) : NULL ;
362         }
363         type *operator--( /* prefix */ )
364         {
365             nodetype *p = (nodetype *) node_iterator::operator--();
366             return p ? &(p->contained()) : NULL ;
367         }
368         type *operator++(int /* postfix */ )
369         {
370             nodetype *p = (nodetype *) node_iterator::operator++(0);
371             return p ? &(p->contained()) : NULL ;
372         }
373         type *operator--(int /* postfix */ )
374         {
375             nodetype *p = (nodetype *) node_iterator::operator--(0);
376             return p ? &(p->contained()) : NULL ;
377         }
378         type &operator*()    // returns reference to contained object
379         {
380             nodetype *p = (nodetype *)( node_iterator::operator->() );
381             return p ? p->contained(): garbage ;
382         }
383     };
384     //-----------------------------------------------------------------
385     template <class nodetype, class type>
386     type iterator_base<nodetype,type>::garbage;
```

Listing 7.19. *listnode.hpp*— The iterator<type> Template

```
387    template <class type>
388    class iterator: public iterator_base< lnode<type>, type >
389    {
390    public:
391        iterator(  void      ): iterator_base<lnode<type>,type>(      ){}
392        iterator(node *first): iterator_base<lnode<type>,type>(first){}
393        iterator<type> &operator= ( node *here )
394        {
395            node_iterator::operator=(here);
396            return *this;
397        }
398        // All other functions inherited from iterator_base
399    };
```

Listing 7.20. *listnode.hpp*— The iterator_c<cls> Template

```
400    template <class cls>
401    class iterator_c: public iterator_base<lnode_c<cls>, cls>
402    {
403    public:
404        iterator_c(  void      ): iterator_base<lnode_c<cls>,cls>(      ){}
405        iterator_c( node *first ): iterator_base<lnode_c<cls>,cls>(first){}
406        iterator_c<cls> &operator=( node *here )
407        {
408            node_iterator::operator=(here);
409            return *this;
410        }
411
412        cls *operator->( void )  // address of contained object which must
413        {                        // be a struct, class, or union
414
415            lnode_c<cls> *p = (lnode_c<cls> *)( node_iterator::operator->());
416            return & p->contained();
417        }
418        // All other functions inherited from iterator_base
419    };
420    #endif // __LISTNODE_HPP
```

Listnode.hpp ends at this point without a test main() subroutine as is usually my practice. I've omitted the main() because it's difficult to test a node class in a stand-alone fashion. The classes in *listnode.hpp* are tested by the main() in the files that hold the stack, queue, and array class definitions discussed below.

7.9 Implementing the Stack Classes and Templates

The refinement of a collection continues with the `ptr_stack` class defined in Listing 7.21. As with the earlier `list_node` class and `lnode<type>` and `lnode_c<cls>` templates, I've created a true base class to hold the functions that are used by both the `stack<type>` and `stack_c<cls>` templates. I then derive classes from this base class in the template definition. The benefits of this approach are, again, less code to maintain—the template classes won't hold a body of almost identical code—and smaller code size—the functions in the base class are inherited by the classes generated from the templates, so versions of these inherited functions won't have to be created as part of the template-generation process.

stack<type> and
stack_c<cls>

The `ptr_stack` class in Listing 7.21 implements a stack of pointers to nodes (or more correctly, a stack of pointers to objects of classes that derive from node). Other than the usual constructors and **operator=**() that chain to the base-class version, three functions need to be provided to modify the default behavior of the collection to support a stack. The first of these is remove(), which just chains to the base-class remove() function, passing it the address of the end-of-list item returned from end().

ptr_stack::

This change modifies the behavior of a collection object so that elements are popped (removed from the end of the list) rather then dequeued (removed from the start of the list). Since remove() is virtual, any function that manipulates a `ptr_stack` object through a collection pointer or reference will pop items from a `stack_ptr` object and dequeue them from a normal collection.

The subroutine in Listing 7.22 (which is part of the test code at the bottom of the listing) demonstrates what I'm talking about. test_collection() is passed a reference to a collection object, not to a stack. (The subroutine assumes a collection of lnode<**int**> objects.) The insert() calls on lines 89 to 92 push objects if the collection is a stack or enqueue them if the collection is a queue. The remove() on line 96 pops an object from a stack and dequeues an object from a queue.

The other two member functions of the `ptr_stack` class in Listing 7.21 add to the ones in a collection rather than modifying existing behavior. These are push() and pop() on lines 22 and 23. They are just in-line aliases for insert() and remove()—they help you implicitly document an addition or removal as a stack operation, at the same time identifying the manipulated collection as a stack, so perform an important function in program maintenance if not in functionality.

ptr_stack::
push(),
ptr_stack:: pop()

The `ptr_stack` class is now made easier to use by defining the stack<type> and stack_c<type> templates in Listings 7.23 and 7.24. The two definitions are almost identical, so I'll explain only the first one—stack<type> in Listing 7.23. The class template starts out with the usual complement of constructors and **operator=**() functions that all just chain to the similar base-class functions. The real work is done in the three functions at the bottom of the definition. find(), on line 124 of Listing 7.23, finds a collection member that matches the incoming specification, but that specification is a contained object (the **int** in lnode<**int**>), not a container (like lnode<**int**>). Given a stack<**int**>, you'd say something like

Listing 7.21. *stack.hpp*— The `ptr_stack` class

```
1    #ifndef __STACK_HPP
2    #define __STACK_HPP
3
4    #include <stdio.h>
5    #include <stdlib.h>
6    #include "listnode.hpp"
7    #include "collect.hpp"
8    //-------------------------------------------------------------------
9    class ptr_stack: public collection        // things unique to a stack
10   {
11   public:
12       ptr_stack( void                    ) : collection(   ) {}
13       ptr_stack( const ptr_stack  &src ) : collection(src) {}
14       ptr_stack( const collection &src ) : collection(src) {}
15       ptr_stack &operator=( const collection &right )
16       {
17           *(collection *)this = right;    // Chain to base-class function
18           return *this;
19       }
20
21       virtual node *remove( void ){ return collection::remove( end() ); }
22       void   push ( node *ele ){ insert( ele );        }
23       node *pop   ( void      ){ return remove();      }
24   };
```

`intstack.find(10)`. The function must encapsulate the incoming argument in an `lnode` in order to call `collection::find()`, and it does so with a cast operation as part of the `collection::find()` call. The lifetime of the temporary that results from the cast is very short, being destroyed when `find()` exits.

The `push()` function on line 126 works in similar ways, but it must use **new** to create the `lnode` container because the container object must continue to exist until the matching pop is executed—an anonymous temporary won't do.

The final member function is `stack<type>::pop()`, on line 131 of Listing 7.23. It calls `ptr_stack::pop()` on line 133, which removes the item from the underlying collection and returns a pointer to it. The contained object is then extracted from the container on line 134. The container is deleted on line 135, and the contained object is then returned.

There is a minor efficiency problem with this code, caused by the fact that the contained object cannot be accessed reliably after the **delete** on line 135 is executed. The initialization on line 134 implicitly calls the copy constructor for class `type` to avoid this problem. I'm using the `contained()` function, which returns a reference to the contained object rather than its value, to avoid a second copy operation. The code

```
type obj = *p;
```

would also work because there is a defined `lnode<type>` to `type` conversion supplied by the `lnode<type>::operator type()` function on line 266 of Listing

Listing 7.22. *stack.hpp*— A Test Routine for The Stack Functions

```
84   #ifdef  __STACK_MAIN
85   void test_collection( collection &s )     // Can manipulate both
86   {                                          // queues and stacks
87       node *p = new lnode<int>( 1 );
88
89       s.insert( p );                         // push if stack, enqueue if queue
90       s.insert( new lnode<int>( 2 ) );
91       s.insert( new lnode<int>( 3 ) );
92       s.insert( new lnode<int>( 4 ) );
93
94       while( !s.empty() )
95       {
96           p = s.remove();                    // pop if a stack, dequeue if a queue
97
98           printf( "Got %d :", int( * (lnode<int> *)( p ) ) );
99           delete p;
100
101          // Use raw node_iterator to print elements.
102          // Assume C++ 2.1 compiler
103
104          for( node_iterator it = s.start();  it ; )
105              printf( "%d ", int( * (lnode<int> *)( it++ ) ) );
106          printf("\n");
107      }
108  }
109  #endif // __STACK_MAIN
```

7.16 on page 380, but this extra conversion requires the compiler to create (and initialize) a temporary that's used only to initialize a second temporary.

Unfortunately, the `return` statement uses a second implicit call to the copy constructor (as well as an implicit delete of `obj`), so that's at least two copy operations. You can't return a reference because you'd be referencing a local variable.

Listing 7.24, implements a stack of `lnode_c<cls>` objects rather than a stack of `lnode<type>` objects. It's virtually identical to `stack<type>`. Note that I could have used a common base class, as I did earlier in the `iterator<type>` and `iterator_c<type>` classes, to eliminate the redundant code. There was so little code involved, though, that it seemed to me a common base class would add complexity.

The final part of *stack.hpp* is a test routine in Listing 7.25 that exercises the foregoing code.

Listing 7.23. *stack.hpp*— The `stack<type>` Template

```
110    template <class type>                         // A stack-of-<type> class
111    class stack : public ptr_stack
112    {
113    public:
114        stack( const stack<type> &src ) : ptr_stack(src) {}
115        stack( const collection &src  ) : ptr_stack(src) {}
116        stack(        void        ) : ptr_stack(   ) {}
117
118        stack &operator=( collection &src )
119        {
120            *((ptr_stack *)this)=src;
121            return *this;
122        }
123
124        node *find( type x ){ return collection::find( lnode<type>(x) ); }
125
126        void push( const type &obj )
127        {
128            ptr_stack::push( (node *)(new lnode<type>(obj)) );
129        }
130
131        type pop( void  )
132        {
133            lnode<type> *p  = (lnode<type> *)(ptr_stack::pop());
134            type        obj = ( *p ).contained();
135            delete p;
136            return obj;
137        }
138    };
```

Listing 7.24. *stack.hpp*— The `stack_c<cls>` Template

```
139    template <class cls>                    // A stack-of-class-<cls> objects
140    class stack_c : public ptr_stack
141    {
142    public:
143        stack_c( const stack_c<cls> &src ) : ptr_stack(src) {}
144        stack_c( const collection &src    ) : ptr_stack(src) {}
145        stack_c(     void                 ) : ptr_stack(   ) {}
146
147        stack_c &operator=( const collection &src )
148        {
149            *((ptr_stack *)this)=src;
150            return *this;
151        }
152
153        node *find( cls x ){ return collection::find( lnode_c<cls>(x) ); }
154
155        void push( const cls &obj )
156        {
157            ptr_stack::push( (node *)(new lnode_c<cls>(obj)) );
158        }
159        cls  pop( void )
160        {
161            lnode_c<cls> *p  = (lnode_c<cls> *)(ptr_stack::pop());
162            cls          obj = *p;
163            delete p;
164            return obj;
165        }
166    };
167    #endif // __STACK_HPP
```

Listing 7.25. *stack.hpp*— A Test Routine for The Stack Functions

```
168    #ifdef   __STACK_MAIN              // Test things
169    #define __FIXED_COMPILE_METHODS // Compile the methods to avoid having
170    #include <tools/fixed.hpp>
171    #include <alloc.h>                 // Borland coreleft defn.
172    //---------------------------------------------------------------------
173    void dotest( void )
174    {
175        stack<int> s;
176        iterator<int> it;
177
178        printf("Test as stack:\n");
179        s.push( 1 );
180        s.push( 2 );
181        s.push( 3 );
182        s.push( 4 );
183
```

→

Listing 7.25. continued. . .

```
184        // Iterate through the stack. The horrible cast converts the node*
185        // returned from the iterator to a pointer to a lnode<int>---the
186        // actual stack type. The next star gets the lnode<int> itself,
187        // the key field of which is then extracted with the (int) cast.
188
189        printf("\nprint  stack with node_iterator: ");
190        node_iterator nit;
191        for(nit = s.start(); nit ;)
192            printf( "%d ", int( * (lnode<int> *)( nit++ ) ) );
193
194        printf("\nprint  stack with iterator<int>: ");
195        for(it = s.start(); it ; printf("%d ", *it++) )
196            ;
197
198        printf("\nprint  cpy  with iterator<int>: ");
199        stack<int> cpy = s; // test copy construction.
200        for(it = cpy.start(); it ; printf("%d ", *it++) )
201            ;
202
203        stack<int> assign;
204        assign = s;              // Test assignment
205        printf("\nprint assign with iterator<int>: ");
206        for(it = assign.start(); it ; printf("%d ", *it++) )
207            ;
208
209        printf("\n(test pop on stack ) Should get 4 3 2 1, Got:");
210        while( !s.empty() )
211            printf( " %d", s.pop() );
212
213        printf("\n(test pop on cpy   ) Should get 4 3 2 1, Got:");
214        while( !cpy.empty() )
215            printf( " %d", cpy.pop() );
216
217        printf("\n(test pop on assign) Should get 4 3 2 1, Got:");
218        while( !assign.empty() )
219            printf( " %d", assign.pop() );
220
221        printf("\nTest stack as collection:\n");
222        test_collection( s );
223
224        s.push( 4  );
225        s.push( 2  );
226        s.push( 1  );
227        s.push( 3  );
228        s.push( 3  );
229        s.push( 16 );
230        s.push( 0  );
231
232        if( s.find( 16 ) )
233            printf("\nFound 16 in array\n");
234
```

➡

Listing 7.25. continued...

```
235      printf("\nTest sorting, initial list is:");
236      for(it = s.start(); it ; printf( "%d ", *it++ ) )
237          ;
238
239      s.sort();
240      printf("\nAfter sort (0 1 2 3 4 16)....:");
241      for(it = s.start(); it ; printf("%d ", *it++) )
242          ;
243
244      if( !s.sort() )
245          printf("\nsort correctly refused to resort sorted list\n");
246      else
247          printf("\nsort incorrectly resorted sorted list\n");
248
249      stack_c<fixed>  fstack;       //       test the stack_c<cls>
250      fstack.push( 4.0 );
251      fstack.push( 3.0 );
252      fstack.push( 2.0 );
253      fstack.push( 1.0 );
254
255      printf("\nTest iterator_c<fixed>,   should read 4.0 3.0 2.0 1.0: ");
256      iterator_c<fixed> it_c;
257      for( it_c = fstack.start(); it_c; printf("%3.1f ", (double)*it_c++) )
258          ;
259
260      printf("\nTest pop, stack_c<fixed>, should read 1.0 2.0 3.0 4.0: ");
261      printf("%3.1f ",   (double) fstack.pop() );
262      printf("%3.1f ",   (double) fstack.pop() );
263      printf("%3.1f ",   (double) fstack.pop() );
264      printf("%3.1f\n", (double) fstack.pop() );
265  }
266
267  void main( void )
268  {
269      printf("Core left: %ld\n", (long)coreleft() );
270      dotest();
271      printf("Core left: %ld\n", (long)coreleft() );
272  }
273  #endif // __STACK_MAIN
```

7.10 The Queue Classes and Templates

ptr_queue

The ptr_queue class and the queue<type> and queue_c<cls> templates are all presented in Listing 7.26. These definitions are almost identical to the stack classes and templates discussed in the previous section, so I won't go into them in depth. The only real differences are the introduction of enqueue() and dequeue() functions on lines 22 and 23 to replace ptr_stack::push() and ptr_stack::pop() and the redefinition of remove() on line 21 to do a dequeue.

Note that the default removal mechanism for a collection is a remove-from-head operation—a dequeue. Though I don't have to redefine remove() in theory, the redefinition guarantees that a queue behaves as a queue, even if the default mechanism is changed in the collection() class. I'm isolating the queue definitions from the collection definition to get better maintenance. Since the remove() function is **inline**, there's no performance penalty.

Listing 7.26. queue.hpp

```
 1   #ifndef __QUEUE_HPP
 2   #define __QUEUE_HPP
 3
 4   #include <stdio.h>
 5   #include <stdlib.h>
 6   #include "listnode.hpp"
 7   #include "collect.hpp"
 8   //-----------------------------------------------------------------
 9   class ptr_queue: public collection        // things unique to a queue
10   {
11   public:
12       ptr_queue( void                ) : collection(   ) {}
13       ptr_queue( const ptr_queue  &src ) : collection(src) {}
14       ptr_queue( const collection &src ) : collection(src) {}
15       ptr_queue &operator=( const collection &right )
16       {
17           *(collection *)this = right;   // Chain to base-class function
18           return *this;
19       }
20
21       virtual node *remove( void ){ return collection::remove( start() ); }
22       void    enqueue( node *ele  ){ insert( ele );          }
23       node *dequeue(    void       ){ return remove();        }
24   };
25   //-----------------------------------------------------------------
26   template <class t>                        // A queue-of-<t> class
27   class queue : public ptr_queue
28   {
29   public:
30       queue( const queue<t>   &src ) : ptr_queue(src) {}
31       queue( const collection &src ) : ptr_queue(src) {}
32       queue(        void       ) : ptr_queue(   ) {}
33
34       queue &operator=( const collection &src )
35       {
36           *((collection *)this)=src;
37           return *this;
38       }
39
40       node *find( t x ){ return collection::find( lnode<t>(x) ); }
41
```

Listing 7.26. continued. . .

```
42        void enqueue( const t &obj )
43        {
44            ptr_queue::enqueue( (node *)(new lnode<t>(obj)) );
45        }
46        t dequeue ( void  )
47        {
48            lnode<t> *p  = (lnode<t> *)(ptr_queue::dequeue());
49            t        obj = ( *p ).contained();
50            delete p;
51            return obj;
52        }
53 };
54 //-----------------------------------------------------------------
55 template <class cls>                    // A queue-of-class-<cls> objects
56 class queue_c : public ptr_queue
57 {
58 public:
59        queue_c( const queue_c<cls> &src ) : ptr_queue(src) {}
60        queue_c( const collection &src   ) : ptr_queue(src) {}
61        queue_c(      void             ) : ptr_queue(   ) {}
62
63        queue_c &operator=( const collection &src )
64        {
65            *( (ptr_queue *)this ) = src;
66            return *this;
67        }
68
69        node *find( cls x ){ return collection::find( lnode_c<cls>(x) ); }
70        void enqueue( const cls &obj )
71        {
72            ptr_queue::enqueue( (node *)(new lnode_c<cls>(obj)) );
73        }
74        cls  dequeue( void )
75        {
76            lnode_c<cls> *p  = (lnode_c<cls> *)(ptr_queue::dequeue());
77            cls          obj = *p;
78            delete p;
79            return obj;
80        }
81 };
82 #endif // __QUEUE_HPP
83 //-----------------------------------------------------------------
84 #ifdef  __QUEUE_MAIN
85
86 void test_collection(collection &s) // Manipulates both queues and stacks
87 {
88        node *p = new lnode<int>( 1 );
89
90        s.insert( p );                            // push if stack, enqueue if queue
91        s.insert( new lnode<int>( 2 ) );
92        s.insert( new lnode<int>( 3 ) );
93        s.insert( new lnode<int>( 4 ) );
94
```

Listing 7.26. continued...

```
 95         while( !s.empty() )
 96         {
 97             p = s.remove();              // pop if a stack, dequeue if a queue
 98
 99             printf( "Got %d :", int( * (lnode<int> *)( p ) ) );
100             delete p;
101
102             // Use iterator to print all elements, assume C++ 2.1 compiler
103
104             for( node_iterator it = s.start();  it ; )
105                 printf( "%d ", int( * (lnode<int> *)( it++ ) ) );
106
107             printf("\n");
108         }
109 }
110 //------------------------------------------------------------------
111 #define __FIXED_COMPILE_METHODS
112 #include <tools/fixed.hpp>
113
114 void main( void )
115 {
116     queue<int> s;
117     iterator<int> it;
118
119     printf("Test as queue:\n");
120     s.enqueue( 1 );
121     s.enqueue( 2 );
122     s.enqueue( 3 );
123     s.enqueue( 4 );
124
125     queue<int> cpy = s; // test copy construction.
126     queue<int> assign;
127     assign = s;            // test assignment.
128
129     // Iterate through the queue. The horrible cast converts the node*
130     // returned from the iterator to a pointer to a lnode<int>---the
131     // actual queue type. The next star gets the lnode<int> itself,
132     // the key field of which is then extracted with the (int) cast.
133     // Generate an iterator locally to test that declaration-time
134     // initialization works.
135
136     printf("\nprint queue with node_iterator: ");
137     node_iterator nit;
138     for(nit = s.start(); nit ;)
139         printf( "%d ", int( * (lnode<int> *)( nit++ ) ) );
140
141     printf("\nprint queue with iterator<int>: ");
142     for(it = s.start(); it ; printf("%d ", *it++) )
143         ;
144
145     printf("\n(test dequeue on queue) Should get 1 2 3 4, Got:");
```

→

Listing 7.26. continued. . .

```
146        while( !s.empty() )
147            printf( " %d", s.dequeue() );
148
149        printf("\n(copy constructor test) Should get 1 2 3 4, Got:");
150        while( !cpy.empty() )
151            printf( " %d", cpy.dequeue() );
152
153        printf("\n(assignment test      ) Should get 1 2 3 4, Got:");
154        while( !assign.empty() )
155            printf( " %d", assign.dequeue() );
156
157        printf("\nTest queue as collection:\n");
158        test_collection( s );
159
160        s.enqueue( 4  );
161        s.enqueue( 2  );
162        s.enqueue( 1  );
163        s.enqueue( 3  );
164        s.enqueue( 3  );
165        s.enqueue( 16 );
166        s.enqueue( 0  );
167
168        if( s.find( 16 ) )
169            printf("\nFound 16 in queue\n");
170
171        printf("\nTest sorting, initial list is:");
172        for(it = s.start(); it ; printf( "%d ", *it++ ) )
173            ;
174
175        s.sort();
176        printf("\nAfter sort (0 1 2 3 4 16)....:");
177        for(it = s.start(); it ; printf("%d ", *it++) )
178            ;
179
180        if( !s.sort() )
181            printf("\nsort correctly refused to resort sorted list\n");
182        else
183            printf("\nsort incorrectly resorted sorted list\n");
184
185        queue_c<fixed>  fqueue;       //       test the queue_c<cls>
186        fqueue.enqueue( 1.0 );
187        fqueue.enqueue( 2.0 );
188        fqueue.enqueue( 3.0 );
189        fqueue.enqueue( 4.0 );
190
191        printf("\nTest iterator_c<fixed>,          "
192                                       "should read 1.0 2.0 3.0 4.0: ");
193        iterator_c<fixed> it_c;
194        for( it_c = fqueue.start(); it_c; printf("%3.1f ", (double)*it_c++))
195            ;
196
```

Listing 7.26. continued. . .

```
197      printf("\nTest dequeue of queue_c<fixed>, "
198                              "should read 1.0 2.0 3.0 4.0: ");
199      printf("%3.1f ", (double) fqueue.dequeue() );
200      printf("%3.1f ", (double) fqueue.dequeue() );
201      printf("%3.1f ", (double) fqueue.dequeue() );
202      printf("%3.1f\n", (double) fqueue.dequeue() );
203  }
204  #endif // __QUEUE_MAIN
```

7.11 Implementing the Array Classes

The final part of the collection classes are the various array classes. As before, I'm eliminating redundant code with a `ptr_array` base class from which the `array<type>` and `array_c<cls>` templates derive—all common subroutines are concentrated into this base class. You can explicitly derive classes from `ptr_array` if your compiler doesn't support templates.

The `ptr_array` class is defined in Listing 7.27. Unlike most of the classes that derive from `collection`, the `ptr_array` class actually has some data in it. Array access is done by means of a `node_iterator` (it—defined on line 13 of Listing 7.27). The iterator is always positioned at the collection element that represents the most recently visited cell of the array. The `cur_index` field on the next line holds the index associated with that cell. The overloads of **operator**=() and `sort()` (on lines 27 and 33 of Listing 7.27) chain to the base-class function, but they also call `ptr_array::rewind()` (declared on line 15) to set the iterator back to the start of the list. In the case of **operator**=(), because all of the current list's elements are destroyed as part of the assignment process—the iterator will point a deleted list element. In the case of `sort()`, the list elements will have moved around—the iterator will still address a valid list element, but that element will be at a different position in the list than it used to be, so the `cur_index` will no longer be synchronized with the iterator. The easy solution is to reset both the iterator and `cur_index` to the start of the sorted list.

The one nontrivial function in the `ptr_array` class is `operator[]()` in Listing 7.28. Since the underlying collection is a list of some sort, **operator**[]() must translate incoming array indexes into a list position. The easiest way to accomplish this feat is to traverse the list starting at the leftmost collection element, counting elements until you find the desired one:

ptr_array
array<type>
array_c<cls>

ptr_array::
operator[]()

Listing 7.27. *array.hpp*— The `ptr_array` Class

```
1   #ifndef __ARRAY_HPP
2   #define __ARRAY_HPP
3
4   #include <stdio.h>
5   #include <stdlib.h>
6   #include "listnode.hpp"
7   #include "collect.hpp"
8
9   class ptr_array : public collection
10  {
11      friend class ptr_array_aux;
12
13      node_iterator it;
14      int           cur_index;
15      void rewind( void )
16      {
17          it        = start();          // Position at ar[0] after copy
18          cur_index = 0;
19      }
20      virtual node *new_object(void) = 0; // Return empty object
21
22  public:
23      ptr_array( const collection &src ) : collection(src) {}
24      ptr_array(  void                 ) : collection(   ) {}
25      ~ptr_array(  void                 )                    {}
26
27      ptr_array &operator=( const collection &src )
28      {
29          *((collection *)this)=src;
30          rewind();
31          return *this;
32      }
33      int sort( void )
34      {
35          int i = collection::sort();
36          rewind();
37          return i;
38      }
39      node *operator[]( int index );
40  };
```

```
node *operator[](int index)    // return pointer to Nth element
{
    iterator it = start();
    for( cur_index = -1; ++cur_index < index ; ++it )
        ;
    return &(*it);      // return address of current object
}
```

An easy optimization searches backward from the end of the list if the desired element is closer to the end than the start of the list. Just modify the earlier `for` loop as follows:

```
for(it = end(), cur_index = size(); --cur_index > index; --it)
    ;
```

The obvious disadvantage of a straight search is that a simple traversal of an array becomes a very inefficient operation—you have to count over from one or the other of the ends of the array for each indexed array element. `operator[]()` does use this mechanism (on lines 77 and 89 of Listing 7.28) as a last resort, but it tries to do things more efficiently if it can.

The strategy is straightforward. The `ptr_array` object's iterator field (`it`, on line 13 of Listing 7.27) is used much like the local `iterator` variable in the earlier example. [You can't make the iterator a **static** local variable of `operator[]()`, because `rewind()` needs to access it.] The `operator[]()` function compares the desired index against the current index (stored in `ptr_array::cur_index`). If the distance from the current position to the desired position is less than the distance from the end of the list to the desired position, then `operator[]()` advances the iterator from its current position to the desired position rather than starting all over again from the head of the list. Otherwise, it counts over from the head or tail of the list as before.

ptr_array::
cur_index

Using this strategy makes a simple traversal like this one:

```
for( i = 0; i < ar.size(); print( ar[i++] ) );
    ;
```

only slightly less efficient than a straight traversal using an explicitly declared iterator.

The `operator[]()` function in Listing 7.28 does the foregoing and a little more as well. The code on lines 50 to 57 handles the case where the desired array element is not in the array—the array isn't big enough. It handles the situation by inserting new elements on line 53 until the array is the correct size. The `new_object()` function, declared **virtual** on line 20 of Listing 7.27, is used to get the new objects. The function must be supplied by a class that derives from `ptr_array`—that is, you can't declare a `ptr_array` object directly; you must derive a class that knows the the array element's type. The following definition demonstrates the process for an array of `lnode<`**int**`>` objects:

ptr_array::
operator[]()

ptr_array::
new_object()

```
struct lnode_int_array : public ptr_array
{
    node *new_object(){ return new lnode<int>(0); }
};

lnode_int_array  ar;    // array of lnode<int> objects
```

As I mentioned back at the beginning of the chapter (on page 347), it might also be convenient to add an overload of `operator[]()` to this derived class.

The array templates, defined in Listing 7.29, do little more than provide the derived-class functions necessary to make the `ptr_array` useful. They provide `new_object()` functions (on lines 99 and 119) and `operator[]()` overloads (on lines 109 and 129) that make the array-access syntax a bit more straightforward—they give access to the `type` object contained in the `lnode<type>` and to the `cls`

Listing 7.28. *array.hpp*— The `ptr_array::`**operator**`[]()` Function

```
41  #ifdef  __ARRAY_COMPILE_METHODS
42  #ifndef max
43  #define max(a,b)  ((a)>(b)?(a):(b))
44  #endif
45
46  node *ptr_array::operator[](int index)
47  {
48      index = max( index, 0 );         // Round negative indexes to zero.
49
50      if( index >= size() )            // Add elements until there are
51      {                                // enough of them.
52          while( size() <= index )
53              insert( new_object() );
54
55          cur_index = index;
56          it        = end();
57      }
58      else
59      {
60          if( !it )                    // Iterator not positioned in list
61          {
62              it = start();
63              cur_index = 0;
64          }
65
66          if( index < cur_index )
67          {
68              // if distance from current index to the desired index is
69              // less than the distance from the start of the array, then
70              // count back from the current index, otherwise count
71              // forward from the start of the array.
72
73              if( (cur_index - index) < index )
74                  for(; index < cur_index ; --it, --cur_index )
75                      ;
76              else
77                  for(it=start(), cur_index=-1; ++cur_index<index ; ++it)
78                      ;
79          }
80          else if( cur_index < index )  // ditto, but end-of-list relative
81          {
82              // if( distance from     <  distance from end
83              //     current index         of the array
84
85              if( (index - cur_index)  <  (size()-index)  )
86                  for(; cur_index < index ; ++it, ++cur_index )
87                      ;
88              else
89                  for(it=end(), cur_index=size(); --cur_index>index; --it)
90                      ;
91          }
92      }
```

→

```
Listing 7.28. continued...
93        return &(*it);        // Address of current object.
94    }
95    #endif // __ARRAY_COMPILE_METHODS
```

object in an lnode_c<cls>. The templates also provide the usual complement of constructors and the operator=() function that chains to the base-class function.

The final part of *array.hpp* are the test routines shown in Listing 7.30. The test_ptr_array() function demonstrates how to use a raw ptr_array object without resorting to templates. (I've used the lnode<**int**> template to create an array element, but it's easy enough to derive a class from list_node yourself if you don't have templates.) The test_array() function on line 176 tests the array<type> template and the test_array_c() function on line 207 tests the array_c<type>.

7.12 Conclusion

So that's a simple class library. The example demonstrates both the good and bad points of C++. The template versions of the classes are easy to use and do very useful things in a simple way. The underlying class definitions are far from simple, though, either to write or to use. The real tradeoff is application-level complexity for class-definition complexity. Since a class is created rather fewer times than it is used, this tradeoff is usually for the better.

Nonetheless, a C++ class library usually takes longer to create than a simple C library that does the same thing. Sometimes this extra time is spent solving problems that should be solved in the C implementation, too—C++ forces you to be more careful than you might be in C, and you tend to think of issues when programming in C++ that you might not think of when doing the same thing in straight C. The complexity of the language's syntax is a real problem, and the extra time spent implementing a C++ application is often the fault of its overly complex syntax.

C++ does provide some help with this last problem, though. Unlike languages like Smalltalk, in which all functions must be methods of some class or another, C++ is a hybrid language in which large parts of a program can be written in a straight procedural language—C. Only those parts of the program in which the benefits of an object-oriented approach are obvious need to use the C++ extensions. I strongly believe that it's a mistake to use classes and derivation just because you can, and one good test of whether a class-based approach is worth the trouble is whether the class is used more than once. Classes that are used only once tend to add more complexity rather than reduce complexity and should generally be avoided. (This last statement, by the way, is heresy to programmers who define "object oriented" to "as much like Smalltalk as possible." I think it makes good sense in the C++ environment, though.)

The other problem with C++ is the language is still a moving target. Many compilers don't support templates, for example, and it's templates that can make

Listing 7.29. *array.hpp*— The `array<type>` and `array_c<cls>` Templates

```
 96    template <class type>
 97    class array : public ptr_array
 98    {
 99         node *new_object(void) { return new lnode<type>; }
100    public:
101         array( const collection &src ) : ptr_array(src) {}
102         array(       void          ) : ptr_array(    ) {}
103        ~array(       void          )                   {}
104         array &operator=( const collection &src )
105         {
106             *(ptr_array*)this = src;
107             return *this;
108         }
109         type &operator[]( int i )
110         {
111             return( (lnode<type>*)(ptr_array::operator[](i)) )->contained();
112         }
113         node *find( type x ){ return collection::find( lnode<type>(x) ); }
114    };
115    //------------------------------------------------------------
116    template <class cls>
117    class array_c : public ptr_array
118    {
119         node *new_object(void) { return new lnode_c<cls>; }
120    public:
121         array_c( const collection &src ) : ptr_array(src) {}
122         array_c(      void          ) : ptr_array(    ) {}
123        ~array_c(      void          )                   {}
124         array_c &operator=( const collection &src )
125         {
126             *(ptr_array*)this = src;
127             return *this;
128         }
129         cls &operator[]( int i )
130         {
131             return( (lnode_c<cls>*)(ptr_array::operator[](i)) )->contained();
132         }
133         node *find( const cls &x )
134         {
135             return collection::find( lnode_c<cls>(x) );
136         }
137    };
```

the difference between easy-to-maintain and hard-to-maintain application. The nontemplate versions of the current library classes are both less useful and harder to maintain than the template versions. For one thing, the application program must explicitly derive classes in order to use the library base classes. This explicit derivation not only adds complexity but also requires application programmers to have considerably more knowledge of classes than they would need to use the templates. The template-expansion process effectively lets the compiler take over the mechanics of derivation, hiding that process from the application programmer.

Templates are not a panacea, though. They can expand to a huge amount of code. C++ programs are typically pretty large. Moreover, templates simply cannot be used in some applications. You must constantly weigh the readability of a C++ implementation against the readability of a functionally equivalent C implementation and make your decisions primarily on the basis of maintenance. This is not to say that an object-oriented approach to design should be abandoned; rather, you must decide whether C++ is the best language for implementing that approach in a particular context.

In sum, C++ is rather a mixed bag. I really like what the language does, but I don't much like the way that the language forces you to do it. C++ has several semantic and syntactic problems that make it hard to read, and these problems coupled, with sometimes inappropriate default behavior, make the C++ learning curve very steep. When written poorly, C++ approaches a write-only language. On the other hand, when used appropriately, the object-oriented approach to program design definitely helps with program maintenance—improving both readability and ease of use—and C++ can make it much easier to use this approach.

Listing 7.30. *array.hpp—* Test Functions

```
138   #ifdef  __ARRAY_MAIN
139   #define __FIXED_COMPILE_METHODS
140   #include <tools/fixed.hpp>
141   #include <alloc.h>              // Borland, coreleft() prototype
142   #define  NUMELE 10
143
144   void test_ptr_array( void )
145   {
146       struct lnode_int_array : public ptr_array
147       {
148           node *new_object(){ return new lnode<int>(0); }
149       public:
150           int &operator[]( int index )
151           {
152               // The following horrific expression saves us from having
153               // to say *(lnode<int> *) ar[0] = 0; to do an assignment in
154               // the code.  Similarly, an "x = *(lnode<int> *) ar[0]" to
155               // access the contained int is also avoided.
156               //
157               // With the current operator[]() in place, a simple
158               // ar[0]=0 or x=ar[0] does the job.
159
160               return ( (lnode<int>*)
161                         (ptr_array::operator[](index)) )->contained();
162           }
163       };
164
165       lnode_int_array      ar;      // An array of lnode<int> objects
166
```

➡

Listing 7.30. continued...

```
167         ar[0] = 0;    // uses lnode<int>::operator=(int)
168         ar[1] = 1;
169         ar[2] = 2;
170
171         printf("%d\n", ar[0] );
172         printf("%d\n", ar[1] );
173         printf("%d\n", ar[2] );
174     }
175
176     void test_array( void )
177     {
178         int i;
179         char buf[80];
180
181         printf("\nTesting array<int>\n");
182
183         array<int> ar;
184
185         for( i = 0; i < NUMELE; ++i )
186             ar[i] = i;
187
188         if( ar.find( NUMELE/2 ) )
189             printf( "found a %d in array\n", NUMELE/2 );
190         else
191             printf( "find doesn't work" );
192
193         while( 1 )
194         {
195             printf("Array is: ");
196             for( i = 0; i < ar.size(); ++i )
197                 printf("%d ", ar[i] );
198             printf("\n");
199
200             printf("Enter desired index: ");
201             if( !gets(buf) || !*buf )
202                 break;
203             printf( "ar[%d]==%d\n", atoi(buf), ar[ atoi(buf) ] );
204         }
205     }
206
207     void test_array_c( void )
208     {
209         int i;
210         char buf[80];
211         array_c<fixed> ar;
212
213         printf("\nTesting array_c<fixed>\n");
214
215         for( i = 0; i < NUMELE; ++i )
216             ar[i] = (double)i;
217
```

Listing 7.30. continued...

```
218        while( 1 )
219        {
220            printf("Array is: ");
221            for( i = 0; i < ar.size(); ++i )
222                printf("%3.1f ", (double)ar[i] );
223            printf("\n");
224
225            printf("Enter desired index: ");
226            if( !gets(buf) || !*buf )
227                break;
228            printf("ar[%d]==%3.1f\n", atoi(buf), (double) ar[ atoi(buf) ]);
229        }
230    }
231
232    void main( void )
233    {
234                                printf("Core left: %ld\n", (long)coreleft() );
235        test_ptr_array();       printf("Core left: %ld\n", (long)coreleft() );
236        test_array();           printf("Core left: %ld\n", (long)coreleft() );
237        test_array_c();         printf("Core left: %ld\n", (long)coreleft() );
238    }
239
240    #endif // __ARRAY_MAIN
241    #endif // __ARRAY_HPP
```

Exception Handling

errors in
constructors,
destructors,
operator overloads

One conundrum with constructors, destructors, and operator overloads is error handling. A constructor, for example, is not called in the normal sense of the word, and cannot return values as a consequence.

Several error-handling strategies are available to you. An operator overload can evaluate to an illegal value or a reserved "error" value, for example. A new overload can evaluate to NULL. Constructors and destructors pose particularly difficult problems, though. It's not a great idea for the constructor to call a global-level error-processing function because you don't want to require the user to provide such a function. A virtual error-processing function is a better strategy because a base class can provide a default version that a user can choose to override. The difficulty with both approaches is that they change the error behavior at a global level—all instances of the class will exhibit the same behavior when a constructor-error occurs. You'd like to be able to have finer control so that error handling can be tailored to specific situations.

use raise(SIGABRT)
to handle
constructor errors

One solution is to use a special-purpose signal such as SIGABRT. Listing A.1 demonstrates the process.

If the user takes no particular action, the raise(SIGABRT) aborts the current program. raise() does not return in this case. If the user disables the signal with a call to

```
signal( SIGABRT, SIG_IGN );
```

then raise() does return, and the constructor itself prints an error message and exits. The user can also install a signal handler to provide special processing:

Listing A.1. Using `raise(SIGABRT)` to Handle Constructor Errors

```
1    class rapunzle
2    {
3        static int error;
4    public:
5        rapunzle( int let_down_hair )
6        {
7            error = 0 ;
8            if( !let_down_hair )      // error
9            {
10               error = 1;
11               raise( SIGABRT );   // Normally aborts program
12               fprintf(stderr,"Error creating class rapunzle\n");
13               exit( 1 );
14           }
15       }
16   }
17   int rapunzle::error = 0;
```

```
my_handler()
{
    if( rapunzle::error )
    {
      fprintf(stderr,"Error creating rapunzle object\n");
      exit( 1 );
    }
}
///...
signal( SIGABRT, my_handler );          // call my_handler
```

The **static member** `rapunzle::error` **tells** `my_handler()` **that** `rapunzle::rapunzle()` **raised** `SIGABRT`.

An alternative strategy uses a member function to report the error:

use member
function to detect
constructor errors

```
class goldilocks
{
    int error;
public:
    goldilocks( )
    {
      error = 0 ;
      if( some_error_condition() )    // error
          error = 1;
      else
          // initialize here.
    }
    construction_ok(){ return error; }
}
```

```
main()
{
    goldilocks x;
    if( x.construction_ok() )
      // error in constructing x;
}
```

You don't want to provide direct access to `rapunzle::error` for all the reasons discussed earlier: Providing read-only access only guarantees data integrity, and access through a member function allows for easy modification of the internal workings of the class.

The `operator int()` function that's discussed in Chapter Four is also a convenient candidate for an error-detection function, provided that it's not used for something else. For example, given these declarations:

```
class mamma_bear
{
    int error;
    mamma_bear()
    {
      error = 0;
      if( /* some error condition */ )
      {
          error = 1;
          return;
      }
    }
public:
    operator int( return !error );
};
```

you can now do this:

```
mamma_bear ursula;
if( !ursula )
    // constructor error
```

A third possibility for error handling is one of the "experimental" language features that has become official only with AT&T's release 3.0. This mechanism, called *exception handling*, uses three new keywords: `throw`, `try`, and `catch`. Since many compilers don't support this mechanism at all, and since there's still a lot of variation of how the compilers that do support it actually do the work, you should use the mechanism with care.

The idea is that an object of a predetermined type is *thrown* from a constructor or similar function when an error is detected. The error is then *caught* by code at an outer scope that is laying in wait for an object of a specific type to pass by it. Several different objects can be thrown to several different error handlers provided that those objects are of different types.

Listing A.2 contains a simple example of this process. The declaration on line 19 is contained inside a `try` block that has attached to it a `catch` block for type `char*`. When the `rudolph` constructor detects an error it throws an object of type `char*` (on line seven) to the handler for `char*` exceptions on line 25. Control is transferred from the `throw` statement on line seven directly to the matching `catch`

exception handling

thrown

caught

throw, try, catch

on line 25. No intervening code is executed, though destructors are called. For example, the destructor for y (declared on line 18 of Listing A.2) is called when an exception is thrown from the x constructor.

Listing A.2. The Exception Mechanism, A Simple Example

```
1    class rudolph
2    {
3    public:
4        rudolph()
5        {
6            if( error() )
7                throw "rudolph";
8
9            // any code found here is not executed if the
10           // error message is thrown
11       }
12   };
13   //------------------------------------------------------------
14   donder()
15   {
16       try
17       {
18           some_object y;
19           rudolph      x;
20
21           // code that uses x goes here, but this code
22           // is not executed if an error message is thrown
23           // from the x constructor.
24       }
25       catch( char *err_msg )
26       {
27           if( strcmp(err_msg,"rudolph")!=0 )
28               throw;
29           else
30           {
31               fprintf( stderr, "%s\n", err_msg );
32               exit( 1 );
33           }
34       }
35   }
```

The final detail in Listing A.2 is the way that the `catch` block determines that the error came from the rudolph constructor (rather than from the some_object constructor, for example) and what it does if not. The `strcmp()` call on line 27 compares the thrown string with the string `"rudolph"`. If they don't match, the `throw` statement on line 49 rethrows the exception, transferring control to a catch statement attached to a outer `try` block. For example, the function that called donder() might look like this

rethrowing exceptions

```
vixen()
{
    try
    {
      donder();
    }
    catch( char* p )
    {
        // Catches char*  exception thrown either by donder()
        // itself or by some function called by donder(). It
        // the current case, it will catch the exception
        // rethrown by the catch statement inside donder().
    }
}
```

The rethrown exception passes back up the path determined by the runtime flow of control to the next `char*` exception handler—the one in the calling routine, `vixen()`.

catch missing, catch(...)

A `catch` statement that uses an ellipsis rather than an explicit type [i.e. `catch(...)`] catches all exceptions. Since `catch` statements are processed in the order that they appear in the source file, you can use `catch(...)` to handle a none-of-the-above case, provided that the `catch(...)` is the last one in the list. Normal `catch` statements that specify a type but follow the `catch(...)` in the list won't ever be activated. If none of the `try` block's `catch` statements match the type of a thrown exception, the exception is rethrown to the outer block as if the following statement were present:

```
try
{
    //...
}
catch(...){ throw; }
```

exception-
identification
classes

derivation used to
specify hierarchical
exceptions

The foregoing approach of throwing a `char*` exception is not a particularly good one. It's too hard to determine where the exception came from or what the exact problem was. There are several ways to solve the problem, two of which are shown in Listing A.3. The first method creates several special-purpose error classes on lines one to four. These rather weird-looking declarations create empty classes—classes with no members. You need to create a class here, but only so that you can throw an object of that class. You won't use the object for anything beyond identification, so there is no need for internal data.

class

The `file_err` class on line one of Listing A.3 specifies a general file error of some sort. The derived classes like `input_err` refine the error information further by specifying what caused the problem. For example, an exception is thrown on line 26 when an input-error occurs. The **throw** statement creates an object of class `input_err`, using the default constructor. That exception is then caught with a

class

`catch(open_err)` statement on line 45 of Listing A.3. Since the `input_err` object isn't used directly—the object's type is sufficient to tell us which error occurred—there's no need to declare a name for the object on line 45 of Listing A.3. (Compare this `catch` statement with the `catch` statement on line 25 of Listing A.2, which does need a name.)

When you use derived classes to identify an exception, as is the case here, both the derived and base class can appear in `catch` statements. This way you can catch all exceptions of one sort (i.e. all file errors) by catching a base-class object or refine the error handling to process specific errors (i.e. a file-open error) by catching a derived-class object. The `catch` file_err on line 49, for example, would normally catch all exceptions of type file_err, including those generated by throwing classes that derive from file_err. Since input_err is caught explicitly for the current `try` block, and since this derived-class `catch` precedes the base-class `catch`, the `catch` file_err on line 49 catches only the output_err, open_err, and file_err exceptions. `catch` statements are processed in the order in which they appear, so the `catch` for a derived class must always precede the one for a base class when both are attached to the same `try` block.

derived and base class can both appear in catch

Listing A.3. Using Classes to Differentiate Exceptions

```
 1   class file_err               {};
 2   class input_err  : file_err  {};
 3   class output_err : file_err  {};
 4   class open_err   : file_err  {};
 5
 6   class some_class
 7   {
 8       FILE *fp;            // a file pointer
 9       char xfer_buf[128]; // transfer buffer
10
11       class error {};      // empty. Error-processing class.
12
13   public:
14       some_class()
15       {
16           if( !(fp = fopen("tmp_file","w")) ) // Note that the open_err()
17               throw open_err();               // used in the throw is a
18                                               // cast operation that
19           else if( /* some other error */ )   // uses the default con-
20               throw error();                  // structor to create an
21       }                                       // open_err object.
22       load()
23       {   /*...*/
24           fread(xfer_buf, 1, sizeof(xfer_buf), fp);
25           if( ferror(fp) )
26               throw input_err();
27       }
28       unload()
29       {   /*...*/
30           fwrite(xfer_buf, 1, sizeof(xfer_buf), fp);
31           if( ferror(fp) )
32               throw output_err();
33       }
34   };
35   //------------------------------------------------------------
36   foo()
37   {
```

➡

Listing A.3. continued...

```
38      try
39      {
40          some_class x;
41
42          x.load();
43          x.unload();
44      }
45      catch( input_err )   // input_err derives from file_err
46      {
47          // catches input error thrown from load()
48      }
49      catch( file_err )
50      {
51          // catches all exceptions of class file_err or of a class
52          // that derives from file_err. Does not catch input_err,
53          // however, because that class is handled explicitly
54          // by the previous catch statement.
55      }
56      catch( some_class::error )
57      {
58          // Catches error from constructor
59      }
60  }
```

The second mechanism demonstrated in Listing A.3 uses a nested, rather than derived, error class. The declaration on line 11 creates a class that's internal to `some_class`. The exception is thrown on line 20 and caught on line 56. Note the scope-resolution operator that's used on line 56 to specify that this is the `error` class whose declaration is nested inside `some_class`. You'd use the same syntax if you wanted to create an object of this class for some reason. Do it like this:

```
some_class::error x;   // Creates an object of
                       // class some_class::error
```

constructor arguments in error-processing classes

Error-processing classes do not have to be empty. Listing A.4 shows you how state data can be used to give a more informative error message in some situations. The constructor for the `mem_err` class declared at the top of the listing is passed a file name and line number to print in an error message. (It's declared as a **struct** since everything's public.)

The `mem_err` object is created by the **throw** statement on line 16, passing the constructor the name of the current source-code file and line numbers made available through the ANSI `__LINE__` and `__FILE__` macros. This information is stored in the thrown object, and is then used when the exception is caught on line 27. The mechanism is effectively passing arguments from the place where the exception is thrown to the handler. Note that you do need to name the incoming object on line 27 since you need to access its contents.

exception specifier

Two loose ends need to be covered before leaving the subject of exception processing. First, you can promise the compiler that only exceptions of a specified type will be thrown by using an *exception specifier*, of which there are two forms:

Listing A.4. Using Members of Exception Class

```
1    struct mem_err  // Global-level exception class
2    {
3        const char *file;
4        int         line;
5        out_of_mem_err( int line_no, const char *file_name ):
6                                    line( line_no ), file( file_name ){}
7    };
8    //------------------------------------------------------------
9    class poo_bah
10   {
11       char *p;
12   public:
13       poo_bah()
14       {
15           if( !(p = new char[10]) )
16               throw mem_err(__LINE__, __FILE__);
17       }
18   };
19   //------------------------------------------------------------
20   main()
21   {
22       try
23       {
24           poo_bah grand;
25           // ...
26       }
27       catch( mem_err &obj )
28       {
29           printf( "Out of memory condition while processing"
30                   "declaration on line %d of source file %s\n",
31                                       obj.line, obj.file );
32       }
33   }
```

An exception specifier with no arguments such as

```
carl()  throw()
{
}
```

tells the compiler that the function throws no exceptions. An exception specifier
that specifies various argument types such as

```
class X;
class Y;
class Z;

philip() throw( X, Y, Z )
{
    //... body of function goes here.
}
```

guarantees that philip() will handle all exceptions except the listed ones (X, Y, and Z). This way you can write a function that calls philip() knowing that unexpected exceptions won't be thrown at you. An unexpected exception is really a hard error in this case, so should terminate the program—indeed the default action.

Unfortunately, the unexpected-exception syntax is overly complicated and somewhat awkward to use. Moreover, the mechanism doesn't work as well as it could because errors are not caught until run time. It's not possible for the compiler to check because the exception specifier (**throw**(X,Y,Z) here) is not considered part of the function's type—the exception information is not built into the function's signature. (This omission probably resulted from exception processing being tacked onto the language as an afterthought rather than being designed in.)

unexpected()

If a philip() throws an unexpected exception at run time, the problem is handled by calling the function unexpected() at run time. The default action for unexpected() is to call abort(), but you can cause it to call a different handler

set_unexpected()

by passing the address of that handler to set_unexpected(). For example:

```
aaaaggghhh()
{
    printf("Unexpected exception thrown by philip()\n")
};

//...
deirdre()
{
    class X; class Y; class Z;
    extern philip() throw(X,Y,Z);

    set_unexpected( aaaaggghhh );
    try
    {
        philip();
    }
    catch( X ) { /*...*/ }
    catch( Y ) { /*...*/ }
    catch( Z ) { /*...*/ }
}
```

To my mind, appending a **catch**(...) to the foregoing list of **catch** statements is a cleaner solution to the problem than using set_unexpected(). The **catch**(...) would function much like the **default** case in a **switch**().

handling errors in the exception mechanism itself

The final loose end handles errors in the exception processing itself. Problems arise in three situations:

- when no **catch** can be found for a thrown exception.
- when a destructor that's called implicitly because a **throw** transfers control outside the block in which an object is declared itself throws an exception.
- when the exception-processing system finds problems with the runtime stack.

terminate()

The compiler responds to all three situations by calling a function called terminate() , which calls abort() by default. As with unexpected(), you can

set_terminate()

modify the terminate() handler by calling set_terminate(), passing it the address of the new handler. That new handler cannot return, however. It should call `abort()` rather than returning.

The exception-processing mechanism is one of the weakest parts of the C++ language. The syntax is difficult and the mechanism is awkward at best. You should keep things under control by observing the following rule of thumb religiously: **An exception should be thrown only when a function cannot return an error status in the normal way because it is not called in the normal way.** For example, constructors, destructors, operator overloads, overloads of `new`, and so forth, are all candidates for exception processing. Never throw a function from a normal function that can return an error status through the standard return mechanism.

making exception
processing tractable

Bibliography

[Budd]   Timothy Budd. *An Introduction to Object-oriented Programming*. Reading, Massachusetts: Addison Wesley, 1991.

[CGaz]   Jeff Taylor. "Quicksorting Linked Lists." *The C Gazette* 5:6 (October/November, 1991), pp. 17–20.

[Cox]   Brad J. Cox and Andrew J. Novobilski. *Object Oriented Programming, An Evolutionary Approach*, 2d. ed. Reading: Addison Wesley, 1991.

[Ellis and Stroustrup]   Margaret A. Ellis and Bjarne Stroustrup. *The Annotated C++ Reference Manual*. Reading: Addison Wesley, 1990. (Also known as the *ARM*.)

[Holub1]   Allen I. Holub. "A Virtual Memory System in C/C++." *Programmer's Journal* 8:5 (September/October, 1990), pp. 40–51.

[Holub2]   Allen I. Holub. "Virtual Memory Paging." *Programmer's Journal* 8:6 (November/December, 1990), p. 47–57.

[K&R]   Brian W. Kernighan and Dennis M. Ritchie. *The C Programming Language*, 2d. Ed. Englewood Cliffs, New Jersey: Prentice Hall, 1988.

[Stroustrup] Bjarne Stroustrup. *The C++ Programming Language*, 2d. Ed. Reading: Addison Wesley, 1991.

Index